# RISK COMMUNICATION

## A Handbook for Communicating Environmental, Safety, and Health Risks

### *Third Edition*

**Used in more than 20 countries by . . .**

- Utilities
- Chemical and oil companies
- Pharmaceutical and biotechnology firms
- State departments of health
- Federal agencies
- Consumer product firms
- Manufacturers
- Agribusinesses
- Consultants
- National associations and societies
- Colleges and universities

◇ ◇ ◇

**NEW in the third edition of *Risk Communication*:**

Bioterrorism and other emergencies

New technologies for risk communication

New laws and regulations that affect risk communication

Effective message crafting

More research-tested risk graphics—do's and don'ts

Facilitated deliberation and alternative dispute resolution

◇ ◇ ◇

**What others have said . . .**

About the first edition (1994)

*"One of the top five 'must read' publications for industry risk communication practitioners"*
—Society for Risk Analysis, Risk Communication Specialty Group

About the second edition (1998)

*"Most thorough coverage of practical issues of any risk communication text"*
—Programme Group Humans Environment Technology, German Research Centre Juelich

*"It's an excellent first handbook for the [occupational health and safety] professional, government regulator, or anyone who is expected to communicate about risk to health and safety"* —Dr. Tim Sly, professor and director, School of Occupational and Public Health, Ryerson Polytechnic University

*". . . a useful book for anyone working in this field"* —Institute for Scientific and Technical Communications

*"The text reads easily, which one might expect from a book on effective communication. Yet the book's smooth flow is an impressive feat given the specialized topic. The authors' credentials shine through in their inclusion of copious references and suggested resources, as well as their attention to detail in editing and presentation"*
—Security Management Organization

# RISK COMMUNICATION

## A Handbook for Communicating Environmental, Safety, and Health Risks

*Third Edition*

R<small>EGINA</small> E. L<small>UNDGREN</small>

A<small>NDREA</small> H. M<small>C</small>M<small>AKIN</small>

Battelle Press

Columbus • Richland

Library of Congress Cataloging-in-Publication Data

Lundgren, Regina E., 1959–
   Risk communication : a handbook for communicating environmental,
safety, and health risks / Regina E. Lundgren, Andrea H. McMakin. — 3rd ed.
     p.  cm.
   Includes bibliographical references and index.
   ISBN 1-57477-142-6  (softcover : alk. paper)
    1. Risk communication—Handbooks, manuals, etc.   I. McMakin,
Andrea H., 1957–   II. Title.

T10.68.L86 2004
658.4´08—dc22

2004047668

Printed in the United States of America

Battelle Press
505 King Avenue
Columbus, Ohio 43201-2693, USA
614-424-6393 or 1-800-451-3543
Fax: 614-424-3819
E-mail: press@battelle.org
Website: www. battelle.org/bookstore

# Preface

*T*he first edition of this book came about because Regina Lundgren had always been fascinated with communication. She started writing novels in the third grade. When she was asked her first day at the University of Washington what she hoped to do with her degree in scientific and technical communication, she replied, "I want to write environmental impact statements." When Pat Hays hired her to work at the Pacific Northwest National Laboratory to do just that, she was overjoyed.

Her fascination with communication led her to pursue an interest in risk communication. That in turn took her from leading the public relations function for an 800-person environmental research and development organization to developing her own consulting and training firm. Since then, she's been on a panel for the first workshop on risk communication for weapons of mass destruction events, developed the risk communication plan for the most sophisticated cancer cluster investigation in the nation's history, crafted one of the first state-level risk communication plans for public health preparedness, and peer reviewed materials for the Centers for Disease Control and Prevention's emergency risk communication training efforts, among other projects for clients in government and industry.

Her earlier work at the Pacific Northwest National Laboratory put her in contact with Andrea McMakin, an accomplished risk communicator who had led environmental risk communication efforts that touched several states. Andrea's background in emergency medicine, master's degree in communication, experience in training scientists and engineers to communicate, and first-hand knowledge of working with the news media as both writer and facilitator made her the perfect co-author for the second and now third edition of this book.

The previous editions of this book have been used by practitioners, students, and teachers of risk communication across the United States and in at least seven other countries. Readers' suggestions and new experiences have helped us make the new edition even more useful in terms of content. We added new information on health risk communication, particularly bioterrorism risk communication. We updated and expanded information on current laws, approaches, audience analysis, computer-based applications, and evaluation. The index is revised and expanded for easier use.

This book was not written in a vacuum. We owe much of our own knowledge to our forebears in risk communication—including Vince Covello, Peter Sandman, Billie Jo Hance, Caron Chess, Baruch Fischhoff, Paul Slovic, Roger Kasperson, Jim Creighton, and many others. Several other experts in science, management, and communication have inspired us by personal example: Pete Mellinger, Emmett Moore, Jack Robinson, Lori Ramonas, Bob Gray, Judith Bradbury, Kristi Branch, Geoff Harvey, Bill Hanf, Marilyn Quadrel, Dan Strom, Darby Stapp, Barb Wise, and Randal Todd.

Regina would like to thank Laurel Grove, who brilliantly edited the first edition, and Kristin Manke, who provided a professional index for the book. Most of all Regina would like to thank her husband Larry and sons Ted and William, who always support her in all she does.

Andrea wishes to acknowledge the advice and review of several experts, including *L.A. Times* reporter David Shaw, science journalists Bill Cannon and Karen Adams, radio reporter Charles Compton, media specialists Greg Koller and Staci Maloof, Portland State University professor Char Word, statistician Greg Piepel, and information technology specialist Don Clark. She also thanks the many communication and public health researchers and information specialists who answered questions and corrected errors.

Regina and Andrea gratefully acknowledge peer review of the second edition by two luminaries in the risk communication field: Caron Chess, Director of Rutgers University's Center for Environmental Communication, and Susan Santos, founder and principal of the health and environmental management and risk communication consultancy FOCUS GROUP. Their insights and suggestions helped us think through several issues while staying true to the experiences of our readers.

We also thank Susan Vianna for the creative design and layout, Kristin Manke for first-rate proofreading and indexing, and Joe Sheldrick, our publisher, for ongoing support and encouragement.

We welcome comments and suggestions from readers; please send them to us in care of our publisher, Battelle Press, at the address on the copyright page.

# Contents

# Tables and Figures

## TABLES

## FIGURES

# RISK
# COMMUNICATION

A Handbook for Communicating
Environmental, Safety, and Health Risks

*Third Edition*

# Introduction

*R*isk communication encompasses many types of messages and processes. It is the poster warning food workers to handle food safely to prevent the spread of *E. coli* bacteria. It is the emergency response worker rallying a community to evacuate amidst the rising flood. It is community representatives sitting down with industry to discuss the siting and operation of a hazardous waste incinerator. Risk communication involves people in all walks of life—parents, children, legislative representatives, regulators, scientists, farmers, industrialists, factory workers, writers. It is part of the science of risk assessment and the process of risk management.

This book was written for those who communicate health, safety, and environmental risks in the United States, primarily:

- the writers, editors, and communication specialists who prepare the messages, coach the speakers, and facilitate public involvement

- the scientists, engineers, and health care professionals who must communicate the results of risk assessments

---◇---

Risk communication involves people in all walks of life—parents, children, legislative representatives, regulators, scientists, farmers, industrialists, factory workers, writers. It is part of the science of risk assessment and the process of risk management.

---

1

- the organization representatives who must present a risk management decision

- those new to the field of risk communication and anyone being asked to communicate risk for the first time.

Because each of these readers may have different needs and questions concerning risk communication, we have divided the book into six parts. Each part or chapter within a part is relatively self-contained; a reader can choose to read some chapters and to skip others of less interest. Part I gives background information necessary to understand the basic theories and practices of risk communication and provides a basis for understanding information in the other parts. Part II tells how to plan a communication effort. Part III gives more in-depth information on different methods of communicating risk and describes how each differs from its counterparts in other areas of communication. Part IV discusses how to evaluate risk communication efforts, including how to measure success. Part V discusses risk communication during and after an emergency, with particular emphasis on bioterrorism events. A list of additional resources, a glossary, and an index are also provided. To emphasize key points, each chapter concludes with a summary section. Chapters that discuss how to apply risk communication (as opposed to those that deal with more theoretical aspects like principles and ethics) end with a checklist, which can be used to help plan and develop your risk communication efforts.

## TO BEGIN

Many of the terms used in this book are defined in ways that differ slightly from usage in other branches of science or communication. A glossary is provided, but as a beginning, we want to explain exactly what we mean by risk communication and how it differs from other forms of technical communication.

Technical communication is the communication of scientific or technical information. Audiences can range from children in a sixth-grade science class, to workers learning a new procedure on a piece of equipment, to scientists reviewing the work of peers. The purpose of technical communication can be to inform, educate, or even occasionally persuade.

Risk communication is a subset of technical communication. As such, it has its own characteristics. At its most basic, it is the communication of some risk. (In this book, it is used to mean the communication of health, safety, or environmental risks.) The audience can be similar to those described for technical communication, but it can also be a wide cross section of the United States. For example, information to present the risk of not wearing seatbelts could have as an audience anyone who will ever ride in a car.

Sometimes, the risk being communicated is frightening to a particular segment of the audience. Other times, the audience is unaware or even apathetic to the risk. In still other cases, the organization communicating the risk is not credible to a portion of the audience or the audience finds the way the risk is being managed to be unacceptable. The strong emotions, or the lack thereof, audiences associate with a risk can make it difficult to communicate.

The purpose of risk communication can also differ from that of technical communication. In dangerous situations, such as floods and tornadoes, risk communication may have to motivate its audience to action. In other situations, the purpose is more appropriately to inform or to encourage the building of consensus (more on this in Chapter 5, "Ethical Issues"). Another difference between risk communication and technical communication is that risk communication more often involves two-way communication, that is, the organization managing the risk and the audience carry on a dialogue. In technical communication, most efforts are designed to disseminate information, not to receive information back from the audience or to include the audience in the decision-making process. An example of two-way technical communication is scientists reviewing the work of peers.

Risk communication comes in many forms (see Figure 1-1). In this book, we generally divide risk

◇

Risk communication comes in many forms (see Figure 1-1). In this book, we generally divide risk communication along functional lines, distinguishing between care communication, crisis communication, and consensus communication.

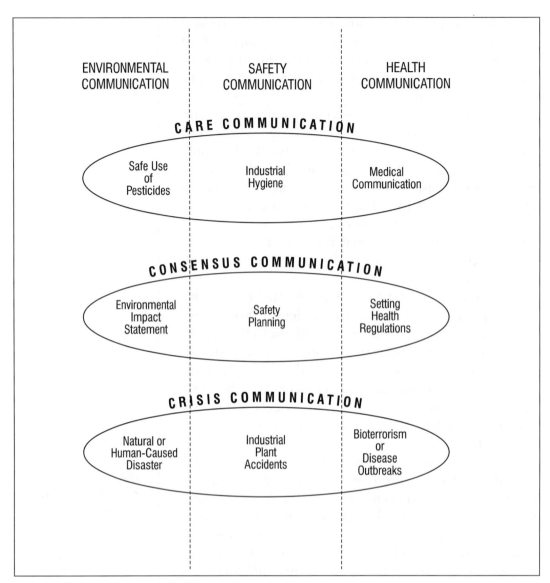

**FIGURE 1-1.** Examples of various types of risk communication.

communication along functional lines, distinguishing between care communication, consensus communication, and crisis communication, which are described in more detail below. While these three forms have elements in common with other forms of technical communication, they always have circumstances that require different tactics, or ways of communicating, to effectively deliver their messages to their respective audiences. For example, consensus communication involves much more audience interaction than do care or crisis communication. Risk communication can also be divided topically, for example, into environmental, safety, and health risk communication.

Care communication is communication about risks for which the danger and the way to manage it have already been well determined through scientific research that is accepted by most of the audience. Another distinguisher is that generally those charged with communicating have little return on investment other than the betterment of human lives. Think of the American Heart Association and local public health agencies.

Two subsets of care communication are health care communication, which seeks to inform and advise the audience about health risks such as smoking or AIDS, and industrial risk communication, which involves informing workers about potential safety and health risks in the workplace. Industrial risk communication can be further divided into ongoing communication about industrial hygiene and individual worker notification, which informs workers of the findings of retrospective mortality studies, where the mortality rates of a set of workers have been evaluated against standards. Examples of these are the longitudinal studies to determine whether painting radium watch dials was hazardous to the workers (i.e., whether they had a higher rate of mortality compared to standards).

Consensus communication is risk communication to inform and encourage groups to work together to reach a decision about how the risk will be managed (prevented or mitigated). An example would be a citizen advisory panel and the owner/operator of the local landfill working together to determine how best to dispose of hazardous chemicals found at the landfill. Consensus communication of risk is also a subset of stakeholder participation, which encourages all those with an interest (stake) in how the risk is managed to be involved in consensus building. Often the agency or organization with the greatest financial stake funds this process. (Stakeholder participation is also generally called public engagement, public involvement, public participation,

◇

Care communication is communication about risks for which the danger and the way to manage it have already been well determined through scientific research that is accepted by most of the audience.

◇

Consensus communication is risk communication to inform and encourage groups to work together to reach a decision about how the risk will be managed (prevented or mitigated).

stakeholder involvement, public consultation, and audience interaction.) Stakeholder involvement, however, can go far beyond risk communication, into the realms of conflict resolution and negotiation. These realms encompass entire disciplines in themselves and hence are beyond the scope of this book.

Crisis communication is risk communication in the face of extreme, sudden danger—an accident at an industrial plant, the impending break in an earthen dam, the outbreak of a deadly disease. This type can include communication both during and after the emergency. (Communication during planning on how to deal with potential emergencies would be either care or consensus communication, depending on how much the audience is involved in the planning.)

## THE RISK COMMUNICATION PROCESS

An overview of the risk communication process will also help explain the concepts presented elsewhere in this book. The process begins with a hazard, a potential or actual danger to the environment or human health or safety. Examples include an oil spill (environment), cigarette smoking (health), and a loose stair tread in an office building (safety). Usually by law but sometimes by commitment, some organization is responsible for managing the risks posed by this hazard, that is, preventing or mitigating any damage (decreasing the probability or lessening the consequences). In the case of an oil spill, the U.S. Environmental Protection Agency, among other organizations, must develop regulations to prevent occurrence and oversees cleanup if preventive measures fail. The American Lung Association has a commitment to eradicate cigarette smoking. The Occupational Safety and Health Administration requires that organizations maintain safe work environments.

Risk management usually begins with a risk assessment. Just how dangerous is the risk? How much of a hazardous chemical has to spill into a river before the water's natural self-cleansing ability is overwhelmed? Can AIDS be spread by contact with infected health care practitioners? How does the way workers use a forklift affect their risks of being injured or of injuring another? Risk assessment is a scientific process that characterizes risk and assesses the probability of occurrence and outcomes. Based on probabilities, it usually tries to answer questions like:

- Who, or what ecosystems, will be harmed?
- How many of them will be harmed?
- How will they be harmed and by how much?
- How long will the harm continue?

Sometimes the risk assessment has a benefit component attached (risk/benefit analysis). This kind of analysis seeks to determine whether any benefits attached to the risk would balance against the harm caused. For example, does the benefit of the potential advancement of science balance against the potential harm of experimenting with radioactive materials? This kind of analysis may or may not include factors other than the strictly scientific evaluation of the risk and benefit.

Information from the risk assessment is used by risk managers to decide what to do about the risk. Their decisions, and often the process by which they decide, are usually communicated to the people who would be or are affected by the risk or to those interested in the risk for other reasons (ethical issues, for example). Sometimes the risk managers try to encourage this audience to take action (care or crisis communication), sometimes they need to educate the audience about the risk so that the audience has the information needed to make a decision (care communication), and sometimes they need to discuss the risk with the audience so that a consensus on a course of action can be reached with all parties speaking the same language (consensus communication).

In the case of consensus communication, the decision about how risks are to be managed is made through stakeholder involvement. This type of management requires risk communication that seeks to

- determine stakeholder perceptions of a variety of factors including the risk, the organization in charge of managing the risk, and the process being used to reach the decision

- inform, not persuade (except in the context of an agreed-upon negotiation)
- balance the needs of competing stakeholders
- assist in reaching a resolution that all parties can live with.

For example, the process of using an environmental impact statement to evaluate a set of alternative actions often begins with a series of stakeholder meetings to encourage individuals and groups to help define what should be evaluated (this part of the process is called scoping). Care communication and crisis communication also need to identify stakeholder perceptions and concerns; however, in these cases the information is used to develop messages that will inform the audience and encourage them to take some course of action. An example of this is the U.S. Environmental Protection Agency's program to communicate the dangers of radon in the home (for example, Weinstein and Sandman 1993).

At any point during the process, the organization that has been communicating may evaluate its risk communication effort to determine successes and failures. What should be done next time? What was most effective for this audience, in this situation? Is there anything that can be generalized to apply to other situations and audiences?

## AUDIENCES, SITUATIONS, AND PURPOSES

The ideas and techniques given in the rest of the book are tools; they are what we and other risk communicators have found to work for a given audience in a given situation with a given purpose. Because risk communication is a relatively new area of study, the limited amount of empirical research available makes finding the one "right solution" impossible, even if there is one right solution to find. Wherever possible, we've cited the work of others as confirmation of our own findings and those of other practitioners in the field. Citations for the research discussed in the text can be found at the end of each chapter. Other sources of information in the area of

───── ◇ ─────

Because risk communication is a relatively new area of study, the limited amount of empirical research available makes finding the one "right solution" impossible, even if there is one right solution to find.

─────────────────

risk communication can be found in Chapter 19, "Resources."

Many of the resources listed discuss such issues as credibility of the organization communicating or managing the risk, fairness of the risk in the audience's eyes, and trust among parties. These issues will be dealt with only as they relate to specific points in the rest of this book; however, they are important issues that heavily affect the ability to communicate risk effectively. Unfortunately, they are often outside the control of most of us who actually communicate risk. When we step in front of an audience, policies made by those far above us and sometimes years in the past have already either forged a bond of trust with the audience or broken it. Likewise, our credibility as risk communicators will depend on the credibility of other risk communicators who previously faced the same audience. Although we cannot change the past, we can be aware of past mistakes or successes and make sure that our own efforts are trustworthy, credible, and fair insofar as we have the authority to make them so. And we must champion the cause of trustworthy, credible, and fair risk management decisions in our own organizations, both because it is ethical and because it is the only way to ensure successful communication.

## REFERENCES

Kasperson, R. E. 1986. "Six Propositions on Public Participation and Their Relevance for Risk Communication." *Risk Analysis*, 6(3):275-281.

Weinstein, N. D., and P. M. Sandman. 1993. "Some Criteria for Evaluating Risk Messages." *Risk Analysis*, 13(1):103-114.

*"Where potential personal harm is concerned, the believability of information provided depends greatly on the degree of trust and confidence in the risk communicator. If the communicator is viewed as having a compromised mandate or a lack of competence, credence in information provided tends to be weakened accordingly. Or if the particular risk has been mismanaged or neglected in the past, skepticism and distrust may greet attempts to communicate risks."*

—Roger E. Kasperson, "Six Propositions on Public Participation and Their Relevance for Risk Communication" (1986, page 277).

# Part
# I

# UNDERSTANDING RISK COMMUNICATION

*T*o understand risk communication, you'll need to understand the approaches to communicating risk, the laws that shape the way we communicate risk today, the constraints to effective risk communication, the ethical issues, and the basic principles of risk communication, which have evolved out of the approaches, laws, constraints, and ethics. Additional sources of information are listed under Chapter 21, "Resources."

◇

*"Learning about risk occurs not in isolated individuals but in a social dynamic, with multiple sources of information, channels of information flow, confirmatory and challenging mechanisms, and linkage with other social issues."*

—R. E. Kasperson, "Hazardous Waste Facility Siting: Community, Firm, and Government Perspectives" (1986, page 131).

# Approaches to Communicating Risk

*T*here are a number of approaches to the process of risk communication and its components, including how messages are sent and received, how conflicts are managed, and how decisions are made. Some of these approaches are communication research methods in themselves, some grew out of research in fields other than communication, and still others are based on traditions across disciplines.

Why should those who are communicating risks learn about the various approaches? Each approach views risk communication from a slightly different perspective, just as different audiences view a risk from different perspectives. The more risk communication perspectives the communicators understand, the more likely they will be able to choose approaches that will meet the needs of their particular situation and audience, and the more likely that their risk communication efforts will succeed.

Are all approaches equally valid? Each approach was developed to illuminate a particular perspective on risk communication. Depending on how broad that perspective is, the approach may be applicable to a variety of situations and audiences. Some approaches, although still widely used in communicating risk, may be outdated given the situations and audiences that face communicators today. For example, the traditional communication method developed by Claude Shannon in 1948 is still used occasionally today to structure risk communication efforts despite the fact that more sophisticated models have been developed that include two-way communication so important to risk communication.

The following discussion of approaches to risk communication presents an overview of twelve of the most common approaches as well as implications for those who are communicating risk and how the approach might be used in various situations.

## COMMUNICATION PROCESS APPROACH

Risk communication is a form of communication that, like other forms, is represented by the traditional model of communication (Shannon 1948). That is, there is a source of communication that generates a message that goes through a channel to a receiver. For example, a regulatory agency (the source) may decide that a chemical poses an unacceptable risk to the public (the message) and issue a press release (the channel) published as a story by the news media (another channel) that is read by members of the local community (the receivers). Various studies in the risk communication literature have looked at the individual components of this model (sources, messages, etc.) to see how changes in any one component affects the others. For example, researchers at the Center for Mass Media Research at Marquette University found that the receiver relied more heavily on different channels for information based on personal emotions such as worry in the wake of a parasite outbreak in drinking water in Milwaukee (Griffin et al. 1994).

The implications for risk communicators are that each of the model components need to be considered when developing risk communication efforts. Will the source of the message be credible with the intended audience? Have the messages been developed in such a way as to be easily understood by the receivers? What channels (methods) are available that reach the intended audiences? What attitudes from the receiver will affect how the message is perceived? Can we plan for effective feedback to evaluate not only the risk communication process but the decision process as well? Additional information in Parts II, III, IV, and V will help risk communicators answer these types of questions for care, consensus, and crisis communications (see Chapter 1, "Introduction" for a description of these types).

## NATIONAL RESEARCH COUNCIL'S APPROACH

In the 1980s, the National Research Council funded an extensive study in the effective communication of risk (NRC 1989). The multiagency panel of experts came to several conclusions. One was that risk communication can be defined as the "interactive process of exchange of information and opinions among individuals, groups, and institutions concerning a risk or potential risk to human health or the environment." The panel saw risk communication as a process by which scientific organizations both disseminate technical information and gather information about the opinions and concerns of nonscientific groups.

More recently, the NRC sponsored a second group of experts to look at how risk assessment (which they called characterization), management, and communication could be improved (NRC 1996). This group found that risk assessment should be directed toward informing decisions and solving problems, and that this consideration of the social context of the risk should start from the very beginning of the risk assessment and continue through management and communication. This group called for early and interactive involvement with those at risk.

The implication for those who communicate risk is that any form of successful risk communication must incorporate that "exchange of information and opinions" and the participation of the stakeholder groups from the beginning. How this exchange is accomplished will vary for each type of risk communication (care, consensus, or crisis). The audience is necessarily involved in exchanging information with those who are communicating and

◇

Risk communication can be defined as the "interactive process of exchange of information and opinions among individuals, groups, and institutions concerning a risk or potential risk to human health or the environment" (NRC 1989).

managing the risk in consensus communication. The exchange can be incorporated into care communication by, at the very least, soliciting audience feedback before and after risk information is distributed. The exchange may be the most difficult in crisis communication. In a crisis, by definition, there is almost never time to bring together representatives of the audience to determine their needs and concerns. One way to solve this problem is to exchange information with the potential audience (those who may be affected by the crisis, for example, the community surrounding a chemical plant) as part of emergency planning efforts.

## MENTAL MODELS APPROACH

The concept of how people understand and view various phenomena, or their mental models of the situation, is grounded in cognitive psychology and artificial intelligence research (Geuter and Stevens 1983). The mental models approach as applied to risk communication comes largely from researchers at Carnegie-Mellon University (Baruch Fischhoff, Granger Morgan, Ann Bostrom, and associates; Morgan et al. 2002). The approach was used successfully in other forms of technical communication, such as computer documentation, before being used to focus risk communication efforts.

Using this approach, communicators begin by determining to which audience the risk communication efforts will be directed. They then interview members of that audience to determine how the audience views the risk. For example, in one of the more publicized efforts, the U.S. Environmental Protection Agency's radon information program, researchers interviewed members of the audience using open-ended questions that gradually became more focused as the interview progressed (from "tell me everything you know about radon" to "tell me more about how it affects you"). Answers from all the participants were used to compile a "mental model," a view of how the audience saw radon, its exposure routes, and dangers. This mental model was compared with the expert model—the model that scientists use to evaluate radon. Researchers followed up with a more focused questionnaire to verify differences between the two models. Risk communication messages were then designed to address the gaps or inconsistencies in the audience's knowledge (Morgan et al. 1992). The intent was not to convince the public to think like scientists but to identify the information the public would need to make an informed decision.

The implication for those who communicate risks is that to really communicate with your audience, you must understand what your audience already believes about the risk. Risk communication messages that do not address key audience concerns or account for existing beliefs will fail. At the very least, all three forms of risk communication (care, consensus, and crisis) must incorporate some audience analysis.

For care communication, which often has as its audience a wide cross section of the population, the communicators will need to understand lifestyle characteristics of each portion of the audience to tailor risk messages. For example, teenagers have been found to be more likely to engage in drunk driving than other age groups. How do their beliefs differ from those of other age groups to make them more likely to drive while drunk?

For consensus communication, the communicators will need to understand the concerns and beliefs of the audience before they can hope to agree on a solution. For example, how do different Native American tribes view the environment and how will these views affect their stance on hazardous waste cleanup?

For crisis communication, communicators need to understand the cultures of the audience to be able to discuss ways to mitigate a crisis. A specific example is the illness that struck Navajo in northern New Mexico and Arizona in 1993 (dubbed the "mystery illness" by the news media because the cause eluded health care professionals for some time). The illness was found to be spread by breathing airborne particles of infected mouse dung, which would seem to be a relatively easy source to avoid. However, because sweeping was part of the religious and cultural activities of the Navajo, and sweeping raised the dust in which the dung was often found, the source proved to be a more insidious one to combat. See

◇

*"In the absence of evidence, no one can predict confidently how to communicate about a risk. Effective and reliable risk communication requires empirical study."*

—Morgan et al.,
*Risk Communication: A Mental Models Approach*
(2002, page 182).

Chapter 8, "Analyze Your Audience," for more information on understanding your audience.

## CRISIS COMMUNICATION APPROACH

The crisis communication approach holds that those who are communicating the risk should use every device to move the audience to appropriate action. For example, in a flood, they should construct messages that cause the audience to evacuate to higher ground while refraining from hindering the work of rescue groups. As one risk communication professional explained, "You only give the audience the information they need to get them to leave. Anything else is extraneous." Given this goal, passing on such information as probability of risk and alternatives seems pointless. This approach holds that the organization knows what is best for the audience and should act as a firm parent in enforcing its opinion.

In an era when those who are affected by a risk are demanding more and more involvement, this approach seems outdated in the extreme. As its name suggests, the only type of risk communication for which it might be valid is crisis communication. However, even in extreme public health emergencies like a bioterrorist attack, the public's demand for information is likely to be higher than this apprach would satisfy. The implication for those who are communicating in a crisis is that persuasion, which is discussed under Chapter 5, "Ethical Issues," is justified in this case and that information given to those at risk should be limited. Our own experience is that people are more likely to change behavior when they know the "why," not just the "what" or "how."

## CONVERGENCE COMMUNICATION APPROACH

Everett Rogers (Rogers and Kincaid 1981) developed a theory that communication (including risk communication) is an iterative long-term process in which the values (culture, experiences, background) of the risk communication organization and the audience affect the process of communication. The organization issues information, the audience processes it to the extent possible and issues its own information ("we don't trust you," "what is this stuff?," "do you want me to do something?"). The organization then processes that information and responds by issuing additional or modified information. The two groups continue to cycle information back and forth, slowly converging onto common ground.

The implication for those communicating risk is that the audience must be involved in the risk communication process, that the process must be a dialogue, not a monologue on the part of the organization. Continuous feedback and interpretation are necessary for communication to be effective. This is true for care and crisis communication, but particularly for consensus communication. For care communication, the dialogue may be with a sample of the intended audience. For crisis communication, the dialogue may be with community members involved in emergency planning efforts. For consensus communication, of course, the dialogue is with the group with which you are trying to reach an agreement.

———— ◇ ————

The audience must be involved in the risk communication process, and the process must be a dialogue, not a monologue on the part of the organization.

## THREE-CHALLENGE APPROACH

This approach gets its name from Rowan (1991), who views risk communication as three challenges:

- knowledge challenge—the audience needs to be able to understand the technical information surrounding the risk assessment

- a process challenge—the audience needs to feel involved in the risk management process

- communications skills challenge—the audience and those who are communicating the risk need to be able to communicate effectively.

Those who are communicating the risk must meet each of these challenges for risk communication efforts to succeed.

The implication for those communicating the risk (whether through care, consensus, or crisis communication) is that both those who are communicating risk and the audience must have excellent communication skills.

If the audience's skills are lacking, those who are communicating the risk will have to compensate with techniques designed to increase comprehensibility.

To meet the knowledge challenge, the technical information will have to be presented in a variety of ways—in information materials (pamphlets, fact sheets, technical reports), in visual representations of risk (graphics, such as simple diagrams, pie charts, conceptual drawings), through face-to-face communication (presentations with vivid projected graphics and handouts), through stakeholder participation (small group discussions with facilitators who are knowledgeable about the risk), and in technology-assisted communication (web sites and interactive models of risk).

To meet the process challenge, the audience will have to be included in how the risk is being managed. For care communication, the audience may be involved by choosing among a variety of preventive or mitigative measures (the risk of dying from heart disease can be reduced by changing to a high-fiber, low-fat diet; exercising; and/or stopping smoking). For consensus communication, the audience may be involved by helping to develop the way the risk management decision will be made (do all stakeholders vote or will representatives develop a decision?), making the decision (working within a group to develop a consensus), and implementing the decision (developing the policies and procedures or actually doing what was decided). For crisis communication, the audience may be involved by helping to develop emergency preparedness plans or assisting in evacuations or other management strategies.

To meet the communications skills challenge, those who are communicating the risk may need to interview the audience to help audience members focus their thoughts or meet with audience members in smaller groups so that members can help each other communicate.

## SOCIAL CONSTRUCTIONIST APPROACH

Similar to the National Research Council approach, this approach focuses on the flow of technical information and values, beliefs, and emotions (Waddell 1995).

Many approaches consider that during a risk assessment, the scientific community provides technical knowledge while the audience or stakeholders provide values, beliefs, and emotions through feedback on the risk communication effort or in the risk management process. The Social Constructionist approach holds that in fact both inputs come from both sides. In other words, the scientific community has values, beliefs, and emotions that subtly affect how risks are assessed and communicated, and the stakeholders often have technical knowledge that could affect the risk assessment and communication process.

The implication for risk communicators is that social context and culture can influence beliefs and actions of all parties. Understanding this context and facilitating an exchange of information, attitudes, values, and perceptions in both directions ("expert" to "stakeholder" and vice versa) can help build better risk decisions, whether in care, consensus, or crisis communication.

## HAZARD PLUS OUTRAGE APPROACH

Noted risk communication expert Peter Sandman, in a number of articles, books, and videos, popularized the approach originally developed through research by Baruch Fischhoff and Paul Slovic that risk should be viewed as hazard plus outrage (Sandman 1987). That is, the audience's view of risk (as opposed to that of the experts assessing the risk) reflects not just the danger of the action (hazard) but also how they feel about the action and, even more important, what emotions they feel about the action (their outrage). Think of the hazard part of the risk as the expert's assessment of the risk—the factors considered in the risk assessment, which may lack emotional aspects of the risk. Think of the outrage part of the risk as the nonexpert's assessment of the risk—the average person's assessment of the risk, which may lack some or all of the factors considered in the risk assessment. If both assessments are in agreement, that is, the expert and nonexpert agree that the risk is substantial (high hazard and high outrage) or insubstantial (low hazard and low outrage), then there is a lesser chance of

> "The Social Constructionist Model suggests that we do not—or should not—develop policy in private by some arhetorical means and then, through rhetoric, attempt to impose that policy on our fellows."
>
> —Craig Waddell, "Defining Sustainable Development: A Case Study in Environmental Communication" (1995, page 201).

controversy. If the two assessments do not agree (high hazard and low outrage or low hazard and high outrage), there is a greater chance of controversy.

The implication for those who are communicating risk (whether in care, consensus, or crisis communication) is that a presentation of technical facts will not necessarily give most audiences the information they want. Indeed, the audience will probably not even listen to those facts until their concerns and feelings have been addressed. You cannot ignore the outrage part of the risk and focus solely on the hazard. This does not mean that you should pretend to agree with the audience's concerns, which would be disastrous to building the levels of credibility needed to communicate risk. Instead it means you must understand the audience's feelings and make sure information addressing those feelings is included in the risk message.

## MENTAL NOISE APPROACH

Dr. Vincent Covello, another luminary in the field of risk communication, cautions his students in course work and workshops to beware of mental noise when communicating risks. The approach is also used by some portions of the U.S. Department of Defense and in public health circles.

This approach holds that when people perceive themselves at risk, their ability to hear and process information decreases dramatically. Under such circumstances, the ability to attend to and retain information is estimated to be 80% less than normal. This limitation is particularly true in sudden, unexpected crises. For example, those responding to the bombing of the Oklahoma City federal building in April 1995 found that both verbal and written information had to be provided, sometimes multiple times, for the victims' families to understand what had happened and what they should do next (Blakeney 2002).

The implication for those communicating risk is that risk information must be carefully packaged and presented, particularly in crisis communication. Proponents of the approach advise no more than three key messages, repeated frequently; reinforcement of verbal and written communications with visuals; and ruthless removal of jargon, technical terms, and acronyms. For additional information on designing risk information materials, see Chapter 13, "Information Materials."

## SOCIAL NETWORK CONTAGION APPROACH

Organizational studies have looked at the way social networks influence behavior and attitudes in the workplace. The results of these studies suggest that who we spend time with affects how we view the world. More recently, this approach has been applied to risk communication efforts (for example, see Scherer and Cho 2003).

The approach holds that, when faced with a risk, people adopt the behaviors and attitudes of others in their social network as a response to the risk. Their network does not need to influence them intentionally; the change may come about gradually as a result of shared time and similar perceptions in other areas. The stronger the social tie and the more frequent the interaction, the more likely the cohesiveness of reaction to the risk.

The implication for those communicating risk is that we must look beyond individuals to their communities when communicating risk. In trying to encourage people to modify risky behaviors (for example, in care communication), getting their social network to endorse or reinforce less risky actions might be more effective than targeting individuals. Involving all members of a social network might be the only way to gain participation in some areas for consensus communication. In crisis communication, partnering with key social leaders may spread the news the fastest. For more information on understanding the needs of the audience, see Chapter 8, "Analyze Your Audience."

## SOCIAL AMPLIFICATION OF RISK APPROACH

This approach grew from a social science perspective and was furthered by internationally known researchers Roger and Jean Kasperson (for example, Kasperson et al.

> We must look beyond individuals to their communities when communicating risk.

1988), as well as Paul Slovic and James Flynn. Slovic, Flynn, and others helped add the concept of stigma to the approach (for example, in Flynn et al. 2001).

The basic theory is that social activities will magnify the consequences of a risk event, often in unexpected ways. Think of a pebble thrown into a lake; the ripples spread far beyond the pebble's initial impact on the water. So too, a risk can spread to impact business sales, regulatory agendas, community opposition, and legal action. These consequences can in turn result in an industry or a community being stigmatized—seen as negative or bad by others who associate with them.

The news media in particular has been credited with amplifying risk consequences. For example, work at several universities in the United Kingdom (Birmingham, East Anglia, Surrey, and Queen's University in Belfast) found that while media coverage often brought in secondary issues associated with risk, government agencies charged with communicating risk usually failed to recognize or address such issues (Department of Health 2003). This dichotomy resulted in stories about the risk growing in number and outrage, without providing any support to its resolution.

The implication for risk communicators is to actively plan for and respond to such ripples, particularly for consensus and crisis communications. Such planning should incorporate a thorough understanding of audiences' needs. See Chapter 8, "Analyze Your Audience," and Chapter 16, "Working with the Media," for more information.

## SOCIAL TRUST APPROACH

The social trust approach also grew from social science research, particularly that of George Cvetkovich and Tim Earle. This approach holds that a person's trust in an institution (for example, a government agency) is built on an understanding of the institution's goals, motives, and actions in relationship to the person's values. In other words, if I perceive based on observed behaviors that the organization managing the risk has the same values I have, I will place my trust in them to appropriately manage the risk. Research has found that the higher the trust, the lower the estimate of risk and the higher the estimate of benefits (Cvetkovich and Winter 2001).

Another aspect of this approach is called the Asymmetry Principle. Researchers found that it is more difficult to create or earn trust than to destroy it. Studies showed that if people do not trust an organization, negative information associated with that organization reinforces their distrust, while positive information is discounted. Fortunately, the converse is also true: If people trust an organization, positive information will reinforce that trust and negative information will be discounted (Cvetkovich et al. 2002).

When the control of risk isn't at the personal level, trust becomes a major and perhaps the most important variable in public acceptance of the risk management approach (Cvetkovich and Winter 2001). This premise is also supported by work by Vincent Covello, who has been credited with the idea that when people perceive themselves to be at risk, they understand and put into practice only those messages that come from sources they perceive as trustworthy and credible. Some researchers believe this perception of trust and credibility comes from the audience's perceptions of the organization's ability to care, commitment to resolving the risk, competence, and honesty. The single biggest contributor to increasing trust and credibility is the organization's ability to care or show empathy.

Implications for those communicating risk is that information alone, no matter how carefully packaged and presented, will not communicate risk effectively if trust and credibility are not established first. Trust and confidence are being shown as increasingly important to how people perceive risks and how they respond to risk management strategies. Unfortunately, how an organization is perceived is often beyond the control of risk communicators. Some techniques for building trust and credibility can be found in Chapter 4, "Constraints to Effective Risk Communication," and Chapter 5, "Ethical Issues."

———— ◇ ————

Trust and confidence are being shown as increasingly important to how people perceive risks and how they respond to risk management strategies.

## IN SUMMARY

No one approach to risk communication can be applied equally well to all the purposes, audiences, and situations for which risk is being communicated. Instead, approaches to risk communication come from a variety of disciplines, each of which can provide insight to those who are communicating the risk. Understanding the various approaches and their implications can give us a repertoire of ways to develop our risk communication efforts, giving us a greater chance of success than if we were communicating without this knowledge.

## REFERENCES

Blakeney, R. L. 2002. "Providing Relief to Families After a Mass Fatality: Roles of the Medical Examiner's Office and the Family Assistance Center." *OVC Bulletin*, November 2002. U.S. Department of Justice, Office of Justice Programs, Office for Victims of Crime, Washington, D.C.

Cvetkovich, G., and P. L. Winter. 2001. "Social Trust and the Management of Risks to Threatened and Endangered Species." Presented at the Annual Meeting of the Society for Risk Analysis, Seattle, Washington, December 2-5, 2001.

Cvetkovich, G., M. Siegrist, R. Murray, and S. Tragesser. 2002. "New Information and Social Trust: Asymmetry and Perseverance of Attributions about Hazard Managers." *Risk Analysis* 22(2):359-367.

Department of Health (of the United Kingdom). 2003. "The Social Amplification of Risk: The Media and the Public." Posted at http://www.doh.gov.uk/risk/riskampl.htm.

Flynn, J., P. Slovic, and H. Kunreuther, editors. 2001. *Risk, Media, and Stigma: Understanding Public Challenges to Modern Science and Technology*. Earthscan, London.

Geuter, G., and A. L. Stevens, editors. 1983. *Mental Models*. Lawrence Erlbaum Associates, Hillsdale, New Jersey.

Griffin, R. J., S. Dunwoody, F. Zabala, and M. Kamerick. 1994. "Public Reliance on Risk Communication Channels in the Wake of the Cryptosporidium Outbreak." Paper presented at the Society for Risk Analysis Annual Meeting, Baltimore, Maryland, December 1994.

Kasperson, R. E., O. Renn, P. Slovic, H. S. Brown, J. Emel, R. Goble, J. X. Kasperson, and S. Ratick. 1988. "The Social Amplification of Risk: A Conceptual Framework." *Risk Analysis* 8:177-187.

Morgan, M. G., B. Fischhoff, A. Bostrom, L. Lave, and C. J. Atman. 1992. "Communicating Risk to the Public." *Environ. Sci. Technol.*, 26(11):2048-2056.

Morgan, M. G., B. Fischhoff, A. Bostrom, and C. J. Atman. 2002. *Risk Communication: A Mental Models Approach.* Cambridge University Press, New York.

NRC (National Research Council). 1989. *Improving Risk Communication.* National Academy Press, Washington, D.C.

NRC (National Research Council). 1996. *Understanding Risk: Informing Decisions in a Democratic Society.* National Academy Press, Washington, D.C.

Rogers, E. M., and D. L. Kincaid. 1981. *Communications Networks: Toward a New Paradigm for Research.* The Free Press, a Division of Macmillan Publishing Company, Inc., New York.

Rowan, K. E. 1991. "Goals, Obstacles, and Strategies in Risk Communication: A Problem-Solving Approach to Improving Communication about Risks." *Journal of Applied Communication Research*, November:300-329.

Sandman, P. M. 1987. "Risk Communication: Facing Public Outrage." *EPA Journal*, November:21-22.

Sandman, P. M. 2003. "Four Kinds of Risk Communication." *The Synergist* (Journal of the American Industrial Hygiene Association), April:26-27.

Scherer, C. W., and H. Cho. 2003. "A Social Contagion Theory of Risk Perception." *Risk Analysis*, 23(2):261–267.

Shannon, C. E. 1948. "A Mathematical Theory of Communication." First published in *Bell System Technical Journal*, Bell Labs, Murray Hill, New Jersey.

Waddell, C. 1995. "Defining Sustainable Development: A Case Study in Environmental Communication." *Technical Communication Quarterly*, 4(2):201-216.

## ADDITIONAL RESOURCES

Hannigan, J. A. 1995. *Environmental Sociology: A Social Constructionist Perspective.* Routledge Press, London.

Johnson, B. B. 1993. "'The Mental Model' Meets 'The Planning Process': Wrestling with Risk Communication Research and Practice." *Risk Analysis*, 13(1):5-8.

"Risk=Hazard+Outrage . . . A Formula for Effective Risk Communication." Videotape course presented by Peter M. Sandman. Available from the American Industrial Hygienists Association, Washington, D.C.

Sandman, P. M. 1989. "Hazard versus Outrage in the Public Perception of Risk." *Effective Risk Communication: The Role and Responsibility of Government and Nongovernment Organizations*, editors V. T. Covello, D. B. McCallum, and M. T. Pavlova, pages 45-49. Plenum Press, New York.

# Laws That Mandate
# Risk Communication

*A*lthough many organizations have realized that it is good business practice to keep communities and interested parties aware of potential risks, risk communication is still often conducted as a result of a law, regulation, or other government inducement. A number of laws and regulations in the United States mandate risk communication as part of the risk assessment and risk management process. Although these laws can run to several volumes, making it difficult for anyone outside of the legal profession to really understand them, those who are communicating risk need to be aware of the laws affecting risk communication efforts and what these laws entail.

Failing to understand the laws and regulations can have several repercussions:

- Some member of your audience (who knows more than you do about the law) may sue your organization for failing to follow due process. This has happened to a number of federal agencies because they took a law or even their own implementing regulations less seriously than did the audience.

◇

Although many organizations have realized that it is good business practice to keep communities and interested parties aware of potential risks, risk communication is still often conducted as a result of a law, regulation, or other government inducement.

- Your arguments for continued or increased funding for risk communication are weakened if you don't know the law. Organizations are more likely to take notice if the risk communication effort is "required" than if it is optional. Optional programs get cut in budget crunches, whereas those required by law usually do not.

- The agency in charge of implementing the regulation may shut down your operations or levy a heavy fine if you are not in compliance.

Below are highlights of some of the major federal laws within the United States. Many states have similar rulings, often with more stringent requirements. In addition, many agencies and organizations have guidelines for implementing the regulations they must comply with most frequently. For example, the National Environmental Policy Act has counterparts in many states (State Environmental Policy Act) and several federal agencies (for example, the U.S. Department of Energy and U.S. Department of Defense) have developed their own policies and procedures to comply with both regulations. Check your state and local laws and how your organization has chosen to implement these laws before beginning your risk communication[1] efforts.

## COMPREHENSIVE ENVIRONMENTAL RESPONSE, COMPENSATION, AND LIABILITY ACT

Also known as CERCLA or Superfund, this Act and its reauthorization (Superfund Amendment and Reauthorization Act, or SARA) require that specific procedures be implemented to assess the release of hazardous substances at inactive waste sites. Those procedures involve the inclusion of "community relations" in the evaluation process. The term "community relations" refers to

---

[1]In this chapter, we sometimes use the terms "risk communication" and "public involvement" interchangeably because many of the regulations use the same term to mean both.

developing a working relationship with the public to determine acceptable ways to clean up the site. Figure 3-1 illustrates how the community relations process fits into the technical process for cleanup. Key communication pieces are as follows:

- Community Relations Plan—The Community Relations Plan is very similar to the communication plan described in Chapter 12, "Develop a Communication Plan." The plan incorporates information about the site (e.g., history, levels of contamination, types of contamination); the community interested in the cleanup (demographic information); their concerns and beliefs about the site; and which communication methods will be used to address these concerns and include the public in the cleanup process. Under U.S. Environmental Protection Agency guidelines, in developing the community relations plan, representatives of the organization responsible for cleanup are required to meet with members of the community to listen to their concerns. These community interviews are generally conducted one-on-one in a location where each member feels comfortable (their home, the local tavern, etc.). The plan is usually updated at least yearly throughout the process, which averages 8 years.

- Administrative Record—The Administrative Record is a set of all documents and other information that were used to make a decision about steps in the cleanup process. It is housed in a public library or other location where the audience can have easy access to it. It is updated at each step in the cleanup process.

- Information Repository—An Information Repository is a file containing site information, documents on site activities, and general information about the Superfund program. It too is housed in a library or other location where the audience can have easy access to it. It is updated regularly (the interval depends on how much activity is going on at the site and could range from weekly to quarterly).

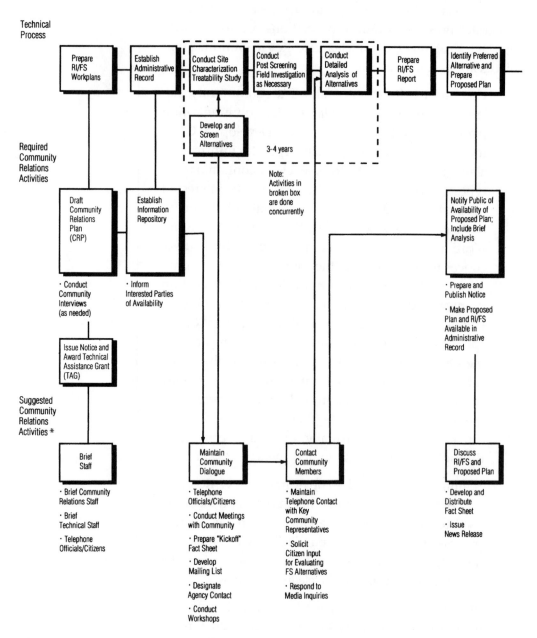

**FIGURE 3-1.** Risk communication and public involvement activities associated with the Superfund cleanup process.

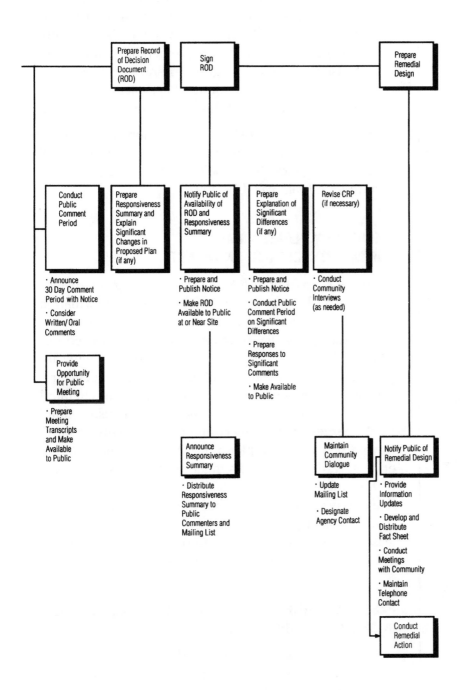

Prepare Record of Decision Document (ROD)

Sign ROD

Prepare Remedial Design

Conduct Public Comment Period

· Announce 30 Day Comment Period with Notice

· Consider Written/Oral Comments

Provide Opportunity for Public Meeting

· Prepare Meeting Transcripts and Make Available to Public

Prepare Responsiveness Summary and Explain Significant Changes in Proposed Plan (if any)

Notify Public of Availability of ROD and Responsiveness Summary

· Prepare and Publish Notice

· Make ROD Available to Public at or Near Site

Announce Responsiveness Summary

· Distribute Responsiveness Summary to Public Commenters and Mailing List

Prepare Explanation of Significant Differences (if any)

· Prepare and Publish Notice

· Conduct Public Comment Period on Significant Differences

· Prepare Responses to Significant Comments

· Make Available to Public

Revise CRP (if necessary)

· Conduct Community Interviews (as needed)

Maintain Community Dialogue

· Update Mailing List

· Designate Agency Contact

Notify Public of Remedial Design

· Provide Information Updates

· Develop and Distribute Fact Sheet

· Conduct Meetings with Community

· Maintain Telephone Contact

Conduct Remedial Action

- Advertisement of Public Involvement Opportunities—Fact sheets, news releases, and proposed plans are some of the devices used to alert the public to opportunities for involvement in how cleanup decisions are made. Figure 3-1 shows the points at which the U.S. Environmental Protection Agency suggests that some of this information be released.

More information on risk communication requirements of Superfund can be found in the U.S. Environmental Protection Agency handbook *Community Relations in Superfund: A Handbook* (EPA 1992).

## EMERGENCY PLANNING AND COMMUNITY RIGHT-TO-KNOW ACT

This Act, a part of SARA, is a free-standing law that requires that the public be provided with information about hazardous chemicals in the community and establishes emergency planning and notification procedures to protect the public from a release of those chemicals. The Act also calls for the creation of state emergency response commissions to guide planning for chemical emergencies. Such state commissions have also created local emergency planning committees to ensure community participation and planning. Organizations that generate hazardous chemicals must produce a list each year of the quantities of chemicals stored at each site and make it available to the public and regulatory agencies. In addition, organizations must report any accidental release of hazardous chemicals to the environment and in some cases file reports on routine emissions as well.

## EXECUTIVE ORDER 12898, ENVIRONMENTAL JUSTICE IN MINORITY POPULATIONS

Presidential or Executive Orders provide requirements to federal government agencies and departments. These agencies and departments in turn often pass along similar requirements to civilian organizations that contract to them. This Order requires that government agencies and departments consider any potentially dis-

---

Organizations that generate hazardous chemicals must produce a list each year of the quantities of chemicals stored at each site and make it available to the public and regulatory agencies. In addition, organizations must report any accidental release of hazardous chemicals to the environment and in some cases file reports on routine emissions as well.

proportionate human health or environmental risks to minority or low-income populations posed by the organization's activities, policies, or programs. As noted in Chapter 5, "Ethical Issues," environmental equity (or environmental justice) has become a rallying cry across the nation as civic organizations have begun to realize that hazardous waste facilities and other industries perceived to be "risky" were apparently more often being sited in minority or low-income areas (for example, see Bullard 1990).

One of the requirements of the Order is for agencies to consider translating crucial public documents and public meetings related to human health or environmental risks for those in the audience with limited skills in English. It also requires that information related to human health or environmental risks is concise, understandable, and readily accessible to the public.

## EXECUTIVE ORDER 13045, REDUCE ENVIRONMENTAL HEALTH AND SAFETY RISKS TO CHILDREN

This Order requires that federal agencies and departments consider the potentially disproportionate health and safety impacts to children from the organization's activities, policies, and programs. For example, an agency considering revising a regulation regarding the use of safety belts in automobiles might need to consider the growing body of evidence indicating that people of shorter stature (such as children) are actually in danger using standard over-the-shoulder safety belts. While the Order does not require risk communication per se, it does require that agencies considering enacting regulations submit risk information specifically related to children. Agencies, and contractors supporting them, need to be aware of this requirement so as to effectively communicate the risks.

*"This executive order says to every federal agency and department: put our children first. We Americans owe our largest responsibility to our smallest citizens. From now on, agencies will have to take a hard look at the special risks and disproportionate impact that standards and safeguards have on our children."*

— Former Vice President Albert Gore, national press conference at the Children's National Medical Center, April 21, 1997.

## NATIONAL ENVIRONMENTAL POLICY ACT

This is the Act that mandates environmental impact statements and other environmental assessments. Under this law, any time a federal agency takes some "major" action (whether it be their own action or the granting of a federal permit or right-of-way), it must consider the impact of that action on the environment. Depending on the potential level of impact, this consideration will be documented in:

- categorical exclusion report—a categorical exclusion report shows that the agency has considered the action and has determined that it obviously won't have an effect on the environment.

- environmental assessment—an environmental assessment is usually written by an outside organization who has analyzed the action and determined that it will or will not have an effect on the environment.

- environmental impact statement—an environmental impact statement is usually written by an outside organization when the federal agency has determined that the action is likely to have a significant impact on the environment.

Many states have similar documentation requirements for actions taken by state agencies.

Each type of assessment has different communication requirements, which become more complex as the assessment becomes more involved. The categorical exclusion report is often simply several standard forms that are filled out and filed. The environmental assessment, although a public document, basically serves to help the agency to decide whether an environmental impact statement is necessary or whether the agency can issue a Finding of No Significant Impact (referred to as a "FONSI"). An environmental assessment should contain information on the need for the proposed action, alternatives to the proposed action, environmental impacts of the proposed action and alternatives, and a listing of agencies and persons consulted in the preparation of the report. Although public involvement is not required for an environmental assessment, some agencies nevertheless issue the report for public comment and consider those comments in determining whether an environmental impact statement will be necessary.

The most complex communication requirements are associated with the environmental impact statement.

Key communication pieces associated with the environmental impact statement are:

- Notice of Intent—the agency must file a notice in the *Federal Register* detailing its intent to prepare an environmental impact statement, the possible content of that statement, and a request for public comments. The notice is usually several paragraphs to several pages long.

- Scoping Meetings—the agency has the option of conducting formal meetings with the public to determine what should be included in the environmental impact statement.

- Publication of a Draft for Comment—the agency must release a draft environmental impact statement for public comment.

- Meeting for Comments on the Draft—during the comment period, the agency usually holds public meetings to collect comments on the draft environmental impact statement.

- Publication of Final Environmental Impact Statement—the agency revises the statement based on comments. A discussion of how the comments were used must be included in the environmental impact statement or as a supplement. Another comment period may follow the issuance of the final environmental impact statement, but usually no additional meetings are held.

- Publication of a Record of Decision—the agency publishes a short statement describing their final decision on the action. The Record of Decision may be posted in the *Federal Register*, mailed to those who commented, and/or placed in a public reading room.

The Council on Environmental Quality issues regulations as to the content and size of environmental impact statements (40 CFR 1500).

## NATURAL RESOURCE DAMAGE ASSESSMENT

A natural resource damage assessment is the process of assessing environmental damage caused by releases of

The most complex communication requirements are associated with the environmental impact statement.

hazardous substances. This process is part of CERCLA. The process determines the condition of a particular part of the environment (including land, fish, wildlife, plants, air, water, groundwater, and drinking water supplies) that is public property (held by federal, state, local, or Native American governments). Natural Resource Trustees (state or federal agencies or Native American nations who act on behalf of the public for these resources) begin the process with a preassessment screen—a review of existing data concerning the resource—to determine whether hazardous substances have been released in sufficient quantity or concentration to damage the resource, whether the resource was damaged, whether data are available or can be obtained to conduct a full assessment, and how quickly it might be possible to restore the resource to its original condition. If the preassessment screen shows that the resource has likely been damaged, an independent organization is usually hired to prepare an assessment plan, more rigorously assess the damage (by studying the resource directly), and report to the Trustees. If the Trustees find that the resource has been detrimentally changed (chemically, physically, or in its viability as a natural resource; legally called injury), the organization or individual responsible for the injury may have to make restitution to them for loss of use of the resource, the cost to assess the injury, and the cost to restore the resource to its original condition (this money is legally called the damage). The public can also sue the Trustees for failing to live up to their responsibilities.

Risk communication, while not mandated specifically for these assessments, can be extremely useful in developing the assessment plan, preparing the final report, and educating the Trustees and the public on the potential risks and damages to the resource and the process of assessing those risks and damages.

## OCCUPATIONAL SAFETY AND HEALTH ACT

The Occupational Safety and Health Act was passed to ensure that "no employee will suffer material impairment of health or functional capacity" as a result of working at a particular occupation. One provision of the Act set up the Occupational Safety and Health Administration, which oversees compliance with the other provisions. One of the Occupational Safety and Health Administration's duties is to set standards for the limits of exposure to potentially hazardous chemicals and other occupational exposures. A number of public involvement activities surround the setting of standards, but, because these activities are conducted only by the Occupational Safety and Health Administration, they are not discussed here. Instead, we focus on the communication requirements placed on the organizations employing workers.

The Occupational Safety and Health Administration has issued regulations in 29 CFR 1910.1200 (referred to as the Hazard Communication Standard or Hazcom) that require employers to explain chemical and physical risks in the work environment to workers. These regulations are the origin for the use of Material Safety Data Sheets (MSDSs), which are generally one- or two-page documents that explain the properties and risks of various chemicals and mitigative measures to prevent injury. The Material Safety Data Sheets are prepared by organizations who manufacture, import, or sell the chemical or combination of chemicals. Over 500,000 products have these sheets.

Although no formalized standard exists for the format of these sheets, the same basic information is captured on each:

- specific chemical identity of the hazardous chemicals involved
- common names for the chemicals
- physical and chemical characteristics of the chemicals
- known acute and chronic health effect and related health information
- exposure limits
- whether the chemical can be considered a carcinogen
- precautionary measures for effective use
- emergency and first aid procedures

---

◇

The Occupational Safety and Health Administration has issued regulations in 29 CFR 1910.1200 that require employers to explain chemical and physical risks to workers.

---

- identification (name, address, and telephone number) for the organization responsible for preparing the sheet.

ANSI Standard No. Z400.1, *Material Safety Data Sheet Preparation*, or the MSDS Form (OSHA 174) can be used as guides to complete such sheets (OSHA 1995). Several commercial firms sell software also devoted to helping the user develop these sheets. Under the Occupational Safety and Health Act, the sheets must be made available to workers who could come in contact with the chemical described.

Specific chemicals are subject to additional regulations, some of which stipulate the training of workers in the use of the chemical. The training must include information on the risks, how to prevent possible exposure to the chemical, and what to do if exposed. Additional information, such as the Material Safety Data Sheets, must also be made available.

One portion of the standard that is often overlooked is the requirement for a "written hazard communication program" that describes what steps will be taken to ensure that workers receive the information about the chemicals in their work environment. The OSHA publication "Chemical Hazard Communication" (OSHA 1995) describes the types of information to be included in the plan such as the ways in which containers of hazardous chemicals will be labeled, how MSDSs will be made available to employees, a list of the hazardous chemicals in each work area, the means by which the employer will inform employees of the hazards of nonroutine activities, and the hazards associated with chemicals in unlabeled pipes. The written program must be available to employees as well as others such as the Director of the National Institute for Occupational Safety and Health.

All federal agencies have been given authority to administer the regulations in their areas. In addition, state agencies can administer their own program if it is approved by the Occupational Safety and Health Administration. The state programs must be at least as stringent as the federal program and are usually more stringent. Check with your organization and state agencies to

———— ◇ ————

One portion of the standard that is often overlooked is the requirement for a "written hazard communication program" that describes what steps will be taken to ensure that workers receive the information about the chemicals in their work environment.

determine which programs apply to your risk communication effort.

## RESOURCE CONSERVATION AND RECOVERY ACT

This Act was passed as an attempt to solve the growing number of problems related to the disposal of solid waste, including hazardous waste. It establishes regulatory standards for the generation, transportation, storage, treatment, and disposal of hazardous waste. Public involvement in this process is encouraged by the Act, but not specified to the extent that it is in the Superfund legislation. Instead, the Act discusses ways for the public to take organizations that do not comply to court. To forestall such litigation, many agencies and organizations have developed their own requirements for risk communication and public involvement. Check with your state and local governments, your organization, and regulatory agencies involved before beginning your risk communication efforts.

## RISK MANAGEMENT PROGRAM RULE

Under the Clean Air Act Amendments of 1990, the U.S. Environmental Protection Agency, in 1996, issued this rule, which requires facilities that use, make, or store hazardous materials to report accident scenarios for each of their facilities and to make this information available to the public and the agency. These accident scenarios include information on the "worst-case scenario" (the most drastic accident that can be envisioned for a facility), an alternate more likely accident, what the facility has done or is doing to prevent such accidents, and plans for emergency responses should the accident occur.

Because of government and industry concern about the potential criminal and terrorist use of chemical data, the agency limited the types of data available to the public and how that data could be accessed. For example, information on the off-site consequences of chemical releases can only be accessed in person at federal reading rooms after showing appropriate identification and no copies of the material can be made.

While even this limited accessibility is a benefit to communities trying to determine potential local hazards, it provides greater incentive for organizations to find ways to communicate risks effectively, as the availability of the information could raise additional questions about local risks.

## PRIVACY RULE

The Health Insurance Portability and Accountability Act of 1996 included a provision directing the U.S. Department of Health and Human Services to develop national standards for electronic health care transactions and the security and privacy of health information. The Privacy Rule, signed in April 2001 with required compliance for April 2003 for all but small health plans (who have until April 2004), outlines administrative steps, policies, and procedures to safeguard individuals' personal, private health information, in electronic or other form, including oral communications.

While this regulation does not mandate risk communication per se, it has effected risk communication in certain cases, particularly where organizations are rigorous in implementing the regulation. Developing strategies to combat certain communicable diseases can be difficult if agency staff refuse to share individual information with the mistaken idea that they will be liable for legal action should they do otherwise. If the risk about which you are communicating must be addressed using private health information, you will want to review this regulation, your state's interpretation or similar regulations, and your organization's policies in this area.

## OTHER GOVERNMENT INDUCEMENTS

Besides laws, government agencies and sometimes private organizations can encourage risk communication activities by issuing funds in the form of grants. When

If the risk about which you are communicating must be addressed using private health information, you will want to review the Privacy Rule, your state's interpretation or similar regulations, and your organization's policies in this area.

$10 million in funding is riding on the development of a risk communication plan, that plan will most likely get written. One of the more recent examples of this tactic is the Public Health Preparedness funding from the U.S. Centers for Disease Control and Prevention (CDC). Each state was allocated a certain amount of money to plan for responding to a public health emergency such as a bioterrorist attack or major disease outbreak, but the money came with the requirement of a grant application that was more of a project plan, divided into areas of focus. Focus Area F constituted risk communication activities, among them a plan on how to communicate during a public health emergency.

To aid states developing such plans, CDC developed a comprehensive training program called CDCynergy, Emergency and Risk Communication. The materials for this program were developed by experts in risk communication, particularly crisis communication, and included videos on specific topics, examples of plans and procedures, and in-depth information on working with the news media and public. Most of the materials for this program are available on a multi-media CD from CDC. No web page for the final version was available at the time this book was published. The beta version was available at http://www.orau.gov/cdcynergy/erc.

## IN SUMMARY

Various laws and regulations can apply to risk communication efforts. Check with federal agencies, state agencies, local governments, and your organization before beginning a risk communication effort to ensure that you understand and are in compliance with the requirements. Table 3-1 shows which laws and regulations might apply in care, consensus, and crisis communication.

**TABLE 3-1**
Applicability of Laws and Regulations to Risk Communication*

| Type of Risk Communication | CERCLA | EPCRA | EO12898 | EO13045 | NEPA | NRDA | OSHA | RCRA | RMP |
|---|---|---|---|---|---|---|---|---|---|
| *Care Communication* | | | | | | | | | |
| Health communication | | | | ✔ | | | ✔ | | |
| Industrial hygiene | | | | | | | ✔ | | |
| Worker notification | | | | | | | ✔ | | |
| *Consensus Communication* | | | | | | | | | |
| Hazardous waste | ✔ | | ✔ | ✔ | | | | ✔ | ✔ |
| Solid waste | | | ✔ | ✔ | | | | ✔ | |
| Environmental issues | ✔ | | ✔ | ✔ | ✔ | ✔ | | ✔ | ✔ |
| *Crisis Communication* | | | | | | | | | |
| Emergency planning | | ✔ | | ✔ | | | | | ✔ |
| Actual crisis | | | | | | ✔ | | | |

*Acronyms are defined as follows:

   CERCLA=Comprehensive Environmental Response, Compensation, and Liability Act

   EPCRA=Emergency Planning and Community Right-to-Know Act

   EO=Executive Order

   NRDA=Natural Resource Damage Assessment

   NEPA=National Environmental Policy Act

   OSHA=Occupational Safety and Health Act

   RCRA=Resource Conservation and Recovery Act

   RMP=Risk Management Program Rule

# REFERENCES

29 CFR (*Code of Federal Regulations*) Part 1910.1200. Occupational Safety and Health Administration, "Hazard Communication." Office of the Federal Register, National Archives and Records Administration, Washington, D.C.

40 CFR (*Code of Federal Regulations*) Parts 1500 to 1508. Council on Environmental Quality, "National Environmental Policy Act Implementing Regulations." Office of the Federal Register, National Archives and Records Administration, Washington, D.C.

Bullard, R. D. 1990. "In Our Backyards: Minority Communities Get Most of the Dumps." *EPA Journal*, 18(1):11-12.

EPA (U.S. Environmental Protection Agency). 1992. *Community Relations in Superfund: A Handbook*. EPA/9230.0-03C, U.S.

Environmental Protection Agency, Office of Emergency and Remedial Response, Washington, D.C.

OSHA (Occupational Safety and Health Administration). 1995. *Chemical Hazard Communication.* OSHA 3084, Occupational Safety and Health Administration, Washington, D.C.

## ADDITIONAL RESOURCES

Baram, M. S., and P. Kenyon. 1986. "Risk Communication and the Law for Chronic Health and Environmental Hazards." *Environmental Professional*, 8(2):165-179.

Carson, J. E. 1992. "On the Preparation of Environmental Impact Statements in the United States of America." *Atmospheric Environment*, 26(15):2759-2769.

EPA (U.S. Environmental Protection Agency). 1989. *Facts About The National Environmental Policy Act.* U.S. Environmental Protection Agency, Enforcement and Compliance Monitoring, Washington, D.C.

Hadden, S. G. 1990. *A Citizen's Right to Know: Risk Communication and Public Policy.* Westview Press, Boulder, Colorado.

Jia, C. Q., A. diGuardo, and D. Mackay. 1996. "Toxic Release Inventories: Opportunities for Improved Presentation and Interpretation." *Environmental Science and Technology*, 30(2):A86-A91.

# Constraints to Effective Risk Communication

*A* number of factors can place limitations on the risk communication effort. In general, the same factors can limit or constrain care, consensus, and crisis communication. Those who are communicating risk need to be aware of these constraints so that they can recognize and overcome the problems to increase their chances of communicating effectively. This chapter discusses the constraints on those who are communicating risk and the constraints that come from the audience, offering advice on how to recognize and overcome the potential problems.

## CONSTRAINTS ON THE COMMUNICATOR

Suppose you're faced with a particularly difficult assignment—explain to a group of mothers that their infants have been inadvertently exposed to a highly toxic chemical that may cause mental retardation, physical disabilities, or even death. You can justifiably expect anger and fear, with people yelling and crying, not to mention the likelihood of lawsuits that could close your organization permanently. You plunge into the task, only to find that these difficulties in communicating this risk information are the least of your worries. What could make them worse? Read on.

## Organizational Constraints

The very organization that has asked you to communicate risks can put any number of roadblocks in your way:
- inadequate resources
- management apathy or hostility
- potential roles dichotomy
- difficult review and approval procedures
- corporate protection requirements
- conflicting organizational requirements
- insufficient information to adequately plan and set schedules.

### Inadequate Resources

To effectively communicate risk, you need the funding, staff, equipment, and space to do the job. Unfortunately, in many organizations, the technical aspects of the risk (the risk assessment and risk management) are given the bulk of these key resources. Many organizations that would never refuse a scientist software to calculate dose quite easily turn down a requisition for desktop publishing equipment that would make it easier and less expensive to create and revise risk messages which are far more readable for the intended audience. With so much attention paid to the analysis of risk, the actual communication can be completely forgotten.

Risk communication is still too new to have much empirical data to show managers and decision-makers the importance of supporting it. One example comes from the *Washington Post* that reported in October 2003 that utilities were coming to realize the importance of communicating risk management to their constituencies. One utility took the brunt of public outcry when it failed to provide prompt and reliable estimates of when power would be restored after a devastating hurricane.

Concerns escalated to the political level, damaging company credibility and exposing the organization to Congressional inquiry (Davenport 2003).

Those of us who are developing risk communication programs based on laws or other regulations can point to these laws, which mandate involving the audience in how the risk is managed, and therefore require risk communication. Organizations ignore or neglect these requirements only at their own peril. Likewise when the entire charter of the organization is based on communicating risks, it may not be hard to argue for adequate resources. In the absence of such legal or organizational mandates, those who are communicating risk in more voluntary programs can use case studies and examples of programs that succeeded or failed and how these affected the organization's ability to do business (for example, see Beierle 2002; Hunt and Monaghan 1992; and Sanderson and Niles 1992).

### Management Apathy or Hostility

Sometimes even when resources are plentiful, risk communication efforts fail because of the lack of support by the organization's managers or other decision-makers. This support is necessary to obtain resources; to conduct many of the activities required in care, consensus, and crisis communication; and to evaluate and improve risk communication efforts. Balch and Sutton (1995), Boiarsky (1991), and Dozier et al. (1995) have pointed out that those who are communicating risk must first reach this internal audience before reaching out to an external audience. Only when the managers support a risk communication effort can that effort succeed.

Sometimes, this lack of support may arise from an apparent apathy. As in the case of having insufficient resources, with the risk assessment and resulting decision taking the spotlight (often justifiably), managers and other decision-makers often seem to find it easy to overlook the risk communication effort. Educating managers on the effects poor communication can have on an organization will sometimes be enough to alert them to the need to support your efforts.

Educating managers on the effects poor communication can have on an organization will sometimes be enough to alert them to the need to support your efforts.

Sometimes, however, the lack of support for risk communication efforts comes from an apparent hostility to the process. Caron Chess, Director of Rutgers University's Center for Environmental Communication, in a presentation at the 1994 Society for Risk Analysis Annual Meeting, described a phenomena called the "Threat Rigidity Response." Simply put, this is how the managers of an organization may react when they feel threatened. This feeling can arise from such situations as the threat of a lawsuit, the perceived potential for negative publicity, or the perceived lack of control of the situation. When so threatened, the managers of an organization become more rigid and more controlling. They tighten controls on their staff, the flow of information, and the decision-making process. This kind of rigid response can make successful risk communication virtually impossible.

Chess found that organizations with certain characteristics are more successful at avoiding this rigid response to a perceived threat and hence are more successful at communicating risk. These characteristics include the following:

- The organization has a mechanism for the upward flow of information.

- The organization has a diffraction of responsibility (communication is everyone's business as opposed to being within the sole purview of a public affairs function).

- The organization has a permeable boundary—there are numerous ways for the community (or audience) to get information about the organization's activities.

In addition, studies of communication organizations by David Dozier and Larissa and James Grunig of the University of Maryland found that communication effectiveness or excellence was heavily influenced by shared expectations between senior management and those charged with communicating for the organization. Other factors included the core knowledge of the communicators and the level of participation allowed by corporate culture. The more knowledgeable the communicator in communication tactics and strategy, and the more participatory the culture, the better was the chance of effective communication (Dozier et al. 1995).

On a routine basis, those who are communicating risk can encourage these types of behaviors and philosophies within their organizations so that hostility to risk communication efforts is less likely to occur. Dozier's work suggests that sometimes "crises" like mergers, change in leadership, new competition, new markets, and new projects open opportunities to convince management to support risk communication activities (Dozier et al. 1995). If hostility does occur, those who are communicating risk can view their management as a hostile audience and use some of the techniques described later in this chapter to deal effectively with hostile audiences. See also Chapter 5, "Ethical Issues," for more information on satisfying the needs of managers.

### Potential Roles Dichotomy

Another constraint the organization can place on those communicating risk is the role that organization is willing to play in the risk communication process. The organization's perception of this role may come from laws and regulations, community expectations, or corporate policy. Table 4-1 summarizes some of the most common roles organizations can play.

Often those in care communication situations find themselves in the educator role—trying to provide information to explain a risk so that people will take

---

**TABLE 4-1**
Example Organizational Roles in Risk Communication

| Role | Expectation | Authority |
|------|-------------|-----------|
| Educator | Explain, inform | To impart knowledge |
| Facilitator | Encourage, support | To point toward solutions |
| Partner | Work with others | To jointly solve problems |
| Manager | Tell them what to do | To prevent or mitigate the risk |
| Regulator | Mete out justice | To enforce decisions |

appropriate steps to protect themselves. In consensus communication, organizations may play the role of facilitator or partner, working with stakeholders to develop an appropriate risk management approach. In crisis communications, organizations may serve as managers, telling audiences exactly what must be done to stop a risk from escalating. After the crisis, other organizations may act as regulators to ensure that future crises are avoided.

Risk communication efforts are constrained when the audience expects a different role from the one the organization is willing to play. For example, if the audience is expecting the organization to partner with them in developing a risk management approach, but the organization attempts to fill a manager role by telling the audience what must be done, both the organization's credibility and its ability to communicate effectively will suffer. When presented with a role dichotomy, audiences often react with anger, hostility, and a general unwillingness to help manage the risk.

For example, a distraught mother called a local agency charged with communicating about air quality issues. A contractor had just finished remediating her home for asbestos in the ceiling. The mother wanted assurances from the agency that it was safe for her child to return to the home. The agency representative explained the potential risks of asbestos and advised her to talk to her contractor to see what had been done to remediate them.

"You sound like a mother," the woman protested. "What would you do? Would you let your child back in the house?"

In this case, the caller wanted to give the agency representative the role of friend and confidante. Perhaps motivated by anxiety, she might have been trying to put a human face on what she perceived as a bureaucracy. But the agency's role was to inform and educate, not facilitate or regulate. Providing advice as a "mother" could even have resulted in legal action later. The lesson: stay within your role. The representative could have responded something like this:

"I am a mother, but I don't think you called me because of that. I think you may have called because you were hoping my organization had information that could help you. Let me make sure I understand what information you're looking for and then I'll try to help you get the answers you need."

One of the best ways to manage this constraint is to identify the organization's role before the risk communication process starts. Know what your organization expects of you and communicate this consistently to your audiences every time. We sometimes recommend that agency representatives who answer public information lines identify their role in the first few seconds of the conversation. You can do this by using your position title, if it communicates what you do to those outside the agency. If it doesn't, you can add an explanatory phrase when introducing yourself. For written materials, include a sentence on the responsibilities of your organization early on to set expectations.

For additional information on developing materials, see Chapter 13, "Information Materials." For more information on being a credible spokesperson, see Chapter 15, "Face-to-Face Communication."

One of the best ways to manage roles dichotomy is to identify the organization's role before the risk communication process starts.

### Difficult Review and Approval Procedures

Another way an organization can constrain the communication of risk is by requiring review and approval procedures that are either inappropriate or too time-consuming. A good example comes from one of the national laboratories. The laboratory had a detailed review and approval procedure for the release of all technical information. This procedure required no less than nine reviews and signatures, as well as review and approval by the U.S. Department of Energy, which funded the laboratory's work. This system was designed to ensure that preliminary technical information generated in innovative research and development activities was not released prematurely. However, the laboratory was asked to act as an independent agency to determine what past doses the public may have received from radioactive releases from a U.S. Department of Energy facility. To maintain its independence in the eyes of its audience, the laboratory needed to be able to release information, sometimes even preliminary data, as quickly as possible. It also needed to distance itself from the U.S. Department of Energy, which many members of the audience did not trust to produce unbiased results. Recognizing these problems, the laboratory tailored its internal review process (fewer signatures required and no U.S. Department of Energy approval) to allow risk to be communicated effectively for that audience.

To show managers and decision-makers that changes are necessary, a complete audience and situation analysis may be all that is required, especially if the audience has already threatened legal action. What reviews does the organization feel are absolutely necessary? Can any be combined? Who does the audience view as credible to review the information? Is this a crisis situation or one in which the audience is particularly hostile? In either of these cases, information will need to be released as quickly as possible. Showing that the audience and the organization's interests are best served by changes and suggesting easy ways to accomplish those changes can result in review and approval procedures that are more appropriate and timely.

### Corporate Protection Requirements

Review and approval procedures are only one way an organization seeks to protect itself. Private companies, in particular, can view information as a competitive advantage. Even if some risk information is provided, other information may be closely guarded for fear of releasing sensitive information that could clue competitors in to company trade secrets.

Since the tragedies of September 11, 2001, organizations have additional concerns about protecting information. Information on where hazardous materials are stored and in what quantities could be used by those with criminal or terrorist intent. Yet it is often this information that is key to understanding risk in communities.

Faced with issues like these, the U.S. Environmental Protection Agency reconsidered its Risk Management Program Rule activities. Where once such information was going to be placed on the Internet in a publicly accessible database, now it is sheltered in public reading rooms and its access carefully controlled. Such access was a compromise between industry fears and public demands. Neither was completely satisfied, but both understood the need.

Risk communicators must carefully consider what information can be released and look for ways to reach satisfactory compromises. As memories of dangers fade, the public will be less willing to allow companies to protect information in the name of security. For additional information on deciding on what information can be released, see Chapter 5, "Ethical Issues." For more information on choosing appropriate communication mechanisms, see Chapter 10, "Determine Appropriate Methods."

### Conflicting Organizational Requirements

Yet another way an organization can constrain those who are communicating risk is by having policies, however well-intentioned, that conflict with the goals of risk communication. For example, a research and development firm had a standing policy that any information given to the public regarding the organization had to be approved of and released by public affairs representatives. Unfortunately, the public affairs staff had the charter for safeguarding the company's reputation and felt that to fulfill this charter they would allow nothing but completely positive information to be released. When risk communicators wanted to add information about the firm to an environmental impact statement, which analyzed both the negative and positive aspects of a risk, the public affairs staff responded, "I just can't let you say that." (This type of response is one reason why public affairs staff are often mistrusted by some members of the audience.) However, communicating risk often requires that some of the worst information about an organization be released.

Before any risk communication project begins, those who are communicating the risk should review organizational requirements to see which will conflict and discuss the potential problems with the staff responsible for implementing the requirements. A little planning and explanation of the purposes of risk communication can help avoid a problem.

Risk communicators must carefully consider what information can be released and look for ways to reach satisfactory compromises. As memories of dangers fade, the public will be less willing to allow companies to protect information in the name of security.

## Insufficient Information to
## Adequately Plan and Set Schedules

As discussed in Part II, "Planning the Risk Communication Effort," a wealth of information is necessary to create a communication plan and set a schedule. In some organizations, this information is closely guarded. Other organizations seem to simply ignore the planning process. After diligently searching, those who are communicating risk may develop schedules based on inadequate or what turns out to be incorrect information, only to find that their schedules cannot be met. For example, suppose your risk communication effort is scheduled to begin after a risk assessment is finished on October 1, with fact sheets to be issued and public meetings to be held shortly thereafter. Notices of where and when the meetings will be held have already been published. However, unbeknownst to you, the risk assessment has been delayed and won't be finished until November 1. You will have to retract your notices and replan. Unfortunately, members of your audience may conclude that this is some kind of delaying tactic, that your organization does not want to release the information. When you finally do get the chance to begin communicating the risk, your credibility will already have suffered.

Plans and schedules that are both realistic and flexible must be developed to effectively communicate risk. Some factors to consider include legal requirements, organizational requirements, the scientific process, ongoing activities within the organization and nation, and audience needs. More specific information to be considered in developing schedules is discussed in Chapter 11, "Set a Schedule."

◇

Plans and schedules that are both realistic and flexible must be developed to effectively communicate risk. Some factors to consider include legal requirements, organizational requirements, the scientific process, ongoing activities within the organization and nation, and audience needs.

## Emotional Constraints

Another type of constraint on those who communicate risk comes from within themselves. Emotions and beliefs can color our attempts to communicate. The three emotional constraints most difficult to overcome are unwillingness to see the public as equal partner in risk decisions, inability to see how stakeholder value systems differ from your own, and the belief that science can never be understood by the public.

### Unwillingness to See the Public as an Equal Partner

In a logical world, many feel, decisions about how to manage a risk would be made by those who really understood the situation. Furthermore, such decisions would be based on scientific principles, economic realities, and logic, not emotions, beliefs, and political leanings. Risk communication, however, cannot be effective unless it considers the emotions, beliefs, and political leanings of the audience.

Working with decision-makers who show this unwillingness can be difficult. Remind them of their goal: to make a decision that will stand the test of time. As a number of court cases have shown, such a decision can only be reached when all parties agree with it, at least to some extent. It does the organization no good to decide on a perfectly logical, scientifically based, economical strategy, only to be tied up in court for years trying to justify it to people who would likely have accepted it in the first place if they had only been consulted!

Overcoming this belief in yourself can be even more difficult. If you find yourself resisting reaching out to those you know are concerned or whom others have suggested should be contacted, ask yourself why. Is it because of the difficulty involved in developing the contacts, or do you feel that the contacts really shouldn't be made at all? Remind yourself that a number of success stories and research (see also Arvai 2003, Beierle 2002, Hunt and Monaghan 1992, and Sanderson and Niles 1992) have shown that making reasonable attempts to consult interested stakeholders results in better, more useful, more lasting solutions.

### Inability to See Differing Value Systems

Everyone has a value system, a method by which they evaluate and chose between alternatives in a given situation. Often, our values are so deeply ingrained that it is difficult to recognize them for what they are. It is even more difficult to recognize that these values differ from the value systems of others. It seems to be a very human tendency to think that everyone else sees things the same way we do.

Value systems play a large role in how any member of the audience views a risk. When constructing risk messages, it is easy to focus attention on matters we feel are important, without thinking through what issues are of importance to the intended audience. To guard against our own biases in framing risk communication messages, those of us who are communicating risk must understand the audience thoroughly. Terryn Barill, a risk communication consultant, recommends interviewing members of the audience and listening to not only the questions they ask but the words they use to help you determine what is most important to them and to then include that information in the risk message (Barill 1991). The techniques in Chapter 8, "Analyze Your Audience," are also designed to help.

### Belief That the Public Cannot Understand Science

Many experts who have devoted years to a field of study feel that the public cannot possibly understand scientific or technical information. As one expert stated when asked for a definition of a term used to present risk, "I have a Ph.D. and I've been studying that for 15 years; I can't possibly explain it to you." When this topic was introduced at a lecture at a university, a professor in the audience asked with great skepticism, "Do you honestly believe that you can explain anything to the general public?" Our answer was, and is, a resounding "Yes!"

Like risk communicators the world over, we have spent our careers explaining scientific information to nontechnical audiences—how a nuclear reactor works, how hydrocarbon contamination can "float" on aquifers, what a risk of $10^{-6}$ means. Presenting each piece of information was a challenge, requiring that we know our audience and have a good command of language. We often had to borrow or develop innovative ways to present the information. But that just proves that it can be done. The techniques described later in Part III, "Putting Risk

◇

"The principal obstacles to understanding are lay [people] time and attention, not intelligence."

—Morgan et al.,
Risk Communication: A
Mental Models Approach
(2002, page 8).

Communication Into Action," are designed to help you present risk information in a variety of ways.

## CONSTRAINTS FROM THE AUDIENCE

Constraints do not just come from within those who are communicating risk or the organization. The audience itself often brings constraints that must be overcome if risks are to be communicated. These constraints include hostility and outrage, panic and denial, apathy, mistrust of risk assessment, disagreements on the acceptable magnitude of risk, lack of faith in science and institutions, and learning disabilities.

### Hostility and Outrage

Many audiences react with hostility toward risk messages. By hostility, we mean anxiety, anger, frustration, and contempt. This can be true in care and crisis communication efforts; however, it seems to particularly plague consensus communication efforts. Peter Sandman, among others, has presented factors that may affect the audience's hostility level. As mentioned under Chapter 2, "Approaches to Communicating Risk," in the discussion of the Hazard Plus Outrage Approach, he sees risk as having two components: hazard, or the scientific aspect of the actual danger, and outrage, or the audience's other concerns about the danger. Factors that influence the level of outrage include the voluntariness of the risk (do they have a choice?), level of dread (how scary is it?), issue of fairness (do they see it as being fair?), and the moral relevance (the more relevant it is to their morality, the more hostility).

In addition to Sandman's outrage factors, there are other reasons that the audience may be hostile (Table 4-2), reasons that have nothing to do with the risk itself. Those who are communicating risk need to be aware of these issues because the higher the level of hostility, the less chance that the audience will hear the risk message, and the less chance that any real communication will take place.

Reasons the Audience Can Be Hostile

| Factors | More Hostility | Less Hostility |
|---|---|---|
| Catastrophic potential | Grouped in time and space | Scattered in time and space |
| Level of familiarity | Uncommon | Very common |
| Level of understanding | Not well understood by science | Well understood by science |
| Level of personal control | Controlled by a distrusted individual | Controlled by the source |
| Voluntariness | Involuntary | Voluntary |
| Effects on children | More likely to affect children | Less likely to affect children |
| Moral relevance | Relevant | Not relevant |
| Timing of effects | Immediate effects | Delayed effects |
| Identity of victims | Closely related | Statistical victims |
| Level of dread | Greatly feared | Apathetic |
| Level of trust in institutions | Distrust | Trust |
| Amount of media attention | Highly popularized | Seldom mentioned |
| History of accidents | Well-known accidents | No accidents |
| Equity (fairness) | Viewed as unfair | Viewed as fair |
| Distribution of benefits | Benefits distributed unequally with risk | Benefits distributed equally with risk |
| Reversibility | Damage irreversible | Damage reversible |
| Personal stake | Strong | Weak |
| Origin | Artificial | Natural |
| Level of uncertainty | Unknown to science | Known to science |
| Tone of message | Too positive | Objective |
| Organizational attitude | Organization ignores | Organization seeks out concerns and acknowledges concerns |
| Degree of change in lifestyle | Sharp change from normal | Little change from normal |
| Degree of understanding of process/data | Process/data presentation too complex | Process/data presentation aimed at audience |

(Adapted from various works by Vincent T. Covello and Peter Sandman, for example, Covello et al. 1988.)

One reason an audience may be hostile is that the organization communicating the risk is seen as not being credible. This was the situation for the U.S. Environmental Protection Agency during the Reagan Administration. The agency was viewed by many as being more often on the side of the polluter than on the side of the environment; hence, anything agency officials said was viewed with great suspicion. There may not be much those who are communicating risk can do once credibility has been lost, except to recognize it and try to keep future risk communication efforts as credible as possible. The trust between organization and audience can be rebuilt slowly, if the relationship is built on trustworthy efforts.

Another reason for audience hostility has to do with the message being viewed as too positive. Most audiences react with hostility if they feel they are merely being placated, if the message is full of trite phrases or facile reassurances, especially in the face of negative information in the press. They don't want to hear, "Trust us; everything is fine." They will often only be satisfied if they or someone they trust has reviewed all the data and reached the same conclusion.

Audiences can also be hostile if their concerns have been ignored. One of the principles of risk communication is to listen and deal with specific concerns (see Chapter 6, "Principles of Risk Communication"). Hance et al. (1988) cite the case of an office building that was contaminated with dioxin (a cancer-causing chemical) after a fire. Although the risk assessment showed the building to be safe for the employees to return to work, and this information was communicated to the employees, the hostility level continued to rise. It turned out the employees' main concern was where to park. The parking garage had also been damaged, and parking wasn't available in the downtown area near the building. The employees were not willing to listen to the message that the workplace was safe and they could return to work until their concerns over parking were addressed. Thus, those who are communicating risk must make sure that risk messages address audience concerns, even if the concerns seem to relate to peripheral issues.

◇

Audiences may react with hostility if the message is viewed as too positive. Most audiences react with hostility if they feel they are merely being placated, if the message is full of trite phrases or facile reassurances, especially in the face of negative information in the press.

Another reason audiences can be hostile is the very human perception that change is bad. For example, in a case where the groundwater in a rural area had been contaminated by chemicals leaching from a landfill, the response from many area residents was, "My grandfather drank from this well, my father drank from this well, and I don't see why I can't." A possible way to overcome this type of attitude is to show not only the dangers of continuing risky behavior but the benefits of changing behavior to something less risky. However, information alone does not generally lead to changes in behavior, as shown by some of the research related to the mental models approach to risk communication (see Chapter 2).

Another reason audiences can be hostile is that they don't understand either the process or the data being communicated. The information may be too technical (full of difficult concepts or laced with acronyms and jargon) or the presentation may not meet their needs (for example, a presentation in English for an audience whose primary language is Spanish). The obvious way to overcome this reason for hostility is to use language and a method that meet the needs of your audience. The information in Part III, "Putting Risk Communication into Action," is designed to help.

### Panic and Denial

Sometimes the nature of the risk and the audience's situation raise an even deadlier response than hostility: panic and denial. Such cases are, we are thankful to say, rare. Panic is the extreme response to a combination of fear, dread, and a lack of perceived control. When audiences panic, it is because they perceive themselves or those they love in imminent, life-threatening danger that they cannot influence. Panic can stop all action to prevent a risk, effectively freezing a person, or cause unproductive actions that can actually make the damage worse. Panic also tends to interfere with cognitive processing, as chemicals flood the brain, preventing risk communication messages from being heard and acted upon.

Beyond panic, however, is denial. Denial occurs when the perceived result of a risk is so horrific that other coping mechanisms break down. We cannot accept that

Panic is the extreme response to a combination of fear, dread, and a lack of perceived control. When audiences panic, it is because they perceive themselves or those they love in imminent, life-threatening danger that they cannot influence. Panic can stop all action to prevent a risk, effectively freezing a person, or cause unproductive actions that can actually make the damage worse.

something so awful has happened or could happen, so we simply refuse to think about it. An audience in denial is deceptively calm. Risk communication messages attempting to increase concern only push those at risk into a deeper denial.

Panic and denial are beyond the skills of most risk communicators to manage. However, those who are communicating risk need to realize that denial and panic are one end of the response spectrum for risks. A thorough understanding of audience needs can help prevent the introduction of risk messages or use of mechanisms (such as a graphic picture or live footage) that could thrust an audience into this difficult psychological area. Chapter 8, "Analyze Your Audience," provides additional information on understanding those with whom you will be communicating.

## Apathy

At times it seems those who are communicating risk simply cannot succeed. Audiences faced with crises may show panic. Audiences in consensus communication situations often exhibit hostility and outrage. Audiences in care communication (and to a lesser degree some crisis communication efforts) are often apathetic.

When an audience is apathetic toward a risk, it is often because what has been deemed a high risk by scientists and government agencies seems impossible or trivial to the audience in question. A good example is the early efforts of the U.S. Environmental Protection Agency to warn of the dangers of radon in homes. Despite a major risk communication effort, the intended audience still did not exhibit a change to less risky behavior, in this case, testing their homes for radon. Only when risk communication researchers did a more thorough audience analysis, using the mental models approach discussed in Chapter 2, did the risk communication effort begin to show some success (Morgan et al. 1992).

When faced with apathy, those who are communicating risk need to conduct as thorough an audience analysis as time and other resources allow. Only by understanding the audience can we hope to identify

When faced with apathy, those who are communicating risk need to conduct as thorough an audience analysis as time and other resources allow.

matters of importance to them, and then to link the risk communication efforts to those important issues. First consider, however, the ethical implications of manipulating your audience (see Chapter 5, "Ethical Issues," for additional information).

## Mistrust of Risk Assessment

As mentioned in Chapter 1, "Introduction," risk communication efforts are built around a process that starts with a risk assessment and ends with a risk management decision and subsequent action. Unfortunately, a number of environmental and civic organizations have over the last few years presented their opinions that any form of risk assessment is so seriously flawed as to prevent its use in all but the most specific of circumstances. Researcher Alon Tal of the Arawa Institute for Environmental Studies in Israel conducted a study of 17 national and 16 local environmental groups to determine their attitudes toward risk assessment. Over 75% of those surveyed felt that risk assessment was a disempowering process (undemocratic), led to regulatory delays, and was used as a ruse for deregulation. Another telling observation was that 58% felt that risk assessments are inescapably biased to underestimate risk, when most risk assessors would agree that assessments are grossly overconservative (Tal 1997).

Faced with such negative perceptions of risk assessment, what can those who are communicating risk hope to accomplish? The key appears to be in understanding what is driving the difficulties. For example, many environmental organizations in Tal's study felt that one of the major flaws in the risk assessment process was the characterization or definition of risk. One way to address this flaw is to involve the audience in the risk characterization process to identify the aspects of the risk to be studied and the study methods. Another area of concern was the ethical dimension of risk. According to Tal, many environmental organizations felt that "risk assessment is fundamentally immoral, consigning people (and in some critiques, ecosystems) to intolerable environmental fates without their consent" (Tal 1997, page 473A). As noted

———— ◇ ————

*"Until these issues are addressed, environmentalists will remain extremely suspicious of risk numbers. Without enhanced scientific validity, they will oppose the growing influence of risk numbers over environmental health decisions. 'Garbage in-garbage out' is a frequently heard aphorism among interviewees."*

—Alon Tal, "Assessing the Environmental Movement's Attitudes Toward Risk Assessment" (1997, page 473A).

earlier, addressing the value systems of your audience can help in this case by adapting the process when possible. For example, risk assessors found a way to show via icons the various steps and assumptions in the risk assessment process when the audience expressed concerns that risks were calculated by a "black box."

## Disagreements on the Acceptable Magnitude of Risk

Scientists, regulators, and risk managers often disagree with the public on the acceptable magnitude of a certain risk. Industry and government standards deem a certain level of risk to be safe, that is, unlikely to cause harm to most people who follow some lifestyle. Unfortunately, the public sometimes sees risk as an all-or-nothing proposition. Any level of risk may seem to be too much. For example, some people do not want to hear that the level of trichloroethylene in their drinking water is below U.S. Environmental Protection Agency standards; they want the level to be zero. Given this attitude, it can be very difficult to communicate risk.

Providing more technical information will not necessarily eliminate this constraint. However, letting the audience see all the data and helping them understand how tradeoffs might be made can help many members of the audience come to terms with the risk. They still may not accept that the risk is necessary and may go on fighting for cleaner water and cleaner air, but they may come to accept the risk communication efforts.

## Lack of Faith in Science and Institutions

A number of researchers have pointed out the decreasing credibility of scientists and government institutions with regard to communicating risk information. Nearly 20 years ago, Roger Kasperson warned that public opinion surveys were showing a steady decrease in confidence in industry and government officials, with a decline of up to 50% in some areas from 1966 to 1980 (Kasperson 1986). Another study found that confidence in government and industry has been declining for the last 30 years (Harris poll as cited by Peters et al. 1997). Unfortunately, many of these same industries and

◇

A number of researchers have pointed out the decreasing credibility of scientists and government institutions with regard to communicating risk information. Nearly 20 years ago, Roger Kasperson warned that public opinion surveys were showing a steady decrease in confidence in industry and government officials, with a decline of up to 50% in some areas from 1966 to 1980 (Kasperson 1986).

government agencies are faced with the challenge of communicating risk information today.

Those who are communicating risk need to be aware of their audience's attitudes toward the organization in charge of the risk communication effort and any associated organizations. In some cases, it may be necessary to partner with someone the audience finds credible to convey the risk message. In a survey to measure how audiences determined trust and credibility of organizations, Peters et al. (1997) found that defying a negative stereotype was the most important factor to improving trust and credibility for government and industry. The researchers cited the example of Johnson and Johnson's strong response in the wake of the Tylenol tampering in 1982, exhibiting more openness than is usually attributed to big industry. In any case, those who are communicating risk need to continue to strive for credible and open risk assessment, management, and communication efforts, for only these will fully rebuild the faith that has been lost through past practices.

## Learning Disabilities

Another difficulty inherent to the audience is the fact that many people reach adulthood lacking a number of learning skills. Much has been written about the growing problem of illiteracy. In addition, the future will see more children moving through the education system with problems associated with having parents who were addicted to drugs or alcohol. Although it is not a learning disability, psychologists also bemoan the fact that today's youth looks to television for its information, entertainment, and role models. All these factors can conspire to make the job of communicating the scientific concepts of risk extremely difficult.

One way around this is to know your audience. If you are communicating the dangers of reusing unsterile needles to a community who never finished high school, is seldom sober, and watches television 15 hours a day, you will need to tailor your message differently than if you are explaining the need to maintain cleanliness to restaurant workers in a mid-western town where everyone graduated from high school. The information presented in Parts II and III should help you determine which techniques are best suited for your audience's needs.

## CONSTRAINTS FOR BOTH COMMUNICATOR AND AUDIENCE

As if these constraints weren't enough, other constraints affect both those who are communicating risk and their audiences: stigma and stability of the knowledge base.

### Stigma

Both the audience and the risk communicator can be affected by the stigma of being at risk. In many cases, the actual physical risk can be exacerbated by the impacts on the economy and society. For example, when a small town in Nevada found itself the focus of a cancer cluster investigation, property values plummeted, people moved to other nearby towns, and tourism took a heavy hit, all because of the perception that something dangerous must be happening there.

Stigma can also affect the psychological well being of the audience. For example, researchers Robin Gregory and Theresa Satterfield found that dairy farmers in the Tillamook River estuary, long admired for its pristine beauty, felt themselves unwelcome by the growing retirement community because their work had resulted in increased fecal coliform bacteria counts in the local rivers. Because the farmers were associated with this increased health risk, they felt they were being accused of moral deficiency by simply earning a living (Gregory and Satterfield 2002).

When those at risk are stigmatized, their level of outrage and hostility rises. This increase in emotion can be seen as a destabilizing influence on risk communication efforts. For example, researcher Theresa Satterfield found that some groups were denied access to public meetings because it was assumed they would be disruptive

(Satterfield 1996). However, for risk communication efforts to succeed, such exclusionary attitudes must be overcome.

Stigma expert James Flynn and colleagues (Flynn et al. 2001) suggest two ways that risk communicators can help to overcome stigma:

1. Reduce perceived risk. It is the perception of the danger that drives stigma. This perception can be managed, at least in part, by creating and maintaining trust in those charged with managing the risk, informing and educating the public about the risk, and educating scientific experts on how to more effectively present risk information without increasing stigma.

2. Reduce the amplification of stigma. Once begun, stigma has a tendency to grow. Educate the media as well as government regulators on the potential effects of over-stating or sensationalizing a risk.

To avoid creating or amplifying stigma, those communicating risk must factor audience concerns into risk communication efforts. As mentioned previously, these include even those concerns that might be seen as tangential to the risk itself. Again, a thorough understanding of audience may be your best approach. See Chapter 8, "Analyze Your Audience," for additional information.

### Stability of the Knowledge Base

Both science and the information your audience has been exposed to change daily. Today's scientific "facts" may be derided in years to come as tales of superstition and ignorance. Once even learned people thought the earth was flat and the sun revolved around the earth. Given the knowledge at the time, this was a logical assumption; our knowledge may be similarly outdated in the future.

In addition, experts on a particular risk often disagree on the magnitude or effects of the risk. The study that you quote extensively can come under fire as being too general or too specific. The experts you bring forth to discuss the risk may be confronted with results of a study by

─────── ◇ ───────

Both science and the information your audience has been exposed to change daily. Today's scientific "facts" may be derided in years to come as tales of superstition and ignorance.

─────────────────

colleagues who directly contradict their findings. These kinds of problems can make the public dubious about any scientific procedure.

Your audience's knowledge base also changes. Two weeks ago when you finished your audience survey, the local news station hadn't aired "complete" coverage of the risk you were trying to communicate. We once watched in dismay while a news broadcast explained why the waste tanks at a nuclear facility (our customer) were "burping" dangerous gases, all the while showing a picture of radiation-suited individuals loading pluto-nium pellets into a nuclear reactor. The spoken story was about the risks associated with storing hazardous and ra-dioactive waste; the visual story was about what a reac-tor looks like. At no time were the tanks or procedures there shown. Those of us who were communicating the risks now had to contend with a number of audience misperceptions.

This constraint can be difficult to overcome because it is often the least within the control of the communicator. Planning ahead, keeping abreast of what is happening in science and the community, and keeping a sense of humor can all help. Planning is discussed further in Part II, "Planning the Risk Communication Effort." Keeping abreast can be enhanced by subscribing to those infor-mation sources most respected by your audience and by whatever branch of science you are communicating about. Read the local newspaper, watch local newscasts, and develop relationships with local print and television news media representatives (see Chapter 8, "Analyze Your Audience," and Chapter 16, "Working with the Media," for more details).

## IN SUMMARY

A number of constraints can hinder the effective communication of risk, including organizational and emotional constraints affecting those who are communi-cating the risk; hostility and outrage, panic and denial, apathy, mistrust of the risk assessment process, disagree-ment on the acceptable magnitude of risk, lack of faith in science and institutions, and learning disabilities for the audience; and stigma and the changing knowledge base for both communicators and audience members. Those who are communicating risk need to recognize potential constraints and act to overcome them for risk communication efforts to succeed.

## REFERENCES

Arvai, J. L. 2003. "Using Risk Communication to Disclose the Outcome of a Participatory Decision-Making Process: Effects on the Perceived Acceptability of Risk-Policy Decisions." *Risk Analysis*, 23(2):281-290.

Balch, G. I., and S. M. Sutton. 1995. "Putting the First Audience First: Conducting Useful Evaluation for a Risk-Related Government Agency." *Risk Analysis*, 15(2):163-168.

Barill, T. 1991. "Communicating Risk to Communities." In *Superfund '90, Proceedings of the 11th National Conference*, p. 98-100. Hazardous Materials Control Research Institute, Washington, D.C.

Beierle, T. C. 2002. "The Quality of Stakeholder-Based Decisions." *Risk Analysis*, 22(4):739-750.

Boiarsky, C. 1991. "Writing for Multiple Readers with Conflicting Needs: An Opportunity for Improving Communication with Regulatory Agencies." In *The Engineered Communication: Designs for Continued Improvement*, Proceedings of the 1991 International Professional Communication Conference, Volume 2, pages 313-317. 91CH3067-4, Institute of Electronics and Electrical Engineers, Washington, D.C.

Covello, V. T., P. M. Sandman, and P. Slovic. 1988. *Risk Communication, Risk Statistics, and Risk Comparisons: A Manual for Plant Managers*. Chemical Manufacturers Association, Washington, D.C.

Davenport, C. 2003. "Utilities Discover Message Matters." *Washington Post*, Monday, October 6, 2003, page B01.

Dozier, D. M., L. A. Grunig, and J. E. Grunig. 1995. *Manager's Guide to Excellence in Public Relations and Communication Management*. Lawrence Erlbaum Associates, Mahwah, New Jersey.

Flynn, J., P. Slovic, and H. Kunreuther, editors. 2001. *Risk, Media, and Stigma: Understanding Challenges to Modern Science and Technology*. Earthscan, London.

Gregory, R. S., and T. A. Satterfield. 2002. "Beyond Perception: The Experience of Risk and Stigma in Community Contexts." *Risk Analysis,* 22(2):347-358.

Hance, B. J., C. Chess, and P. M. Sandman. 1988. *Improving Dialogue with Communities: A Risk Communication Manual for Government.* New Jersey Department of Environmental Protection, Division of Science and Research, Trenton, New Jersey.

Hunt, B., and J. Monaghan. 1992. "How Public Issues Shape Environmental Restoration Plans—Experiences with Colorado UMTRA Projects." *ER '91: Proceedings of the Environmental Restoration Conference for the U.S. Department of Energy.* U.S. Department of Energy, Washington, D.C.

Kasperson, R. E. 1986. "Six Propositions on Public Participation and Their Relevance for Risk Communication." *Risk Analysis,* 6(3):275-281.

Morgan, G., B. Fischhoff, A. Bostrom, L. Lave, and C. J. Atman. 1992. "Communicating Risk to the Public." *Environ. Sci. Technol.,* 26(11):2048-2056.

Peters, R. G., V. T. Covello, and D. B. McCallum. 1997. "The Determinants of Trust and Credibility in Environmental Risk Communication: An Empirical Study." *Risk Analysis,* 17(1):43-54.

Sanderson, W., and K. Niles. 1992. "Effective Outreach is Good Public Policy." *ER '91: Proceedings of the Environmental Restoration Conference for the U.S. Department of Energy.* U.S. Department of Energy, Washington, D.C.

Satterfield, T. A. 1996. "Pawns, Victims, or Heroes: The Negotiation of Stigma and the Plight of Oregon's Loggers." *Journal of Social Issues,* 52(1):71-83.

Tal, A. 1997. "Assessing the Environmental Movement's Attitudes Toward Risk Assessment." *Environ. Sci. Technol.,* 31(10):470A-476A.

## ADDITIONAL RESOURCES

Chess, C., P. M. Sandman, and M. R. Greenberg. 1990. *Empowering Agencies to Communicate about Environmental Risk: Suggestions for Overcoming Organizational Barriers.* Rutgers University, Cook College, Environmental Communication Research Program, New Brunswick, New Jersey.

Hadden, S. G. 1990. "Institutional Barriers to Risk Communication." *Risk Analysis*, 9:301-308.

Hance, B. J., C. Chess, and P. M. Sandman. 1988. *Improving Dialogue with Communities: A Risk Communication Manual for Government*. New Jersey Department of Environmental Protection, Division of Science and Research, Trenton, New Jersey.

"Risk=Hazard+Outrage . . . A Formula for Effective Risk Communication." Videotape course presented by Peter M. Sandman. Available from the American Industrial Hygienists Association, Washington, D.C.

Sandman, P. M. 1989. "Hazard Versus Outrage in the Public Perception of Risk." *Effective Risk Communication: The Role and Responsibility of Government and Nongovernment Organizations*, editors V. T. Covello, D. B. McCallum, and M. T. Pavlova, pages 45-49. Plenum Press, New York.

# Ethical Issues

ε thics can be a difficult subject. One reason for this is that each of us has our own ethical code, our own morality, that has been shaped by our experiences and beliefs. This personal code makes ethical issues subjective: what is an issue for me may not be one for you. Another reason is that ethics is a philosophical study with its own language and concepts. Although we are not ethicists, we wanted to provide a general overview of some of the ethical issues often faced, either directly or indirectly, by those who are communicating risk. Therefore, this chapter discusses potential ethical issues and associated decisions. It does not tell you what decision to make, but rather helps you weigh the potential outcomes of the possible choices.

Producing any form of technical communication can result in ethical difficulties. Questions like how much information to release, to whom should it be released, and who makes those decisions are connected with the dissemination of any type of information. The Society for Technical Communication, the largest professional society for those who communicate scientific or technical information, publishes "Ethical Principles for Technical

The Society for Technical Communication, the largest professional society for those who communicate scientific or technical information, publishes "Ethical Principles for Technical Communicators" (STC 1998) that recognize such ethical issues as complying with regulations, honesty, confidentiality, and fairness.

Communicators" (STC 1998) that recognize such ethical issues as complying with regulations, honesty, confidentiality, and fairness.

The communication of risk carries additional potential ethical issues, such as when and how much information should be released, whether the use of persuasion is appropriate, and the relationship between public danger versus private interests. Such ethical issues can arise in care, consensus, and crisis communication. Ethical issues in risk communication can be divided into three areas: social ethics, organizational ethics, and personal ethics.

## SOCIAL ETHICS

Social ethics comprise the code of conduct by which society judges our behavior. As a society evolves and changes, so will its ethics and the resultant behavior. Risk communication has also evolved to meet changing societal demands. However, the influence of society on the communication of risk can itself be an ethical issue. Other social ethical issues related to risk communication are how the risk idiom is used, by whom, and when; whether the risk is being applied equally to all ethnic and social groups; who should bear the consequences if messages are misunderstood; and the issue of stigma.

### The Sociopolitical Environment's Influence

Society has changed over the years, especially in the way in which it views risks and how risk decisions are made. Joseph Beck, social scientist and former Congressional and presidential advisor, attributes these changes in public involvement to changes in governance ideologies. Until the 1950s, he says, the United States insisted on strong national governance, or federalism. The threat of Communism and the Cold War in the 1950s led to a change in the education system, in which the "virtues of the national government being controlled by its peoples was (sic) firmly entrenched in the minds of the largest mass of school children ever taught in any school system in the world" (Beck 1991, page 1). As this group moved

———— ◇ ————

The threat of Communism and the Cold War in the 1950s led to a change in the education system, in which the "virtues of the national government being controlled by its peoples was (sic) firmly entrenched in the minds of the largest mass of school children ever taught in any school system in the world" (Beck 1991, page 1).

through the educational system and into the larger society, they made sure that this view of government by the people was upheld. A good example, according to Beck, is the way this group mounted an effort that resulted in the American abandonment of the Vietnam War.

James Creighton of Creighton and Creighton, the consulting firm responsible for many of the Bonneville Power Administration's successes in the area of risk communication and public involvement, has also observed changes in society in the areas of public involvement and risk communication. His focus was on how the public decided to accept any particular decision, such as how a risk will be managed. According to Creighton, in the 1950s, the public felt a decision was acceptable if they had been informed about it. All an organization had to do was produce the proper information and disseminate it widely. In the 1960s and 1970s, society's views changed: now the public felt that it must be heard first before a decision could be made. Agencies moved into the age of public involvement, but mostly in the form of written testimony and formal hearings. Beginning in the 1980s and continuing today, Creighton says, society feels that it must actually influence the decision. This has led to a form of public involvement that is referred to as consensus building, trying to get all parties to agree on a decision before it is implemented and involving the public in all aspects of risk assessment, management, and communication (Creighton 1992).

More recently, Granger Morgan and his associates from Carnegie-Mellon University laid out historical stages through which organizations have viewed their charter to assess, communicate, and manage risks:

- All we have to do is get the numbers right.
- All we have to do is tell our audience the numbers.
- All we have to do is explain what we mean by the numbers.
- All we have to do is show our audience that they've accepted similar risks in the past.
- All we have to do is show our audience it's a good deal for them.

- All we have to do is treat our audience nicely.

- All we have to do is make our audience partners (Morgan et al. 2002).

If these researchers are correct, and we believe they are, these changes in society can pose a number of ethical issues. If the public demands the right to be involved in risk decisions throughout the cycle of assessment, management, and communication, then is it appropriate for organizations to stick to the old ways of making decisions and informing the public afterward? Is it right to take public testimony but simply go on with whatever decision the organization hoped for to begin with? Is it prudent to exclude public participation in a crisis? Should the mandates of such agencies as the U.S. Environmental Protection Agency and local health departments be changed to allow and encourage them to bring the public more fully into the decision-making process?

The choice for those who are communicating risk is whether or not to involve interested participants in the full cycle of assessment, management, and communication of risk and to what extent. Admittedly, this involvement will be different in care, consensus, and crisis communication; however, each type can carry some kind of involvement. Table 5-1 shows the advantages and disadvantages of each choice. For a more in-depth discussion of public involvement, see Chapter 17, "Stakeholder Participation."

## The Use of the Risk Idiom

On a slightly smaller scale is the ethical issue of who determines what is a risk and to whom the risk will be communicated. Audiences often take umbrage at the terms "insignificant" or "negligible" when applied to the magnitude of risk, yet these are terms experts often use to generalize complicated risk assessment calculations. Who decided that the risk was insignificant? Was the judgment based on scientific principles alone or were the audience's values considered? Who decided what part of the information was to be disseminated if not the entire set of assessment calculations? Who decided who would

Who decided what part of the information was to be disseminated if not the entire set of assessment calculations? Who decided who would receive the information? These issues derive from the ethical questions of power and fairness.

**TABLE 5-1**
Advantages and Disadvantages of Involving the Public in Risk Assessment, Management, and Communication

### *INVOLVE* THE PUBLIC

**Advantages**
- Because public participates in risk decision, decision is likely to last.
- Project schedules and budgets less likely to be affected later by lawsuits.
- Can increase organization's credibility.
- Provides organization with broader information net.

**Disadvantages**
- Risk managers may resist because of fear of loss of control.
- Lack of organizational commitment can result in loss of credibility.
- Requires more time at the beginning of the process.

### *DON'T* INVOLVE THE PUBLIC

**Advantages**
- Organization won't have to change the way it does business.
- No chance of loss of control.

**Disadvantages**
- Risk analysis, decision, and communication can be held up in court indefinitely, delaying project schedules and increasing budgets.
- Organization's credibility decreases.
- Loss of potential information critical to understanding risk.

receive the information? These issues derive from the ethical questions of power and fairness.

The choice for those who are communicating risk is to determine how soon to become involved in the risk assessment process as the audience's representative. While the expert who is assessing the risk (and who may be communicating it) is involved from the beginning, the technical communicator, risk manager, or public affairs person is sometimes not involved until the risk assessment has been completed. In either case, those who are communicating risk must determine audience concerns and perceptions of the risk and help decide how to factor these concerns and perceptions into the risk assessment process. Concerns and perceptions can be factored in at several stages in the process (Table 5-2), or not at all, leaving the risk communication efforts to compensate. In many situations, the best stage to factor in audience

**TABLE 5-2**

Stages When Audience Concerns and Perceptions Can Be
Factored into the Risk Assessment or Risk Communication Efforts*

| Stage | Advantages of Consideration | Disadvantages of Consideration |
|---|---|---|
| Risk assessment planning | • Less likely to delay schedule or increase budget<br>• Concerns integrated throughout process | • Because risk is not fully understood, integration in planning may be difficult and require changes later |
| Scenario development | • Suggest additional or different scenarios | • Potentially increase time and cost to explore more options |
| Data collection | • Can suggest additional data sources | • Potentially increase time and cost to explore more options |
| Analysis | • Provide audience-specific review of data and results | • Potentially increase time and cost to explore more options |
| Risk communication | • Communication more likely to be understood | • Assessment less likely to be accepted if this is the only place of involvement<br>• May require more resources in communication |

*Note that some agencies advise that risk assessment, risk management, and risk communication will be most successful if the audience is involved in all stages of the process (NRC 1996).

concerns and perceptions is during the planning of the risk assessment because concerns and perceptions can be more easily integrated without a delay in schedule or an increase in budget. Another stage is when the scenarios (i.e., the lifestyle characteristics and other factors to be considered in the calculation of risk) are being developed (for example, the risk to children from ingesting apple products coated with a pesticide). At this stage, the audience concerns and perceptions may point to different scenarios than those being considered by the experts, and revision may give the risk assessment more credibility for the audience.

Another stage at which audience concerns and perceptions can be factored into the risk assessment is in the choice of data to be collected. Using the example of the children ingesting apple products, perhaps the expert had decided not to collect data on preschool children because of the potential dangers associated with testing chemicals on humans and the greater expense of other data collection methods. If an analysis of audience concerns and perceptions shows that the danger to preschool children is the main concern, innovative methods may have to be developed so that these data will have to be collected and this concern can be addressed.

Another stage in which concerns and perceptions can be factored in is how the scenarios and data are analyzed. Is there a particular method that will be more credible with the audience? The latest generation of environmental and health risk software (FRAMES, ARAMS, 3MRA) include graphical interfaces that allow stakeholders to manipulate data and set up analyses. Also, many audiences find the assessment more believable if more than one group of experts analyzed the information and reached similar conclusions. On the other hand, some members of the audience will be satisfied only if their chosen expert has conducted the analysis.

Audience concerns and perceptions must be factored into the risk communication effort, if nowhere else. Those who are communicating risk must know to whom they are communicating and what information that audience requires or risk communication efforts will likely fail. However, if audience concerns and perceptions have not been considered earlier in the process, those who are communicating the risk will likely have a much more difficult job of explaining (and justifying) the risk information.

## Fairness of the Risk

One social ethical issue of growing concern is whether the risk is spread equitably over all ethnic and social groups. According to Dr. Robert Bullard, Director of the Environmental Justice Resource Center, Clark Atlanta University, and author of *Dumping in Dixie: Race, Class, and Environmental Quality* (Bullard 1990), "People of color (African Americans, Latinos, Asians, and Native Americans) have borne a disproportionate burden in the siting of municipal landfills, incinerators, and hazardous waste treatment, storage, and disposal facilities" (Bullard 1992, page 11). In the early 1990s, Congress passed legis-

⸻ ◇ ⸻

*"People of color (African Americans, Latinos, Asians, and Native Americans) have borne a disproportionate burden in the siting of municipal landfills, incinerators, and hazardous waste treatment, storage, and disposal facilities."*

—Robert Bullard, "In Our Backyards: Minority Communities Get Most of the Dumps" (1992, page 11).

lation to ensure that future efforts to site potential environmental risks such as factories and landfills considered the equity of the risk. The term coined was "environmental equity" or "environmental justice" (see Chapter 3, "Laws That Mandate Risk Communication" for more information on the Executive Order that mandates environmental justice).

Because of recent laws, environmental equity is often considered (or ignored) long before any risk communication effort begins. On the other hand, poor risk communication, accompanied by unresponsive risk management, may cause those at risk to perceive a lack of equity. In either case, those who are communicating risk need to be aware of the potential issue because of its potential effect on risk communication efforts. If the audience's perception is that the risk is being shared inequitably, the level of anger and hostility will rise, making any risk communication effort (care, consensus, or crisis) extremely difficult. (Angry people do not listen.) One way to lessen the anger and hostility is to give the audience a role in how the risk is being assessed and/or managed. For example, if the concern is that the fumes from the siting of a sewage plant will pass over a particular neighborhood, possibly endangering the inhabitants, those inhabitants could be involved in assessing the risk of breathing the fumes (perhaps by determining scenarios or data to be collected) or operating community air monitoring stations to ensure that the releases do not go over an agreed-upon level.

## Consequences of Multiple Meanings

Another ethical issue within society is what happens when messages are misunderstood. Who is to blame when a worker misunderstands a safety procedure and is injured? Is it the fault of the worker for not reading properly, the organization for failing to properly train the worker, the manufacturer of the equipment involved, or the communicator who wrote a message that could be misunderstood?

In any given situation, any message can be misunderstood. No matter how much we analyze our audience, there will always be someone within it who misinterprets the risk message. For example, at a public meeting on the proposed siting of a wind energy project (windmills to generate electricity), the representative of the company making the proposal spoke at length about how the windmills were constructed and how they would be arranged on the site. At one point he made the statement, "We have to site the windmills so far apart because when the wind hits them, they take 25% out of the wind and the wind needs time to recover before it hits the next windmill for maximum efficiency." A member of the audience later expressed a concern: "But if you take away some of the wind, won't there be less air for the rest of us?" The spokesperson was talking about velocity, but the member of the audience was thinking in terms of volume.

The choice for those who are communicating risk is how much information about the audience to collect. What information is necessary to understand how the audience thinks? A principle of technical communication related to gathering information about the audience is "audience, purpose, use." For risk communication, this equates to know your audience, know why you are communicating with them (purpose), and know how they plan to use the information. In Chapter 8, "Analyze Your Audience," we rank gathering information on the audience into three tiers: baseline, midline, and comprehensive. In choosing the appropriate tier, consider your resources (time, money, staff), the purpose of your risk communication effort (care, consensus, or crisis), and your specific objectives. Also consider pretesting your messages to identify and correct as many potential misunderstandings as possible before wide dissemination.

## The Issue of Stigma

As mentioned in Chapter 4, "Constraints to Effective Risk Communication," communities or individuals facing certain risks can also face societal disapproval or stigmatizing behavior. A child born to a mother with AIDS may be avoided by neighbors uneducated in the transmission mechanisms. A scenic coastal area may lose

◇

In any given situation, any message can be misunderstood. No matter how much we analyze our audience, there will always be someone within it who misinterprets the risk message.

tourist trade after an oil spill blackens beaches farther north.

Those at risk and organizations charged with managing the risks are often quick to blame the news media for such stigma. While sensationalized stories in the public view can increase stigma, so can other factors. For example, researchers Theresa Satterfield and Robin Gregory found that risk mitigation measures, such as protective barriers around a hazardous waste site, actually increased perceptions of risk and thus stigma (Gregory and Satterfield 2002).

More pointedly, a major contributor to stigma can be the careless use of risk information by otherwise conscientious scientists. Even civic-minded organizations have been known to manipulate risk information to make their point about the perceived dangers of a particular substance. For example, when the National Resources Defense Fund protested the use of the chemical Alar on apples and their story was prominently featured on national television, prices for the fruit plummeted.

The question for those communicating risk is how to present information appropriately for various segments of the audience without raising undue concern. Those at risk must understand their situation if they are to take appropriate action to eliminate or minimize the potential impacts. Those charged with managing the risk must understand the magnitude of the risk and potential management mechanisms. James Flynn, expert on the topic of stigma, advises educating risk assessment scientists and the news media on how stigma can impact communities (Flynn et al. 2001). Even if this education is impossible given the particular circumstances, risk communicators must understand their audiences. See Chapter 8, "Analyze Your Audience," for additional information.

## ORGANIZATIONAL ETHICS

Besides the societal scheme of ethics, agencies and corporations have their own organizational ethics. In many organizations, it is now standard practice for a newly hired employee to be required to read the organization's code of ethics and sign a formal statement promising to abide by it. In others, the code is less formal and may even take some deciphering by the new employee. Nevertheless, some such code exists, formal or informal, within every organization. Organizational ethical issues relate to how that code handles such issues as the legitimacy of representation, designation of first audience, release of information, and attitude toward compliance with regulations.

## Legitimacy of Representation

Legitimacy of representation refers to who is trusted to speak for whom—for the organization or for the audience—and whether the information being presented on the risk actually represents the risk. An organization usually has rules as to who is allowed to represent it before external audiences, how that person is prepared, and how the information to be presented is tailored for release. In some organizations, only staff in the public affairs department are allowed to speak for the organization. In others, managers or staff knowledgeable in a particular area are allowed to present information, as long as they have received training in such areas as public speaking and media relations. In rare cases, anyone who happens to be in the right (or wrong?) place at the right time will end up as the organization's spokesperson.

Usually, the information presented is passed through some sort of organizational screening review first. This review can range from a grammar check or presentation dry run to ensure that the information is in standard English, to a complex system in which a written version of the planned speech or a draft of an article is reviewed by the legal office, line or project managers, peer reviewers, and communications specialists.

The choices for those who are communicating risk are who to send to a particular audience, how to train that person, and how to ensure the information presented meets the audience's needs. The choice of spokesperson is among an expert on the risk, a person who has a high level of accountability in managing the risk (risk manager), a communications specialist (technical communicator, public relations specialist, or public information officer), or a celebrity (someone the audience knows and trusts). Table 5-3 shows which audiences are likely to accept each spokesperson and areas in which each spokesperson may need training. For more information on choosing a spokesperson, see Chapter 16, "Working with the Media." For more information on determining audience needs, see Chapter 8, "Analyze Your Audience."

A related ethical issue is who the organization accepts as having the right to speak for the audience. For example, a group or individual may step forward and claim to be representatives of "the public." They may act as if they are the ONLY representatives of the public and their views are the only legitimate ones. However, seldom does any one group or individual encompass all aspects of an audience.

The choice for those who are communicating risk is how to determine who represents the audience. The way to make this choice is to know all the components of your audience. For example, in assessing the risk of developing carpal tunnel syndrome among those who use computers, components of the audience could be divided into job categories related to computer use—computer programmers and database managers, secretaries and

> A related ethical issue is who the organization accepts as having the right to speak for the audience. For example, a group or individual may step forward and claim to be representatives of "the public." They may act as if they are the ONLY representatives of the public and their views are the only legitimate ones. However, seldom does any one group or individual encompass all aspects of an audience.

**TABLE 5-3**
Matching Spokespersons to Audience Characteristics

| Audience Characteristics | Spokesperson | Potential Training Needed |
|---|---|---|
| • Are interested in technical details<br>• Are not particularly hostile<br>• Have at least a basic understanding of the risk | Expert | Public speaking<br>Media relations |
| • Are interested in who's accountable<br>• Are hostile<br>• Have a basic understanding of the risk | Risk Manager | Public speaking<br>Media relations<br>Risk assessment |
| • Are interested in passing information on to others (e.g., news media)<br>• Are not particularly hostile<br>• Have little understanding of the risk | Communications Specialist | Risk assessment* |
| • Have some general knowledge of risk area<br>• Are apathetic to or unaware of specific risk | Celebrity | Risk assessment |

*Assumes that communications specialists have backgrounds in public speaking and media relations.

clerks, other nonclerical professionals, and managers. The members of each of these components view computer use differently (and may stand at greater or lesser risk). In choosing who represents the audience, those who are communicating risk may want to choose at least one representative from each of these components. More information on audience analysis can be found in Chapter 8, "Analyze Your Audience."

## Designation of Primary Audience

Another potential ethical issue within the organization is the designation, either formally or informally, of the "primary audience." The primary audience is that segment of the audience with the highest priority in the risk communication effort. In many cases, the needs of this segment of the audience are considered above the needs of other audience segments. When resources are scarce, the needs of the primary audience are often the only needs considered.

The choice of primary audience should be based on several considerations, such as:

- which segment of the audience is most at risk

- which segment of the audience has the least information with which to make choices on how to manage the risk

- which segment of the audience will be most involved in making choices on how to manage the risk (including those that must be involved for legal reasons).

In many situations, the first aspect, which segment of the audience is most at risk, would be the primary consideration. However, in some organizations, the third aspect becomes the most, and sometimes the only, aspect of importance. In other words, those who are communicating risk are forced to communicate in such a way as to meet only the needs of internal senior management who will make a final decision concerning the risk, an audience who are likely not part of the audience at risk. When only this segment of the audience has its needs met, the risk communication effort will fail. However, if this audience is ignored, risk communication efforts will lack the needed support to succeed (see Chapter 4, "Constraints to Effective Risk Communication," for more information). For example, in an organization responding to an external audit of a safety program, appeasing internal management can come before fixing some of the problems identified.

The dilemma for those who are communicating risk is how to meet the needs of all audiences. Carolyn Boiarsky, a communication consultant for industry and government, suggests holding a meeting of those who are communicating risk, subject matter experts, and senior management to understand the context of the risk communication effort and align internal approaches. She also suggests designing an appropriate format for documentation of risk in which information for particular audiences is separated into sections or placed in an appendix that can be skimmed or ignored by less interested readers (Boiarsky 1991).

## Releasing Information

Another ethical issue within organizations is the release of information. There are two aspects to this issue. First, audiences generally want as much information as they can get as early in the process as possible. However, organizations often release as little as possible as late as possible, for several good reasons. One is that early risk information—information gathered shortly after the risk has been identified—hasn't been subjected to the kind of peer review necessary to ensure the validity of scientific results. Another reason is that much risk information is either classified in some way (releasing it before a certain time would be detrimental to national security) or proprietary (early release would damage the organization's financial or competitive standing). However, the question arises of whether it is right to put scientific, national, or organizational interests before those of the people at risk.

The choice for those who are communicating risk is to determine when and how much information to release. The choice should be based on organizational, legal, and audience requirements. The risk communication

First, audiences generally want as much information as they can get as early in the process as possible. However, organizations often release as little as possible as late as possible, for several good reasons.

literature advocates releasing as much information as possible as soon as possible. However, if this is your choice, remember to release that information with sufficient caveats as to its stage of scientific uncertainty. One caveat of our own, however: if you are releasing information associated with some legal proceedings (a lawsuit, compliance with the National Environmental Policy Act, or meeting some other legal commitment), be mindful of your legal responsibilities. One federal agency released an environmental impact statement for a nuclear plant that would use an innovative method of producing isotopes. To protect themselves (and because this was standard procedure for the organization preparing the statement), they put a lengthy disclaimer on the inside cover of the document. The disclaimer basically said that the information in the statement was so preliminary that no one in the organization or the agency was willing to be accountable for anything in the environmental impact statement! Based largely on that disclaimer, an environmental activist group promptly sued the agency for failing to live up to due process of law. Because of this lawsuit, the project was scrapped entirely.

The second aspect of releasing information that can be an ethical issue is the archiving and possible release of draft information. This is information that led up to the preliminary results—draft input on scenarios to be considered, hand calculations of various types, even the first drafts of the risk communication messages. Those who are communicating risk (as well as others in the risk assessment process) often file a number of early "drafts," most of which are never intended to be read by anyone outside the group assessing and communicating the risk and which may contain proprietary or even embarrassing information (some reviewers can be quite scathing in their comments on drafts). However, when a lawsuit has been filed against an organization, these drafts may be some of the first information to be requested for use in court. In addition, the Privacy Rule for individual health information (see Chapter 3, "Laws That Mandate Risk Communication") describes ways to manage some risk information. So, the question is: should an organization limit the amount of this type of information that can be kept on file, or would this limitation be a form of censorship?

The choice for those who are communicating risk is how many drafts should be archived, understanding the needs of the audience and the needs of others within the organization who are using the information. If the organization has a policy that is too limited for audience and risk assessment purposes (for example, a policy that only final versions of documents are kept), those who are communicating risk may need to work to advocate a change in policy. For example, an external panel of experts overseeing an effort to determine radiation doses received by a population near a government nuclear facility had trouble finding unclassified information. When it became apparent that it was inappropriate to declassify all the necessary information, they requested the government to grant certain members high-level security clearances so they could review the information and assure the public that no pertinent data was being left out of the assessment. See Chapter 4, "Constraints to Effective Risk Communication," for more information on dealing with restrictive review procedures or lack of management support.

## Attitude toward Compliance with Regulations

Another ethical issue that may arise in organizations is the attitude toward compliance with regulations. Most organizations have wisely chosen to follow regulations, and those that have decided otherwise face legal as well as ethical difficulties that are beyond the scope of this book. Almost as important as following a regulation, however, is the way in which the regulation is followed. When compliance is viewed as an onerous duty at best or a way to subvert democracy at the very worst, risk communication, and all other efforts, can only suffer. For example, the staff for one government contractor refers to their response to Freedom of Information Act requests as "malicious compliance." That is, when a public group has to resort to threatening to sue in order to get necessary risk information, the organization dumps every piece of unanalyzed, unfiltered raw data onto the group

"Communicator's Serenity Prayer: 'Grant us the serenity to compromise with the publics we cannot change, the courage to persuade the publics we can change (when it is socially responsible to do so), and the wisdom to know the difference.'"

—David Dozier and Larissa and James Grunig, *Manager's Guide to Excellence in Public Relations and Communication Management* (1995, page 14).

in hopes this truckload of information will take the group so long to decipher that they will no longer have the resources to "bother" the organization. This approach further frustrates and alienates the audience.

The choice for those who are communicating risk is how to comply with regulations in such a way as to assist the risk communication effort. As with many of the ethical questions faced by communicators, the issue is to balance the needs of the organization with those of the audience. One key to this is understanding and respecting the audience. The information in Chapter 8, "Analyze Your Audience," should provide some useful guidelines.

## PERSONAL ETHICS

Another area that must be considered is your own personal ethics. What do you believe is the right way to present risk information? What do you believe your role as the communicator of risk should be? What is your personal code of honor and what would you do if following it conflicted with following your organization's code of ethics?

### Using Persuasion

One of the ways to present risk information is by using persuasion, which purposefully presents risk information with the intent of forcing an opinion on the audience. At its worst, persuasive arguments are used to alarm the audience and motivate them to action for fear of loss of life or livelihood. Those who communicate risk in this way often justify it by saying that in some situations, such as a crisis, time is limited and risks are high; therefore, the risk communicator should use every communication tool to get people to do what is best for them. But even in a crisis does any organization have the right to tell others what is best?

The choice for those who are communicating risk is whether persuasion is justified in their situations. Situations in which persuasion has been justified by risk

◇

*". . . The power to change behavior carries the immense ethical responsibility to use this power wisely."*

—David B. McCallum, "Risk Communication: A Tool for Behavior Change" (1995, page 65).

communicators are those that have one or more of the following characteristics:

- at least some component of the audience is in immediate danger of injury or death (as in crisis situations)

- those at risk are not the same as those engaged in the behavior and have little control over those engaged in the behavior (for example, unborn babies of alcoholic mothers)

- the audience consists of fewer than 10 people who all feel that they are social equals of the risk communicator (in a small group of equal standing, there is more likelihood that the audience will consider the arguments and not feel as if they are being coerced)

- the audience has specifically asked to be persuaded (for example, by inviting a speaker in for a lively debate).

### The Role of the Communicator

◇

*"Those charged with making and implementing policies governing our affairs must understand the limits of science as well as its promise, and scientists must learn the limits of policy, the processes by which policies are established in a democratic society, and how to communicate scientific information to the policy process."*

—American Institute of Biological Sciences, 1994.

Another personal ethical question is, "What should my role be in the communication of risk information?" Should we be disseminators of information, the conduit through which technical information flows and the audience's needs are communicated back to the decision-maker? Should we "sell" the risk decision? Or should our knowledge of the audience and communication methods help the decision-maker determine what the ultimate decision should be?

Your choice of role will depend on organizational and personal factors. If the organization recognizes that those who are communicating risk are a vital part of the risk assessment team, the range of roles available will be wider than in a organization that views risk communication as a necessary evil. Some audiences will want to interact only with decision-makers and hence limit interactions with others who might communicate risk. In addition, some risk communicators may not have the skills necessary to fill a larger role or have not realized that a larger role can exist.

## Organizational Ethics or Personal Ethics?

Perhaps the most difficult ethical dilemma comes when personal ethics conflict with organizational ethics. The organization has asked you to downplay, ignore, or, worse, to cover up some risk information that, if released, could prevent the injury or death of a number of people. Yet you have a certain loyalty to the organization that issues your paycheck. Which do you listen to—your organization's need to protect itself (and perhaps your job) or your conscience's need to ensure that no one is hurt? Examples of this can be seen in some classic disasters—the engineering staff who warned about the integrity of the O rings before the explosion on the space shuttle *Challenger*, and the medical staff who warned of potential problems with silicone-gel breast implants.

Oftentimes, the dilemma isn't as clear cut as this. Sometimes the organization simply wishes to limit the amount of information provided to an audience concerning a particular risk. How much information is the right amount? Which pieces will the audience feel are necessary? When faced with such dilemmas, the communicator really has three choices: follow organizational dictates, step down from the work in question, or find someone who will recognize the problem and give it the attention it deserves. Sometimes this person is a higher-level manager within the same organization (and we encourage you to try this avenue first if at all possible). Sometimes it is an outside agency with oversight over your organization. If all else fails, you can turn "whistle-blower" and tell your story to the media. This may make you a celebrity in the short run; however, despite laws that stipulate no harassment of whistleblowers, telling your story to the press may have disastrous results for your career. Organizations take a dim view of those who break corporate dictates, however justifiably.

## IN SUMMARY

This short discussion has covered only a few of the ethical issues that can face those who are communicating risk. Many more might be added. Being aware of these issues and how they might be resolved can help those who are communicating risk meet the challenges of communicating risk in an ethical manner.

## REFERENCES

Beck, J. E. 1991. "Public Involvement Through Negotiation, Mediation, and Arbitration." Seminar presented to staff, November 25, 1991, Pacific Northwest National Laboratory, Richland, Washington.

Boiarsky, C. 1991. "Writing for Multiple Readers with Conflicting Needs: An Opportunity for Improving Communications with Regulatory Agencies." In *The Engineered Communication: Designs for Continued Improvement*, Proceedings of the 1991 International Professional Communication Conference, pages 313-317. 91CH3067-4, Institute of Electronic and Electrical Engineers, Washington, D.C.

Bullard, R. D. 1990. *Dumping in Dixie: Race, Class, and Environmental Quality*. Westview Press, Boulder, Colorado.

Bullard, R. D. 1992. "In Our Backyards: Minority Communities Get Most of the Dumps." *EPA Journal*, 18(1):11-12.

Creighton, J. 1992. "What Does it Take for a Decision to 'Count?'" Presentation to U.S. Department of Energy, Richland Operations Office, Richland, Washington. Creighton and Creighton, Palo Alto, California.

Dozier, D. M., L. A. Grunig, and J. E. Grunig. 1995. *Manager's Guide to Excellence in Public Relations and Communication Management*. Lawrence Erlbaum Associates, Mahwah, New Jersey.

Flynn, J., P. Slovic, and H. Kunreuther, editors. 2001. *Risk, Media, and Stigma: Understanding Challenges to Modern Science and Technology*. Earthscan, London.

Gregory, R. S., and T. A. Satterfield. 2002. "Beyond Perception: The Experience of Risk and Stigma in Community Contexts." *Risk Analysis*, 22(2):347-358.

McCallum, D. B. 1995. "Risk Communication: A Tool for Behavior Change." *NIDA Research Monograph*, 155:65-89.

Morgan, M. G., B. Fischhoff, A. Bostrom, and C. J. Atman. 2002. *Risk Communication: A Mental Models Approach*. Cambridge University Press, New York.

NRC (National Research Council). 1996. *Understanding Risk: Informing Decisions in a Democratic Society.* National Academy Press, Washington, D.C.

STC (Society for Technical Communication). 1998. "Ethical Principles for Technical Communicators." http://www.stc.org/ethical.asp

## ADDITIONAL RESOURCES

Chess, C., P. M. Sandman, and M. R. Greenberg. 1990. *Empowering Agencies to Communicate about Environmental Risk: Suggestions for Overcoming Organizational Barriers.* Rutgers University, Cook College, Environmental Communication Research Program, New Brunswick, New Jersey.

Covello, V. T., D. B. McCallum, and M. T. Pavlova. 1989. "Principles and Guidelines for Improving Risk Communication." *Effective Risk Communication: The Role and Responsibility of Government and Nongovernment Organizations*, editors V. T. Covello, D. B. McCallum, and M. T. Pavlova, pages 3-16. Plenum Press, New York.

Gelobter, M. 1992. "Expanding the Dialogue: Have Minorities Benefited . . ? A Forum." *EPA Journal*, 18(1):32.

Kasperson, R. E. 1986. "Hazardous Waste Facility Siting: Community, Firm, and Governmental Perspectives." *Hazards: Technology and Fairness*, pages 118-144. National Academy of Engineering/National Academy Press, Washington, D.C.

Morgan, M. G., and L. B. Lave. 1990. "Ethical Considerations in Risk Communication Practice and Research." *Risk Analysis*, 10(3):355-358.

# Principles of
# Risk Communication

The risk communication literature discusses a number of principles regarding how best to communicate risk. Two that have been covered extensively are the fact that the audience must find the communicating organization credible and trustworthy and the fact that the audience must be allowed to participate in the risk management decision. Because following both of these principles is often outside the control of those who are communicating the risk, we will not discuss them here.

The following principles, then, focus on those aspects of risk communication that are within the purview of those who are communicating risk, the principles related to the risk communication process, risk communication presentation, and risk comparison. Unless specifically noted, these principles apply equally to care, consensus, and crisis communication. For more information on risk communication principles, consult Chapter 21, "Resources."

## PRINCIPLES OF PROCESS

Principles of process relate to the process of planning and conducting a risk communication effort. They are ways of setting up the risk communication process that help ensure that the effort achieves its objectives.

## Know Your Communication Limits and Purpose

To effectively communicate risk, you must know why you are communicating and any limitations to your ability to communicate risk. Your communication limits may be defined by:

- regulatory requirements—for example, the U.S. Environmental Protection Agency specifies what community relations activities are to be conducted for Superfund cleanup sites (see Chapter 3, "Laws That Mandate Risk Communication")

- organizational requirements—for example, some organizations cannot allow preliminary risk data to be released for proprietary reasons (see Chapter 4, "Constraints to Effective Risk Communication")

- audience requirements—for example, some members of the audience may have difficulty in reading or processing information (see Chapter 4, "Constraints to Effective Risk Communication").

These kinds of limits affect how you can communicate risk.

Another way to think about this principle is "don't promise what you can't deliver." Define the audience's role at the beginning and frequently during the process so that both the audience and your organization knows what to expect. If you and your audience understand why you are communicating about the risk and the limits to that communication, you will be less likely to promise what you can't deliver and they will be less likely to demand a bigger role than they can legally have. See Chapter 7, "Determine Purpose and Objectives," for more information on setting purposes and determining limits.

Violating this principle can increase hostility in the audience, making it more difficult for the organization to communicate credibly and effectively. An example of violating this principle comes from one of the U.S.

Define the audience's role at the beginning and frequently during the process so that both the audience and your organization knows what to expect.

Department of Energy's defense production laboratories (those laboratories whose research has focused on better ways to produce nuclear weapons). A group of citizens who lived in the area near the laboratory were concerned about the risk of having nuclear materials so close and distressed that their local economy was driven by making better bombs. They petitioned for and received funding from a philanthropical organization to study alternative uses for the laboratory. The communication process between the laboratory and the concerned citizens had never been good—suspicion was strong on both sides. However, even as the laboratory had begun to communicate risk more effectively, opening their doors to tours and inviting comments on activities, the citizens group was trying to identify ways to change the laboratory, with no input from the laboratory or the U.S. Department of Energy. When the citizens group comes up with its recommendations, will anyone listen? And if the recommendations fail to get the hearing the group feels is deserved, what kind of communication will be possible then? In a situation like this, it would have been best if the laboratory and U.S. Department of Energy had gone to the citizens group as soon as the grant was received and discussed what options were possible given department funding and mandate. With expectations set, the group could have developed strategies within existing constraints.

## Whenever Possible, Pretest Your Message

Audience analysis should be part of every effort to communicate risk. Factors such as reading level, knowledge of the subject, and level of hostility must be considered if risk is to be communicated effectively. Whenever possible, however, the message should also be pretested—reviewed by a group representing the intended audience—before dissemination, to determine that the audience analysis information was correct and that the risk message achieves the desired results.

Pretest even before the message is designed by asking your potential audience about issues to be covered, concerns to be addressed, and levels of information needed.

Pretest the risk communication message prototype before dissemination to make sure you have addressed the concerns and aren't alienating anyone with the presentation. Test between communication rounds so that you can build on your efforts and refine them (Arkin 1989). More information on pretesting is presented in Chapter 8, "Analyze Your Audience."

### Communicate Early, Often, and Fully

This principle has two aspects: timing of communication and amount of information released. Risk communication must be timed to involve the audience throughout the process, not only during a crisis or once in the life of a project. As mentioned previously (see Chapter 5, "Ethical Issues"), many members of the audience will expect to be involved from the beginning. In fact, many will consider such involvement their right. Denying them this opportunity will increase hostility and make risk communication more difficult. Therefore, risk communication should begin as soon as a risk has been identified and continue as new information becomes available. If no new information becomes available in a timely manner, let the audience know that the risk is still being studied and that they haven't been forgotten. The length of time between communications will vary by risk and level of interest from the audience. A risk that seriously threatens entire communities and has the audience extremely concerned will require more frequent communications (hourly to daily, as in a flood) than will a risk that results in less immediate danger to an audience that is unconcerned (quarterly to yearly).

The second aspect involves the amount of information released. As noted in Chapter 4, "Constraints to Effective Risk Communication," many organizations find it difficult to release information about a risk because of national security or proprietary concerns. However, withholding information, even to confirm the accuracy of the data, can make the audience suspect that the organization is trying to hide something, eroding its credibility, increasing hostility, and generally making risk communication more difficult. Therefore, don't restrict information. When in

If no new information becomes available in a timely manner, let the audience know that the risk is still being studied and that they haven't been forgotten.

doubt, ask your audience what level and type of information they want and provide as much of it as you can within organization and resource constraints.

An example of how this principle has been implemented comes from the New York City Department of Health. When the West Nile virus outbreak hit in 1999, they developed a detailed response plan that allowed them to communicate early. To allow them to communicate often, they also used multiple communication channels (including TV and radio public service announcements), extensive media outreach and announcements during daily mayoral press conferences, brochures and fact sheets prepared in ten languages, posters placed throughout the city, bill inserts mailed with the cooperation of city utilities, hotlines staffed around the clock, a web site, and town-hall public meetings. To ensure they were communicating fully, they provided information that answered peoples' questions, explained protective measures people could take to reduce their risk, and described what the city was doing. As a result, communication efforts went more smoothly than what might otherwise have been the case (Covello et al. 2001).

### Remember That Perception is Reality

This principle can be difficult for some technical experts to apply. To them, reality is built on carefully constructed, tested, scientific truths, not someone's possibly uninformed perceptions. However, such regulatory agencies as the U.S. Environmental Protection Agency sometimes make decisions based heavily on the audience's perception, not just the technical aspects.

For example, at a garbage dump near Spokane, Washington, dangerous chemicals had the potential to leak into the groundwater and from there to the drinking water supply. A scientific study of alternative treatment methods recommended the use of capping, that is, pouring cement over the dump and monitoring it to ensure nothing leaked out, as the most cost-effective treatment. However, during the public review of the study and recommendations, the public overwhelmingly preferred the alternative of pumping out some waste, treating the remaining waste, and then capping. Although this alternative did not significantly lessen the risk and significantly increased the cost, it was the alternative chosen by the U.S. Environmental Protection Agency. The moral: risk assessments and subsequent decisions are not based on the technical aspects of the risk alone. Audience perceptions and concerns must be considered if risk decisions, and their communication, are to be successful.

## PRINCIPLES OF PRESENTATION

Another set of principles addresses how to present the risk information in ways that best communicate the risk to the intended audience.

### Know Your Audience

You cannot communicate unless you know to whom you are communicating. This is the one principle you should always follow; if you follow it, you will be in a position to know how to apply any of the other principles. In fact, knowing your audience is crucial to knowing what risk communication methods to use. For example, if you know that your audience wants to see the risk information immediately, you might forego the principle of pretesting so that you can release the information more quickly. And you might use the method of informing the news media rather than using a method that could take longer (such as holding a public meeting 30 days after announcing it in the paper). For more information on this issue, see Chapter 8, "Analyze Your Audience."

### Don't Limit Yourself to One Form, One Method

Any audience for a risk communication message will be made up of a variety of segments, each with different levels of knowledge about the risk, of interest in the risk, and of being at risk. Because of these factors, no single method of communication is likely to meet the needs of your entire audience. You will need to find methods that best meet the needs of each segment. For example, in a community near a Superfund site in Alaska, we found that the written word was the best approach for a large segment of the population because other forms of communication (radio and television) were subject to outages during inclement weather and the library was the one place almost everyone eventually visited. For those in more rural areas, who came into town only for major community events such as fairs, we also developed a traveling exhibit. See Chapter 10, "Determine the Appropriate Methods," for more information on which methods best serve which segments of the audience.

## Simplify Language and Presentation, Not Content

When trying to communicate the complex issues behind a risk, it is easy to leave out information that seems to be overly technical. Unfortunately, by simplifying the content of a risk message, you may leave out key information that your audience would need to make a decision. Your audience will understand the concepts better, and be better informed about the risk, if you simplify the way you present the content instead of the content itself. Any technical subject can be understood by the public if it is presented properly. Technical communicators have made careers out of this fact. The audience doesn't have to understand it at the same level as the risk expert, but they can understand it well enough to make an informed decision.

## Be Objective, Not Subjective

Quantify information whenever possible. Avoid words like "significant," "negligible," and "minor." They beg the questions, "significant to whom? under what conditions? based on what evidence?" Whenever possible, give examples, numbers that can be put in perspective, and concrete information.

## Communicate Honestly, Clearly, and Compassionately

To communicate honestly, you must differentiate between opinions and facts. Any risk communication message, whether spoken, written in a report, or printed on a bulletin board, can be questioned by the audience. Responding credibly to a question about a fact is much easier than substantiating an opinion.

To communicate clearly, you must present information at your audience's level of understanding. Audiences reject information that is too difficult for them, either by refusing to acknowledge it or by becoming hostile. On the other hand, audiences may become hostile when information is too easy for them, because they feel patronized.

To communicate compassionately, don't ignore audience concerns, even ones that seem to be based on information about something other than the risk itself. A scientist we once worked with was wonderful about listening to his audience. He attended every public meeting, pored over letters and comments, and carefully categorized every comment. Unfortunately, he then identified groups of comments that he felt were ridiculous: "That's a stupid comment, I won't sink to that level to answer it. This one is clearly out of scope, it doesn't have anything to do with the risk. This comment is purely emotional." The audience's concerns won't go away simply because you refuse to deal with them. On the contrary, they will likely keep coming up until you are forced to deal with them, perhaps under less favorable conditions such as a lawsuit. Better to deal with them as soon as they are aired, show your audience that you are listening, and allow them to move on to other questions that may more directly involve the risk itself. How you deal with them depends on the risk communication method. In print messages and computer-based applications, use a question-and-answer format with the questions being their concerns and the answers your responses or incorporate your responses into a graphic. In face-to-face methods and stakeholder participation, respond directly to questions and concerns as you hear them.

### Listen and Deal with Specific Concerns

Besides dealing with the emotions behind concerns, listen to what people are saying about the risk itself. Then deal with each specific concern you hear. Don't discount concerns that seem based on faulty scientific information or are peripheral to the situation. A good example comes from a scientist who was asked to speak about atmospheric fallout at a public meeting. After explaining the process and associated risks, the scientist asked if there were any questions. A man from the back of the room rose and identified himself as a local farmer: "You tell me that I have this plutonium stuff all over my crops. What exactly does that mean? Can I still sell my crops? Can I eat them myself? Should I let my children play outside? I don't know who to trust anymore!" The scientist responded, "Excuse me, sir, but it's strontium-90, not plutonium."

Now, the scientist was just trying to correct a technical mistake. However, as you can imagine, the level of hostility in that room skyrocketed. No one listened to anything else the scientist had to say. It would have been far more effective for the risk communication process if the scientist had recognized the underlying confusion and fear and said something like, "I understand why you might not know where to turn. There's a lot of information out there, but there's also a lot of misinformation. Let's see what I can do to clarify a few points. For one thing, it's not plutonium, it's strontium-90, and what that means is . . . ."

Besides dealing with the emotions behind concerns, listen to what people are saying about the risk itself. Then deal with each specific concern you hear. Don't discount concerns that seem based on faulty scientific information or are peripheral to the situation.

## Convey the Same Information to All Segments of Your Audience

As mentioned previously, different segments of your audience will have different needs—for information, for involvement, and for responding to the risk. To communicate effectively, you must communicate with each segment in a way that meets those needs. However, as Callaghan (1989) found, you can change the method and amount of detail, but you can't change the basic information or you will lose trust and your efforts will be useless. You must provide the same information to each segment to retain credibility.

## Deal with Uncertainty

In communicating about risks, you can never present results as definitive; no study is ever the final word. Instead, you must discuss sources of uncertainty, such as how the data were gathered, how they were analyzed, and how the results were interpreted. The sources of uncertainty and how you communicate about them vary among care, consensus, and crisis risk assessments. In care communication situations, the risk assessment has been conducted and found to be credible by most of the audience. Sources of uncertainty, then, are less important and may be discussed very little if at all. In consensus communication, the audience will probably be involved in determining how the risk is analyzed and may help determine which types of uncertainty are acceptable. Therefore, sources of uncertainty become well understood and may be discussed less and less as time goes on. In some types of crisis communication, the risk is obvious and the areas of uncertainty can be left out of messages unless a particular audience has requested them. In other types of crisis communication, for example in a terrorist attack, the risk and final consequences may be less well defined. In such cases, the uncertainty may lie in our response to the crisis. Risk communicators must be open with what they do not know and stress what they do know and what they are doing to resolve the uncertainties.

In cases where uncertainty is to be discussed, the process of assessing the risk should be discussed first to frame where the sources of uncertainty can be found. In data gathering for an environmental risk assessment, for example, were the data gathered over the same time period, or are you comparing between years? Were the same collection methods used each time? Were the data always gathered in the same location? In data analysis for a safety risk assessment, which methods were used? How reliable are they? Are they new methods or ones that have stood the test of time? For interpreting the results of a health assessment, what was the basis for determining significance? How certain are the standards or limits used? Who determined whether these standards actually protected human health? Your audience will often want the answer to one particular question, "Is it safe?" Although they may not like answers with caveats attached, they will be even less happy if they are given an answer that later turns out to be wrong because of the uncertainties involved. See Chapter 14 concerning the pictorial representation of risk for more information on portraying uncertainty and probability.

# PRINCIPLES FOR COMPARING RISKS

In risk communication efforts, comparing risks can be helpful but challenging. As you try to present information at a level that your audience understands, comparisons look like an easy answer. Unfortunately, what little empirical research has been devoted to this area is complicated, confusing, and contradictory (see for example Johnson 2002, which provides a frank discussion of compounding influences). Much of the advice that follows is based on informed opinions of risk communication researchers and practitioners. The best way to choose which of these principles or methods to apply is to know your audience and pretest messages.

Risk communication researchers and practitioners agree that some types of comparisons can alienate certain segments of the audience. Unfortunately, which comparisons are best for which audiences has yet to be determined. Covello et al. (1988) listed ways to compare risks according to which methods might be most acceptable with most audiences (Table 6-1). However, studies at Carnegie-Mellon University and elsewhere (for example, Roth et al. 1990) have shown that some of these methods may in fact be more acceptable to certain audiences than Covello et al. originally thought.

**TABLE 6-1**
Acceptability of Risk Comparisons*

| Most Acceptable | Less Desirable | Even Less Desirable | Rarely Acceptable |
|---|---|---|---|
| Same risk at different times | Doing something vs. not doing it | Average risk vs. peak risk at a particular time or location | Risk vs. cost |
| Risk vs. standard | Alternative ways of lessening risk | Risk from one source of harm vs. risk from all sources of that harm | Risk vs. benefit |
| Different estimates of the same risk | Risk in one place vs. risks in another place | Occupational risk vs. environmental risk | Risk vs. other specific causes of same harm |

*Adapted from Covello et al. (1988).

## Use Analogies, but Don't Trivialize

According to the Presidential/Congressional Commission on Risk Assessment and Risk Management (1997) and our own experience, most people, including physicians and some risk assessment experts, do not easily relate to terms like $10^{-6}$ or E-6 when describing risk. Analogies can help put these risks in perspective. For example, a risk of one in a million ($10^{-6}$) is equivalent to 30 seconds in a year, 1 inch in 16 miles, or 1 drop in 16 gallons (Commission 1997).

Using analogies, however, can be problematic for several reasons. One reason is that risk is such a multi-faceted situation that it is difficult to find something completely analogous with which to compare it. For example, the analogies discussed in the previous paragraph, while endorsed by the Presidential/Congressional Commission, deal with volume or distance, not toxicity, and may in fact confuse some of the audience.

Another reason analogies can be problematic is that they can come across as trivial. As you try to compare a technical concept of risk to something that is more familiar to your audience, it's easy to find something that may look too simplistic. For example, you might say that the risk of contracting cancer from being exposed to a certain chemical is as small as one piece of toilet paper in a roll stretched from New York to San Francisco. This does present the concept that the risk is very small, but you seem to have compared someone's life to a roll of toilet paper, a comparison that will offend at least some if not all members of your audience.

## Use Ranges

You can express a risk by using a range of numbers. (Unfortunately, some studies show that this can be problematic—again, know your audience.) One end of the range may represent a level that has been determined to be "safe," the other end may represent a level that has been determined to be risky, and another number may represent the findings of your risk assessment. Audiences can then compare your risk assessment find-

---

◇

Analogies can help put risks in perspective. For example, a risk of one in a million ($10^{-6}$) is equivalent to 30 seconds in a year, 1 inch in 16 miles, or 1 drop in 16 gallons (Commission 1997).

---

ings with those in the range. This method of risk comparison is especially good for hostile audiences in that your audience can determine for themselves where the risk falls on a hazard scale, and you do not have to decide "significance" for them, a practice that can lead to increased hostility. However, be careful to explain the ranges—why were they chosen, by whom, and what do they mean to your audience? This further explanation helps put the risk in perspective.

## Compare to Standards

A number of standards have been developed by regulatory agencies and interested groups to describe levels at which certain risks can cause certain levels of harm. One of the most often used at Superfund sites, for example, is the Interim Primary Drinking Water Standards mandated by the U.S. Environmental Protection Agency. These standards show what level of contaminant is considered safe in drinking water supplies. You could compare the results of your risk assessment to such a standard. If your results are higher than the standard, you are showing your audience that they should be concerned. If your results are lower than the standard, you are showing your audience that they probably have no reason for concern. One caution, however: recent studies have shown that this rule is only as good as the standard used. If your audience already feels the standard is too low or high, comparing to it may not be your best choice.

## Compare to Other Estimates of the Same Risk

For any particular risk, a number of assessments are usually performed. For example, government researchers, university researchers, and independent researchers hired by concerned citizen groups may all study a particular risk. In addition, some risks have been studied by the same organization over many years. You can compare the results of each of the studies. If the results are similar, you are reinforcing the risk assessment. If the results vary widely, you are reinforcing recognition of the uncertainties involved. This type of comparison has been called "Dueling Ph.D.'s," which points to a possible problem. If having too many studies or contradictory studies will confuse or alienate your audience ("I knew it—these scientists will say anything!"), you may want to try another way of comparing the risk.

## Compare Traits

Another way to compare risks is to base the comparison on different traits of segments of your audience. Use age groups (risk to infants versus risk to senior citizens), geographic regions (risk on the East Coast versus risk on the West Coast), or lifestyles (risk to the avid sportsman versus risk to the farmer, risk to the farmer versus risk to the city dweller). This personalizes the risk for each member of your audience by allowing them to determine which trait best applies. Those at lesser risk may find this determination comforting. Those at greater risk may be motivated to find ways to lessen their risk.

## Don't Compare Risks with Different Levels of Associated Outrage

The term outrage refers to the feelings of anger and frustration often associated with certain risks. (For a more in-depth discussion, see Chapter 4, "Constraints to Effective Risk Communication.") Risks that are high in outrage include those that are imposed, government controlled, seen as unfair by the audience, from an untrustworthy source, artificial, exotic, associated with disasters, dreaded, undetectable, or not scientifically well understood. Nuclear power is a prime example of a high-outrage risk, being imposed, government controlled, artificial, exotic, associated with disasters like those at Chornobyl and Three-Mile Island, dreaded, undetectable (the radiation is), and relatively new. In contrast, smoking cigarettes is voluntary, familiar, detectable, and scientifically well understood, so outrage is generally lower. The reasoning behind this principle is that when you compare something like the high-outrage risk of contracting cancer from radiation exposure from nuclear power to the low-outrage risk of contracting cancer from smoking cigarettes, you alienate your audience. Your audience will see the two as totally different risks, having nothing to do with each other.

However, studies at Carnegie-Mellon University (Roth et al. 1990) indicate that some audiences will not be alienated by such comparisons. They will, in fact, learn from such comparisons and even find them comforting, if the high-outrage risk they were concerned about is actually lower than the low-outrage risk. Unfortunately, the research has not delineated exactly which audiences these are. So, for now, it is probably best to avoid comparing high-outrage and low-outrage risks.

## Explain Reductions in Magnitude

One of the common misperceptions among those at risk is that a reduction in magnitude (one chance in a thousand to one chance in a million) is the same as a linear reduction (10,000 to 9,999). While research in this area is quite complicated, one suggestion is to illustrate this concept graphically. The Presidential/Congressional Commission on Risk Assessment and Risk Management (1997) recommends bar charts to show the radical differences between these scales. See Chapter 14 for additional information on pictorial representation of risk.

## IN SUMMARY

Risk communication is still far from being a science. The principles that have been developed through years of study still can be distilled into two maxims: know your audience and know your situation. Understand what your audience needs to know (what they want to know and what you need to tell them to help deal with the risk), how they want to receive that information, and what you can do within certain constraints. The other principles can then be followed as they apply to your audience and situation. Part II, "Planning the Risk Communication Effort," deals with the issues of audience and situation.

# REFERENCES

Arkin, E. B. 1989. "Translation of Risk Information for the Public: Message Development." *Effective Risk Communication: The Role and Responsibility of Government and Nongovernment Organizations*, editors V. T. Covello, D. B. McCallum, and M. T. Pavlova, pages 127-135. Plenum Press, New York.

Callaghan, J. D. 1989. "Reaching Target Audiences with Risk Information." *Effective Risk Communication: The Role and Responsibility of Government and Nongovernment Organizations*, editors V. T. Covello, D. B. McCallum, and M. T. Pavlova, pages 137-142. Plenum Press, New York.

Covello, V. T., P. M. Sandman, and P. Slovic. 1988. *Risk Communication, Risk Statistics, and Risk Comparisons: A Manual for Plant Managers*. Chemical Manufacturers Association, Washington, D.C.

Covello, V. T., R. G. Peters, J. G. Wojtecki, and R. C. Hyde. 2001. "Risk Communication, the West Nile Virus Epidemic, and Bioterrorism: Responding to the Communication Challenges Posed by the Intentional or Unintentional Release of a Pathogen in an Urban Setting." *Journal of Urban Health: Bulletin of the New York Academy of Medicine*, 78(2):382-391.

Johnson, B. B. 2002. "Stability and Inoculation of Risk Comparisons' Effects Under Conflict: Replicating and Extending the 'Asbestos Jury' Study by Slovic et al." *Risk Analysis*, 22(4):777-788.

Morgan, G., B. Fischhoff, A. Bostrom, L. Lave, and C. J. Atman. 1992. "Communicating Risk to the Public." *Environ. Sci. Technol.*, 26(11):2048-2056.

Presidential/Congressional Commission on Risk Assessment and Risk Management. 1997. *Risk Assessment and Risk Management in Regulatory Decision-Making*. Volume 2, Commission on Risk Assessment and Risk Management, Washington, D.C.

Roth, E., M. G. Morgan, B. Fischhoff, L. Lave, and A. Bostrom. 1990. "What Do We Know About Making Risk Comparisons?" *Risk Analysis*, 10(3):375-387.

# ADDITIONAL RESOURCES

Covello, V. T., and F. W. Allen. 1988. *Seven Cardinal Rules of Risk Communication*. OPA-87-020, U.S. Environmental Protection Agency, Washington, D.C.

Covello, V. T., D. B. McCallum, and M. T. Pavlova. 1989. "Principles and Guidelines for Improving Risk Communication." *Effective Risk Communication: The Role and Responsibility of Government and Nongovernment Organizations*, editors V. T. Covello, D. B. McCallum, and M. T. Pavlova, pages 3-16. Plenum Press, New York.

Hance, B. J., C. Chess, and P. M. Sandman. 1988. *Improving Dialogue with Communities: A Risk Communication Manual for Government*. New Jersey Department of Environmental Protection, Division of Science and Research, Trenton, New Jersey.

Hance, B. J., C. Chess, and P. M. Sandman. 1990. *Industry Risk Communication Manual*. CRC Press/Lewis Publishers, Boca Raton, Florida.

NRC (National Research Council). 1989. *Improving Risk Communication*. National Academy Press, Washington, D.C.

# Part
# II

# PLANNING THE RISK COMMUNICATION EFFORT

**F**or any effort to be effective, a certain amount of planning is needed. To plan a risk communication effort, whether a one-time message or a variety of messages for a variety of audiences over a longer time, you need to determine your purpose and objectives, analyze your audience, develop messages, determine the proper method, set a schedule, and pull all these pieces together into a comprehensive plan. Having a risk communication plan can help you focus your efforts and keep all those involved in assessing, communicating, and managing the risk informed so that they can work together as a team.

—————— ◇ ——————

*"Attention to details (e.g., dress, language used in risk communication materials, meeting location, and room arrangement) is often critical to effective risk communication."*
—Vincent T. Covello, David B. McCallum, and Maria Pavlova, "Principles and Guidelines for Improving Risk Communication" (1989, page 9).

# Determine Purpose and Objectives

*T*wo variables you have to consider in communicating risk are why you are communicating the risk (purpose) and what you hope to gain by it (objective). The purpose is a general statement. It answers "why" questions. Why are we communicating? Why are we educating this group? Why are we trying to build consensus? Objectives are statements of specific, measurable details to be accomplished. Objectives often answer "how" questions. How will we communicate? How often will we communicate? How many messages will we use? For example, if your purpose is to decrease teenage smoking, one of your objectives might be to have 50% of your audience stop smoking by June 15.

When you have determined your purpose and objectives, formalize them by writing them down and getting concurrence from all those involved in the project, as high up in the organization as you can. This formal agreement can help you communicate risk more effectively because it:

- gives everyone a common ground upon which to build

- lets upper management know why you're doing what you're doing

———— ◇ ————

Two variables you have to consider in communicating risk are why you are communicating the risk (purpose) and what you hope to gain by it (objective).

• gives you a yardstick for measuring success.

When you're determining purpose and objectives, there are a number of factors to be considered.

## FACTORS THAT INFLUENCE PURPOSE AND OBJECTIVES

Your purpose and objectives may at first seem obvious. You are communicating to provide the audience with information they need to make a decision about a risk to their health or safety or the environment. However, your purpose and objectives are necessarily influenced by a number of factors, including legal issues, organizational requirements, the risk itself, and audience requirements. These factors must be consciously considered in determining your purpose and objectives or you may find yourself in conflict with something that could seriously impair, if not cancel, your entire effort. For example, if the purpose and objectives of your risk communication effort at a Superfund site conflict with the communication requirements for these sites mandated by the U.S. Environmental Protection Agency, your organization will be liable for strict financial penalties.

### Legal Issues

Several legal issues may influence your choice of purpose and objectives. Chief among these are the laws that may dictate your risk communication efforts. We describe some of the major United States laws and their requirements in Chapter 3, "Laws That Mandate Risk Communication." They include the Comprehensive Environmental Response, Compensation, and Liability Act (CERCLA); the National Environmental Policy Act (NEPA); and the requirements set forth by the Occupational Safety and Health Administration (OSHA). In addition, many government agencies have policies regarding how risk communication will be conducted or how the public will be involved in risk management decisions.

For example, in late 1992 the U.S. Department of Energy's Office of Environmental Management first issued a policy on public involvement/communication that specified involving the audience fully in decisions related to the environmental cleanup of the department's sites. In 2001, the U.S. Centers for Disease Control and Prevention issued guidance for risk communication activities as part of multi-million dollar grants to the states. These kinds of requirements must be considered when planning a risk communication effort because they generally provide guidance and sometimes specify activities that must be conducted. If the purpose and objectives of risk communication efforts that fall under these legal requirements differ from what is specified, special arrangements such as legal waivers or exemptions may be necessary.

## Organizational Requirements

After considering the legal issues that may affect your efforts, you also need to consider your own organization's requirements and policies regarding the communication of risk, the involvement of the public, the release of information, and the development of communication materials and processes in general. The policies may be formal, or they may be in the form of tradition ("we always do it this way").

Check with those in charge of communication in your organization to determine what they expect from risk communication efforts. For example, do they feel that the only proper purpose for communication efforts is to advertise the organization or otherwise make it look good? Is one of their objectives dissemination of information to key political figures who might be able to influence the future of the organization? You'll need to be aware of these issues before you determine exactly what you should do to communicate risk. How you handle their expectations depends on your philosophy concerning the communication of risk. For example, if you agree that promoting the organization should be part of the risk communication effort, then you will include that as a purpose with associated objectives. If you

◇

After considering the legal issues that may affect your efforts, you also need to consider your own organization's requirements and policies regarding the communication of risk, the involvement of the public, the release of information, and the development of communication materials and processes in general. The policies may be formal, or they may be in the form of tradition ("we always do it this way").

disagree, then you may try to convince those in charge that your audience will want more from a risk communication effort, perhaps by showing how risk communication has helped speed the implementation of projects by avoiding costly and time-consuming legal battles (see Chapter 4, "Constraints to Effective Risk Communication," for more information on how this might be accomplished).

## The Risk Itself

As mentioned in Part I, your risk communication efforts will probably fall into one of three categories: care communication (for situations in which the risk is no longer in doubt), consensus communication (for situations in which the audience will help assess and/or manage the risk), or crisis communication (for an immediate risk). Each of these has its own requirements for communication.

Care communication risks include the risks from using tobacco, contracting the AIDS virus, and failing to wear protective clothing when handling hazardous materials in the workplace. Most experts agree that these risks are dangerous to human health (although they may disagree about the magnitude or specific exposure routes). When communicating about these risks, it isn't necessary to review the possible dangers. The dangers are recognized. The purpose, then, is to alert your audience and provide information that will encourage them to change to less risky behaviors.

Consensus communication involves risks in which the audience and the decision-maker must reach an agreement over how the risk will be assessed or managed. Examples include operation of a hazardous waste incinerator, siting of electrical power transmission lines, and cleanup of a Superfund site. Often no consensus has been reached about what constitutes safe or dangerous levels of exposure or about the acceptability of the risk to those affected by it. The purpose of risk communication in such cases is to build consensus as a basis for making a risk management decision.

Crisis communication relates to those risks brought about by an emergency: a chemical plant fire, an earthquake, a train derailment. Again, the danger is clearly recognizable. In these situations, there is no time to develop advisory groups to assess ways of dealing with the risk (although such groups may have been involved in the emergency planning process long before the actual crisis). The purpose of crisis communication is to alert your audience to the danger and provide alternatives to minimize the risk.

In addition to your communication type, another consideration in determining your purpose and objectives is the relative newness of the risk and its visibility to your audience (how risky it seems; Figure 7-1). If the risk is relatively new and not very visible, you will have to first raise awareness before you can communicate more technical information, encourage behavior changes, or build consensus. If this risk is something that has been discussed for years and has been visible for some time, the audience may be apathetic, and you may have to find new ways to awaken audience interest and concern. You might use new information to pique audience interest or

◇

In determining your purpose and objectives, consider the relative newness of the risk and its visibility to your audience.

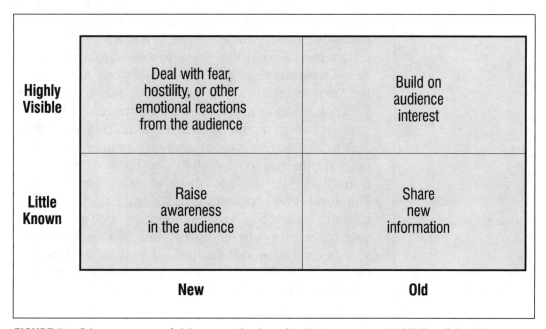

| | New | Old |
|---|---|---|
| **Highly Visible** | Deal with fear, hostility, or other emotional reactions from the audience | Build on audience interest |
| **Little Known** | Raise awareness in the audience | Share new information |

**FIGURE 7-1.** Primary purpose of risk communication related to newness and visibility of the risk.

present the older information in relation to something your audience is now concerned about. If this risk is relatively new and highly visible, you may have to deal with fear and hostility before effective risk communication can take place. Begin by acknowledging and addressing audience concerns so that they can move beyond the fear and hostility to understanding the risk itself.

## Audience Requirements

The fact that audience requirements are last on the list does not imply that they are the least important. They may in fact be the most important, because the audience's needs and concerns heavily affect any type of risk communication. Therefore, what the audience wants from you should be among the first things you consider in determining your purpose and objectives.

What does your audience want from the risk communication effort? The specific answer to this question will differ for each effort; however, the question can be answered generally for each category of risk communication. For care communication, your audience generally wants to know about any risks that would prevent their living a good life (enjoyable, long, and worry free) and about how they can minimize those risks. For consensus communication, your audience generally wants to contribute to a decision about how to assess and manage the risk. Depending on how concerned your audience is, they may want to make a larger or smaller contribution. For crisis communication, your audience generally wants to learn how to minimize their risk as quickly as possible.

Another way to look at audience requirements is to consider the relationships between those who are communicating the risk and those at risk. Kasperson and Palmlund (1989) present purposes and objectives of risk communication based on relationships such as doctor to patient, employer to employee, and government or private organization to community. Consider the information in Table 7-1 if your risk communication effort is based on one of these relationships.

---◇---

The fact that audience requirements are last on the list does not imply that they are the least important. They may in fact be the most important, because the audience's needs and concerns heavily affect any type of risk communication.

**TABLE 7-1**

Risk Communication Purposes Based on Job Relationships

| Doctor to Patient | Employer to Employee | Organization to Community |
|---|---|---|
| Change behavior | Inform | Encourage involvement in decision-making |
| Increase responsibility for living a healthy life | Motivate to action | Motivate to action |

(Adapted from Kasperson and Palmlund 1989)

## CHECKLIST FOR DETERMINING PURPOSE AND OBJECTIVES

The purpose and objectives of my risk communication effort are based on:

❑ associated legal requirements

❑ organizational requirements for

    ❑ public involvement

    ❑ release of information

    ❑ development of communication materials and processes

❑ type of risk communication

    ❑ care

    ❑ consensus

    ❑ crisis

❑ newness of the risk

❑ visibility of the risk

❑ audience requirements

    ❑ functional relationships between my organization and the audience

    ❑ doctor to patient

    ❑ employer to employee

    ❑ organization to community.

The purpose and objectives are agreed upon by those involved in the risk communication effort:

❏ those assessing the risk

❏ those managing the risk

❏ those communicating the risk.


❏ The purpose and objectives and agreement have been documented.


## REFERENCES

Kasperson, R. E., and I. Palmlund. 1989. "Evaluating Risk Communications." *Effective Risk Communication: The Role and Responsibility of Government and Nongovernment Organizations*, editors V. T. Covello, D. B. McCallum, and M. T. Pavlova, pages 143-158. Plenum Press, New York.

## ADDITIONAL RESOURCES

Rowan, K. E. 1991. "Goals, Obstacles, and Strategies in Risk Communication: A Problem-Solving Approach to Improving Communication about Risks." *Journal of Applied Communication Research*, November:300-329.

Santos, S. L. 1990. "Developing a Risk Communication Strategy." *Management and Operations*, November:45-49.

# Analyze Your Audience

*W*henever we communicate, we make assumptions about our audience. When we talk to our spouses about our children, we can use nicknames and allusions to past behavior because we can assume that our spouses will know the children and situations. When we discuss our jobs with our managers, we assume they know what we do. When we communicate risk to a broad audience, however, we cannot make such assumptions, because the audience can be divided into segments, each with its own characteristics and needs.

Whom are we communicating with? Although answering this question is a must in communicating risk (or any information for that matter), some risk communication efforts are still conducted with a total lack of information about the audience. Instead, communication efforts are based on one of two assumptions: either the people we are communicating with are just like us or they are somehow different.

We don't do too badly if the audience really is the same as we are. Scientists generally communicate well with other scientists. Managers generally communicate well with other managers. Within each group there is a common language, a shared way of viewing the world. In addition, some scientists have found effective ways of communicating with managers and vice versa. However, once we step very far outside this shared vision, effective communication becomes much more difficult.

Suppose you are vacationing in a country where English is seldom spoken and you know little of the local language. You notice that the elevator door in your hotel is stuck open on the fifth floor. Being a good risk communicator, you try to alert the first hotel employee that you see to the potential danger. To your chagrin, you find that the helpful chambermaid doesn't speak a word of English.

Obviously, your usual mode of communication will not work. You cannot explain to her that the risk of people falling to their deaths is approximately 3E-6. You cannot hand her Poole's latest paper discussing all the possible ways in which open elevator doors can cause increased morbidity and reduced life spans. You cannot hold an open public forum and take depositions and written comments for a 45-day period.

You have to try something different. You could draw a picture, you could take her out and show her the door, you could wander in search of someone to translate. Doubtless there are also other ways that you could convey your message. The most effective ways, of course, will be those that address her needs. For example, if she has been told NOT to fraternize with guests and to do her work more quickly, she will probably avoid or ignore you as much as she can to get on with her work, a behavior for which you will have to compensate if you are to succeed in your communication efforts.

Audience analysis (i.e., determining the audience's characteristics and needs) is a tool too often neglected in risk communication. In almost every case in which communication efforts failed, inadequate or faulty audience analysis is at least partly to blame. *You have to know to whom you are communicating if you are to communicate with any hope of success!*

◇

Audience analysis (i.e., determining the audience's characteristics and needs) is a tool too often neglected in risk communication. In almost every case in which communication efforts failed, inadequate or faulty audience analysis is at least partly to blame. *You have to know to whom you are communicating if you are to communicate with any hope of success!*

## BEGIN WITH PURPOSE AND OBJECTIVES

You can begin to develop an understanding of your audience by looking at your purpose and objectives. Why are you communicating risk? If you are conducting care communication—risk communication in which the risk is not in doubt—you are generally communicating to increase awareness and change behavior. Whose behavior are you trying to change: a group of workers, a specific group in a community, an entire community, or a specific group across the country? If you are conducting consensus communication—risk communication to reach agreement about the way a risk is assessed or managed—you are generally communicating to encourage consensus building. Who must reach that consensus: a federal agency, its contractors, concerned citizens groups, industry representatives? If you are conducting crisis communication—risk communication relative to an immediate threat—you are generally communicating to alert the audience and provide ways to minimize the risk. Who is at risk: several communities, one community, specific people within that community? Answering these questions will give you a basic knowledge about who you are trying to reach.

## CHOOSE A LEVEL OF ANALYSIS

After examining your purpose and objectives, you have limited knowledge of your audience. How much you more fully analyze your audience will depend on several factors within and without your organization. Factors within your organization include funding, schedule, availability of staff and information sources, and approvals required. The first three are fairly self-explanatory. The more funding available, the more you may be able to use for audience analysis, and the more detailed can your analysis be. The more time available, the more detailed your analysis can be. More staff and resources will also help you achieve a more detailed analysis. However, the fourth factor, approvals required, merits additional discussion.

After examining your purpose and objectives, you have limited knowledge of your audience. How much you more fully analyze your audience will depend on several factors within and without your organization. Factors within your organization include funding, schedule, availability of staff and information sources, and approvals required.

Approvals for some of the audience analysis techniques discussed in this chapter can be difficult to obtain. If you are a federal agency or government contractor, for example, any survey with more than 10 participants will require approval by the U.S. Office of Management and Budget. This approval can take some time. In addition, because of liability and privacy issues, many organizations also have approval requirements for "human subjects research," which may include any form of questioning. Legal offices and public affairs departments may also have to approve any discussions with people outside the organization. Before you start any audience analysis, find out which approvals will be necessary, how long they will take, and who makes the final decision. Also find out if anyone else has been through this maze and whether you can follow their path. Then draw yourself a map of that path with all its turnings so that you not only make it through the maze, but can plan for future efforts.

Factors outside your organization to consider when choosing an appropriate level of audience analysis are those that derive from your purpose and objectives and from the audience itself. What you have to communicate and what you hope to accomplish affect the amount of information you need about your audience. More information is always better than less; however, if your purpose is merely to raise awareness, you may need less information than if your purpose is to change behavior patterns. To raise awareness, you may need to know only reading or education levels and preferred ways of communicating. To change behavior, you need a more complete psychological profile, including why the members of your audience are practicing the behavior to begin with, their feelings about the risk, and what would motivate them to change.

Not surprisingly, your audience also influences your choice of levels of audience analysis. Are the members of the audience spread over wide areas? If so, do you have the time and funding to reach each area? Do they differ greatly in other ways (for example, are some highly educated while others failed to finish high school)? Do you have the time and funding to fully analyze each segment

> Before you start any audience analysis, find out which approvals will be necessary, how long they will take, and who makes the final decision.

or will you have to do one in depth or both more shallowly? Is the audience already so hostile to your organization or efforts that they won't be willing to be interviewed? In that case, you will have to use less direct methods to gather information. Do you already know that they have reading difficulties that require you to use methods that would not require them to read surveys or write? Some of these questions are a little like the question of whether the chicken or the egg came first—you need to know the information before you can properly analyze their needs, but you can only get the information after doing some sort of analysis.

Audience analysis efforts can generally be divided into three levels:

- Baseline Audience Analysis—includes information largely related to the audience's ability to comprehend the communication, such as reading ability, preferred methods of communication, and level of hostility. At least a baseline audience analysis should be conducted for any risk communication effort. However, for crisis communication, it may be the only level needed.

- Midline Audience Analysis—includes baseline information plus information about socioeconomic status, demographics, and cultural information, such as age, gender, and occupations. A midline audience analysis will usually suffice for care communication in which the purpose is to increase awareness.

- Comprehensive Audience Analysis—includes baseline and midline information plus psychological factors, such as motivations and mental models of risk. A comprehensive audience analysis is usually necessary in consensus communication and care communication in which the purpose is to change behavior.

The cost and time associated with any level depends largely on how the information is gathered, but both generally increase with each level of effort. A baseline audience analysis will usually take one person working full-time between 4 hours and 2 weeks, a midline 1 week to 1 month, and a comprehensive 3 weeks to 2 months.

Since the publication of the second edition of this book, the U.S. Environmental Protection Agency (EPA) issued an excellent resource for audience analysis. *Community Culture and the Environment: A Guide to Understanding a Sense of Place* (EPA 2002) is designed to provide "a process and set of tools for defining and understanding the human dimension of an environmental issue" (page 3). While focused on helping the EPA foster community-based environmental protection, the guide's process could be applied to any health intervention at a community level. The approach is flexible, but if used to its full extent, the resulting analysis would be beyond comprehensive. Some of the characteristics suggested for analysis include:

- Community boundaries—natural, physical, administrative, social, and economic characteristics that distinguish one community from another.

- Community capacity and activism—how local leaders and citizens influence local decisions.

- Communication interaction and information flow—how people interact and exchange information.

- Demographic information—population description.

- Economic conditions and employment—history, present, and future of the local economy.

- Education—the level of schooling achieved and the role of education in the community.

- Environmental (or health) awareness and values—knowledge, concerns, and perceptions and how these influence daily life.

- Governance—how decisions are made from the local to federal levels.

- Infrastructure and public services—roads, schools, police, fire, etc.

- Local identity—quality of life issues, history, art, and local traditions.

- Local leisure and recreation—how community members spend their free time.

- Natural resources and landscapes—natural features of the area.

- Property ownership, management, and planning—who owns land and who is responsible for land-use planning.

- Public safety and health—personal safety and health issues.

- Religious and spiritual practices—importance, variety, and beliefs associated with local religions and spiritual practices.

Many of these characteristics are also noted in Tables 8-1, 8-2, and 8-3 for the baseline, midline, and comprehensive audience analysis, respectively.

## DETERMINE KEY AUDIENCE CHARACTERISTICS

Once you have determined the appropriate level of analysis (considering organizational and audience factors), make a detailed list of the characteristics you need to know. Refer to Tables 8-1, 8-2, and 8-3 for suggestions. Depending on your specific situation, you may want to add characteristics to these lists or delete some. For example, if you will not be developing written materials, then reading level is not a characteristic you will need to determine. Each level of analysis builds on the last; that is, the midline includes everything in the baseline, and the comprehensive includes everything in the baseline and midline.

## DETERMINE HOW TO FIND
## AUDIENCE ANALYSIS INFORMATION

There are many ways to gather the audience analysis information listed above. The best way is to go out and talk to your audience, actually meet them face to face. This can be done by conducting interviews, conducting surveys (face-to-face or less directly through the mail),

There are many ways to gather audience analysis information. The best way is to go out and talk to your audience, actually meet them face to face.

**TABLE 8-1**
Key Audience Characteristics for the Baseline Audience Analysis

| Characteristics | Questions to Ask Yourself | How Answers Affect Risk Communication |
|---|---|---|
| Experience with the risk | Is risk new to the audience or something they've been living with for a long time? | If new, build awareness first. If familiar, build on known concepts. |
| Experience with organization communicating risk | Are they familiar with the organization? Do they find it credible? | If unfamiliar, explain organization's role. If familiar and credible, build on good will. If familiar but not credible, use outside spokesperson. |
| Background in risk subject matter | How much do they understand about the risk scientifically? | If little, provide explanation. If a great deal, build on concepts. |
| Reading level | At what level do they read? | If lower level, simplify language, organization, and sentence and paragraph structure. At higher level, can use more complex. |
| People they trust and believe | Whom do they trust and believe? | Choose that person as spokesperson. |
| Information sources | Where do they get information (television news, newspapers, radio, family networks, experience)? | Use that source to disseminate risk messages. |
| Education level | What is the highest level of education completed? What is the range? | If higher levels, use more complex concepts. If lower levels, provide basic information. |
| Group size | How many people are in the audience? | If larger audience, use a method like television. If smaller audience, use more intimate method like meetings. |
| Goals/expectations for risk communication process | What do they expect to happen when you communicate risk? | Whenever possible, match or exceed their goals and expectations. |
| Their role in the risk communication process | Based on laws and organization's requirements, what can the audience's role be? | Whenever possible, involve them in the way they want to be involved. |
| Their "hot buttons" | Are there words and concepts that infuriate them? | Avoid those words. Find other ways to discuss concepts. |

**TABLE 8-2**
Key Audience Characteristics for the Midline Audience Analysis

| Characteristics | Questions to Ask Yourself | How Answers Affect Risk Communication |
|---|---|---|
| Age | What age range do they fall into? What 5-yr range has the most people in it? | Consider possible concerns—families, careers, retirement. |
| Culture | How many different cultures make up the audience? How does each view the world? | Address different views. |
| Gender | Are they mostly male or female? | Consider how gender affects risk probability. |
| Turnover within the community (yearly) | Is this a transient community or one with deep local ties? | If transient, use self-contained messages. If more stable, build on previous messages. |
| Preferred social institutions | Where do they go to relax? To play? To worship? | Determine possible concerns. Use preferred locations to hold meetings. |
| Length/history of involvement | How long have they been involved with the risk? Has the involvement been one of passive listening, consensus building, or reactive argument? | If passive, build on concepts and encourage activity. If consensus building, provide information and encourage involvement. If reactive, acknowledge concerns to lower hostility and encourage activity. |
| Jobs/occupations | Where do they work? What do they do there? Is the risk part of their workplace? | If jobs relate to risk, focus on how to mitigate. If not, determine possible concerns. |
| Geographic areas | How near is the risk? | If close to risk, provide information to mitigate. In general, determine possible concerns. If large geographic area, use method like television. If smaller area, use more intimate method like meetings. |

**TABLE 8-3**
Key Audience Characteristics for the Comprehensive Audience Analysis

| Characteristics | Questions to Ask Yourself | How Answers Affect Risk Communication |
|---|---|---|
| Concerns and feelings about risk | What kinds of concerns do they have? How do they feel about the risk (angry, frustrated, apathetic)? | Address concerns and feelings in risk messages. |
| Experience with other risks | Have they had good examples you can build on? Bad examples to overcome? | If good, build on. If bad, acknowledge and begin with basic risk information. |
| Exposure to news media or other coverage | Have they seen comprehensive coverage or tabloid-style journalism? | If comprehensive, build on. If tabloid, acknowledge and begin with basic risk information. |
| Effect of the risk on them | How do the experts think the risk can affect them? How does the audience think it can affect them? | If two views differ, address misconceptions to correct. If two views identical, build on concepts. |
| Their control over the risk | Can they mitigate the risk or must they live with it? | If mitigate, give ways. If no control, try to empower with knowledge. |
| Goals of organized groups | What are they trying to accomplish? | Determine possible concerns and feelings. |

sponsoring members of the audience as advisors, hosting focus groups, or pretesting prototype risk messages with audience members. These direct methods often provide the most current, risk- and situation-specific information. Unfortunately, these methods are not often used in risk communication efforts for several reasons:

- The members of the audience are so dispersed or in such large numbers that it is impossible to meet them all or even representatives.

- The costs and time involved are prohibitive in a given situation.

- The audience is hostile and refuses to associate with anyone connected with the risk or its assessment, management, or communication.

- The very idea of actually meeting with the audience terrifies some members of the organization that is conducting the risk communication effort.

If these reasons apply in your situation, you may have to choose other methods of gathering audience information.

Less-direct methods of gathering audience information include using surrogate audiences and consulting existing sources of information. Surrogate audiences are people to whom you have easy access who seem to approximate the general audience you are trying to reach. If, for example, you were trying to construct a risk message for a distant community, but had no time to fly there and conduct a more direct analysis, you might find a local community that seems similar and interview or survey people there. The danger in using this method is that you are forced to make assumptions based on very little information. These assumptions may prove wrong and cause your risk communication efforts to be less than successful. However, some audience information is generally better than none.

Another way to use surrogate audiences is to look to the risk communication literature to find examples of audiences that have been studied in detail and seem to match your audience (based on your purpose and objectives). J. D. Callaghan (1989), for example, divided audiences into the scientific/medical community,

———— ◇ ————

Surrogate audiences are people to whom you have easy access who seem to approximate the general audience you are trying to reach.

government agencies, a specific community, and the public (which would include a number of communities). He determined characteristics for each of these audiences and used that information to tailor risk messages. His advice for each was:

- To present risk effectively to the scientific/medical community, work through professional societies and conferences, personal communication, and impartial databases. Use simple English (as opposed to the scholarly writing often seen in professional journals), with references for additional information. Target mailings to society members and develop special interest groups within societies. Begin a newsletter on your risk that includes both scientific information and clearly labeled opinions, and develop traveling seminars that could be given to society groups.

- To present risk effectively to government agencies, provide in-depth information at the beginning. Use information packages that consist of a position statement in nonspecialist language, backed up by research information. Have a scientist or other expert in the field present the information to the group. Identify the decision-makers and those that will offer advice and concentrate on key individuals who will be able to influence others.

- For communities, use more personal communication. Use open meetings with a skillful moderator. Follow up with stories in union and company publications, and with video or classroom instructional materials.

- For the public in which there is little or no hostility, use the news media (press conferences, news releases, interviews, video and audio tapes, and media hotlines; see Chapter 16 for more information). If there is hostility, send credible experts to radio and television talk shows, radio call-in shows, and major public forums. Also submit articles to the newspapers for the opinion-editorial page and stories to magazines, which can be reprinted and sent to specific segments of the audience.

Another indirect method of gathering audience analysis information is to use existing sources of information:

- Staff sociologists—many large organizations have on staff a group of social scientists who compile information about the local community and other people with whom the organization comes into contact regularly. They can provide a wealth of information for audience analysis. If your organization doesn't have such a staff, and you have time and money, you can hire social scientists (from colleges and universities or independent consulting firms) to develop surveys, interview key audience members, and compile information to meet your needs. Sometimes graduate or undergraduate classes will do the research for you for the experience and/or a nominal fee as a class project.

- Environmental impact statements—many environmental impact statements incorporate information about the local communities and economy. While they won't give you sufficient information for a comprehensive audience analysis, they can be a source of information for the baseline and midline analyses. Sources include local libraries and government document repositories. Some documents are now available online as well.

- Documentation of work for the Comprehensive Environmental Response, Compensation, and Liability Act (CERCLA or Superfund)—by law, a Superfund site must have a community relations plan. This plan should include information about the community (and thus the audience with whom the environmental cleanup contractor must communicate). Sources include local libraries, government document repositories, the U.S. Environmental Protection Agency, and the Internet.

- The Internet—nearly every community and group has a web site, which can provide a wealth of information, often in the language and style preferred in the area.

- Census data—these data cover demographics, economic trends, and education levels. Sources include local libraries, government repositories, and the Internet.

- Local television station and radio station advertising profiles—stations need to know to whom they are broadcasting to attract advertising and viewers or listeners. They may be willing to share this information with you if you explain why you need it. They may charge a fee.

- Local newspapers and magazines advertising profiles—these media also need to know their readership to attract advertising and increase subscriptions. They may be willing to share this information with you if you explain why you need it. They may also charge a fee.

- State or local political groups—again, these organizations need to know their constituencies to be reelected. They may be willing to share this information with you if you explain why you need it.

- Health care agencies and cancer centers—public affairs or communications groups within larger health care agencies often have to communicate to a large group and will have developed community profiles. They may share these if you explain why you need the information.

- Chambers of Commerce or other community economic development organizations—these organizations also conduct community research to provide information that might attract new businesses to the area. They may be willing to share if the purpose of your risk communication effort will assist the community.

- Letters to the editor in the local newspaper—these will tell you what the local concerns are and which groups are most vocal.

- Market analysis information—firms such as Gallup, Harris, and Opinion Research conduct surveys and interviews to gather information for marketing purposes. They may be willing to share existing information for a fee and can develop specific surveys and interviews to meet your needs. These tailored services can be more expensive than using your own staff, but may be cost and time effective for large risk communication efforts.

- Related information materials—in consensus communication and sometimes in care communication, other organizations besides yours will also be communicating about the risk. These organizations may in fact be part of the audience. Look at how they frame questions, what factors seem important to them, the language they use. This information can give you important clues to answer your audience analysis questions.

- Job descriptions—for communication focused on specific types of workers, job descriptions can indicate education levels preferred, years of experience, and other factors useful in analyzing that audience.

Which sources you use to gather information concerning your audience depends not only on your situation (time, funding, organizational support) but also on whether you are conducting care, consensus, or crisis communication. For care communication, useful sources differ depending on whether you are conducting health care communication (in which human health in general is at risk) or industrial risk communication (in which worker health or safety is at risk). Industrial risk communication can be divided into industrial hygiene and individual worker notification. The less-direct sources of audience analysis information most useful for each of these types of risk communication are shown in Table 8-4.

A possible issue with using these indirect methods is the validity of the information. The less direct, that is, the farther the source is from the original (your audience itself), the more likely that information is actually interpretation or at least partly assumed. To compensate for this problem, use multiple sources of information to confirm audience characteristics and needs.

Which sources you use to gather information concerning your audience depends not only on your situation (time, funding, organizational support) but also on whether you are conducting care, consensus, or crisis communication.

**TABLE 8-4**

Less-Direct Sources Most Useful for Audience Analysis for Various Types of Risk Communication

| Type of Risk Communication | Most Useful Source |
|---|---|
| *Care Communication* | |
|    Health Care (heterogeneous audience) | Market analysis information |
| | Health care agencies |
| | |
|    Health Care (homogeneous audience) | Surrogate audience |
| | Advertising profiles |
| | Internet |
| | Census data |
|   Industrial Risk | |
|     Industrial Hygiene | Job descriptions |
|     Worker Notification | Surrogate audience |
| | |
| *Consensus Communication* | None—direct contact required for this type of |
| | communication to succeed |
| | |
| *Crisis Communication\** | Staff sociologists |
| | Environmental impact statements |
| | CERCLA documentation |
| | Political groups |
| | Letters to the editor |

*Crisis communication sources also depend on the timing of the analysis. Sources listed are most useful before the crisis, during emergency planning. During a crisis, use whatever sources are immediately available, including surrogate audiences.

## INCORPORATE AUDIENCE ANALYSIS INFORMATION INTO RISK COMMUNICATION EFFORTS

Once you get all this information, what do you do with it? Audience analysis information is used to tailor risk messages to meet specific audience and situational needs. The information can tell you what media to use, how much audience interaction is needed, and what concerns must be addressed, among other factors (Table 8-5).

Audience analysis information is also often used to determine the proper "style" for written messages. Many organizations use computer software like "style-checkers," or apply readability formulas. While these will give you written messages that conform to a particular grade

**TABLE 8-5**

Using Audience Analysis Information to Tailor Risk Messages

| Information Learned | How to Tailor the Message |
|---|---|
| Audience unaware | Use graphic method—high color, compelling visuals and theme. |
| Audience apathetic (or feels like victims) | Open risk assessment and management process to stakeholder participation. Show where past interactions have made a difference. Provide choices. |
| Audience well informed | Build on past information. |
| Audience hostile | Acknowledge concerns and feelings. Identify common ground. Open risk assessment and management process to stakeholder participation. |
| Audience highly educated | Use more sophisticated language and structure. |
| Audience not highly educated | Use less sophisticated language and structure. Make structure highly visible, not subtle. |
| Who the audience trusts | Use that person to present risk information. |
| Where the audience feels comfortable | Hold meetings in that location. |
| The method by which the audience gets most of its information | Use that method to convey your message. |
| Who makes up the audience | Ensure that the message reaches each member. |
| How the audience wants to be involved in risk assessment or management | If at all possible given time, funding, and organizational constraints, involve the audience in the way they want to be involved. |
| Misconceptions of risk or process | Acknowledge misconceptions. Provide facts to fill gaps in knowledge and correct false impressions. |
| Audience concerns | Acknowledge concerns and provide relevant facts. |

or reading level, they may also give you messages that are flat, boring, and monotonic.

Recent studies have shown that the concept loading, or number of concepts, and the placement of those concepts in the sentence is far more important to readability and comprehension than the length of words or their number in a sentence. Take for example the following sentence:

> *Because of differences in lifestyles, certain members of this group, particularly infants and the elderly, are more likely to be affected.*

This sentence would be rated at about the tenth grade reading level according to the Fog Index, a readability formula developed by Robert Gunning and Douglas Mueller. After all, it contains 21 words, several with three or more syllables. However, according to the theories of concept loading and placement, this sentence should be readable at a much lower level. There are three main concepts, with one clarifier, each contained in its own phrase or component of the sentence. With any skill, the communicator can stack such phrases so that each sentence and paragraph builds on the next.

## CHECKLIST FOR AUDIENCE ANALYSIS

Based on the purpose and objectives, general audience, and organizational constraints, the most appropriate level of audience analysis is:

- ❑ baseline
- ❑ midline
- ❑ comprehensive.

The list of key characteristics to be analyzed was based on the:

- ❑ purpose and objectives
- ❑ general audience
- ❑ level of analysis.

Based on:

❏ time

❏ funding

❏ availability of staff

❏ approvals required

audience analysis information will be gathered by:

❏ direct methods

    ❏ interviews

    ❏ surveys

    ❏ focus groups

❏ less-direct methods

    ❏ surrogate audiences

    ❏ existing sources of information.

For direct methods:

❏ necessary approvals have been determined

❏ necessary approvals have been received.

For less-direct methods:

❏ multiple sources were used to confirm audience information.

Audience analysis information was used to:

❏ tailor risk communication strategies

❏ determine appropriate

    ❏ language

    ❏ sentence structure

    ❏ organization.

## REFERENCES

Callaghan, J. D. 1989. "Reaching Target Audiences with Risk Information." *Effective Risk Communication: The Role and Responsibility of Government and Nongovernment Organizations,* editors V. T. Covello, D. B. McCallum, and M. T. Pavlova, pages 137-142. Plenum Press, New York.

EPA (U.S. Environmental Protection Agency). 2002. *Community Culture and the Environment: A Guide to Understanding a Sense of Place.* EPA 842-B-01-003, Office of Water, Washington, D.C.

## ADDITIONAL RESOURCES

Arkin, E. B. 1989. "Translation of Risk Information for the Public: Message Development." *Effective Risk Communication: The Role and Responsibility of Government and Nongovernment Organizations*, editors V. T. Covello, D. B. McCallum, and M. T. Pavlova, pages 127-135. Plenum Press, New York.

Babbie, E. 1973. *Survey Research Methods.* Wadsworth Publishing Company, Belmont, California.

Barke, Dr. Richard P., School of Public Policy, Georgia Institute of Technology, Atlanta, Georgia 30332, (404) 894-6843. Surveys on how specific audiences see risk.

Butler, L. M. 1995. *The "Sondeo" A Rapid Reconnaissance Approach for Situational Assessment.* Community Ventures, A Western Regional Extension Publication, WREP0127, Washington State University, Pullman, Washington.

Hodges, M. 1992. "How Scientists See Risk." *Research Horizons*, Summer 1992, page 22-24. Georgia Institute of Technology, Atlanta, Georgia.

International Association for Public Participation, P.O. Box 10146, Alexandria, Virginia 22310, (800) 644-4273 or (703) 971-0090, http://www.pin.org/iap2.htm.

McDonough, M. H. 1984. "Audience Analysis Techniques." *Supplements to a Guide to Cultural and Environmental Interpretation.* U.S. Army Corps of Engineers, Waterways Experiment Station, Vicksburg, Massachusetts.

Pearsall, T. E. 1969. *Audience Analysis for Technical Writing.* Glencoe Press, Beverly Hills, California.

Santos, S. L. 1990. "Developing a Risk Communication Strategy." *Management and Operations*, November:45-49.

Warren, T. L. 1993. "Three Approaches to Reader Analysis." *Technical Communication*, 40(1):81-88.

Weinstein, N. D., and P. M. Sandman. 1993. "Some Criteria for Evaluating Risk Messages." *Risk Analysis*, 13(1):103-114.

# Develop Your Message

*W*hen conveying risk-related information, it often helps to develop key messages as part of the planning process. Messages help focus all communication participants on the most important information and how to convey it. In care communication, messages usually convey the essential nature of a risk and what people can do to avoid or reduce it. In consensus communication, a stakeholder group may want to develop its own messages when recommending policy or actions to be taken by decision makers. In crisis communication, making all organizational participants aware of the key messages (even if they evolve during the crisis) can make recovery actions more effective, reduce confusion, and increase organizational credibility. In a crisis, key messages are especially important for media spokespeople and those who staff phone hotlines.

Message development in risk communication is not the same as developing a catchy slogan in an advertising campaign. Message development is not manipulative, nor is it a substitute for audience analysis or public participation. The point is not to try to bombard people with what you think they ought to know, but to understand

Message development is not manipulative, nor is it a substitute for audience analysis or public participation.

what they want and need to know and addressing those things in a clear, concise way.

The following sections discuss what people want to know about risks and how to craft messages for various risk situations.

## INFORMATION PEOPLE WANT

Recent research has pointed to some key pieces of information people are most likely to want to know when faced with an unfamiliar risk. Though some people don't seek information out of fear or out of inability to process the risk, many others want to know everything (Lion et al. 2002). In general, people are interested in the following types of information:

- **Description of the risk.** People want to go beyond technical descriptions to familiar analogies. Thus, risk communicators may want to provide example analogies to aid risk understanding.

- **Risk consequences.** This includes effects and the level of danger associated with the risk.

- **Level of control about the risk and its consequences.** People want to know the answers to questions such as, "What should I do?" and "What are agencies doing?"

- **Exposure information.** This includes risk intensity, duration, acceptable risk levels and how they are measured, how long the exposing agent is dangerous, how long it persists, and how it accumulates in the body.

People with higher levels of education also wanted to know how research on the risk was conducted; those with lower education were interested only in the results of the research. The advantages of the risk were uniformly ranked as among the least important information (Lion et al. 2002).

Additional research has focused on how people process risk messages. A group of university researchers led by LeeAnn Kahlor of the Center for Health Systems Research and Analysis in Wisconsin found that the less people knew about a risk, the more likely they were to process information in a systematic matter. Such systematic processing was methodical and evaluative. This type of processing tends to lead to attitudes that are more stable and resistant to change, which can help crisis preparedness and consensus communication efforts. It may also lead to behavior changes, which can help crisis response and care communication efforts. To encourage systematic processing, risk communicators need to include what audience members *perceive* they need to know, or audiences will not attend to the information (Kahlor et al. 2003).

## MENTAL MODELS

The mental models approach, described in Chapter 2, "Approaches to Communicating Risk," can be used to develop accurate risk messages. Because the time involved can be extensive, this approach is most appropriate for care and consensus communication and for the planning phase of crisis communication.

Messages are developed after conducting interviews that show how people understand and view the risks associated with various phenomena. The approach is not designed to persuade people that risks are small and under control, but rather to supply laypeople with the accurate information they need to make informed, independent judgments about risks to health, safety, and the environment. Morgan et al. (2002) describe a six-step process to learn what people believe and what information they need to make the decisions they face:

- **Create an expert model of the risk, using an influence diagram.** This is a scientifically accurate model of the processes that determine the nature and magnitude of the risk. Figures 9-1 and 9-2 show two examples, for Lyme disease and HIV/AIDS.

- **Conduct mental models interviews.** Using the expert model, ask questions to find out people's beliefs about the hazard, expressed in their own terms.

- **Conduct structured interviews.** Interview larger groups of people using a questionnaire that

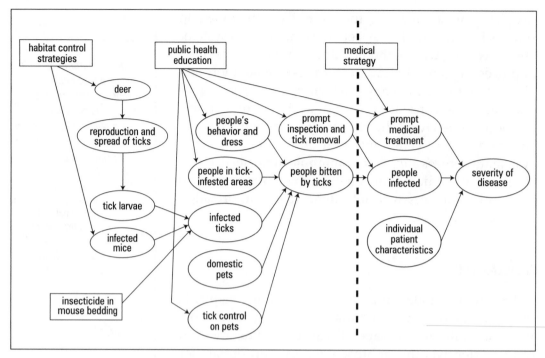

**FIGURE 9-1.** Simplified expert model of the risk of infection from Lyme disease. The part to the left of the vertical dashed line deals with exposure processes; the right, effects processes.

(Source: Morgan et al. (2002). Reprinted with the permission of Cambridge University Press.)

captures the beliefs in the open-ended interviews, to determine the prevalence of the beliefs in a larger population.

- **Compare the responses with the expert understanding of the risk.**

- **Draft risk communication.** Use the results from the interviews, along with an analysis of the decisions people face, to address the most significant incorrect beliefs and knowledge gaps.

- **Evaluate communication.** Test and refine the communication with various groups until the communication is understood as intended.

The goal of this process is neither to persuade people that they should make decisions the way scientists do, nor to transform people into scientists. It's to make sure people have the scientifically, technically, and medically accurate information they need to make their own decisions.

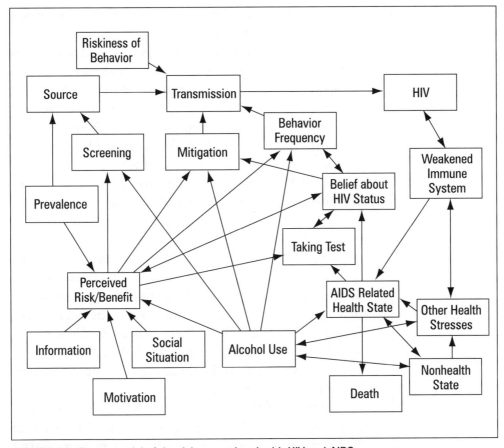

**FIGURE 9-2.** Expert model of the risks associated with HIV and AIDS.
(Source: Fischhoff and Downs (1997). Reprinted with the permission of Cambridge University Press.)

Invariably, this process reveals inaccurate (and often unexpected) beliefs that must be addressed in risk communication. For example, interviewers found that some people believe that houses containing radon are permanently contaminated, and that radon remediation in homes is impossible or prohibitively expensive. Thus, argues Granger Morgan and his colleagues, the central message in the U.S. Environmental Protection Agency's 1986 *Citizens' Guide to Radon*—"You should test your house for radon"—may have been undermined by the public belief that testing was futile (Morgan et al. 2002). Better messages would have been that radon decays over time and that inexpensive devices are available to monitor radon levels in homes.

When the mental models process was used with teens for HIV/AIDS awareness, it showed that teens already understood the big picture about HIV/AIDS, but needed information gaps filled and misconceptions corrected. Thus, rather than repeating familiar HIV/AIDS facts, communication materials were addressed with messages such as, "Knowing your partner is not enough to prevent HIV," "The more times you have sex with an HIV infected person, the more likely you are to get HIV," and "The only way to know if you have HIV is to be tested."

A mental models process about climate change risks led to communication materials that directly addressed common misconceptions. The materials used messages such as, "Climate change and the loss of the ozone layer are two different problems that are not very closely connected," "Using aerosol spray cans has almost no effect on climate change," and "Nuclear power does not contribute to climate change."

A mental models process about health risks from electric power fields led to messages such as, "The strength of electric fields decreases rapidly as you move away from them." Figure 14-1 later in this book shows an illustration that was created to convey this message.

As with any one technique, the mental models approach has its limitations. In one study, mental models interviews were used to design materials to inform electroplater workers in England about their chemical exposure risks. Workers who received the revised risk information showed a better understanding of long-term health effects and were more aware of precautions to take in the plating shop that were not based on direct experience (Petts et al. 2002). However, the researchers also raised several cautions about the mental models approach. For example, the approach may incorrectly assume that all expert beliefs are consistent, may undervalue layperson knowledge and belief, and may skip over behavioral and organizational culture issues, especially in the workplace. The researchers endorsed the user-centered approach for designing risk information, but with these added guidelines:

- Focus not only on what people believe, but why and how they reduce risks.
- Include divergent views related to demographics, length of work experience, and disability.
- Realize that there may be more than one expert model, for example, occupational health experts and factory inspectors, and that the expert model of hazards and risk reduction may not be better than those held by an industry worker.
- In presenting risk information, answer key questions, such as: How might this happen? What can it to do me? How can I protect myself?
- Test whether new risk messages affect behavior, not just improve understanding.

## MESSAGE MAPPING

Risk communication consultant and Columbia University professor Vince Covello has developed the concept of a message map. It's a template for displaying detailed, hierarchically organized responses to anticipated questions or concerns. Message maps are one way to make sure everyone understands the organization's messages for high-concern or controversial issues.

Message maps should be created with interested and affected parties, including scientists, communication specialists, and policy experts as applicable. Broad involvement will reveal a diversity of viewpoints, but the end goal is to come up with messages and supporting points with which everyone agrees.

Start by developing a list of anticipated questions, to identify common sets of underlying concerns. Develop key messages in response to the underlying concerns and questions. Each key message should have up to three supporting facts associated with it. To reduce confusion and increase comprehension and retention, Covello recommends limiting the number of key messages and keeping them at a middle-school level of readability.

Table 9-1 shows an example of a message map to answer the question, "How contagious is smallpox?"

A message map is a template for displaying detailed, hierarchically organized responses to anticipated questions or concerns.

**TABLE 9-1**

Sample Message Map

| Draft Message Map<br>Stakeholder: General Public<br>Question: How contagious is smallpox? | | |
|---|---|---|
| **Key Message 1**<br>Smallpox spreads slowly compared to measles or the flu. | **Key Message 2**<br>This allows time for us to trace contacts and vaccinate those people who have come in contact. | **Key Message 3**<br>Vaccination within 3 to 4 days of contact will generally prevent the disease. |
| **Supporting Fact 1-1**<br>People are only infectious when the rash appears and they are ill. | **Supporting Fact 2-1**<br>The incubation period for the disease is 10-14 days. | **Supporting Fact 3-1**<br>People who have never been vaccinated are the most important ones to vaccinate. |
| **Supporting Fact 1-2**<br>It requires hours of face-to-face contact. | **Supporting Fact 2-2**<br>Resources for finding people are available. | **Supporting Fact 3-2**<br>Adults who were vaccinated as children may still have some immunity to smallpox. |
| **Supporting Fact 1-3**<br>There are no asymptomatic carriers. | **Supporting Fact 2-3**<br>Finding people who have been exposed and vaccinating them is the successful approach. | **Supporting Fact 3-3**<br>Adequate vaccine is on hand and the supply is increasing. |

(Source: Center for Risk Communication and ORISE (2003).)

## HEALTH RISK COMMUNICATION

Public health-related messages are similar to other risk messages, but with the added goal of human behavioral change. Though health messages often contain an element of persuasion, they should still be based on understanding the audience's concerns, needs, and incentives to act. Health communication researcher Kim Witte and her colleagues recommend a detailed process for audience analysis and message development, based on communication research (Witte et al. 2001):

- Identify the health threat, recommended response, and target audience.

- Conduct formative research about the target audience's beliefs about the threat, including beliefs to change, reinforce, or introduce. Develop one or more audience profiles of "typical" members of your target audience, including lifestyle practices, cultural beliefs, religious values, and so on.

- List the source, channel, and message preferences, making sure they fit with the audience's values, demographic characteristics, and needs.

- Determine the stage of change readiness (unaware of or apathetic about the health threat, considering change, preparing to change, action, behavior maintenance) for your profiled audience members and describe ideas for moving them into the next stage.

- Develop and test messages using the above research and using communication theories that address persuasion and behavior change.

- Deliver the message and measure belief and/or behavior change results.

The University of Toronto's Health Communication Unit promotes the following tips for health message development, also based on communication research:

- **Capture and maintain the audience's attention.** The more you can engage the audience to think about the message, the more likely they are to change knowledge, attitudes, and behaviors. Consider using emotionally involving scenes, vivid visuals, and lively language.

- **Give the strongest points at the beginning of the message.** This is the information most critical for convincing the audience to adopt the recommended behavior.

- **Have a clear message.** People should easily understand the actions you are asking them to take and the incentive for taking them.

- **Specify a reasonably easy action.** Instead of telling people to stop smoking, which many people will ignore as unattainable, you could ask them to sign a pledge card, commit to a smoke-free week, or give them tips for the first day of smoking cessation. It also helps to show role models demonstrating the desired behavior.

- **Use incentives effectively.** Use a variety of incentives, including physical, economic, psychological, social, and moral. Make sure the audience cares about the incentives and thinks they are likely to occur if the behavior changes.

- **Provide good evidence for threats and benefits.** People who are already interested tend to respond to expert quotes, documentation, and statistics. People who are not involved are more likely to respond to dramatized case examples and testimonials.

- **Use believable messages.** Don't make extreme claims or use extreme examples.

- **Use an appropriate tone for the audience and topic.** A serious tone is safest, but don't preach or dictate. Some audiences may respond to a light, humorous, ironic, or dramatic tone.

- **Use an appropriate appeal for the audience.** Consider rational appeals for audiences already interested in the topic and emotional ones for the apathetic.

- **Don't offend.** Don't blame the victim for unhealthy behavior. Help people overcome their environments instead.

- **Display the organization's identity prominently with each message.** Identity elements could include an organization's name, a positioning statement or platform, a logo, a slogan, and sometimes an image. Identity elements help people remember and link the campaign messages over time.

- **Choose messengers who are viewed as credible sources of information by the intended audiences.** Messengers are those who deliver information, demonstrate behavior, or provide a testimonial. Messengers could range from celebrities to public officials to victims to successful role models. Messenger credibility is enhanced by perceived expertise and honesty, as well as being viewed as similar to the target audience.

# CRISIS COMMUNICATION

The Centers for Disease Control and Prevention et al. (2003) recommend the following process for message development during a crisis, especially one involving an infectious disease or other public health issue.

- **Describe the audiences you want to reach.** This includes their relationship to the event, their demographics (age, language, education, culture) and their level of outrage, based on risk communication principles.

- **Define the purpose of the message(s).** Purposes could include giving facts and updates, rallying people to action, clarifying event status, addressing rumors, and responding to media requests.

- **Identify the delivery method.** This could include media, the Internet, a spokesperson, recorded phone messages, public meetings, and so on.

Once you've identified the audience, message purpose, and delivery method, construct messages using the following components:

- Expression of empathy

- Facts and/or call to action

- What isn't known and the process to get answers

- Statement of commitment from the organization

- Referrals to others for more information

- Next scheduled update.

Keep the content easy to understand and free of jargon. Convey what science knows and doesn't yet know about the risk. The tone should create a sense of urgency to take action when appropriate and reassure people that answers are being sought, without confusing or alarming them.

Experiences after the Oklahoma City bombing and other mass casualty events show that people's ability to process information in the face of tragedy decreases significantly. In such cases, messages need to be simple and few in number, and any verbal messages must be reinforced in writing (Blakeney 2002).

> In crisis communication, the tone should create a sense of urgency to take action when appropriate and reassure people that answers are being sought, without confusing or alarming them.

In a media or hotline situation, spokespeople and other organization representatives should practice answering questions that reflect the messages. It's especially important to make sure everyone is "singing off the same page" when more than one agency or organization is involved, because receiving conflicting information from various agencies confuses people and diminishes trust. For more information about responding to questions in crises, see Part V, "Bioterrorism and Other Emergencies."

## CHECKLIST FOR MESSAGE DEVELOPMENT

When developing and delivering messages:

❑ the purpose of the message has been identified

❑ the appropriate approach for care, consensus, or crisis communication has been chosen

❑ audiences and their knowledge, beliefs, concerns, and barriers to action have been analyzed, with their input

❑ special attention has been paid to misperceptions and knowledge gaps, as well as beliefs to be reinforced

❑ message content and delivery are based on an understanding of the audience and are pretested

❑ evaluation methods are in place to determine the effectiveness of messages and modify them if necessary.

## REFERENCES

Association of State and Territorial Health Officials. 2002. *Responding to the Communication Challenges Posed by Bioterrorism and Emerging Infectious Diseases.* Washington, D.C.

Blakeney, R. L. 2002. "Providing Relief to Families After a Mass Fatality: Roles of the Medical Examiner's Office and the Family Assistance Center." *OVC Bulletin*, November 2002.

Centers for Disease Control and Prevention, Agency for Toxic Substances and Disease Registry, Oak Ridge Institute for Science and Education, and the Prospect Center of the American Institutes of Research. 2003. *Emergency Risk*

*Communication CDCynergy* (CD-ROM). Online at http://www.orau.gov/cdcynergy/erc/.

Fischhoff, B., and J. Downs. 1997. "Accentuate the Relevant." *Psychological Science*, 8(3):1-5.

Kahlor, L., S. Dunwoody, R. J. Griffin, K. Neuwirth, and J. Giese. 2003. "Studying Heuristic-Systematic Processing of Risk Communication." *Risk Analysis*, 23(2):355-368.

Lion, R., R. M. Meertens, and I. Bot. 2002. "Priorities in Information Desire About Unknown Risks." *Risk Analysis*, 22(4):765-776.

Morgan, M. G., B. Fischhoff, A. Bostrom, and C. J. Atman. 2002. *Risk Communication: A Mental Models Approach.* Cambridge University Press, Cambridge, UK.

Petts, J., S. McAlpine, J. Homan, S. Sadhra, H. Pattison, and S. MacRae. 2002. *Development of a Methodology to Design and Evaluate Effective Risk Messages; Electroplating Case Study. Prepared by the University of Birmingham for the Health and Safety Executive of Great Britain.* Edgbaston, Birmingham, UK. Contract Research Report No. 400. Online at http://www.hse.gov.uk/research/crr_htm/2002/crr02400.htm.

Witte, K., G. Meyer, and D. Martell. 2001. *Effective Health Risk Messages: A Step-by-Step Guide.* Sage Publications, Inc., Thousand Oaks, California.

## ADDITIONAL RESOURCES

The Health Communication Unit at the Centre for Health Promotion, University of Toronto. Online at http://www.thcu.ca/index.htm.

# Determine the Appropriate Methods

*Y*ou know what you're trying to communicate and why and to whom you will be presenting the risk information. Now you need to decide how to communicate your message. Which methods of communication will best meet both your purpose and objectives and your audience's needs? (Usually, no one method will meet the needs of every segment of your audience.) The basic categories to choose from include information materials, visual representation of risk, face-to-face communication, working with the media, stakeholder participation, and technology-assisted communication. How each of these relate to purpose and objectives and audience's needs is discussed below, as well as the time involved and how much technical knowledge is needed to effectively present risk information. More information on using each of the methods can be found in Part III.

## INFORMATION MATERIALS

Information materials are those that your audience will need to read. These materials may have pictures and other graphical elements, and range in size from a partial-page advertisement to a multivolume environmental impact statement. Examples include newsletters, fact sheets, brochures, booklets, pamphlets, displays, advertisements, posters, trade journal articles, popular press articles, and technical reports.

Information materials have the advantage of being able to include a wealth of information. They also can be expanded or condensed to meet audience needs (for instance, a technical report can be condensed into a journal article or news release, depending on the audience). Information materials used to be some of the most inexpensive to produce but rising paper and distribution costs can make widespread availability expensive, unless you opt for putting the materials on CD.

However, information materials can be a comfortable form of communication for some members of the audience—they are more familiar than a computer station and allow the reader to carry away something for later reference. So, if your objectives are to disseminate a large amount of risk information and to economically meet the needs of various segments of your audience, the information materials may be the best choice.

On the other hand, some information materials can be difficult for some members of the audience to comprehend. When writing such messages, it is too easy to resort to jargon and overly technical language ("if they don't understand it, they can look it up"). In addition, the length of information materials (either too short or too long) can deter some readers. So, if your purpose is to raise awareness of an issue or to communicate with people who have difficulty reading, information materials may not be the best choice.

Depending on their length, the amount of research needed, the approval process, and the method of printing, information materials can usually fit into any schedule. For broad, quick dissemination, newspaper articles are excellent because newspapers have a large readership and generally are published daily; however, you often do not control content or timing (see Chapter 16 for additional information). Fact sheets and pamphlets can also usually be prepared relatively quickly. For a risk that will take some time to resolve and that includes audience involvement throughout, such as the cleanup of a waste site, a newsletter may be the best choice, supplemented by a variety of other methods.

To prepare any form of information material, some technical knowledge is necessary. A technical writer can prepare the information and have experts review it for technical accuracy, or the experts can prepare the message and have a technical communications specialist or risk communicator review it to ensure that it meets the audience's needs. Although there may be a fine line between being overly technical and overly simplistic, it is possible to present technical information in a way that the public can understand. Lay readers may not understand the information in the same way that a expert with 35 years of experience in the field understands it, but they can understand it at a level that allows them to make an informed decision about the risk. See Chapter 19 for advice on how to pretest such materials to ensure they meet audience needs.

## VISUAL REPRESENTATION OF RISK

Risk can also be communicated through the use of graphical elements and relatively little text to carry simple risk messages. Examples include posters, displays, direct advertising, videotapes, and television; however, virtually all forms of risk communication make some use of pictorial representation of risk.

Visual representations have the advantage of being memorable. Think of traffic safety signs. The use of graphical elements like color, shape, and imagery along with compelling language can bring simple risk messages to life with stunning clarity. Visuals may be culture-specific; however, because they contain very little written information, they can usually be more easily translated into another language than other information materials. They can be placed where your audience lives, works, and plays—on television in programs or commercials, on posters in work cafeterias, on buses and bulletin boards. So, if your purpose is to raise awareness, pictorial representations may be the best choice.

——— ◇ ———

Risk can also be communicated through the use of graphical elements and relatively little text to carry simple risk messages. Examples include posters, displays, direct advertising, videotapes, and television; however, virtually all forms of risk communication make some use of pictorial representation of risk.

Visual representations, by their very nature, can carry only limited information. They therefore cannot answer as many of the questions audiences may have about the risk as some other forms of risk communication. Because the style of these pictures is sometimes associated with persuasive communications (like product advertisements), they may fail to attract or may even put off certain elements of the audience ("oh, it's just more hype"). If they are overused, they lose their impact and tend to be ignored. Even television programming, which can overcome some of these problems, is often viewed as merely entertainment, so that the risk messages often get lost among the commercials for crunchy munchies or the laugh track from the currently popular sitcom. So, if your purpose is to inform your audience, visual representations cannot be your only choice of method.

Visual representations can take some time to produce. Although organizations who regularly produce public service announcements for television can turn them out in a few weeks, those of us with more limited staff and budgets often cannot match this schedule. Coordinating the production of graphics or video can take a significant amount of time. Nonetheless, to meet your audience's needs and your purpose and objectives, you may want to investigate how much time and money is necessary for the production of visual messages. Contact your public affairs or communications departments, or look in the telephone directory under photography or advertising services, to get cost and time estimates.

Even though the technical message is usually somewhat limited, some technical knowledge is necessary to produce most visual representations. To ensure that the message is technically correct and does not imply something that is incorrect, have people with technical backgrounds review the message and graphics. Knowledge of graphic design, however, is critical to ensure that these messages carry the impact intended. If you do not have a background in graphic design, contact your organization's art department or consult the telephone directory under advertising, graphic art services, or graphic designers. See Chapter 14 for more information on the visual representation of risk.

## FACE-TO-FACE COMMUNICATION

Face-to-face communication involves someone speaking directly to the audience or listening while the audience speaks. Usually the audience and the speaker do not interact, except perhaps to ask questions. (Cases in which the audience can interact are classified in this book as stakeholder participation.) Examples include one-to-one discussions such as between a doctor and a patient or between employees; presentations to clubs, societies, and citizens groups whether as a single speaker or as part of a speakers bureau; talks in educational settings such as grade school, college classes, or training courses; tours and demonstrations; video; audience interviews; and information fairs.

Face-to-face communication has the advantage of having an identifiable human representative of the organization or another credible person presenting the risk information, personalizing the risk information. (Of course, if the presenter lacks credibility, the presentation can have a negative effect!) Face-to-face communication generally offers the opportunity of immediate audience feedback, if not through questions then through the audience's visible reaction to certain statements. Some audience analysis information is generally available beforehand to the presenter (who can ask questions of the person arranging or hosting the presentation), allowing each presentation to be individually tailored. You can also target specific groups to receive an oral message, whereas you may have no way of knowing whether the people to whom you sent a written message ever read it. Face-to-face communication can also be presented in the language of the audience. So, if your objectives are to present information in a forum that allows immediate feedback and to target specific groups, face-to-face communication may be your best choice.

On the other hand, face-to-face messages can also be easily misunderstood. Audiences may be too overwhelmed or hostile to ask questions that would clarify misunderstandings. Particularly angry audiences can make a presentation into a political forum and generally refuse to listen. Oral presentations alone also give the audience nothing to refer to later. So, if you have a particularly angry audience, or one that needs long-term information, face-to-face communication may not be satisfactory or sufficient.

Face-to-face communication can fit into nearly any schedule. For quickly disseminating information, a press conference or radio announcement would be best. For a longer-term effort, a continuing series of presentations to a variety of organizations and societies might serve to reinforce the message and keep the audience up to date. To reinforce any face-to-face communication, encourage health-care professionals to disseminate risk information to their clients at risk.

Advanced technical knowledge is usually necessary to present oral risk information convincingly. However, the ability to speak in a manner that entertains as well as informs is also necessary. No matter how well-educated, an expert who has trouble speaking before groups is a poor choice for spokesperson. So is a professional speech maker with only superficial knowledge of the risk. The best person to present oral risk information is one whom the audience will find credible and whom the organization responsible for communicating risk finds an acceptable representative. For more information on choosing a spokesperson, see Chapter 15, "Face-to-Face Communication."

## WORKING WITH THE MEDIA

Mass media methods usually involve the use of sources such as television, newspapers, radio, and magazines to communicate risk information to broad audiences. Such sources can be powerful because they reach large audiences and can be memorable and credible sources for many people. Television and radio are particularly useful sources in crisis communication situations where people need continuously updated information quickly.

A key disadvantage of mass media is that, except in paid advertisements and other limited circumstances, the media source often controls the content and timing of the story. Because of time and space constraints and the missions of media organizations, aired or published stories on risk-related issues may not contain the emphasis or depth of information that those who communicate risk would like to see. Thus the media should not be relied upon as the sole source of information in planning risk communication efforts.

Because of its wide reach and powerful impact, the use of mass media should be considered carefully as risk communication plans are being prepared. Even a small amount of negative coverage can torpedo the best-planned effort and destroy trust and credibility among the audiences and participants you are trying to reach. On the other hand, productive relationships with media representatives can lead to a more informed, solution-oriented public.

Schedules for planning and implementing media interactions and products can vary widely. On one hand, it may take only a half hour to talk with a reporter about a specific topic and perhaps follow up by sending background materials. In a crisis situation, you are usually working within a short time frame to prevent or mitigate a problem. The time involved in a crisis communication situation may be driven in part by a prescribed series of steps designated in company procedures. The unplanned nature of a crisis, however, makes timing unpredictable. Media followup after a crisis event, especially if an organization was perceived as mishandling the situation, may require much more time than it took to communicate during the actual crisis.

A formal event such as a press conference may require several days to plan and coordinate. Working cooperatively with a local newspaper to communicate about an issue that affects the community may span several weeks or months. Creating your own media messages for a public health campaign usually requires weeks or months of coordination and production.

Developing mutually productive working relationships with reporters is an ongoing effort for many organizations. Though this means vigilantly contacting media representatives to update them on breaking news

◇

Mass media approaches usually involve the use of sources such as television, newspapers, radio, and magazines to communicate risk information to broad audiences. Such sources can be powerful because they reach large audiences and can be memorable and credible sources for many people. Television and radio are particularly useful sources in crisis communication situations where people need continuously updated information quickly.

or to suggest story ideas at appropriate times, the result-ing quality of the media coverage often is well worth the time involved.

Many organizations require approvals of internal management when employees are working with exter-nal media professionals. When planning media interac-tions, include appropriate time up front for approvals, including review of any information materials you plan to give to the media. Be aware that additional time may be necessary to search for or revise materials to be suit-able for a particular medium. For example, newspapers may want a "people" photo rather than a technical illus-tration. Television reporters may ask if you can provide high-quality video clips or, more likely, ask to shoot their own footage.

Several kinds of costs are involved in media interac-tions, depending on the type and duration of the activ-ity. First are labor costs. Often a specialist trained in media relations is needed to plan and coordinate efforts, including creating media plans. There is also the time of those who are talking with media representatives. Production costs are necessary for creating materials such as press releases, press kits, advertisements and public notices, photos, and video footage. Formal events such as press conferences may require room and equip-ment rental.

Working with the media does not have to be expen-sive. Even a small organization can communicate impor-tant risk information to an audience of thousands through one radio, television, or newspaper interview—for only the few minutes it takes to speak with a reporter. The key in budgeting for media interactions, as in other types of communication activities, is to define your goals and target specific activities to meet them. Media spe-cialists or consultants can help you do this for greatest value within a budget that you specify. Chapter 16, "Working with the Media," gives examples of ways to work with media representatives in specific situations.

Those who are communicating directly with media representatives should have at a minimum a basic tech-nical knowledge of the risk situation so that they can an-swer technical questions with accuracy and credibility.

Equally important, however, are an understanding of media organizations and the ability to use language that the media outlet's audience will understand and relate to. When the person speaking is officially representing the company's position, follow the guidance in the section called "Choose the Appropriate Spokesperson," in Chapter 15. Chapter 16 provides guidance in understanding media practices and in using appropriately targeted language.

Those who are producing materials for media use should have professional skills to create high-quality products for the target medium. A person with subject-matter knowledge of the issue being portrayed should review the materials for technical accuracy.

## STAKEHOLDER PARTICIPATION

Stakeholder participation involves the audience in some way in the discussion, analysis, or management of the risk. Examples include advisory committees, facilitated deliberation, alternative dispute resolution, focus groups, community-operated environmental monitoring, and formal hearings in which the audience is invited to give testimony.

The advantage of stakeholder participation is that the audience can see for themselves exactly what is known about the risk, how the risk will be managed, and how decisions are reached. Because they can participate in the risk decision, it is likely to be more acceptable and lasting. Stakeholder participation can be structured to accommodate a variety of audiences, including those that are hostile or have difficulty reading or understanding other forms of communication. So, if one of your objectives is to increase the chances that your risk decision will be one that meets the needs of the audience, stakeholder participation may be the best choice.

However, stakeholder participation can be a frightening proposition to some risk managers. They fear loss of control over the risk decision, instead of seeing that the audience's input can be invaluable to a lasting, equitable decision. If there is no commitment to stakeholder participation from those who are analyzing the risk,

◇

Stakeholder participation involves the audience in some way in the discussion, analysis, or management of the risk. Examples include advisory committees, facilitated deliberation, alternative dispute resolution, focus groups, community-operated environmental monitoring, and formal hearings in which the audience is invited to give testimony.

managing the risk, or making the decision, the effort can be devastating to an organization's credibility, and hamper any future risk communication or management efforts. Stakeholder participation is generally more costly than simply issuing a technical report or holding a press conference. So, unless your organization is completely committed to letting the audience interact in a way that is meaningful to that audience, stakeholder participation is a very poor choice. See Figure 10-1 to determine whether stakeholder participation can be used effectively in your situation.

Stakeholder participation is usually a long-term proposition. Unless the structure for interaction is already functioning (such as an advisory committee), one cannot be put in place quickly enough to release urgent information. Stakeholder participation can usually only be used effectively when the risk management and risk communication effort will occur over time.

Little technical knowledge about the risk is required to set up stakeholder participation; however, technical staff and management must participate for the interaction to have meaning. In addition, knowledge about stakeholder participation (sometimes called public involvement) is necessary to structure the interactions effectively. Groups such as the International Association for Public Participation have evolved to develop and disseminate information concerning stakeholder participation. See Chapter 21, "Resources," for contact information. See Chapter 17, "Stakeholder Participation," for additional information on involving stakeholders in risk efforts.

## TECHNOLOGY-ASSISTED COMMUNICATION

A relatively new way to communicate risk, technology-assisted communication uses high technology to disseminate risk information or allow a member of the audience to query and receive a variety of information about the risk. For example, one application allows audience members to evaluate a number of factors to help experts identify the technologies that are more acceptable to the public for cleaning up a waste site.

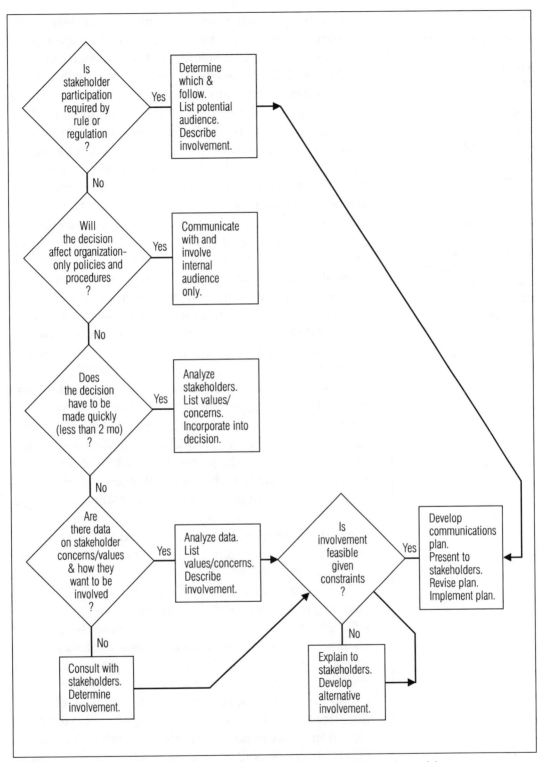

**FIGURE 10-1.** Determining when to use stakeholder participation to communicate risk.

A relatively new way to communicate risk, technology-assisted communication uses high technology to disseminate risk information or allow a member of the audience to query and receive a variety of information about the risk. For example, one application allows audience members to evaluate a number of factors to help experts identify the technologies that are more acceptable to the public for cleaning up a waste site.

Technology-assisted communication has the advantage of being able to disseminate an incredible amount of information, which each member of the audience can tailor to their individual needs. It appeals especially to the "technophiles," those among us who always have to have the latest toys and gadgets technology has to offer. Once developed, technology-assisted communication can be updated and revised more easily than materials developed through any of the other risk communication methods so that it is always current, a plus in the area of risk, which can change hourly. If graphic elements are properly built in, these applications can be as eye-catching as full-color ads or displays, yet carry as much information as traditional information materials or even more. With current computer capabilities, even speeches and video can be incorporated, making the applications incredibly versatile. So, if your objectives are to allow people to see all the data and develop their own perceptions of the risk or to disseminate information quickly, technology-assisted communication may be a good choice.

However, technology-assisted communication has several disadvantages. Those applications that must run on a fairly sophisticated computer make mass dissemination impractical. In addition, computer use in the United States is less than universal, making it difficult to reach all audiences with a computer-based application. Also, certain members of the audience still find using a computer intimidating. So, unless your audience is fairly computer-literate and has ready access to the appropriate equipment, technology-assisted communication may not be the best choice.

Technology-assisted communication is becoming more easy to produce every day. However, some applications still cannot be developed in time to meet the goals of short-term schedules. In addition, unlike information materials that are eventually used up, these applications must be kept up to date or audiences will lose interest.

Some applications, such as web sites, require relatively little technical knowledge of computers to develop. Depending on the purpose of the site, little risk information is needed as well (for example, setting up a computer bulletin board to log in stakeholder comments on an environmental impact statement). However, a computer application that incorporates risk modeling requires a great deal of technical knowledge, not only about the risk but about the application. Often such models are developed by teams, with each member specializing in a particular area such as technical communication, computer programming, and risk assessment. If your organization does not have such experts, contact colleges and universities for help. See Chapter 18, "Technology-Assisted Communication," for additional information.

## CHECKLIST FOR DETERMINING METHODS

If the purpose of the risk communication effort was:

❏ to increase the audience's awareness of the risk, the methods considered included

  ❏ visual representation of risk

  ❏ face-to-face communication

  ❏ technology-assisted communication.

❏ to inform the audience, the methods considered included:

  ❏ information materials

  ❏ face-to-face communication

  ❏ technology-assisted communication.

❏ to build consensus between the audience and the organization assessing or managing the risk, stakeholder participation was the method of choice

❏ to change behavior for the risk, the methods considered included:

  ❏ information materials

  ❏ face-to-face communication

  ❏ visual representation of risk.

## ADDITIONAL RESOURCES

Sachsman, D. B., M. R. Greenberg, and P. M. Sandman, editors. 1988. *Environmental Reporter's Handbook*. Rutgers University, Cook College, Environmental Communication Research Program, New Jersey Agricultural Experiment Station, New Brunswick, New Jersey.

Sandman, P. M., D. B. Sachsman, and M. R. Greenberg. 1988. *The Environmental News Source: Providing Environmental Risk Information to the Media*. New Jersey Institute of Technology, Hazardous Substance Management Research Center, Risk Communication Project, Newark, New Jersey.

Santos, S. L. 1990. "Developing a Risk Communication Strategy." *Management and Operations*, November:45-49.

# Set a Schedule

Once you know what you hope to accomplish, who you are doing it for, and how you will do it, you need to determine when you will do it. Setting a schedule for risk communication efforts requires that you consider a number of factors, such as legal requirements, organizational requirements, the scientific process, other ongoing activities, and audience needs.

## LEGAL REQUIREMENTS

Legal considerations are usually the first item that must be considered if the organization conducting the risk communication effort is to avoid litigation. As discussed in Chapter 3, "Laws That Mandate Risk Communication," many risk communication efforts are the result of laws, which usually prescribe schedules as well. One of the better delineated schedules can be found in the Superfund laws and associated advice from the U.S. Environmental Protection Agency (see Figure 3-1 in Chapter 3; EPA 1992).

Legal considerations are usually the first item that must be considered if the organization conducting the risk communication effort is to avoid litigation.

Federal, state, and local laws and regulations may specify schedules for risk communication milestones. Consult your legal department, a law firm, or a local risk-related government agency to determine which apply in your case.

## ORGANIZATIONAL REQUIREMENTS

After legal requirements have been determined, consider the requirements of your organization. What kinds of reviews will be necessary for any risk communication message to be sent out? How long will each take? Make a calendar for yourself so that you can follow your way through these requirements and plan for them. Look for requirements such as

- scientific review—to verify that the information about the risk is correct and the most current available

- editorial review—to make sure that the way the information is presented will be understood by the audience

- management review—to make sure that the information being presented is what the organization wants to present

- sensitivity review—to make sure that the information being presented does not compromise national security or business interests

- legal review—to make sure that the information does not compromise the organization relative to a law with which the organization must comply

- patents review—to make sure that the information being presented does not give away intellectual property and make it difficult for the organization to patent a certain idea or device

- public affairs review—to make sure the information will not embarrass the organization.

The purpose and objectives you have developed for your risk communication efforts also affect the schedule.

The purpose and objectives you have developed for your risk communication efforts also affect the schedule.

What frequency or duration is needed to achieve this purpose? If your purpose is to raise awareness, a short-term burst of activity that focuses on several methods would provide the most visibility. If your purpose is to build consensus so that your audience and the organization analyzing or managing the risk can come to a decision, you may want to conduct the activities over a longer time, providing different information as it is needed in the consensus-building process.

## THE SCIENTIFIC PROCESS

Your communication efforts will most likely have to coincide with certain aspects of the scientific process. Once a risk has been identified, you must alert those at risk, then follow up with more information as the assessment continues. While those who are assessing the risk may not be able to give you exact dates when they will know certain information, they should have a schedule showing what steps will take place. Make sure you are aware of that schedule and any changes to it as you plan (and update) your risk communication schedule.

—— ◇ ——

*Your communication efforts will most likely have to coincide with certain aspects of the scientific process. Once a risk has been identified, you must alert those at risk, then follow up with more information as the assessment continues.*

## ONGOING ACTIVITIES

The next item to consider is what else is going on within your organization, the community, and the nation, so that you can put your risk communication efforts in context. What other kinds of information will be released from your organization at the same time you are planning to release your risk communication information? For example, if the organization plans to announce the results of a 10-year study on cancer-causing chemicals, you may want to delay releasing your information about one of the chemicals so that you can incorporate the latest data. On the other hand, if the results of the 10-year study confirm your information on risk, you may want to bring your message out first and use the study as reinforcement.

What will be happening in the community during your risk communication efforts? In one effort, we were trying to determine when to hold the first public meeting near a Superfund site in central Alaska. We hoped for a certain week in October, only to find that that week was part of moose season, an extremely popular event for the community. So, even though we didn't want to wait to release information, we tried for another time to meet the needs of our audience and make our efforts more effective.

What will be happening in the nation during your communication efforts? This is much harder to predict. However, if your organization is dependent on federal funding, and an election in which your funding is an issue is imminent, you should wait until after the election to promise funds to a citizens group to act as advisors in your risk assessment, management, and communication activities. While other national trends are harder to foresee, try to at least determine your organization's agenda for the next few months at the national level.

## AUDIENCE NEEDS

To determine audience needs, consider the information from your audience analysis and the timing and severity of the risk. If you are in a crisis situation, obviously the audience needs as much pertinent information as possible as soon as possible. They need straightforward answers to such questions as:

- "What happened?"

- "How dangerous is it?"

- "How could it affect me or people or things I care about?"

- "What can I do?"

If the risk is a longer-term one, such as those related to the cleanup of a hazardous waste site, your schedule will be longer and more complex. You will need to answer the same types of questions, but with more detail and in a variety of ways. The answers are likely to change over time as more information becomes available so you will need to continue to issue messages. (This happens during a crisis as well, but on a much smaller scale and in a compressed time frame.)

If your audience must first become aware of the issue before developing a motivation or decision to act, your schedule will also be affected. Cole's 1993 article, "Perspective: Birth of a Notion," describes a seven-step process that we all go through to make a decision. Tables 11-1, 11-2, and 11-3 show these steps relative to examples of care, consensus, and crisis communication, respectively, and how the risk communication process might support the decision process.

The amount of time it takes to go through each of these steps in the decision process differs slightly for each individual and more greatly for the different types of risk communication. For care communication, the process can take weeks to months. For consensus communication, the process can take months to years. For crisis communication, the process can take hours to days. To determine which step most of your audience has reached for a particular risk, pretest risk messages or consult with audience representatives.

## CHECKLIST FOR SETTING SCHEDULES

The schedule is based on:
- ❏ legal requirements associated with the risk communication effort
- ❏ number and timing of organizational reviews
- ❏ purpose of the risk communication effort
- ❏ objectives of the risk communication effort
- ❏ schedule of the risk assessment
- ❏ activities within the organization
- ❏ activities within the community
- ❏ activities within the nation
- ❏ audience's point in the decision process.

If the purpose of the risk communication effort is to increase awareness, the schedule is as short as possible, given other constraints and audience needs.

**TABLE 11-1**

Risk Communication as Part of the Individual's Decision Process: Care Communication

*(Risk is radon in the home; audience is homeowners; decision process from Cole 1993)*

| Step in Decision Process | Individual's Thoughts | Example Risk Communication Activities |
|---|---|---|
| Dawning awareness | "Boy, there sure are a lot of stories around about radon being dangerous." | Put posters in hardware stores, develop relationships with reporters, send speakers to local organizations. |
| Sense of urgency | "Maybe I better have the house checked." | Encourage news stories, place ads in papers and magazines. |
| Discovery of choices | "Looks like I can write away for an EPA test kit or hire a contractor." | Mail fliers to homeowners, staff hotlines, put up web site. |
| Wishful thinking | "Maybe I could just sell the house and move to Florida." | Continue activities, highlighting choices. |
| Weighing of choices | "The test kit is free, the contractor will cost $100. I'm not technically inclined." | Continue activities, highlighting benefits of protective action and consequences of inaction. |
| Intellectual stand | "I think a contractor is best because they are experts." | Continue activities to ensure action is taken. |
| Responsible judgment | "I'll call the contractor this morning and schedule an appointment to have the house tested." | Evaluate risk communication program. |

**TABLE 11-2**

Risk Communication as Part of the Individual's Decision Process: Consensus Communication

*(Risk is hazardous waste incinerator; audience is interested stakeholders; decision process from Cole 1993)*

| Step in Decision Process | Individual's Thoughts | Example Risk Communication Activities |
|---|---|---|
| Dawning awareness | "They're going to build WHAT?" | Build partnerships with civic and environmental groups, Native American nations, and other interested stakeholders. |
| Sense of urgency | "Not in my backyard!" | Present messages in multiple formats on how to become involved. Make decision-makers accessible. |
| Discovery of choices | "There's got to be a better place. Maybe I should join that citizens group that's looking at sites." | Present messages in multiple formats concerning choices and soliciting ideas. Facilitate citizens group meetings. |
| Wishful thinking | "Maybe we could just truck the waste to New York." | Work with citizens group to develop criteria to screen choices. Continue dialogue with all stakeholders. |
| Weighing of choices | "We've got three sites that look safe. One wants the plant for economic reasons, but is near a National Park. The other two don't really want it, but the environments there are less sensitive." | Provide print and face-to-face messages on choices. Have organization and citizens group evaluate choices together. |
| Intellectual stand | "We understand all the technical facts and the organization's stand. We've decided to give Site 2 economic incentives to accept the plant." | Provide messages in multiple formats to stakeholders regarding choices weighed and decision made by group and organization. |
| Responsible judgment | "We'll work with the community at Site 2 to determine what the incentives should be." | Solicit community input on incentives. |

**TABLE 11-3**

Risk Communication as Part of the Individual's Decision Process: Crisis Communication

*(Risk is flood; audience is community at risk; decision process from Cole 1993)*

| Step in Decision Process | Individual's Thoughts | Example Risk Communication Activities |
|---|---|---|
| Dawning awareness | "The river is really rising from all this rain." | Provide information to news media describing risk and choices. Alert emergency responders. |
| Sense of urgency | "I wonder if it could reach the house." | Continue updates to news media and send volunteers to speak to the community. |
| Discovery of choices | "I could board up the lower floor and move upstairs, lay in a stock of sand and sandbags, or just evacuate." | Continue updates to news media, have volunteers urge consideration of choices. |
| Wishful thinking | "Maybe the river won't get this high." | Continue updates and use of volunteers. Stress urgency. |
| Weighing of choices | "Moving upstairs might not be enough. I probably couldn't fill enough sandbags by myself. I hate to leave everything behind." | Provide visual images of shelters, highlighting safety features. Provide information on duration and consequences. |
| Intellectual stand | "It's better for me to live than to risk being swept away by the flood." | Continue updates and volunteers until danger is past. |
| Responsible judgment | "I'll pack what I can and evacuate." | After emergency, evaluate risk communication effort. |

If the purpose of the risk communication effort is to inform the audience or change behavior, the schedule allows for the:

❑ introduction of the risk

❑ additional information given over time.

If the purpose of the risk communication effort is to build consensus, the schedule allows for the dissemination of risk information in support of the consensus-building process:

❑ before activities

❑ during activities

❑ after activities.

## REFERENCES

Cole, A. 1993. "Perspective: Birth of a Notion." *Modern Maturity*, Feb-Mar:9-10.

EPA (U.S. Environmental Protection Agency). 1992. *Community Relations in Superfund: A Handbook.* EPA/540/G-88/002, U.S. Environmental Protection Agency, Office of Emergency and Remedial Response, Washington, D.C.

# Develop a
# Communication Plan

*N*ow that you have determined your purpose and objectives, analyzed your audience, chosen your methods, and set your schedule, you need to put them all together into a comprehensive plan. Why not just keep the information in your head, notes on your desk, or a file in your computer? There are several reasons:

- A written plan is less likely to be lost than miscellaneous notes or files.

- At some point in the risk communication process, someone either inside or outside the organization may challenge your methods or approach. Having a comprehensive plan is a good defense.

- Having a formal plan that has been accepted (through signatures if necessary) by management can be handy in setting priorities and getting timely approvals for specific activities.

- Because formal plans are more organized, easier to review, and imply a more formal effort, the efforts they describe are more likely to receive the necessary funding and resources than those in nebulous plans.

- It is easier to evaluate the results of formal plans, because you can relate results directly back to your purpose and objectives, schedule, and audience.

The elements to include in a communication plan and how to bring all the elements together are discussed in the remainder of this chapter.

## WHAT TO INCLUDE IN A COMMUNICATION PLAN

A variety of information contributes to a comprehensive communication plan, as shown in the outline in Figure 12-1. You may also want to include other elements, depending on your organization's requirements. For example, Chapter 20, "What is Different about Emergency Risk Communication?," includes specific aspects for communication plans related to emergency response.

The introduction of the plan should discuss why you are writing the plan (purpose), what kinds of activities are covered by the plan (scope), background material on the risk being communicated, the reason your organization is communicating about the risk (authority), and the purpose and objectives of your effort (see Chapter 7 for more information on setting these). This information leads into the next section on audience.

The audience profile section describes what you know about the audience and how you learned it (see Chapter 8). The audience profile section can also discuss how segments of the audience differ. For example, in a care communication effort in which you are informing a community about the potential of fecal coliform bacteria in their well water, the audience might be segmented by level of risk—those who have wells with high readings of the bacteria, those who have wells with minimum readings, those who have wells free of the bacteria, and other interested community members. Each of these groups could differ in the kinds of information they need to make informed decisions regarding their risk. In a consensus communication effort, audiences might be segmented by the amount of involvement they desire in the decision-making process. Each of these groups could

> The introduction of the plan should discuss why you are writing the plan (purpose), what kinds of activities are covered by the plan (scope), background material on the risk being communicated, the reason your organization is communicating about the risk (authority), and the purpose and objectives of your effort (see Chapter 7 for more information on setting these).

```
Introduction
    Purpose of the plan
    Scope of the plan
    Background on the risk
        What is the risk?
        Who is affected by it?
    Authority
        Under what authority (law or organizational mandate) is the risk being
            communicated?
    Purpose of the risk communication effort
    Specific objectives

Audience Profile
    How audience information was gathered
    Key audience characteristics

Risk Communication Strategies

Evaluation Strategies

Schedule and Resources
    Detailed schedule that identifies tasks and people responsible for
        completing them
    Estimated budget
    Other resources to be used (equipment, meeting rooms, etc.)

Internal Communication
    How progress will be documented
    Approvals needed/received

Signoff Page
    Names, job titles, and signatures of key staff acknowledging that they have read
    and concur with the plan
```

**FIGURE 12-1.** Outline of a risk communication plan.

differ in the risk communication method used. In other cases, audiences might be segmented by comprehension level (for example, uneducated to highly educated) or geographic distribution (for example, those who can come to local public meetings and those outside the local area). In these cases, the difference between the audience segments isn't so much kind of information, but the way in which it is delivered. This section of the plan notes such key differences that will affect the risk communication effort described in the following section.

Risk communication strategies take what you learned about the audience and your purpose and objectives and lay out the methods you will use to reach each of the segments of your audience (see Chapter 10 for more information on methods). These strategies are closely aligned with the evaluation strategies (see Chapter 19 for additional information).

The schedule and resources section describes what you need to implement the strategies you laid out and how long it will take to fully implement them. Make sure you include resources other than funding. For example, if you are conducting a consensus communication effort, you might need space for the group to meet, audiovisual equipment to make presentations, and clerical support to type meeting minutes, among other resources. For additional information on setting a schedule, see Chapter 11.

The internal communication section describes how your organization will be kept apprised of the risk communication effort. Will you do monthly reports, send electronic mail messages at key points in the effort, give presentations to interested groups within the organization? Even if your organization does not require you to provide such updates, consider doing so to help ensure that your activities are visible and valued by your colleagues and management. Such visibility can help when additional resources are needed for this effort or future efforts.

The last item on the figure, the signoff page, is particularly important because it confirms organizational support. Get acceptance of the plan (as indicated by the signature) from all those involved in the risk communication effort or having to approve of the risk communication process or materials. Discuss the plan with and get acceptance of it from staff who are conducting the risk assessment and anyone involved with communicating the risk or approving its communication. Get signatures from managers of technical staff conducting the risk assessment, those in charge of making any decision based on the risk assessment results, managers in the public affairs and/or communications departments, and managers of staff involved in the risk communication effort.

You want the acceptance of these managers as well as their staff because the managers will have to approve staff time and resources (which their staff may not be able to commit to alone), the managers need to be aware of what their staff is doing, and the managers are likely to be the ones who have to answer questions from the public or outside organizations regarding your efforts and therefore need to be informed about them.

## DEVELOPING RISK COMMUNICATION STRATEGIES

A number of methods can be used to plan complex projects. Four of the most useful methods in planning a risk communication effort are using storyboarding, following the guidelines recommended by the U.S. Environmental Protection Agency for Community Relations Plans under Superfund, using an audience focus, and using a technique that combines the elements of strategic planning and public involvement.

### Storyboarding as a Planning Tool

Storyboarding is a technique that has been applied to organizing the content of a variety of communication products. It can also be used to develop the entire communication effort. This technique is most useful in planning care or consensus communication efforts and probably cannot be used in crisis communication because it takes time and requires a team of staff to work together, which may be difficult to accommodate in some schedules.

A storyboard can be any large flat surface to which pieces of paper can be affixed with tape, nonpermanent adhesive, pins, or tacks. The process starts with all those involved (those who are communicating the risk as well as other technical experts, managers, support staff, and even members of the audience, if you can arrange it) brainstorming ideas. Someone not involved in the risk communication effort should facilitate the session. The ideas can relate to any part of the process: audience, particular messages, how to distribute them. The facilitator should let the ideas flow and not censor them, even if

A number of methods can be used to plan complex projects. Four of the most useful methods in planning a risk communication effort are using storyboarding, following the guidelines recommended by the U.S. Environmental Protection Agency for Community Relations Plans under Superfund, using an audience focus, and using a technique that combines the elements of strategic planning and public involvement.

they are impractical or impossible. The facilitator or participants write each idea on a separate piece of paper and affix it to the board.

When the group runs out of ideas, the facilitator helps them begin to organize the ideas into the elements discussed in the outline in Figure 12-1. Use larger or different-colored cards to indicate categories. The facilitator will move the ideas into the categories, encouraging discussion. From the discussion, the group can begin to weed out infeasible or contradictory ideas.

Once the ideas have been categorized, the facilitator works with the group to organize the ideas within each category. The ideas can be put in any order that makes sense for your situation. For example, if one category was audience information, you could organize it by various segments of the audience. You now have a detailed list of strategies to be covered in the plan and used in your risk communication effort.

## Communication Planning Using the CERCLA Approach

The U.S. Environmental Protection Agency's publication *Community Relations in Superfund: A Handbook* (EPA 1992) is an invaluable resource for developing community relations plans (and communication plans) that meet the requirements of the Comprehensive Environmental Response, Compensation, and Liability Act (CERCLA or Superfund). This publication lists elements that should be included (these elements look much like the outline in Figure 12-1) and gives an example of a community relations plan. While the method described in the publication is most applicable to planning a risk communication effort related to CERCLA, it can also be used to plan care, consensus, and crisis communication.

In general, communication planning under CERCLA requires that those who are responsible for cleaning up a Superfund site (or conducting the care, consensus, or crisis communication) interview members of the public and organizations who might be interested in or affected by the cleanup (or the risk being communicated). Much the same information is gathered as during audience analysis, and it is used to plan appropriate strategies for com-

In general, communication planning under CERCLA requires that those who are responsible for cleaning up a Superfund site interview members of the public and organizations who might be interested in or affected by the cleanup. Much the same information is gathered as during audience analysis, and it is used to plan appropriate strategies for communicating risk information.

municating risk information. The number of interviews needed depends on the number of people who may be interested or affected. (For crisis communication, this method is best used in planning a crisis response rather than during the actual crisis.)

The publication from the U.S. Environmental Protection Agency also gives examples of methods of communicating information, such as fact sheets, news releases, and announcements of public meetings.

A more in-depth approach similar to this one is to develop a "mental model" of how the audience and experts view the risk and then focus on reinforcing appropriate messages and correcting misperceptions. This approach is particularly useful for care communication. More information on this approach can be found in Chapters 2 and 9.

## Using an Audience Focus

Another technique to identify strategies is to focus on the needs of various segments of your audience. This can be accomplished several ways. James Creighton, public involvement specialist and consultant responsible for many of the Bonneville Power Administration's successes in risk communication, uses an "onion diagram" (Figure 12-2). The center of the onion represents the risk and each of the rings represent audience segments. In care and crisis communication, the audiences closest to the center are those most at risk. In consensus communication (as in the example in Figure 12-2), the audiences closest to the center are those who want to be the most heavily involved in making the decision.

For any risk communication effort, a slightly different set of specific audiences will be in each of the rings. For example, in a consensus communication effort in which citizens of the Pacific Northwest would be asked to determine potential ways to mitigate risks to the salmon population:

1. The inner-most circle would include the agency charged with making the decision and most likely the Native American tribes who rely on the fish for subsistence, economic development, and

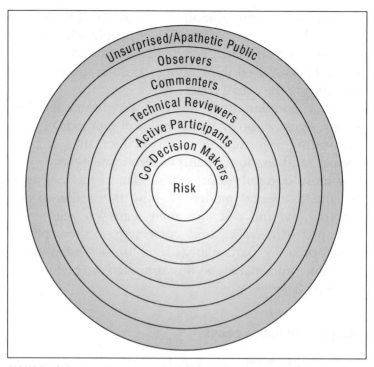

**FIGURE 12-2.** Audience-centered technique for communication planning. (Adapted from various works by James Creighton.)

ceremonial purposes but who must be consulted under a government-to-government agreement (co-decision makers).

2. The next circle (active participants) would include others with economic interests (other commercial fishers or those in the tourist industry) and environmental groups.

3. The next circle (technical reviewers) would include other related regulatory agencies.

4. The next circle (commenters) would include interested residents of communities along the rivers.

5. The next circle (observers) would include the rest of the residents of the Pacific Northwest.

Each of these audience segments will want a different type of involvement.

In general, as you move inward through the rings, the more communication effort is expended. Using the example above, the residents of the Pacific Northwest (observers) would probably be satisfied to read information in the news media about the ongoing activities. If something they read increases concerns, those who are most concerned will join the audience in the next ring. The residents of river communities will probably want additional information, such as direct-mail pamphlets and presentations to local organizations, while those with economic or environmental interests will want more direct involvement in making the decision, such as participating in workshops or on advisory committees. The Native American tribes will expect to be consulted and to actively help make the decision.

Another way to plan for audience needs is to use a situational assessment. According to researchers David Dozier and James and Larissa Grunig, who studied excellence in public relations and communications organizations (Dozier et al. 1995), audiences can be segmented into the following groups (adapted for use in risk communication) based on their situation in relation to the risk and the organization communicating about the risk:

- Nonpublic—those members of the audience who are not affected by the risk or the organization communicating the risk and vice versa

- Latent public—audience affected by the risk but don't realize it

- Aware public—audience both affected by the risk and knowledgeable of the fact

- Active public—audience organized to do something about the risk.

Dozier and his colleagues warn that organizations often focus communication efforts solely on the last group. Ignoring the other groups, however, can have serious consequences. By the time ignored members become active, their views are often negative, entrenched, and oppositional. While each segment of the audience may be reached using different methods and schedules, better to cultivate all segments early in the risk communication process.

Another way to view audiences is by what causes them to be interested in the risk. One crisis communication

Ignoring any component of your audience can have serious consequences.

manual developed for the state of California by a team of experts, including risk communication luminary Peter Sandman (OES 2001), divides audiences into the following segments:

- Residential community—people living near the risk, who have a personal or familial interest in health, safety, the environment, or quality of life in the area
- Business/commercial community—businesses that may be affected by the risk, who are concerned about loss of revenue, infrastructure availability, and protection of employees, as well as personal safety
- Industrial community—businesses that could be affected and who could affect the risk (for example, chemical tanks being targeted by terrorists), who are concerned with the same things as other businesses, as well as security issues
- Your organization—the staff and management who are charged with analyzing, managing, and/or communicating risk, who need to understand the effort as well as the risk
- Other organizations—the staff and management of organizations teaming with you in analyzing, managing, and/or communicating about the risk, who need to be able to explain and implement their roles.

The types of information and communication mechanisms may differ for each of these groups as well.

Using one of these three audience-focused approaches for your risk communication effort can help ensure that all segments of the audience are considered in planning and implementation.

## Strategic Planning for Risk Communication

Social scientists at Battelle have developed a method that combines elements of strategic planning with the ideals of public involvement to create plans for a variety of efforts, including risk communication. Strategic planning identifies an organization's strengths and weaknesses, opportunities to reach goals, and threats to those opportunities. Public involvement is incorporated by interviewing people who are interested in or affected by an organization to learn whether they view the organization in the same way as the organization views itself. This method is most useful in planning care communication efforts but can also be used in planning for a response to a crisis.

To use this method, start by identifying the values of your organization. What does your organization believe in, what is its mission, what is its purpose for being? Then state what the organization hopes to accomplish and how you will know when it has been accomplished. Next list the purposes and objectives of your risk communication effort. Looking at these and the information you developed in the previous steps, you can begin a situational analysis. What is the current situation? What assumptions did you make when planning for it? What are the strengths and weaknesses of your organization? What opportunities are available to you as you try to communicate risk? Is there anything that could prevent you from taking those opportunities? Who is your audience? What are the key issues?

From this analysis, your strategies for risk communication should start to emerge. Discuss your strategies and the information you have developed in the previous steps with representative members of your audience. Do they see the organization in the same way you did? Do they agree with your strategies for communicating risk? What suggestions can they offer to make your program stronger? Incorporate these suggestions into a final plan, using the outline in Figure 12-1.

## CHECKLIST FOR COMMUNICATION PLANNING

❏❏The plan includes the elements outlined in Figure 12-1.

❏❏All segments of the audience have been considered in planning.

The plan has been agreed to by:
   ❏ those who are communicating the risk
   ❏ those who are assessing the risk

❏ those who are managing the risk.

The plan has received the signatures of the:

❏ managers of those who are communicating the risk
❏ managers of those who are assessing the risk
❏ managers of those who are managing the risk.

## REFERENCES

Dozier, D. M., L. A. Grunig, and J. E. Grunig. 1995. *Managers Guide to Excellence in Public Relations and Communication Management*. Lawrence Erlbaum Associates, Publishers, Mahwah, New Jersey.

EPA (U.S. Environmental Protection Agency). 1992. *Community Relations in Superfund: A Handbook*. EPA/540/G-88/002, U.S. Environmental Protection Agency, Office of Emergency and Remedial Response, Washington, D.C.

OES (Governor's Office of Emergency Services). 2001. *Risk Communication Guide for State and Local Agencies*. Office of Emergency Services, Sacramento, California.

## ADDITIONAL RESOURCES

McCallum, D. B. 1995. "Risk Communication: A Tool for Behavior Change." *NIDA Research Monograph*, 155:65-89.

Shyette, B., and S. Pastor. 1989. "Community Assessment: A Planned Approach to Addressing Health and Environmental Concerns." *Superfund '89: Proceedings of the 10th National Conference*, pages 635-641. Hazardous Materials Control Research Institute, Washington, D.C.

*Part*

# III

# PUTTING
# RISK COMMUNICATION
# INTO ACTION

Each method (information materials, pictorial representation, face-to-face communication, working with the media, stakeholder participation, or computer-based application) has its own idiosyncrasies when used as a method for risk communication. Knowing these differences can help make the risk communication process more effective.

◇

*"The farther away we get from individual contact, the more room there is for confusion and misunderstanding."*

—Thomas Wilson, "Interactions Between Community/Local Government and Federal Programs" (1989, page 78).

# Information Materials

*T*he written message in the form of information materials has long been a staple of the communication world. The advantages and disadvantages of using information materials are discussed in Chapter 10, "Determine the Appropriate Methods." There are a number of ways to communicate risk via information materials, including newsletters; pamphlets, booklets, and fact sheets; posters, advertisements, and displays; articles in professional or trade journals, popular press magazines, and newspapers; and technical reports. Specific advice on each of these types of information materials is provided below, focusing on how these materials differ from those used in other types of communication efforts. First, however, there are some principles for constructing information materials.

## CONSTRUCTING INFORMATION MATERIALS

Whatever the form of the information material, those who are communicating risk must consider what infor-

Whatever the form of the information material, those who are communicating risk must consider what information to include, how to organize messages, appropriate language, and the use of the narrative style.

mation to include, how to organize messages, appropriate language, and the use of the narrative style.

## Information to Be Included

For information materials, a number of techniques can be used to present content in a way that your audience will understand. Remember, however, that the primary rule is to know your audience. Take or leave the other rules as they fit your audience's needs and situation. Figure 13-1 lists the kinds of information that might be included in information materials. The paragraphs following the figure describe this information in more detail. Depending on the length and scope of the information material (for example, an advertisement versus a technical report), these elements may be a single word or symbol or represent entire sections or chapters.

---

- Goals and content of the information material
- Nature of the risk
- Alternatives to the action that are causing the risk and any risks associated with these alternatives
- Uncertainties in the risk assessment
- How the risk will be managed
- Benefits of the risk
- Actions that the audience can take to mitigate or manage exposure to the risk
- Contact point
- Glossary
- Conversion table
- "Helpful hints"
- Index
- List of related information

---

**FIGURE 13-1.** Information to include in written risk communication messages.

- For materials over two pages long, summarize the goals and content of the information material. What is the purpose of this communication? What does it contain? This information is particularly important when you are using a variety of methods because it allows the audience to choose the risk communication message that best meets their needs. For example, if a member of the audience wants information on methods for testing a home for radon, and your pamphlet states that it describes what radon is and why the audience should test for it, the audience member will know to look elsewhere for the information on testing. Information on goals and content also helps guide readers through the risk information.

- Describe the nature of the risk and what the risk entails. What is the risk? Who is at risk? Put the risk in context. For example, is the risk similar to other risks with which the audience is more familiar?

- Discuss alternatives to the action that is causing the risk and any risks associated with these alternatives. For care communication, what alternatives does the audience have to living with the risk? Are there any risks associated with those alternatives? For consensus communication, what alternatives are being evaluated in making a decision? What criteria are being used to evaluate the alternatives? For crisis communication, alternatives focus on different actions that can be taken to mitigate the risk.

- Discuss uncertainties in the risk assessment. How were the data collected? How were they analyzed? See Chapter 6, "Principles of Risk Communication," for more information on uncertainties. See Chapter 14 for ways to portray uncertainties visually.

Discuss uncertainties in the risk assessment. How were the data collected? How were they analyzed?

- Explain how the risk will be managed. Risks are managed differently in care, consensus, and crisis communication. For care communication, it is usually the audience who must manage the risk, for example, by following safety procedures (although government agencies may be charged with monitoring a public health risk). For consensus communication, the audience and the organization charged with making a decision about the risk work to build consensus on how the risk will be managed, for example, by agreeing to operate a network of measurement devices around a hazardous waste site to monitor releases. For crisis communication, local and federal agencies as well as individuals and organizations may be involved in managing the crisis situation.

- Describe any benefits of the risk. Will anything good result from people being exposed to this risk? For example, hormone therapy in post-menopausal woman helps bone density and regulates hormonal systems but may contribute to greater chances of breast and uterine cancer. Be very leery of how you use this information. If the benefits are all to one group or the nebulous "science" or "humankind," and the risks are all to another group, the group at risk may not care how much their risks benefit others. Let your audience's desire to know this information be your guide in deciding whether to include it in an information material.

- Present actions your audience can take to mitigate or manage exposure to the risk. Can they change their behavior? Can they write to Congress? Can they provide comments on the material? Can they be involved in the risk assessment or risk management process? Knowing what they can do empowers your audience. The less they feel like victims, the less hostility you will have to combat.

- Always include the name, phone number, if possible, and address of someone to contact directly. If you cannot provide a personal contact, a hotline or web site will sometimes suffice. List the same contact in all your risk communication materials because the audience will feel more comfortable knowing that there is one reliable source available to answer their questions. If you include a phone number, make sure that number is answered 24 hours every day, either by a person or an answering system. Answering only

Always include the name, phone number, if possible, and address of someone to contact directly. If you cannot provide a personal contact, a hotline or web site will sometimes suffice.

during business hours isn't enough because many people don't have access to a phone on which they can make personal calls during that time. In addition, especially for care and crisis communication, it can be potentially life-threatening for someone to wait for an answer to a question.

- For anything more than 20 pages long, include a glossary (with definitions of all necessary abbreviations, acronyms, and technical terms). (For those less than 20 pages, avoid acronyms and abbreviations and define technical terms in text.) In general, for any risk communication message, avoid acronyms and abbreviations. The exceptions are terms that are commonly used more frequently as acronyms than as the spelled-out versions (for example, many people readily identify NASA, but have to think about National Aeronautics and Space Administration) and phrases used several times per page. When in doubt, spell it out.

- Include a method to convert metric units. Although many schools are teaching the metric standard, many adults not directly involved in scientific pursuits are still uncomfortable with metric units. However, many federal agencies (for example, the U.S. Department of Energy) now require that the primary units used in their information materials be metric. If you have only a few measurements, use analogies or metric units with English units in parentheses. If doing this conversion repeatedly will severely interrupt your text, use metric units and include a conversion table in your glossary.

- In information materials that cannot avoid being technical, include a section of "helpful hints" that explains things like scientific notation, uncertainties in tables and graphs, use of "less than" and "greater than" symbols, and other technical conventions. Readers who have a high level of technical knowledge can ignore the section while those with a lower level can use it to decipher the information.

- In documents longer than 40 pages, include an index so that readers can find specific information. Most members of your audience have limited time to devote to reading, so anything you can do to help them find the information they want quickly will encourage them to read your information. In general, indexes should contain key words, phrases, and ideas from the text.

- End with a list of related information. Telling your audience where to find other sources will help them obtain the exact information they want and encourage them to learn more about the risk. Point them to both your organization's publications and those prepared by other organizations.

## Organizing Material for Information Materials

The way you organize your material will in large part depend on the form of the information material and your audience's needs. Fact sheets and technical reports are necessarily organized differently. However, one point is important for all forms: discuss how the risk was determined before you present extensive data on the risk itself. Provide a summary of results by all means, especially for those readers who want only that information. However, don't jump into information on exposure calculations before you have discussed the process by which that information was developed or you will confuse your readers. Explaining the risk assessment process before the data gives your audience a context for the data and allows them to make a more informed decision regarding the risk. For consensus communication, particularly in cases in which the audience has a high level of skepticism or hostility toward the risk or the organization charged with managing the risk, it is equally important to discuss the process by which the decision will be made. Include information on how the audience has been and will be involved in the decision process.

## Language for Information Materials

The language you use depends primarily on your audience. Reading level, education, feelings concerning the risk, and experience with risks and science in general and with this risk specifically affect the audience's ability to process the message. Some general rules apply to most situations:

- Avoid any kind of language that might give your audience the feeling that they have no control. "Victims" process information less effectively and react with greater hostility. If you are trying to build consensus about the location of a hazardous waste incinerator, don't say "The facility will be sited in . . ." when you mean "The facility would or could be sited in . . ." If the decision hasn't yet been made, keep verbs conditional.

- Don't present estimates as facts. Many experts seem to confuse the results of their computer modeling with real life, making statements like, "The resulting harm to the affected population was 10 additional deaths from cancer per year." This makes it sound as if 10 people have already died, when, more likely, the information being communicated is an estimate produced by a computer modeling effort, given certain assumptions and a range of uncertainties. Give your audience the information to judge what the model results mean.

- Avoid scientific notation, mathematic formulas, and exponents. While you can explain some of these to a certain extent, just the fact that they are used at all will scare some readers into avoiding your message. It is true that tables of very small and very large numbers quickly become unwieldy if scientific notation ($1 \times 10^{-6}$) or engineering notation (1E-6) aren't used. However, depending on audience perceptions, a table with endless rows of zeroes can make the risk numbers much more obvious and frequently less threatening than a table filled with exponents. Also avoid the convention used in many technical journals of using a superscript -1 to mean "per" ($1\ d^{-1}$ for 1/d or 1 per day). Many members of your audience will find this notation incomprehensible. Instead, use the phase "one per day."

———— ◇ ————

Avoid scientific notation, mathematic formulas, and exponents. While you can explain some of these to a certain extent, just the fact that they are used at all will scare some readers into avoiding your message.

- Define how you're using the word "conservative" (or avoid using it) in relationship to exposure calculations. While the scientific community usually uses this term to indicate that the risk was overestimated, common usage, for example, in the finance industry, is to indicate an underestimate ("He's worth, conservatively, $1.5 million"). Therefore, many members of your audience will interpret the term as the opposite of what is intended. Either define the term or use terms like "cautious" to explain the process.

- Use culture-appropriate terms. Know your audience and what they consider acceptable words. For example, members of the Confederated Tribes and Bands of the Yakama Indian Nation are Native Americans, not Indians. And many tribes do not want to be called stakeholders because they have a government-to-government relationship with state and federal agencies. As in any form of communication, avoid sexist and racist terms.

Some organizations encourage the use of reading levels to gauge the appropriateness of information materials to present a risk message to an audience. Various formulas, such as Dale-Chall, Fry, Flesch Grade Level, Flesch Reading Ease, Fog Index, SMOG, FORCAST, Powers-Somner-Kearl, Spache, and Klesch-Kincard, allow the writer to calculate the comprehensibility of text at certain grade levels. Most formulas look at number of syllables or letters per word, number of words per sentence, and number of sentences per paragraph. Others factor in phrases and clauses. As mentioned in Chapter 8, "Analyze Your Audience," such formulas are not the best indicators of whether material is comprehensible. Pretesting risk messages is usually the better choice.

### Narrative Style in Information Materials

A relatively new approach to developing information materials is to use "narrative style." This style consists of presenting the risk information in the form of a personal story instead of or in addition to presenting exposure calculations or other data. The story structure helps the audience understand the risk by simplifying it and focusing on cause and effect. Golding, Krimsky, and Plough (1992) evaluated the narrative style versus what they call "the technical style" in each's ability to (1) encourage the audience to continue reading, (2) enhance knowledge, and (3) motivate the reader to action. They found that both forms enhanced knowledge equally well but that more readers kept reading the narrative. Unfortunately, neither style was likely to motivate the reader to action. In the case of the narrative style, one possible reason for this lack of motivation is that the audience may not have identified themselves closely enough with the person in the story, pointing to the need to understand your audience before using this technique.

George Cvetkovich of Western Washington University, a researcher in the area of public perceptions of risk and public policy, offers some suggestions for optimizing the power of the narrative in risk communication. He advises checking narratives for:

- Involvement—is the message interesting to the audience?

- Relevance—does the audience think the message applies to them?

- Ability—can the audience understand the information being presented and can they act in the way being modeled in the story?

To check narratives for these factors, use audience analysis information to guide you in preparing a prototype message and take the prototype to representative members of your audience for review. Ask them the questions related to involvement, relevance, and ability. If the answers are "yes," the narrative will probably have the results you intended. If the answers are "no," you will need to redesign the narrative.

## GUIDELINES FOR SPECIFIC TYPES OF INFORMATION MATERIALS

Information materials can range from the short two-page fact sheet or quarter-page ad in a magazine to the

◇

A relatively new approach to developing information materials is to use "narrative style." This style consists of presenting the risk information in the form of a personal story instead of or in addition to presenting exposure calculations or other data.

multivolume environmental impact statement. What follows are guidelines for some of the more commonly used types of information materials for communicating risk.

## Newsletters

Newsletters are a common form of risk communication. Newsletters are especially good for long-term projects with a relatively stable audience (stable meaning that the audience consists of mostly the same people throughout the communication process) who are interested in the project/risk being described. E-mailed versions are becoming more popular.

Each issue of a newsletter consists of a series of articles related to a specific risk or type of risk. For example, many Superfund sites send a newsletter to interested members of the communities near the site to keep them informed of the progress of cleanup and the risks entailed. Many health care centers also have newsletters describing healthy lifestyles for their patients. While the exact content of a newsletter will depend on the audience and the risk, some general rules apply:

- When first developing a newsletter, allow time in your schedule for approvals from all agencies involved. Because a newsletter often serves as a reflection of the organization over a long period of time, this type of risk communication often requires a number of approvals before the first issue is published, and sometimes for subsequent issues.

- Develop and maintain mailing lists. Be sure to include as many members of your audience as possible in your distribution. Include in each issue a coupon or other method for requesting to be added to or removed from the newsletter distribution. Maintain an accurate mailing list by updating names and addresses at least quarterly. If your audience is already hostile, spelling names wrong, sending information to the wrong address, or forgetting some members entirely won't help.

- Avoid the use of acronyms and abbreviations. Like newspapers, newsletters are seldom read straight through from front to back. Audience members pick stories and headlines that interest them. They won't know where to look for a definition if they first come across an acronym on page 6 and the acronym was spelled out in some other story on page 3.

- Encourage people to read by using compelling headlines and graphic elements. Use design elements appropriately to encourage your audience to pick up the newsletter and read it.

- Be consistent. One of the advantages of newsletters is that subsequent issues will be sent to the same audience (although one that grows with your mailing list) over time. Use the same words to describe the same place or situation (for example, don't call your environmental cleanup areas source areas in one issue and sites in another). For consensus communication efforts involving a decision process, show readers the process each time with the current stage highlighted. Also, watch content. If in issue one you run a story about the new sewer plant opening next April, don't forget to follow up with the grand opening. Lack of consistency can lead to lack of credibility for your entire effort.

## Pamphlets, Booklets, and Fact Sheets

Pamphlets, booklets, and fact sheets are good for short-term, one-message communication efforts or for covering one aspect of a complex risk. Because they are short, they attract those who are put off by longer information materials. A few points to remember for risk communication messages:

- Focus these short forms to meet specific needs. By their very nature, pamphlets, booklets, and fact sheets have a limited amount of space. Cover only one limited subject in each. Your audience's needs will determine which subjects should be included.

- Make these forms self-contained. Pamphlets, booklets, and fact sheets are meant to be picked up, carried away, and read quickly. Although information

Pamphlets, booklets, and fact sheets are good for short-term, one-message communication efforts or for covering one aspect of a complex risk. Because they are short, they attract those who are put off by longer information materials.

on contact points and ways to get additional information should be part of the message, your audience should need nothing more than what they are holding to understand the point you are trying to make about the risk.

- If the message is part of a series, strive for visual consistency. Try for a "family look" to the publications (similar use of type styles and design) so that your audience will begin to recognize them and, with any luck, become comfortable with them. The higher the comfort level, the more likely your audience will be to read them.

- Distribute these materials where your audience lives. Use a direct mail approach, but don't overlook the power of placing packets in locations where your audience is likely to pick them up and read them. Medical offices, libraries, local businesses, community centers, church vestibules, even local chambers of commerce are places where your audience may see and pick up such information.

### Posters, Advertisements, and Displays

American society is increasingly visually oriented. Posters, advertisements, and displays are a form of information material geared to appeal to this visual orientation. While the message they can carry will be limited to the space available, and the creativity of the designer, these information materials can strongly reinforce key concepts if certain guidelines are followed:

- Any written message in posters, advertisements, or displays should be in the language of the audience. Text should be at the audience's reading level and address audience concerns. The message should also be written in a language other than English if the audience speaks English only as a second language. If different members of the audience speak different native languages, similar displays should present the information in each language.

American society is increasingly visually oriented. Posters, advertisements, and displays are a form of information material geared to appeal to this visual orientation. While the message they can carry will be limited to the space available, and the creativity of the designer, these information materials can strongly reinforce key concepts if certain guidelines are followed.

- The message should be simple and clear. This seems obvious, especially given the limited space in display visuals. However, it is frequently violated, sometimes with disastrous results. For example, to advertise its safety campaign, an industrial plant posted a sign outside its gates along the main route for commuters. The sign was covered in text, all in capital letters, and several different colors, with slogans and statistics about lost-workday accidents. Although its placement suggested that it was meant to be read quickly as workers drove home, workers had to slow down to see what it had to say, so that the safety sign actually caused accidents. In general, display visuals are meant to be read quickly, so keep them simple.

- All graphic elements should reinforce the risk message. Too many display visuals offer mixed messages. A billboard outside a chemical manufacturing firm warned workers to remember safety as they went to work. The bold, black lettering and sober message spoke of a serious concern; however, the pastel painting of two happy children picking wildflowers that appeared beneath the lettering contradicted the seriousness of the message. A simple, easy-to-remember slogan would have carried more weight.

- Put display visuals where the audience will see them. Where does your audience work and play? Where are they most likely to be exposed to the risk? That's where your messages belong. Putting a message about the dangers of unsafely operating a forklift in the secretarial pool may reach a number of people, but not likely the workers who are at risk. Better to put the poster in a place where your audience will be thinking about the risk, such as where the machines are parked.

- Always include sources of additional information. While display visuals are particularly good at raising audience awareness of a risk, many members of the audience will find the limited message inadequate and want more information. Always be sure to point them in a direction that will reinforce your message. This could be an address or phone number for your organization or a sheet they can tear off with various contact points. Including this information helps empower your audience to take action.

## Articles

If written by someone knowledgeable about the risk who can communicate well, articles in professional or trade journals, popular press magazines, and newspapers can be very effective in communicating risk to a variety of audiences. However, in some cases, the actual content is often out of the control of those who are communicating the risk. (See Chapter 16 for information on working with the media.) If you are writing the article:

- Make sure the publication's readers match your intended audience. If you don't reach the people you were trying to reach, it does little for your risk communication efforts. Most journal and newspaper publishers will tell you who reads their publications.

- Consider professional journals. For certain occupational risks, for example, carpal tunnel syndrome, your audience may well be members of professional societies or unions. A well-written article in their publication may reach your intended audience faster than some other forms of communication.

## Technical Reports

Although intimidating for many readers, technical reports are needed for those who want to see more detailed data to form their own opinions. Technical reports can meet the needs of several segments of your audience—the expert who has extensive technical information or wants it, the reader with some background in the risk who wants additional in-depth information, and the neophyte who is interested in this type of information. To meet the needs of these segments of your audience, organize the document from the back to the front. That

If written by someone knowledgeable about the risk who can communicate well, articles in professional or trade journals, popular press magazines, and newspapers can be very effective in communicating risk to a variety of audiences.

is, place the technical detail—computer runs, tables of supporting data, lists of standards, and quality assurance data—in appendixes or supporting documents. This information will serve the expert. Then, use the information as a basis for a report that can be read at the tenth-grade level; this will generally serve the reader with some background in the risk. Use the report information as a basis for a summary with a minimum of technical terminology; this summary should be able to be read at the sixth-grade level. This will serve the needs of the neophyte. (We use reading levels here as a guide to content and style, not to imply that all interested readers read at the tenth-grade level or that all neophytes read at the sixth-grade level.)

As mentioned in the section on what to include in written risk communication messages, be sure to include helpful hints, a glossary, and an index to help all readers. Provide additional information-identifying devices, such as introductions that summarize key points for each major section; transitions between sections, paragraphs, and sentences; and paragraphs with topic sentences. Craft sentences and paragraphs so that familiar information comes first, with more difficult and newer information coming later.

——— ◇ ———

Although intimidating for many readers, technical reports are needed for those who want to see more detailed data to form their own opinions. Technical reports can meet the needs of several segments of your audience—the expert who has extensive technical information or wants it, the reader with some background in the risk who wants additional in-depth information, and the neophyte who is interested in this type of information.

## CHECKLIST FOR INFORMATION MATERIALS

❏ The information is tailored for the intended audience.

The information material includes information on any of the following that will meet audience needs:
    ❏ goals and content
    ❏ the nature of the risk
    ❏ alternatives
    ❏ uncertainties
    ❏ risk management
    ❏ risk benefits
    ❏ audience actions
    ❏ contact information
    ❏ glossary

❑ metric conversion

❑ "helpful hints"

❑ index

❑ list of related information.

❑ The message discusses how the data were developed before the data themselves.

The wording in the message:

❑ does not present the audience as victims

❑ distinguishes between estimates and facts

❑ avoids scientific notation

❑ avoids mathematic formulas

❑ avoids exponents

❑ avoids or defines the term "conservative"

❑ does not use racist or sexist terms or other terms the audience might find offensive.

If the message uses narrative style, it will:

❑ involve the audience

❑ be relevant to the audience

❑ be within the audience's ability to understand and act upon.

For newsletters:

❑ time has been allowed for approvals

❑ the mailing list has been developed

❑ there is a mechanism for updating the mailing list.

The text of the newsletter:

❑ avoids acronyms and abbreviations

❑ uses compelling headlines and graphic elements

❑ is consistent from issue to issue.

For pamphlets, booklets, and fact sheets:

❑ each has been focused to meet specific audience needs

❑ each is self-contained

- all strive for consistency
- each has been distributed where the audience lives.

For posters, advertisements, and displays:
- the text portions are written in a language the audience will understand
- text messages are clear and simple
- all graphics reinforce the message
- visuals will be displayed in locations where the audience will see and heed them
- information is included about where the audience can get additional information.

For articles:
- the article is written for publications that will reach the audience
- the article will be in professional journals where appropriate.

For technical reports:
- the report is structured to meet audience needs
- the report uses language and organization that lead the reader through the report.

## REFERENCES

Golding, D., S. Krimsky, and A. Plough. 1992. "The Narrative versus Technical Style in Risk Communication." *Risk Analysis*, 12(2).

## ADDITIONAL RESOURCES

Kolin, J. L., and P. C. Kolin. 1985. "Instructions." *Models for Technical Writing*. St. Martins Press, New York.

No author. 1982. "Indexes." *The Chicago Manual of Style*, pages 511-560. The University of Chicago Press, Chicago.

# Visual Representation of Risks

From hieroglyphics on cave walls to camera cell phones, humans have always gravitated toward visuals to communicate. It is not surprising, then, that when people are trying to understand and make decisions about risks, they often want to see various aspects of the risk in visual or graphical formats.

Those who communicate risk should be aware of the power of well-chosen visuals to help people understand and think about risks.

The human brain has a remarkable capacity to assimilate visual information. People have been shown to "take in" more than 600 pictures without any particular effort and then, with more than 98% accuracy, distinguish them from different pictures that are added to the original 600 (Shepard 1967).

Visuals have been shown to help people understand and remember content (Graber 1990; Lang 1995; Shepherd 1967). For example, consumer comprehension of nutrition information on product labels was improved when bar graphs and pie charts, rather than words only, were used (Geiger et al. 1991). Carefully chosen pictures make information transmission more rapid, realistic, and

> *"What is important is the ability to intuit and communicate the human meaning of data."*
>
> —Lawrence Wallack, Director, Berkeley Media Studies Group, "Media Advocacy and Public Health: Power for Prevention" (1993, page viii).

213

accurate than is possible in purely verbal messages (Graber 1990).

Visuals help clarify abstract concepts, which often are inherent in risk-related information. One study found that people making mental comparisons involving abstract concepts increased their response times when pictures, rather than words, were used (Paivio 1978). Good visuals help audiences construct mental models of abstract or complex concepts (Graber 1990). A typical study tested people's comprehension and problem solving, with and without graphics, about how lightening is created (Mayer et al. 1996). People who were given captioned figures along with explanatory text showed increased comprehension and problem solving than those who received the text only.

Beyond improving comprehension and recall, visuals can help people put facts into context. Numerical information in pictorial formats such as charts can make it easier to get a more holistic (bigger picture) view than with numbers alone, helping users gain more insights into the information (Lacerda 1986). Graphics also reveal data patterns that may go undetected otherwise (Tufte 1990).

This chapter describes ways to represent risk-related information visually—whether in photos, pictures, illustrations, graphs, charts, tables, labels, or other forms. Those who are communicating risk often use visual representations of risks in explanatory materials such as displays, posters, fliers, fact sheets, flip charts, slides or overhead transparencies, newsletters, booklets, product labels, media sources such as television, newspapers, and the Internet, and multimedia programs such as CDs, DVDs, and interactive kiosks. There are almost an unlimited number of options for portraying risk information visually. The key is to tailor the design and use of the format to the needs of the interested individuals or groups. No one presentation format fits all people and situations. Our intent is to give those who are communicating risk some ideas, tools, and guidelines for communicating risk information pictorially.

One important caveat is that the way risks are presented is only one aspect of the way people perceive and act on risks. Some risk experts believe that if they can just find the right way to portray a risk, the public will draw the same conclusions about the risk as do the technical experts (or policy experts, risk managers, plant managers, or government and public health officials). As described in Chapter 4, "Constraints to Effective Risk Communication," many other factors affect the way people respond to risks, such as the nature of the risk and the trustworthiness of those explaining it (Bord and O'Connor 1992; Johnson et al. 1992; Slovic 1987). The way quantitative information is presented, though important, is only one contributing factor.

Regardless of the role of pictorial representations, they can serve as powerful tools to help people understand various aspects of risks and their alternatives. In portraying risks visually, those who are communicating risk should aim for approaches that are clear, comprehensible, nonmanipulative, and useful for making decisions. This chapter draws on research and practice to recommend practical approaches for communicating risk. For simplicity, the words *graphic*, *visual*, and *pictorial representation* are used interchangeably unless specified.

## DESIGN VISUALS FOR SPECIFIC AUDIENCES AND USES

In deciding which aspects of a risk to portray and how to present them, you will need to identify three things: what people want to know, what they need to know to make an informed decision, and how the visual information will be used.

The first step is to analyze your audience's information needs. Different people may want different kinds of information about a risk. In one study of local river contamination, state regulators wanted to know whether the contamination levels would rise over the legal limits, and under what conditions. Farmers wanted to know the potential effects of irrigating their crops with the water. Native American tribes were concerned about how the environmental problems could affect future generations. They also wanted to know whether tribal members whose diets were heavily dependent on locally caught fish were more at risk. Those involved with the

*"Good design should take into account how, when, and where the information is used."*

— Edward R. Tufte, "Visual Explanations: Images and Quantities, Evidence and Narrative" (1997, page 115).

river contamination study worked closely with the stakeholders throughout the study to make sure that the results would portray all of these aspects of the risk. Thus, the study contained graphics for different conditions throughout time, showing contaminant levels for various kinds of river uses.

Follow the advice for audience analysis in Chapter 8, "Analyze Your Audience." The results will help you determine what you may want to show visually, and in what format.

In many communication efforts, especially in care-based communication efforts, it is necessary to go beyond what people want to know. Include what people need to know—but may not think to ask—about the risk to knowledgeably evaluate it. The mental models research approach described in Part I, "Understanding Risk Communication," is one way to identify important factual misperceptions or information gaps about a given risk that must be addressed in communication materials.

Carnegie-Mellon University used the mental models approach in developing a brochure about electric and magnetic fields. The brochure covers the typical issues about possible health effects and how to avoid them. But the brochure also visually depicts specific information to help people understand risks from electric and magnetic fields, including the strength of fields from various sources, how the strength is affected by proximity to the source, how fields are measured, the stages of an electric power system, ways science gets evidence about health effects, and the concept of dose and exposure (Carnegie-Mellon University 1995). Figure 14-1 shows one such depiction from the brochure. This particular graphic and accompanying explanation were added when it was discovered through testing that laypeople typically underestimated the rate at which the strength of fields decreased with increasing distance from their sources (Morgan et al. 1990).

In addition to identifying what people want and need to know, another factor for designing visuals is to determine where and how the visual will be used. Table 14-1 shows some considerations for various presentation options.

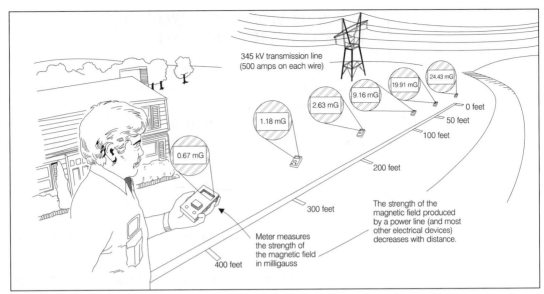

**FIGURE 14-1.** Illustration from a brochure on health risks of electric and magnetic fields. The figure shows how the strength of a 60-Hz magnetic field decreases with distance from a 345-kV transmission line.

(Source: Carnegie-Mellon University 1995; used with permission of the author.)

---

**TABLE 14-1**
Considerations for Showing Visuals in Various Media

| Where Graphics Will Appear | Considerations |
| --- | --- |
| Printed information materials (newsletters, fliers, fact sheets, brochures, booklets) | Such materials usually provide the most detailed explanation of risks; people can read on their own "turf" at a convenient time. Can typically use more detailed visuals, and a wider variety, than in other media, because there is room for explanation. Often the only media where number-intensive graphs, charts, flowcharts, and tables are appropriate. |
| Posters and displays | Typically designed to get attention and convey a few key messages quickly. If displayed at a public forum to discuss the risk, can contain more explanation. Graphics must be clearly legible from at least a couple of feet away or more. Message of graphic should be quickly apparent. Pictures, simple graphics are most effective. |
| Presentations | Make sure the entire audience can see all aspects of the visuals being shown, or use handouts. Tailor visual content to background, knowledge, interests of majority of audience members. Use supplementary print materials for those who want more information. |
| News media | Usually aimed at a broad, general audience. Graphics are typically designed to attract attention and convey a single key point. Keep visuals simple, uncluttered. For TV, consider showing people dealing with the risk. For newspapers, consider picture-oriented visuals (such as icons or symbols) that represent how the risk is carried or mitigated. See Chapter 16, "Working with the Media," for more information. |
| Web-delivered and other technology-related communication, media | Often interactive and tailored to specific interests. Good opportunity to present visuals at several levels, such as a summary graphic, more detailed visuals, and explanations for those who want to "drill down" to learn more. Good for multi-showing movement, including animations, virtual reality, video clips, streaming video. See Chapter 18, "Technology-Assisted Communication," for more. |

## MATCH THE VISUAL PORTRAYAL TO THE INFORMATION TO BE CONVEYED

Not every type of risk or aspect of it lends itself to pictorial representation. How do you determine when a visual representation of risk is needed, and how do you decide the best way to show it? Some common kinds of risk information that lend themselves to pictorial representations include

- the nature of the risk and its effects

- how large or significant the risk is

- how likely the risk is to occur and the chances that it will affect themselves or others

- how much the risk has increased or decreased over time

- alternatives to the risk, and the benefits and dangers associated with alternatives.

Table 14-2 shows potential ways to address each of these factors visually. As described in the next sections, select the approach(es) based on an audience analysis and on pretesting.

One way to plan visuals is to pose a series of questions that address the key issues, then determine how to answer them visually. An example of how to use that process is shown here. Key questions were used to guide the selection of visuals for an annual school safety report (St. Clair 1956):

- How do the accident statistics of our locality compare with those on a national basis or with those in similar communities? A line graph was suggested for comparing the local accident rate with the national rate.

- Has progress in accident prevention over the last year been made? A bar graph was suggested for comparing relative magnitudes: reduction in accidents in the current year, compared with past years.

- What shortages are noticeable in our safety education? A line graph to show the norm, and a bar chart to show deviations, were suggested for showing

**TABLE 14-2**
Options for Portraying Various Aspects of Risk Visually

| Risk Information | Options for Visual Format |
|---|---|
| The risk and its effects | If the effects of the risk can be seen (such as a visible health effect, effect on plants and foods, etc.), depict them in a photo or illustration to help people identify the risk. Also consider showing conditions leading to or indicating a risk, such as blocked fire doors in an industrial plant, high-power lines for electromagnetic fields (previous Figure 14-1), skull and crossbones indicating poison on warning labels, or people demonstrating unhealthy or unsafe behaviors and their consequences. |
| Size and significance of the risk | Show the risk in the affected population, using numbers or charts. Show the risk over time, increasing or decreasing, such as in a line graph or bar chart. Compare judiciously with other similar risks to show relative magnitudes (see Table 14-3 and Chapter 6, "Principles for Comparing Risks.") Consider including a recommended "action" level—a point at which people may want to take action to mitigate the risk (see Table 14-13). |
| Likelihood of risk for specific people | Show probabilities and uncertainties for various conditions. Consider phrasing as "X in Y chances of occurring" under certain conditions. Tables, charts, and graphs can show various risk levels for various situations (see Figure 14-6). "If-then" flowcharts can help people walk themselves through the risk probabilities (see Figures 14-8 and 14-9). |
| Change over time | Use graphs, charts, or pictograms (small pictures representing the risk) to indicate trends over time. Consider several different representations if many variables are involved, such as conditions that change the risk over time. |
| Alternatives to the risk, with corresponding benefits and dangers | Compare alternatives with pros and cons of each. Consider using tables if there are shared variables among the alternatives and the alternatives are being compared in a similar way (costs, environmental effects, health effects, etc.). If the alternatives are not easily comparable, use formats that do not invite comparison on the same scales. |

accident trends that may need attention in the up-coming year.

- What special emphasis should be made during the next school year? A pictograph was suggested for symbolizing the curriculum areas requiring more safety emphasis.

As the example suggests, sometimes the best approach is to show as many aspects of the risk as possible, giving people more information and choices. It may be helpful to use several graphics, each highlighting a certain aspect of the risk. One study found that a presentation that included the most information scored as well as or better than other formats on almost all measures of communication success (Weinstein et al. 1989). There was no evidence that respondents were confused by the amount of information.

A seemingly obvious (but too often ignored) guideline is to make sure the graphic supports the information being conveyed. Journalism professor and risk communication researcher Robert Griffin uses the example of a 1996 story in the *Milwaukee Journal Sentinel* about the disproportionate upturn in suicides among older citizens from 1980 through 1994 (Griffin 1999). The story stated that though people aged 65 and older accounted for only 13% of the population, they accounted for nearly 20% of all suicides. The accompanying graphic, however (Figure 14-2), seems to show that suicides are more common in younger age groups. Instead, Griffin said, the reporter should have used two charts: one showing per capita suicides in each age group in 1994 and another for 1980. That approach would have given the reader two baselines: the relative populations and the prevalence of suicides over time.

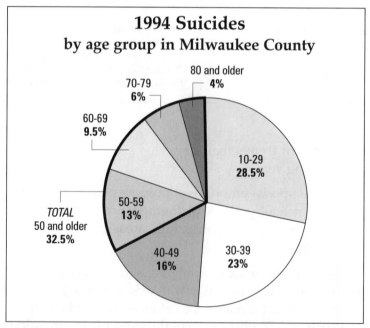

**FIGURE 14-2.** Suicides by age group in Milwaukee County. This figure inadvertently made a different point than the one the reporter intended.
(Source: *Milwaukee Journal Sentinel* 1996, in Griffin 1999.)

## PRETEST GRAPHICS WITH THOSE WHO WILL USE THEM

After you have researched your audience, identified the uses of your graphics, and prepared an initial set of graphics, the next step is to pretest them with people who represent your target audiences. Pretesting graphics is usually done as part of a broader evaluation of messages and/or materials. For example, it is common to pretest an entire brochure or oral presentation containing graphic elements. Pretesting typically provides feedback on the graphic elements as well as other aspects of the message and presentation. Here, we focus on how to get the most out of pretesting for graphics.

Use interviews, discussion groups, and other techniques to get maximum information. (See "Whenever Possible, Pretest Your Message" in Chapter 6, "Principles of Risk Communication.")

Ask people what they think each pictorial graphic means. The answer will help you determine whether your graphics are meeting their objectives. Ask whether anything in the pictures, tables, or charts is unclear, misleading, confusing, incomplete, or inaccurate. Ask what feelings are evoked and what words come to mind when viewing specific graphics. In addition, ask people about their overall reactions to the graphics. You may discover that some graphics come across as patronizing, scary, or overly technical, or that they carry an unintended message.

After hearing from your audience, make decisions about how to modify your graphics, add more, or eliminate them to meet your audience's needs and your communication objectives.

What does pretesting reveal about graphic representations? The following is an example of some comments and changes resulting from pretesting of an information booklet about environmental risks (Pacific Northwest National Laboratory 1994, 1995). The booklet was designed for the general public. Feedback came from students, teachers, agricultural representatives, state regulators, health department officials and practitioners, environmental advocates, and other community members.

*"Poorly designed or produced visuals are worse than no visual at all."*

— Peter J. Hager and H. J. Scheiber, "Designing and Delivering Scientific, Technical, and Managerial Presentations" (1997, page 171).

- People wanted to compare the existing contaminant amounts to an existing standard. Wherever applicable, regulatory safety limits for contaminants in drinking water, air, and food were included in the applicable illustrations and tables. Figure 14-3 shows an example of a redesigned map.

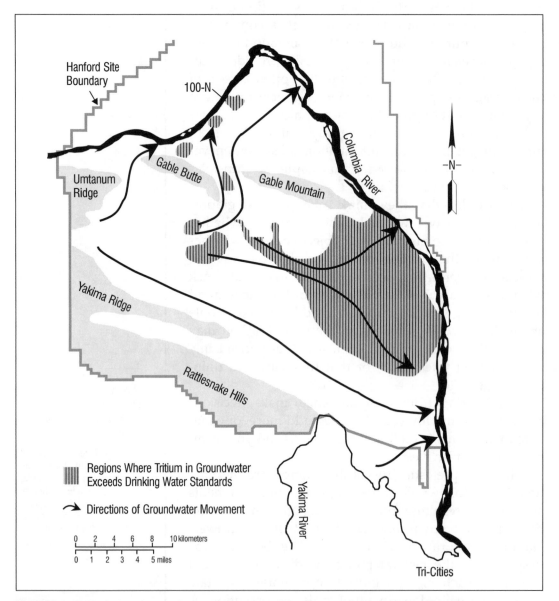

**FIGURE 14-3.** Redesigned map of groundwater contamination on a federal site in 1994. The map shows areas where drinking water standards were exceeded in past years.

(Source: Pacific Northwest Laboratory 1995.)

- People wanted more orientation and clarification of maps. Maps showing contamination locations were clarified to show the direction of contaminant movement (see Figure 14-3). A small state map was included to help the reader locate the smaller geographic area shown on the map (Figure 14-4).

- Some people thought that photos of families enjoying the outdoors were not representative of actual conditions, and that they appeared to put an overly "happy face" on a serious issue. Such photos were replaced with more informative ones such as workers gathering river water samples.

- People had trouble understanding illustrations that included numbers such as, for contaminant levels and quantitative exposure effects over time, regardless of which graphic format was used to convey this information. These illustrations were eliminated and discussed narratively in the text instead.

- People wanted to put events in a historical context and see at a glance when certain cleanup actions

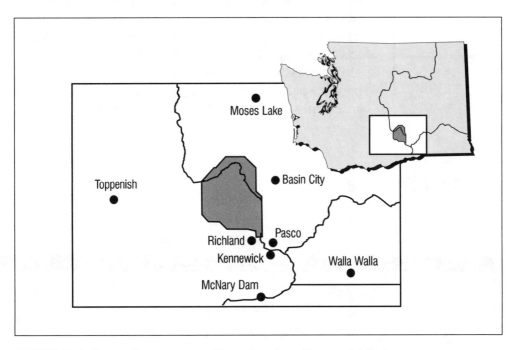

**FIGURE 14-4.** "Locator" state map used in conjunction with more detailed map.
(Source: Pacific Northwest Laboratory 1995.)

would be completed. Visual timelines (Figure 14-5) were added to show key dates and events.

- A table of numerical environmental monitoring results was seen as reference-type information that would be useful only for certain readers. The table was moved to the back so that its more detailed nature would not interrupt the narrative "story" before it.

## USING VISUALS TO PERSONALIZE RISK INFORMATION

People often want to know what risks mean to themselves or to their family members. Visual displays can help personalize risk information.

Photos are effective for realistically depicting visible risk characteristics that can affect individuals. Health professionals often use photos in brochures or posters to show patients warning signs of certain health conditions that they should watch for. For example, photos can be used to accurately show early gum disease and potential skin cancer signs. County extension agents and pesticide control officials use photos to indicate damage done by certain pests, as well as to help people recognize the effects of improperly applied pesticides on plants.

In successful smoking cessation guides targeting Spanish speakers in the United States, Latino readers consistently remembered an explicit photo showing a

## Hanford timeline

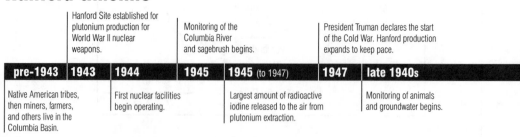

**FIGURE 14-5.** Timeline of dates and events. The timeline provided a historical context for explaining risks associated with a contaminated site.

(Source: Pacific Northwest Laboratory 1995.)

normal and a cancerous lung (Institutos Nacionales de la Salud e Instituto Nacional del Cáncer 2002). Readers told the booklet developers that the photo of the cancerous lung served as a powerful motivator to stop smoking by reminding them how bad smoking is for your health.

Another way to personalize risk information is to show people various conditions associated with the risk and how those might apply to specific individuals. One information booklet used the chart in Figure 14-6 to help people determine their own exposure to radiation from various sources. During pretesting, people consistently rated this chart as one of the most useful pieces in the booklet.

The University of Rochester used a similar personalized approach in its self-test for nicotine addiction, which appears in a smoking cessation guide (Figure 14-7). A score of five or higher indicates possible nicotine addiction.

A regional study funded by the U.S. Centers for Disease Control and Prevention used the "roadmap" in Figure 14-8 that people could follow to find their own radiation dose from past radiation releases, based on demographic and lifestyle factors. Once people identified "their" category, they could find their own radiation dose in the ranges given in a corresponding chart (Figure 14-9). People who viewed these graphics indicated that they were easy to follow and provided helpful information.

| Hanford nuclear production reaches its peak. Operations release large amounts of radioactive and chemical waste materials to soil, groundwater, and the Columbia River. | | Hanford's nuclear production facilities close down. | | A scientific study estimates radiation doses the public may have received as a result of past Hanford releases. | |
|---|---|---|---|---|---|
| **1955** (to 1965) | **1960** (to 1975) | **1964** (to 1989) | **1965** | **1987** (to 1990) | **1989** (to present) |
| | After leaks are discovered from single-shell tanks holding highly radioactive waste, the waste is evaporated or pumped into safer, new double-shell tanks. | | President Johnson announces a decreased national need for weapons materials. | | Health study begins to determine whether there is more thyroid disease than usual in people who lived downwind of Hanford in the 1940s and 1950s. The study is scheduled for completion in 1998. Hanford's new mission is cleanup and development of new technologies to support national needs. |

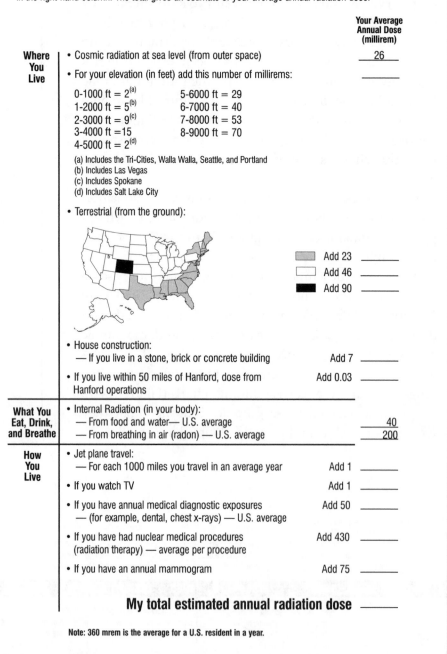

# What's My Radiation Dose?

Use this simple chart to see how much radiation exposure you receive each year. Fill in the numbers in the right-hand column. The total gives an estimate of your average annual radiation dose.

|  |  | Your Average Annual Dose (millirem) |
|---|---|---|
| **Where You Live** | • Cosmic radiation at sea level (from outer space) | 26 |
|  | • For your elevation (in feet) add this number of millirems: | _____ |

0-1000 ft = 2[a]          5-6000 ft = 29
1-2000 ft = 5[b]          6-7000 ft = 40
2-3000 ft = 9[c]          7-8000 ft = 53
3-4000 ft = 15             8-9000 ft = 70
4-5000 ft = 2[d]

(a) Includes the Tri-Cities, Walla Walla, Seattle, and Portland
(b) Includes Las Vegas
(c) Includes Spokane
(d) Includes Salt Lake City

• Terrestrial (from the ground):

Add 23 _____
Add 46 _____
Add 90 _____

• House construction:
— If you live in a stone, brick or concrete building          Add 7 _____

• If you live within 50 miles of Hanford, dose from          Add 0.03 _____
Hanford operations

**What You Eat, Drink, and Breathe**
• Internal Radiation (in your body):
— From food and water— U.S. average          40
— From breathing in air (radon) — U.S. average          200

**How You Live**
• Jet plane travel:
— For each 1000 miles you travel in an average year          Add 1 _____

• If you watch TV          Add 1 _____

• If you have annual medical diagnostic exposures          Add 50 _____
— (for example, dental, chest x-rays) — U.S. average

• If you have had nuclear medical procedures          Add 430 _____
(radiation therapy) — average per procedure

• If you have an annual mammogram          Add 75 _____

## My total estimated annual radiation dose _____

Note: 360 mrem is the average for a U.S. resident in a year.

**FIGURE 14-6.** Chart used to help people determine their own radiation dose from various sources.
(Source: Pacific Northwest Laboratory 1994.)

**Nicotine Addiction Self-Test**

Circle one answer for each question.

| |  |  |
|---|---|---|
| Do you usually smoke your first cigarette of the day within 30 minutes of waking up? | No | Yes |
| Do you find it hard not to smoke in places where it's not allowed, such as at the library, theatre or doctor's office? | No | Yes |
| Do you smoke 10 or more cigarettes per day? | No | Yes |
| Do you smoke 25 cigarettes per day? | No | Yes |
| Do you smoke more during the morning than during the rest of the day? | No | Yes |
| Do you smoke even when you are so ill that you are in bed most of the day? | No | Yes |

Give yourself one point for each question answered "Yes."
What was your total score? _____ points.

The higher your score, the higher your addiction level. If you scored five or higher, you may be highly addicted to the nicotine in cigarettes. Nicotine replacement therapy or Zyban® may be especially helpful for you.

**No matter how addicted you are, you *can* stop smoking!**

**FIGURE 14-7.** Nicotine addiction self-test.
(Source: University of Rochester 2001.)

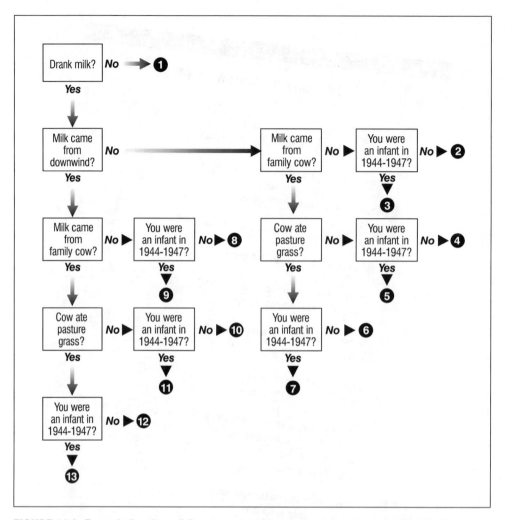

**FIGURE 14-8.** Example "roadmap." By answering the questions, people could identify the category into which they best fit, as indicated by numbered circles.

(Source: Technical Steering Panel 1990.)

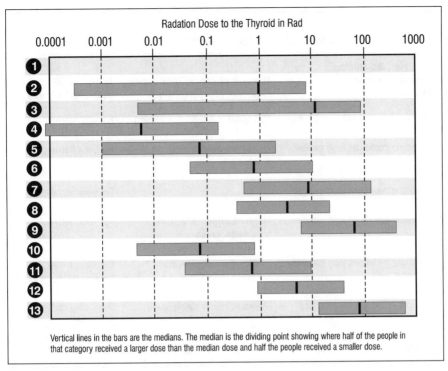

Radation Dose to the Thyroid in Rad

Vertical lines in the bars are the medians. The median is the dividing point showing where half of the people in that category received a larger dose than the median dose and half the people received a smaller dose.

**FIGURE 14-9.** Range of possible radiation doses by category. The numbers in the circles correspond to those in Figure 14-8.

(Source: Technical Steering Panel 1990.)

## COMPARING RISKS IN VISUAL FORMATS

Laypersons and experts often want to know how risks, especially unfamiliar ones, compare with a more common risk or with alternatives. Visuals can be used to compare magnitudes, effects, and alternatives on a common numeric scale, for example.

In one study, people appreciated seeing the health risks from geologic radon and asbestos compared with health risks from smoking (Weinstein et al. 1989). The subjects stated that the comparison helped them understand the data and reduced ambiguity about the risk. The authors noted that the comparison was appropriate because smoking increases the risks from both radon and asbestos.

Table 14-3 shows another way to depict radon risk for smokers by comparing it to other common hazards. The U.S. Environmental Protection Agency uses this table to

**TABLE 14-3**

Home Radon Risk for Smokers and Corresponding Recommendations

| Radon Level | If 1,000 people who smoked were exposed to this level over a lifetime . . . | The risk of cancer from radon exposure compares to . . . | WHAT TO DO: Stop Smoking and . . . |
|---|---|---|---|
| 20 pCi/L | About 135 people could get lung cancer | 100 times the risk of drowning | Fix your home |
| 10 pCi/L | About 71 people could get lung cancer | 100 times the risk of dying in a home fire | Fix your home |
| 8 pCi/L | About 57 people could get lung cancer | | Fix your home |
| 4 pCi/L | About 29 people could get lung cancer | 100 times the risk of dying in an airplane crash | Fix your home |
| 2 pCi/L | About 15 people could get lung cancer | 2 times the risk of dying in a car crash | Consider fixing between 2 and 4 pCi/L |
| 1.3 pCi/L | About 9 people could get lung cancer | (Average indoor radon level) | (Reducing radon levels below 2 pCi/L is |
| 0.4 pCi/L | About 3 people could get lung cancer | (Average indoor radon level) | difficult) |

(Source: U.S. Environmental Protection Agency et al. 1992.)

help citizens understand their risk of radon in the home and to recommend action. (An accompanying table, not shown here, depicts risks for the non-smoker.)

It is important to note that using comparisons to clarify risks can lead to confusion and outrage rather than illumination, as researchers and practitioners have discovered. Follow the advice in "Principles for Comparing Risks," in Chapter 6, "Principles of Risk Communication." And, as we have emphasized, the best foundation for making a decision about comparisons is to analyze your audience and pretest the information before disseminating it.

## DEPICTING PROBABILITY AND UNCERTAINTY

Risk communicators often struggle with how to present two particular characteristics of risks: probability and uncertainty. Deaths, disease, or injuries can happen at various levels or under various conditions.

*Probability* is how likely the event is to occur. An example of explaining probability is telling someone that they have a 1 in 10 chance of getting a certain kind of cancer in their lifetime. Identifying the probability that something will happen is often based on known and unknown factors. The known factors for predicting cancer occurrence could include age, gender, and smoking habits.

*Uncertainty* represents the factors about a hazard that are not completely known. For example, it is often impossible to say what caused a specific person to contract cancer because the disease may have been triggered by numerous factors, many of which medical science does not yet fully understand.

Research in how people respond to probabilities and uncertainties varies widely in its results, and some of the results conflict with each other. This conundrum is both frustrating and intriguing for those who must communicate such characteristics! Our approach here is to present some of the salient research results and suggest guidance that may be considered for various risk communication situations.

## Presenting Probability

In explaining probability, an odds ratio often is used, meaning a fraction with the numerator depicting the chance of something happening and the denominator depicting the total number of possibilities. For example, the odds ratio of 1/10 indicates that there is a 1 in 10 chance that a certain thing will happen.

Even if people understand the magnitude of the probability, there is no guarantee how they will respond. In genetic counseling, for example, some clients focus on the denominator of the odds ratio—the large number of people who do not get a negative genetic trait—and are reassured. But other clients focus on the numerator and are frightened by the image of that one person among the many who does suffer harm (Weinstein et al. 1994).

One study showed that people preferred probability estimates using human figures (Figure 14-10) rather than bar graphs (Figure 14-11) (Schapira et al. 2001). People said they could identify with human figures and that the

◇

*Probability* is how likely the event is to occur. *Uncertainty* represents the factors about a hazard that are not completely known.

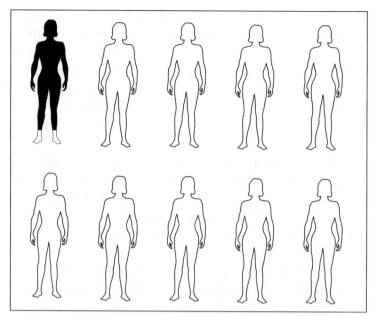

**FIGURE 14-10.** Human figures used in risk estimates. The highlighted female figure among a total of 10 represents the 9% lifetime risk of breast cancer for a 50-year-old woman. This depiction was preferred over the bar chart in Figure 14-11.

(Source: Schapira et al. 2001; used with permission.)

**FIGURE 14-11.** Risk estimate in bar graph format. This figure represents the same information in the previous figure, but in a different format.

(Source: Schapira et al. 2001; used with permission.)

information was more understandable and carried more impact than the bar graph. However, when comparing more than one kind of risk at the same time (cancer, heart disease, stroke), people preferred a vertical bar graph such as that shown in Figure 14-12.

One caution when using human figures such as in Figure 14-10 is not to cross out victims with the letter "X."

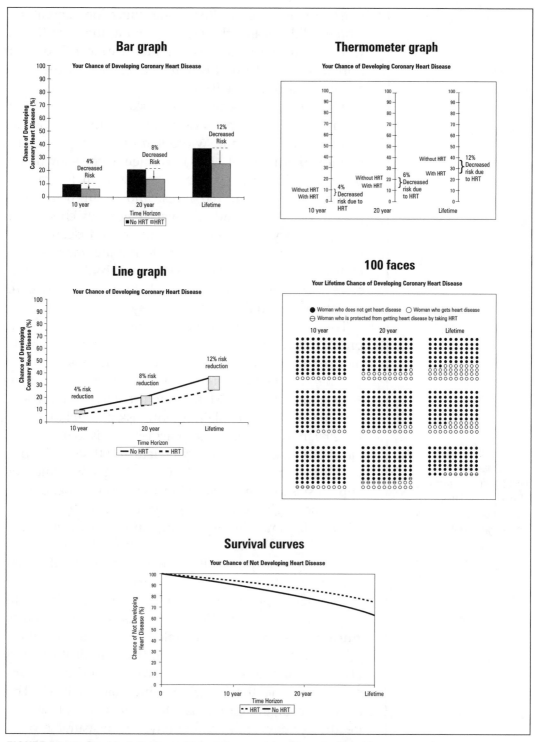

**FIGURE 14-12.** Graphical displays of heart disease risk with and without hormone replacement therapy. Women preferred the bar graph (first display) over the other formats.

(Source: Fortin et al. 2001; used with permission.)

In a study by the Duke Risk Communication Laboratory, women did not like the idea of having the stick figure women who were affected by breast cancer "x'd" out (Lipkus and Hollands 1999). It's better to color them in, as shown in Figure 14-10.

In another study, women were asked to choose among several graphical formats for communicating the risk of heart disease with and without hormone replacement therapy (Fortin et al. 2001). Women were shown the same risk information portrayed in bar graph, line graph, thermometer graph, 100 faces, and a survival curve (Figure 14-12). Respondents overwhelmingly choose the bar graph, saying it was basic, simple, and clearer than the other formats. They also preferred lifetime risk estimates over 10- or 20-year horizons and absolute over relative risks. And they wanted to see a narrative explanation with the graphic displays.

These studies suggest that for single estimates of risk probabilities, human figures may be best, with bar charts more effective for risk probability comparisons.

The Presidential/Congressional Commission on Risk Assessment and Risk Management (1997) suggests several approaches to explaining low-risk probabilities that have been found helpful in practice. One is to use analogies—one-in-a-million is equivalent to 30 seconds in a year, 1 inch in 16 miles, or 1 drop in 16 gallons. Another approach is to express risk in terms of the number of persons who might be affected per year or per hypothetical 70-year lifetime. In explaining and portraying these kinds of probabilities, it is important to clarify that the one-in-a-million probability is not an estimate of actual risk, but a statistical upper boundary.

Another approach for conveying probabilities is to convert units of population to periods per event, such as 1 death expected in 3,500 people. The city of Columbus, Ohio, did an analysis estimating that one death would occur in Columbus in 204 years from an additional cancer risk at the theoretical one-in-a-million level. The analysis compared that risk to frequencies of several deaths per day or every few days for measurable risks, such as ordinary rates of heart disease, cancer, homicide, and automobile collisions. The mayor of Columbus

---

◇

Human figures may be best for single estimates of risk probabilities, with bar charts more effective for risk probability comparisons.

---

stated that the analogy helps citizens understand the magnitude of the effects on the community caused by federal or state regulations concerning the environment, transportation, labor, or education (Presidential/Congressional Commission 1997). This approach is similar to the one portrayed in Table 14-3.

We have two cautions in showing probabilities. Despite these and other examples shown effective in practice, conflicting studies show that people respond differently to portrayal of risk probabilities than they do to other kinds of risk information (Schapira et al. 2001; Weinstein et al. 1994). Pretesting your information, as described in "Pretest Graphics with Those Who Will Use Them," will provide insights for the best approach. The second caution is to avoid attempting to influence people by downplaying or highlighting the magnitude of the risk. This is especially true in consensus communication efforts, where the goal is to present the risk as objectively as possible so people can evaluate it for themselves.

——— ◇ ———

Avoid attempting to influence people by downplaying or highlighting the magnitude of the risk.

## Presenting Uncertainty

Risk assessment is not an exact science, and as such carries with it many uncertainties. Uncertainty is often shown as a range of risk estimates or potential consequences, depending on various factors such as the demographics of the population at risk.

Unfortunately, people are unfamiliar with uncertainty in risk assessment and in science in general, making the job of the risk communicator all the more challenging. In one study, up to 20% of respondents reading news stories about risks had difficulty recognizing the presentation of uncertainty in the form of a range of risk estimates (Johnson and Slovic 1995), as opposed to a single number that represented the risk level. Again, pretesting various visual formats (and narratives) that reflect uncertainty should reveal any such confusion.

As with probabilities, the way the information is presented affects how people perceive it. Research has shown that people see risks with uncertainties as greater (1) if the risks are more ambiguous, (2) when the unfavorable risk evidence is presented last, (3) when the most unfavorable risk studies were performed most recently, and (4) when some aspect of the risk is substantially negative (Viscusi et al. 1991). Risk communicators should be aware of these factors when presenting uncertainty. The goal is not to present the uncertainty in the most favorable format to persuade people, but to present it as objectively as possible.

In dealing with uncertainty, risk managers and communicators also grapple with the issue of credibility. Acknowledging uncertainty has been shown to increase the perceived trustworthiness of the information sources (by admitting that they don't know the exact number) but less competent (they aren't smart enough to figure it out) (Johnson and Slovic 1995). One respondent, upon viewing uncertainty presentations hypothetically published by a U.S. government organization, labeled the agency "honest imbeciles"—a dubious distinction!

We agree with practitioners who advocate dealing with uncertainty head-on. It is best to acknowledge uncertainty; explain why it exists; describe what, if anything, can be done to get a better handle on it; and explain how the risk can be reduced in the mean time.

## Consider Using Action Levels

For crisis and care communication efforts, where it is prudent to take a specific action even when uncertainty exists, some specialists advise using an action standard. Table 14-3 shows an example of action standards, where recommendations corresponding to various radon levels are given. If the risk gets to that level, the reader is advised to take action.

A graphic called a risk ladder has been shown effective in explaining risks and recommending associated action levels. Risk ladders help people "anchor" a risk to upper- and lower-bound reference points. Including an action standard with the risks increases the likelihood that people will follow recommendations (Weinstein et al. 1989). Figure 14-13 shows a risk ladder conveying a range of radon risks and associated action levels.

Risk ladders help people anchor a risk to upper- and lower-bound reference points.

**Cancer Death from Lifetime Radon Exposure**

| **Radon Level** (pCi/L) | **Extra Cancer Deaths** (out of 1000 people) | **Equivalent Smoking Risk** | **Advice** |
|---|---|---|---|
| **100** | **500 in 1000** | 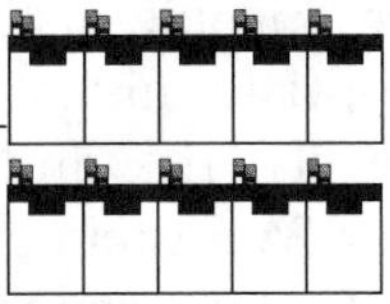 *10 packs per day* | **HIGH TO VERY HIGH RADON LEVELS** Measurements near the upper end of this range are much higher than the EPA action guideline. Exposure to such levels is very dangerous. For residents living in homes at the higher end of this range, action should be taken within the next couple weeks to substantially reduce their exposure. If prompt action is not possible or is not effective, they should consider moving until the radon levels are reduced. Exposure to levels at the lower end of the range is also unsafe. Residents living in homes at these levels should act to reduce the readings within the next couple of months. |
| **40** | **200 in 1000** | | |
| **20** | **100 in 1000** | 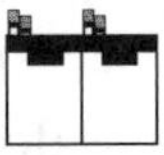 *2 packs per day* | **MODERATE TO HIGH RADON LEVELS** Measurements in this range are above the EPA action guideline. Exposure to these levels is a significant risk if it extends over many years. Residents should carefully evaluate the causes of their elevated levels and make plans to reduce the levels permanently. To minimize the cumulative risk, this permanent action should be completed in the next year or two. In the meantime, residents may want to avoid prolonged exposure to areas of the home where the levels are the highest. |
| **10** | **50 in 1000** | | |
| **4** | **20 in 1000** | 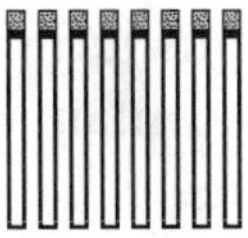 *8 cigarettes per day* | **At 4 pCi/L or above, EPA recommends that you reduce your radon level.** **LOW TO MODERATE RADON LEVELS** Measurements in this range fall below the EPA action guideline. Radon levels at the lower end of this range present a low health risk. Radon levels at the higher end of this range, extended over a lifetime, present a moderate health risk. Any plan to lower the levels should be carefully evaluated to be sure that it is likely to be effective, since it is often difficult to reduce levels below this range. Many authorities do not recommend trying to reduce levels in this range, especially for homes near the lower end. Residents who decide to try to reduce their levels below this range can take several years to act without adding significantly to their risk. |
| **2** | **10 in 1000** | | |
| **1** | **5 in 1000** | 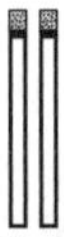 *8 cigarettes per day* | |
| **0.5** | **2.5 in 1000** | | **VERY LOW TO LOW RADON LEVELS** Measurements at this range are no higher than the outdoor "background" level in many areas. Exposure to these levels does not call for action. Even at these low levels, there is a small risk associated with lifetime exposure to radon. However, authorities agree efforts to reduce radon levels still further are likely to be expensive and ineffective. |
| **0.1** | **0.5 in 1000** | | |

**FIGURE 14-13.** Risk ladder about radon. Radon levels are compared with the number of extra cancer deaths and, for perspective, an equivalent number of cigarettes smoked. The "advice" column recommends associated action (or no action) levels.

(Source: Lipkus and Hollands 1999, page 152; used with permission of the author.)

This risk ladder communicates both risk magnitude, relative risk, an action standard (4 picocuries per liter), and advice about how to interpret the risk and what action to take, if any. Studies showed that the risk ladder in Figure 14-13 helped people distinguish among risk levels, identify appropriate mitigation intentions in accordance with their level of risk, and feel confident that they understand the risk (Weinstein et al. 1989).

One interesting finding was that people's perceptions of threat are influenced by the location of the risk on the ladder, more so than the numbers themselves (Sandman et al. 1994). Thus if the communication goal is to get people to pay attention to a risk that they may be apathetic about, placing a risk closer to the top of the ladder will increase perceived risk. A downside of risk ladders is that they may suggests a dichotomy, whereby people may feel that everything up to the action level is safe, and everything beyond it is dangerous. The actual situation is more often a continuum, and those who communicate risk should convey this. For example, the risk ladder in Figure 14-13, despite including an action level at 4 picocuries per liter, also contains explanations with the advice given at each stage.

## Cumulative Distribution Functions: The Potential for Misinterpretation

Some risks contain characteristics of both probability and uncertainty, such as the chance of a certain disease showing up over time in a given community near a toxic waste site. The chances that someone in the community will get cancer from exposure to the waste site may vary from small to large, with the most likely point on the range shown with a certain degree of confidence.

One statistical format that has been used to show this type of portrayal is called a cumulative distribution function, as shown in Figure 14-14. The horizontal axis depicts a range—it could be a range of exposures, potential health effects, or other type of data. The vertical axis depicts the percent of elements in the range that corresponds to a particular number in the range. For example, this figure shows that 50% of people received

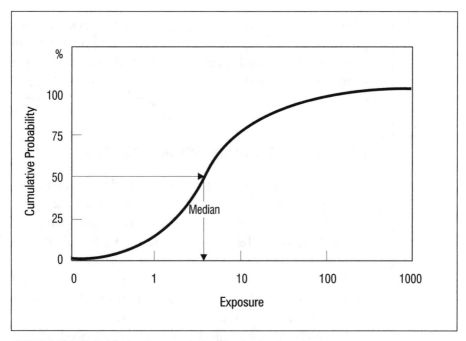

**FIGURE 14-14.** Example of a cumulative distribution function.

an exposure between 1 and 10 (units are not specified in this generic example).

Risk communicators should carefully consider and pretest such graphics to determine whether they add value or increase confusion. Ibrekk and Morgan (1987) found that cumulative distribution functions with no explanation were dramatically misinterpreted by laypeople. In cumulative distribution functions that used the statistical concept of a mean, people thought the mean was much higher than indicated on the graph and often misidentified the maximum as the mean.

The difficulty in communicating with the cumulative distribution function was corroborated in a multi-year environmental risk study funded by the U.S. Centers for Disease Control and Prevention (Technical Steering Panel 1990). Citizens typically did not use or refer to the data shown in cumulative distribution functions. Not one media outlet printed or aired that form of graphic, though it was provided to dozens internationally. Instead, many people focused on the highest (worst-case) number for the risk, regardless of the repeated emphasis of how unlikely it was and how few people were affected by it at that level. A more used portrayal was a series of ranges with the median risk levels within each range, as shown in Figure 14-9.

## ETHICAL PORTRAYAL OF RISK INFORMATION

Many risk communication experts feel that persuasive messages such as fear appeals are manipulative and that people should simply be given the facts and allowed to make their own decisions. Yet beyond being blatantly persuasive, risk information can be portrayed in ways that are arguably deceptive. Here, we focus on several ethical factors that risk communicators should consider when portraying visual aspects of risks.

Researchers have found that the format used to present statistical information influences people's perception of the likelihood of events (e.g., Britton 1991; Halpern et al. 1989). In his classic books describing the visual display of quantitative information, Yale University professor Edward Tufte describes how various design "tricks" are used to circumvent what he calls graphical integrity (Tufte 1983). Two of most common faults that risk communicators should be aware of are

- using pictorial representations that are out of proportion to the actual numerical quantities represented, especially when depicting increases or decreases

- using purely decorative design elements (which Tufte calls "chartjunk") that obscure the meaning of data.

Orcutt and Turner (1993) provided an interesting example of data manipulation in a health-related situation. They showed how major news magazines selectively used and displayed government survey data to manufacture a youth "cocaine epidemic" in the mid-1980s. Figure 14-15 shows an adapted version of the data and the treatment imposed by the news magazines.

---

The format used to present statistical information influences people's perception of the likelihood of events.

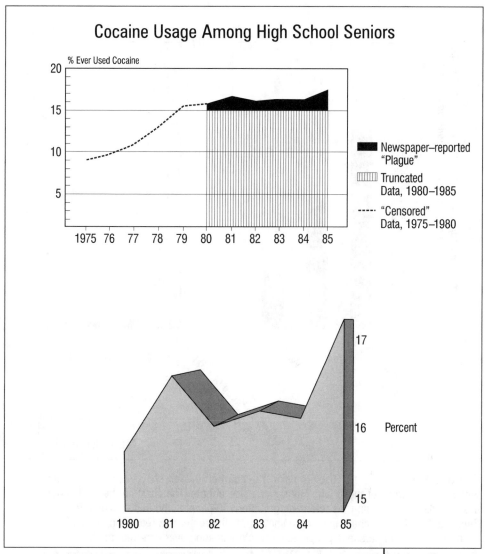

**FIGURE 14-15.** Deceptive use of data. The figure on the top shows the original data depicting a trend over time. The figure on the bottom shows how these data were improperly used to depict a different trend. Only certain data from the figure on top were used, and the scale was compressed to accentuate the peaks and thus "reveal" a cocaine "epidemic." (Source: Orcutt and Turner 1993.)

Another problem that can lead to data manipulation, especially when describing the effect of various medical treatments, is using different reference classes, or more specifically, using relative risks vs. absolute risks. Figure 14-16 shows these comparisons. The two charts both show the effect of treatment with aspirin and warfarin

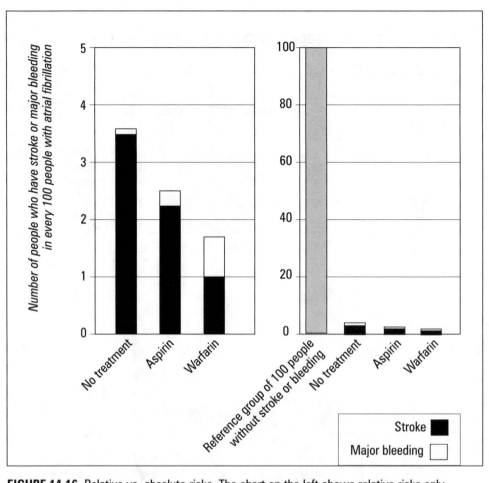

**FIGURE 14-16.** Relative vs. absolute risks. The chart on the left shows relative risks only within a small group of those who had serious side effects. The chart on the right shows absolute data by including the reference group of 100 people who had no side effects. Because the left-hand chart appears to show a much greater risk reduction, it could be used deceptively to persuade people to choose medication over non-treatment.

(Source: Gigerenzer and Edwards 2003; BMJ 327:741-744; reprinted with permission of the BMJ Publishing Group and the authors.)

(an anticoagulant) in patients with atrial fibrillation. The chart on the left shows only those who had a stroke or major bleeding as a result. It appears that aspirin and warfarin decreased the chance of having serious side effects by up to 50%, making it more likely that patients would choose to be treated with medication. In fact, pharmaceutical claims are all too often guilty of this kind of comparison because the risk reduction appears so significant.

The chart on the right, however, which includes the reference group of 100 people, gives a different perspective. It shows that, compared with the reference group of 100, only about 2% reduced their side effects by taking aspirin or warfarin. One could thus conclude that taking medication doesn't make much of a difference because most people in the reference group suffered no ill effects, whether they received treatment or not. In fact, many risk communication professionals advocate using absolute vs. relative risks because absolute risk is less misleading and allows people to make a more informed decision (Gigerenzer and Edwards 2003).

Beyond the deliberate misuse of graphics to manipulate, graphics can be used carelessly. This can lead to the obscuring of important information and, consequently, faulty and even tragic decisions. Edward Tufte makes a convincing argument that improperly designed pictorial displays linking O-ring damage and temperature failed to clearly convey the risk that led to the 1986 space shuttle *Challenger* explosion (Tufte 1997). As evidence, he shows a series of O-ring-related figures exemplifying lack of clarity in depicting cause and effect, improper ordering of data, and deceptive "chartjunk."

Tufte also blasts the misuse of PowerPoint® slides as a potential contributor to the *Columbia* space shuttle disaster in 2003. The National Aeronautics and Space Administration (NASA) used the slides, which summarized engineering studies about possible tile damage on the *Columbia*, as rationale not to investigate the tiles further during flight. Calling the slide presentations a "PowerPoint festival of bureaucratic hyperrationalism," Tufte says that the overwhelming levels of bulleted hierarchies, "grid prisons" surrounding spreadsheet entries, and the fact that the reasoning is broken up into "stupefying fragments" among many slides helped obscure what the data really showed—that the tile problem could indeed cause significant heat damage (Tufte 2003).

The lesson here is to realize that design can affect people's perception of the information being conveyed. If you feel that a certain graphic may be perceived differently as a result of various formats, pretest different variations of the graphic to determine to what extent the

———— ◇ ————

*"Information displays should serve the analytic purpose at hand; if the substantive matter is a possible cause-effect relationship, then graphs should organize data so as to illuminate such a link."*

—Edward R. Tufte, "Visual Explanations: Images and Quantities, Evidence and Narrative" (1997, page 49).

design affects audience perceptions. The goal is to design a graphic that presents risk-related information as clearly and objectively as possible. At the same time, the graphic form should portray factual information, such as measured quantities of contaminants, in ways that are consistently understood across your target audiences.

## USING VISUAL INFORMATION IN GROUP DECISION-MAKING

Showing risk information and alternatives visually can be a very powerful tool for consensus communication that involves group decision-making. For example, community members may be considering installing a dam on a local river. They may wish to visualize the potential effects of the dam on the local economy, recreational use, and fish spawning habits. Viewing these effects visually can provide a common foundation for members to discuss alternatives and tradeoffs.

Computer-assisted decision software systems also can be effective. With interactive computer graphics, such systems can show, sometimes in real time, the effects when certain factors are varied. For instance, using the example above, with proper input data the system could create a graph estimating the decrease or increase in the fish population with a new dam. It could chart the amount of electricity produced over time. It could show estimated costs and savings associated with and without the dam. (Chapter 18, "Technology-Assisted Communication," gives more information on using computers for consensus communication.)

One company specializing in environmental work has had some success with a user-friendly graphic interface that allows nonspecialists to see the workings of a risk assessment computer model. The interface shows the process by which the input (factors that influence the risk, such as lifestyle habits) affects the resulting risk assessment, and by how much.

## CHECKLIST FOR VISUAL REPRESENTATION OF RISK

In depicting risk-related information in visual formats,

❑ the target audiences and uses of graphics formats have been identified

❑ visuals have been designed to portray specific aspects of a risk

❑ visuals have been personalized to the extent possible

❑ visuals with quantitative elements remain true to the original data

❑ probability and uncertainty have been depicted appropriately

❑ graphics have been pretested and modified in response to comments.

## REFERENCES

Bord, R. J., and R. E. O'Connor. 1992. "Determinants of Risk Perceptions of a Hazardous Waste Site." *Risk Analysis*, 12:411-416.

Britton, R. L. 1991. *The Influence of Presentation Format on Interpretation of Paternity Test Results: Due Process or Deception?* Unpublished master's dissertation, University of California, Irvine.

Carnegie-Mellon University. 1995. *Fields from Electric Power*. Department of Engineering and Public Policy, Pittsburgh, Pennsylvania.

Fortin, J. M., L. K. Hirota, B. E. Bond, A. M. O'Connor, and N. F. Col. 2001. "Identifying Patient Preferences for Communicating Risk Estimates: A Descriptive Pilot Study." *BMC Medical Informatics and Decision Making*, 1:2. Online at http://www.biomedcentral.com/1472-6947/1/2.

Geiger, C. J., B. W. Wise, C. R. M. Parent, and R. G. Hanson. 1991. "Review of Nutrition Labeling Formats." *Journal of the American Dietetic Association*, 91(7): 808-815.

Gigerenzer, G. and A. Edwards. 2003. "Simple Tools for Understanding Risks: From Innumeracy to Insight." *BMJ*, 327:741-744

(September 27). Online at http://bmj.bmjjournals.com/cgi/content/full/327/7417/741#REF21.

Graber, D. 1990. "Seeing is Remembering: How Visuals Contribute to Learning from Television News." *Journal of Communication*, 40:134-155.

Griffin, R. J. 1999. "Using Systematic Thinking to Choose and Evaluate Evidence." In *Communicating Uncertainty: Media Coverage of New and Controversial Science*. pages 225 - 248. Editors S. M. Friedman, S. Dunwoody, and C. L. Rogers. Lawrence Erlbaum Associates, Mahwah, New Jersey.

Hager, P. J., and H. J. Scheiber. 1997. *Designing and Delivering Scientific, Technical, and Managerial Presentations*. John Wiley & Sons, Inc. New York.

Halpern, D. F., S. Blackman, and B. Salzman. 1989. "Using Statistical Risk Information to Assess Oral Contraceptive Safety." *Applied Cognitive Psychology*, 3:251-260.

Ibrekk, H. and M. G. Morgan. 1987. "Graphical Communication of Uncertain Quantities to Nontechnical People." *Risk Analysis*, 7:519-529.

Institutos Nacionales de la Salud e Instituto Nacional del Cáncer. 2002. *No Lo Deje Para Mañana, Deje De Fumar Hoy. Guía Para Dejar De Fumar*. Publicación de los NIH 02-3001.

Johnson, B. B., P. M. Sandman, and P. M. Miller. 1992. "Testing the Role of Technical Information in Public Risk Perception." *Risk – Issues in Health & Safety*, pages 341-364.

Johnson, B. B., and P. Slovic. 1995. "Presenting Uncertainty in Health Risk Assessment: Initial Studies of its Effects on Risk Perception and Trust." *Risk Analysis*, 15:485-494.

Lacerda, F. W. 1986. *Comparative Advantages of Graphic Versus Numeric Representation of Quantitative Data*. Unpublished doctoral dissertation, University of Virginia Polytechnic Institute and State University, Blacksburg, Virginia.

Lang, A. 1995. "Defining Audio/Video Redundancy from a Limited-Capacity Information Processing Perspective." *Communication Research*, 22:86-115.

Lipkus, I. M., and J. G. Hollands. 1999. "The Visual Communication of Risk." *Journal of the National Cancer Institute Monographs*, 25:149-163.

Mayer, R. E., W. Bove, A. Bryman, R. Mars, and L. Tapangco. 1996. "When Less is More: Meaningful Learning from Visual and Verbal Summaries of Science Textbook Lessons." *Journal of Educational Psychology*, 88:64-73.

Morgan, M. G., H. K. Florig, I. Nair, C. Cortes, K. Marsh, and K. Pavlosky. 1990. "Lay Understanding of Low-Frequency Electric and Magnetic Fields." *Bioelectromagnetics,* 11:313-335.

Orcutt, J. D., and J. B. Turner. 1993. "Shocking Numbers and Graphic Accounts: Quantified Images of Drug Problems in the Print Media." *Social Problems,* 40:190-206.

Pacific Northwest National Laboratory. 1994. *In Summary: Environmental Report 1993.* Prepared for the U.S. Department of Energy, Richland, Washington.

Pacific Northwest National Laboratory. 1995. *Hanford: Your Environment and Your Health.* Prepared for the U.S. Department of Energy, Richland, Washington.

Paivio, A. 1978. "Mental Comparisons Involving Abstract Attributes." *Memory and Cognition,* 6(3):199-208.

Presidential/Congressional Commission on Risk Assessment and Risk Management. 1997. *Risk Assessment and Risk Management in Regulatory Decision-Making.* Final Report, Volume 2, Washington, D.C.

Sandman, P. M., N. D. Weinstein, and P. Miller. 1994. "High Risk or Low: How Location on a 'Risk Ladder' Affects Perceived Risk." *Risk Analysis,* 14(1):35-45.

Schapira, M. M., A. B. Nattinger, and C. A. McHorney. 2001. "Frequency or Probability? A Qualitative Study of Risk Communication Formats Used in Health Care." *Medical Decision Making,* 21:459-467.

Shepard, R. N. 1967. "Recognition Memory for Words, Sentences, and Pictures." *Journal of Verbal Learning and Verbal Behavior,* 6:156-163.

Slovic, P. 1987. "Perception of Risk." *Science,* 236:280-285.

St. Clair, R. A. 1956. *Presenting School Safety Facts: A Format for Graphic Presentation of Accident Data in the Annual Safety Report.* Unpublished thesis, Stout State College, Menomonie, Wisconsin.

Technical Steering Panel. 1990. *Initial Hanford Radiation Dose Estimates.* Washington Department of Ecology, Office of Nuclear and Mixed Waste, Olympia, Washington.

Tufte, E. R. 1983. *The Visual Display of Quantitative Information.* Graphics Press, Cheshire, Connecticut.

Tufte, E. R. 1990. *Envisioning Information.* Graphics Press, Cheshire, Connecticut.

Tufte, E. R. 1997. *Visual Explanations: Images and Quantities, Evidence and Narrative.* Graphics Press, Cheshire, Connecticut.

Tufte, E. R. 2003. *The Cognitive Style of PowerPoint*. Graphics Press, Cheshire, Connecticut.

U.S. Environmental Protection Agency, U.S. Department of Health and Human Services, and U.S. Public Health Service. 1992. *A Citizen's Guide to Radon (Second Edition): The Guide to Protecting Yourself and Your Family from Radon*. U.S. Government Printing Office, Washington, D.C.

University of Rochester School of Medicine and Dentistry. 2001. *Clear Horizons: A Quit Smoking Guide Especially for Those 50 and Over*. The Smoking Research Program, James P. Wilmot Cancer Center and Department of Community and Preventive Medicine, Rochester, New York.

Viscusi, W. K., W. A. Magat, and J. Huber. 1991. "Communication of Ambiguous Risk Information." *Theory and Decision*, 31:159-173.

Wallack, L., L. Dorfman, D. Jernigan, and M. Themba. 1993. *Media Advocacy and Public Health: Power for Prevention*. Sage Publications, Newbury Park, California.

Weinstein, N. D., P. M. Sandman, and W. K. Hallman. 1994. "Testing a Visual Display to Explain Small Probabilities." *Risk Analysis*, 14:895-896.

Weinstein, N. D., P. M. Sandman, and N. E. Roberts. 1989. *Communicating Effectively About Risk Magnitudes*. EPA 230/08-89-064, U.S. Environmental Protection Agency, Office of Policy Planning and Evaluation, Washington, D.C.

## ADDITIONAL RESOURCES

Covello, V. T., P. M. Sandman, and P. Slovic. 1988. *Risk Communication, Risk Statistics, and Risk Comparisons: A Manual for Plant Managers*. Chemical Manufacturers Association, Washington, D.C.

Gray, Jr., J. G. 1986. *Strategies and Skills of Technical Presentations: A Guide for Professionals in Business and Industry*. Greenwood Press, Inc., Westport, Connecticut.

Maibach, E., and R. Parrot (Eds.). 1995. *Designing Health Messages: Approaches from Communication Theory and Public Health Practice*. Sage Publications, Newbury Park, California.

Raines, C. 1989. *Visual Aids in Business*. Crisp Publications, Inc., Ontario, Canada.

Sandman, P. M., and N. D. Weinstein. 1994. *Communicating Effectively About Risk Magnitudes: Bottom Line Conclusions and Recommendations for Practitioners*. EPA-230-R-94-902, U.S. Environmental Protection Agency, Washington, D.C.

# Face-to-Face
# Communication

*A*nother way to communicate risk is face-to-face through some form of oral presentation. Face-to-face communication includes a wide range of activities such as:

- one-to-one interactions (health care professional to patient, employee to employee, peer to peer, neighbor to neighbor)

- small group settings (speaking before clubs, societies, organizations)

- speakers bureaus

- facility tours

- demonstrations of activities related to preventing, analyzing, or monitoring risk

- video presentations

- audience interviews to elicit concerns or perceptions

- information fairs

- large formal learning situations (grade school to college courses, continuing education courses, training seminars).

In this book, we differentiate face-to-face communication from stakeholder participation in that usually only one of the groups involved (either those who are communicating risk or the audience at risk) does most if not all of the talking (one-way communication). Formal hearings and other kinds of group interactions involving two-way communication are described in Chapter 17, "Stakeholder Participation."

The advantages and disadvantages of using face-to-face communication are discussed in Chapter 10, "Determine the Appropriate Methods." This chapter discusses specific aspects of constructing face-to-face messages, focusing on issues specific to risk communication, and provides guidelines for specific types of face-to-face risk communication activities.

## CONSTRUCTING FACE-TO-FACE MESSAGES

Many people have learned about effective ways to speak or listen to their audiences in face-to-face interactions, perhaps through such organizations as the Toastmasters International. However, for risk communication, a few points should be emphasized. Key to these points is the choice of who will lead the face-to-face interaction.

### Choose the Appropriate Spokesperson

Whether the audience will be doing most of the talking (as in an audience interview) or the organization's speaker will be doing most of the talking, those who are communicating risk have several choices as to who will lead the effort. Sometimes those in charge of the risk communication program will be the spokespeople for their organization. In other cases, other managers or experts will represent the organization. In still other cases, those outside the organization will speak to the issue. How do you know when to choose a spokesperson and which kind to choose? The two key criteria in choosing a spokesperson are audience acceptability and organizational acceptability.

## Audience Acceptability

A number of factors affect whether your audience will find the spokesperson acceptable. Will they find the person credible—that is, will they believe what the person has to say? Credibility has to do with credentials related to the risk (does the person have an advanced degree in the subject matter or many years' experience in the field?), the audience's past experience with the person or organization doing the communicating (do they trust anyone from that organization?), and the speakers ability to demonstrate a caring attitude. Credibility is important regardless of whether the audience or the spokesperson will be doing most of the talking. (See Chapter 5 for additional information on choosing a spokesperson.)

Is the person able to respond to their concerns? This issue is particularly important in settings where the audience will be able to ask questions. If their concerns are largely technical, a scientist or engineer is best. If they have management concerns, a manager with accountability for decision-making is best. Using multiple experts can be effective if the room is arranged to allow them to interact with each other and the audience (for example, by sitting at curved or circular tables) and the experts are responsive to each other. However, this approach can fail if audiences see it as the organization's attempt to "gang up on them" or perceive that the experts are arguing with each other.

Can the person speak in a way the audience will find acceptable? As noted below in the guidelines section, the most appropriate leader of the interaction (regardless of who will be doing most of the speaking) will be one who can speak in the language of the audience. This ability includes the ability to speak in languages other than English if that is preferred by the audience as well as the ability to find innovative ways to describe highly technical information. In addition, the spokesperson should be cognizant of nonverbal communication—for example, his or her stance, hand movements, and facial expressions. This body language can be just as important to acceptability as content and delivery of the speech. For example, Vince Covello, renowned risk communication researcher and consultant, recommends that in risk communication situations in which there is low trust in the communicating organization and high concern over the risk that speakers refrain from nodding their heads while listening to audience concerns. Instead of being perceived as active listening, this behavior is often perceived by concerned audiences as agreeing with an accusation. The spokesperson must be aware of these subtle clues to be effective in communicating risk information.

From an audience's perspective, then, the best spokesperson is one who is credible, responsive to concerns, and a believable speaker.

### Organizational Acceptability

A number of factors also affect whether your organization finds the person an acceptable representative. For cases in which the audience will be doing most of the talking, is the person a good listener? Can that person sit still and note concerns even when these concerns seem to contradict scientific precepts or organizational requirements? For cases in which the spokesperson will be doing most of the talking, is the person able to make speeches? Has the person been trained in public speaking, specifically in media relations and answering tough questions? Can the person speak earnestly? Most importantly from the organizational perspective, does the person understand the organization's rules and philosophy as well as the work that is being done in connection with the risk? Depending on your organization, a host of other factors may also affect the decision. Check with management and the public affairs office of your organization before making a choice.

### Finding the Right Person

Once you know what criteria your spokesperson must meet, there are a number of places you can find your spokesperson. You can choose health care professionals; recognized experts in the field, either inside or outside your organization; risk managers; line managers; public affairs staff; or celebrities. Each group has its own benefits and liabilities.

Health care professionals can be extremely credible to the audience and can usually be responsive to technical concerns related to health and some environmental risks, although some see environmental risks in much the same way as do their patients. For example, risk researchers found in a large-scale study at several major cities across the United States that physicians were the most trusted source of chemical risk information (McCallum et al. 1991). In addition, unless health care professionals are concerned with the risk themselves, either by being associated with the organization or seeing the effects of the risk among their patients, these professionals may find themselves too busy to represent your organization. Their busy schedules especially conflict in the case of activities that require frequent interactions (such as audience interviews) or a long-term commitment (such as being the lead speaker for a speakers bureau).

Experts inside the organization will understand the risk and the organization, but may not be credible to the audience. Experts outside the organization will probably be credible and will understand the risk but, like the health care professionals, they may be too busy or too costly to represent your organization. Also, the very act of your employing them may make them less credible in your audience's eyes. In addition, they may not understand organizational concerns.

Risk and line managers understand the risk and the organization. They will be able to address at least some of the audience's concerns. However, they may not be credible to the audience. For situations in which the audience will be doing most of the talking (such as audience interviews), they may be unable to separate themselves from the risk assessment process or organizational needs to listen without trying to correct misperceptions.

Public affairs staff will understand organizational concerns and, depending on the person and the level of technical understanding, may be able to discuss the scientific aspects of the risk. However, in many cases, they will have no credibility in the eyes of a hostile audience because of the unfortunate stereotype of the public affairs person as the manipulative Madison Avenue type. The expertise of public affairs staff in making speeches is

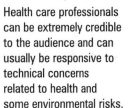

Health care professionals can be extremely credible to the audience and can usually be responsive to technical concerns related to health and some environmental risks.

often best used to facilitate meetings and presentations, and to coach speakers.

Celebrity spokespersons have been used in care communication situations as well as to lobby for a certain constituency in consensus communication. Celebrities generally neither understand the organization nor the risk; they are not particularly credible with the audience, unless they can make some claim to have experienced the risk first hand. If they do not have such a motivation as having experienced the risk (and hence are willing to donate their time to promote its prevention or mitigation), they can be very expensive to hire. However, their high-visibility position can serve to create awareness of a particular risk and even perhaps to motivate an audience to action. A prime example of this power is the highly successful campaign to stop smoking that featured the late Yul Brenner, star of stage and screen, in a television public service announcement in which he discussed how smoking had in fact shortened his illustrious career and his life.

Table 5-3 in Chapter 5, "Ethical Issues," provides additional information on choosing the appropriate spokesperson.

### Give the Audience Something to Take Away

One of the drawbacks of face-to-face communication is that, unless the members of your audience are good at taking notes, they will have nothing to take away from the presentation to help them remember key points. Even though some people learn by listening, most need visual reinforcement. Unless you reinforce the presentation with written materials such as fact sheets (one-page handouts that emphasize key points), the audience may not take away, or retain, the information you intended.

### Reinforce Your Message with Visual Aids

Whenever possible, include visual aids as part of the face-to-face interaction. These visuals must be readable from the back of the room in group settings and readable at arm's length for more intimate settings. Regardless of

---

◇

Unless you reinforce the presentation with written materials such as fact sheets (one-page handouts that emphasize key points), the audience may not take away, or retain, the information you intended.

---

an expert design, creative use of color, and clever wording, your visuals are useless if they must be prefaced by the apology, "Now, I know you probably can't see this, but what it shows is . . . ". Use words or short phrases to emphasize key points and show the audience how concepts fit together. Use photographs, drawings, and graphs to further illustrate key ideas. See Chapter 14 for additional information on using pictorial representations of risk.

◇ Whenever possible, include visual aids as part of the face-to-face interaction.

## Speak in the Language of the Audience

The speaker should use words and phrases that the audience will understand. At a public meeting held concerning the siting of a proposed wind energy farm, the spokesperson for the organization proposing the farm had obviously gone to great trouble to develop slides and an oral presentation that would present the facts to his audience. Unfortunately, when it came to describing the design of the farm, a factor that concerned audience members, he described heights and distances in "rotor diameters." In one of his opening remarks, he had stated that a rotor diameter was so many feet; however, it was rather unrealistic to expect that his audience (1) would have taken note of that fact, which concerned a foreign concept to begin with; (2) would remember the fact until he began using it again; and (3) would be able to do the math in their heads. It would have been far simpler for everyone if he had given the distances in feet. As it was, his audience became more and more hostile with each mention of the term, until it became obvious to even the spokesperson that many of them were no longer listening.

Whenever possible, the speaker should speak in the language of the audience. If the audience speaks a non-standard English, however, by all means have the speaker use standard English. Your message will not be credible if they feel you are trying to speak down to them. If English is not the audience's main language, as is the case in many Hispanic neighborhoods, for example, find a spokesperson (yourself or someone else who is credible) who can speak in the primary language.

## Don't Promise What You Can't Deliver

When you as a speaker get a question from your audience that you can't answer, offer to get back to them with an answer only if you can realistically find that answer. Too often speakers promise information that they won't be able to find in a timely manner or that they forget is classified or proprietary. As you try to respond to your audience, it's easy to promise to give information, knowing that you personally probably won't be held to task later by the often unknown audience member. However, that audience member will remember the lapse and let others know that your organization failed to live up to a promise, eroding your credibility. If you do make a promise for information, find out how to contact the person who wanted the information and make it a point to get back to them within one or two days.

Be careful, too, that you don't promise something that your organization is unable to give. For example, if the request from the audience is to hold more public meetings, and you gladly agree without checking whether your organization has the time or resources needed, you may not be able to keep your promise. Breaking such promises, as you can imagine, is a sure way to increase audience hostility toward the organization and erode credibility.

## GUIDELINES FOR SPECIFIC TYPES OF FACE-TO-FACE COMMUNICATION

The following information is provided for specific types of face-to-face risk communication activities.

### Speaking Engagements

Speaking engagements are one of the most common forms of face-to-face risk communication. To ensure that the audience understands the message being delivered, consider the following guidelines:

- Coach staff with little speaking experience—sometimes the spokesperson who will best meet both audience and organizational needs happens to have with little or no speaking experience. Such people need coaching to be effective. Simply writing a script for them generally doesn't work. Those words came from someone else, and the neophyte speaker will probably not be comfortable with them. In addition, repeating someone else's ideas won't help them when they get unanticipated questions from the audience. It is therefore best to train the spokesperson in how to be an effective speaker. Courses like those offered by the Dale Carnegie Foundation or Toastmasters can be extremely helpful in getting novice speakers over the fear of facing an audience. In-house courses offered by knowledgeable communicators are also helpful, because they can be tailored to specific situations and organizational needs. The speaker should also be prepared with information on how to deal with hostile audiences, working with the news media if that is expected, and the basic principles of risk communication.

- Practice the presentation—even an experienced speaker should practice the presentation if at all possible. Use similar lighting, acoustics, and room size. Include in the practice audience people who will listen for technical details, audience concerns, and legal issues. Have the practice audience listen for content, and watch body language. One speaker had a tendency to push up his glasses with his middle finger while speaking. When he was told to practice in front of a mirror, he saw the gesture and easily remembered not to use it, for fear of offending his audience.

- Practice answering questions as well—using the information you gleaned from the audience analysis, anticipate what questions might be raised. Answer as many questions as possible in the presentation itself. If the audience might want additional details, develop appropriate answers and have them ready if the audience asks for them. Have the practice au-

---

◇

Speaking engagements are one of the most common forms of face-to-face risk communication.

---

dience ask questions. Practice too dealing with hostility and the news media (see Chapter 16).

- Strive for an accessible, comfortable setting—these points are particularly important to the credibility of a risk communication presentation. The setting or place of the face-to-face interaction should be accessible to the audience and comfortable for them. By comfortable, we don't mean that the seats should be soft and have plenty of leg room, although this is always nice. Rather, we mean that the setting should be in a neutral location, one that doesn't evoke negative feelings. For example, a federal agency near our home holds all its public meetings in its own auditorium, which is a nice facility with good lighting and fairly comfortable seats. However, the facility can be used in only one configuration—raised stage at one end and theater-style seating that encourages an "us versus them" perception. This design, and the fact that the agency often comes under fire for its decisions at these meetings, make other facilities more appropriate.

- Dress to suit the setting—for a formal presentation before the city's business leaders, a business suit would be appropriate. For a speech at a lodge picnic, more casual attire is warranted. Speakers should not try to dress exactly like the audience unless it is the way he or she normally dresses. Audiences generally react more favorably to speakers who are being genuine than to ones who are attempting to be something they are not.

- Consider acoustics and lighting—make sure that the acoustics and lighting are adequate for the kind of presentation planned. Make sure the speaker can be heard to the back of the audience. If the speaker will need a microphone, make sure that he or she knows how to use it and has the controls within reach. If the speaker is using overhead transparencies or projected slides as visual aids, make sure the lights can be dimmed so that the audience can see them and still see each other and the speaker. A completely darkened room can be a safety hazard and can also encourage some members of the audience to fall asleep. Also make sure that the speaker or an associate can reach the dimmer switch in mid-presentation if need be. That way, the lighting can be easily increased to see where a question is coming from.

- Know your equipment—for slides, transparencies, a flip chart, or any other kind of visual aid, make sure that the speaker knows the location of any associated equipment and how to make it work. Bring spare parts such as light bulbs and extension cords. That way you can help ensure that the presentation will go on despite possible problems with equipment. Also make sure that someone is available who knows how to work the heating, ventilation, and air conditioning system. Tempers in even the most moderate audience will flare if the room is too hot or too cold.

## Speakers Bureaus

Instead of waiting to be asked to make presentations, many organizations in charge of risk communication efforts have developed a speakers bureau, a group of speakers known for their expertise in a given subject who can be contacted to give free or low-cost speeches for local communities and organizations. The speakers can all belong to a given organization, or they may be experts the organization has contracted to provide the service. When developing a speakers bureau for the purpose of communicating about risks:

- Choose speakers who will be credible with a wide range of potential audiences—the experts in your bureau must be able to speak before virtually any stakeholder group who might request a presentation. Therefore, it is necessary to select speakers who will be credible to the widest possible audience. Depending on your audience's needs, such speakers might include health care professionals, scientists, engineers, regulators, risk managers, or college or university staff.

◇

Instead of waiting to be asked to make presentations, many organizations in charge of risk communication efforts have developed a speakers bureau, a group of speakers known for their expertise in a given subject who can be contacted to give free or low-cost speeches for local communities and organizations.

- Ensure that the speakers have been appropriately trained—the speakers who make up the bureau will by necessity be experts in their fields. They will, however, most likely need additional training in appropriate risk communication principles and techniques as well as the risk communication effort they are supporting.

- If possible, develop consistent materials to support their presentations—as with the speaking engagement described above, ensure that your speakers go out armed with appropriate information materials to leave with their audiences and that their visual aids are appropriate to the situation. If, however, your intended audience is highly hostile to the organization in charge of communicating the risk, avoid providing materials that publicize the organization. Your speakers may be more credible, and the risk message will be more likely to be received, if there is some perceived distance between the speaker and the organization.

## Tours and Demonstrations

Tours and demonstrations are another way to communicate risk in face-to-face interactions. In a tour, some segment of the audience is invited to view a facility or site that is perceived as contributing to a risk. In a demonstration, the audience views or participates in an activity designed to assess, prevent, monitor, or mitigate a risk. Regardless of the form, several guidelines can be applied:

Tours and demonstrations are another way to communicate risk in face-to-face interactions. In a tour, some segment of the audience is invited to view a facility or site that is perceived as contributing to a risk.

- Make sure tours and demonstrations are open. Don't exclude some segment of your audience. Hold the tours and demonstrations at times when it is possible for the audience to attend. For example, if many members of your audience work full time, plan the tour or demonstration before or after their work hours or on weekends.

- Make sure tours and demonstrations are easily accessible to all members of your audience. For example, have wheelchairs and make sure elevators are available to take them between floors. Have someone fluent in sign language available to assist the hearing impaired. Make sure people know in advance what kind of footwear and/or clothing to wear if that is important. For example, walking over rough terrain can be difficult in the high heels some women might wear to a tour unless prewarned. Tell your audience how much walking is involved and in what kind of situations so they can be prepared.

- Be as careful choosing a tour or demonstration leader as you would someone who was giving an oral presentation. Make sure the person is acceptable to both your audience and your organization, can answer audience concerns and questions, and is able to speak at your audience's level.

- Determine what you hope to gain by the tour. Are you trying to persuade your audience that what you are doing is perfectly safe? (See Chapter 5, "Ethical Issues," for the dangers in using persuasion.) Are you trying to raise awareness of an issue? Are you trying to give your audience information on which to base some decision? Make sure that the tour or demonstration reinforces the purpose and doesn't detract from it.

- Consider organizational and audience needs. Make sure that what you are going to show your audience doesn't compromise proprietary or classified information and that the information you are presenting meets your audience's needs. For example, if what your audience really wants to know is how your organization trains its workers, showing them the beautifully landscaped grounds won't meet their needs and may make them angry. A manager at a hazardous waste incinerator took the local garden club on a tour of the plant. One of the women asked him just how dangerous the smoke she saw coming out of a stack was to breathe. The manager, acting in an unfortunately patronizing fashion, told her not to worry about it, that it was no more dangerous than eating a peanut butter sandwich. She hit him with her purse. Consider your audience carefully, listen to their questions, probe for underlying concerns, and answer questions honestly and courteously.

- Practice the tour and demonstration. Practice what the tour leader will say and how the tour or demonstration will be given. Have the practice audience listen as outsiders would. Sometimes concepts that seem clear from within the organization can seem foreign or can be totally misconstrued by your audience. A chemical manufacturing plant had been criticized for failing to take safety issues seriously, despite an excellent safety record, well-documented and applied procedures, and a well-trained workforce. Managers opened the plant to a particularly vocal activist group and carefully explained all the precautions that had been taken. After the tour, the leader of the activist group reported to the press waiting outside the gates, "Well, now we know there's something really unsafe—look at all the attention they're paying to safety!" Analyze your audience carefully in developing your tour or demonstration.

### Video Presentations

Video combines many of the features of information materials and face-to-face communication. It can be used in a variety of situations such as formal learning environments or in-home study. A video can carry more information than some other more visual forms of risk communication such as posters or displays, but the narration of the video adds a dimension of human contact not unlike an oral presentation. Therefore, the content of a video should follow the general guidelines for constructing information materials. The delivery, as in the spokesperson and visual aids, in the video should follow the general guidelines for constructing face-to-face messages.

Videos can be expensive to produce—up to several thousand dollars per minute of finished footage for high-end productions. Therefore, you should have a very specific purpose for the video that can't be accomplished otherwise (for example, depicting a hazardous situation that would be unsafe to show people directly). This reason should include movement; if you don't need to show movement, you can get a similar affect through a presentation with still photography.

Give your video as long a shelf life as possible by writing the script in ways that don't make your content out of date next week. Focus on longer-term, enduring issues related to your risk so that the video can be used in a variety of situations.

Use experienced script writers and videographers. Remember that videos are like television—audiences focus more on (and remember) what is shown than what is said. Make the script and visuals flow together for greater impact.

For successful risk communication videos, always consider the needs of your audience:

- How will the video be distributed? Other types of information materials like pamphlets and newsletters can be easily mailed or handed out at information fairs. The relatively higher costs of producing videos (often up to $10 per copy) generally make mass distribution infeasible. The exception may be when video is used as part of a CD or Internet presentation. Make sure you have a ready distribution network, such as through health care professionals, the school system, or a professional organization, before developing a video.

- Where will the video be shown? Just as important as distribution is the setting in which the video will be shown. If the video will be used as part of a formal learning environment (public school system, college, organization training course), it will need to complement other materials and information such as learning objectives, student workbooks, and tests. If the video will be shown as part of an oral presentation, the speech and other materials should likewise be complementary. If the video will be shown in a home environment, on the other hand, it will need to be more self-contained and more comprehensive.

- Will there be a spokesperson present to answer questions? The chief disadvantage of a video as a form of face-to-face communication is that, unless a spokesperson is present at the showing, there is no opportunity for the audience to ask questions. If the video will always be used with a spokesperson present, it may not have to be as comprehensive as a video that will be used without a spokesperson present.

One other factor to consider in video production particularly is the quality of the video. Again, consider your audience. While high-caliber video production companies are generally available to produce videos that rival some of Hollywood's most impressive films in the areas of special effects and acting ability, such a high-gloss production may in fact alienate some audiences, particularly those who might be hostile to the organization producing the video. Such audiences will see a high-quality video production as a Madison Avenue cover-up. Also, some audiences still equate videos with high price tags, although in fact the price has fallen considerably with the advances in technology. Such audiences will also be alienated by high-end video, especially when produced by a government organization with taxpayer funding. In these cases, it may be better to opt for a more simple production or to use another method to communicate about risk.

### Audience Interviews

Interviewing the audience to understand their concerns and perceptions can be an effective form of face-to-face interaction in that it provides those who are communicating risk the opportunity to better understand their audience and it provides the audience with the opportunity to share their concerns. Audience interviews can be a particularly effective way to begin consensus communication efforts.

An audience interview is similar to conducting a survey, but the questions should be more open-ended. For example, a survey question concerning the audience's perception of home pesticide use might ask the person to rank pest control methods against others on a quantitative scale. In an audience interview, the spokesperson for the organization communicating risk might simply re-

Interviewing the audience to understand their concerns and perceptions can be an effective form of face-to-face interaction in that it provides those who are communicating risk the opportunity to better understand their audience and it provides the audience with the opportunity to share their concerns.

quest, "Tell me how you control pests." Like surveys, however, the order of the questions, and the manner in which they are asked, will have a profound effect on the answers given. In general, move from the general to the specific, from topics that are positive or neutral in perception to those that are more likely to be received with hostility or some other negative reaction.

Other guidelines on audience interviews include the following:

- Be inclusive—try to ensure that you are interviewing the full range of your audience. One way to do this is to start with a known list of possible interviewees and, as the final question in each interview, ask if there is anyone else who should be interviewed. The first few interviews will provide a wealth of new names, but gradually you will begin to see the same names coming up again and again. This is a sign that you've reached a good majority of your intended audience. Another approach is to use focus groups (see Chapter 17 for additional information).

- Make your audience comfortable—make sure the place for the interview is one that is comfortable for each interviewee. It is usually best to conduct each interview separately, in the interviewee's home or location of their choice. Dress casually, but professionally. Let them do most of the talking.

- Explain the process before starting the interview—help them understand why you are conducting the interview, how the results will be used, and how they will know that their concerns have been heard. Ask permission before audiotaping, taking notes, or otherwise recording the information from the interview. If possible, give them the opportunity to see and correct anything you record regarding their concerns or perceptions.

- Consider carefully before correcting apparent misconceptions or misperceptions—it can be very tempting to jump in and correct a misconception or argue over a perception, particularly in cases in which the interviewee is clearly upset about the issue. Correcting the person you're talking with after they make a statement may anger or embarrass them. Either way, they may not want to speak candidly. They may even want to stop the interview. In addition, such correction can be a form of persuasion. Review the information in Chapter 5, "Ethical Issues," on the use of persuasion before interviews and decide how you will handle such situations should they arise.

## Information Fairs

An information fair is a grouping of tables or booths staffed by organizations charged with communicating a particular risk or set of risks. Those interested in the risk can circulate through the fair and choose to talk to or select information materials from various organizations of interest to them. These organizations may also put on demonstrations of how risks can be prevented, analyzed, or monitored. The fair can be for employees of a given organization (for safety and health care communication) or for a local community (for environmental, safety, or health care communication or the planning stages of crisis communication). The fair can also be used to provide information to start a consensus communication effort.

Information fairs are another hybrid of information material and face-to-face interaction. Use the guidelines on information materials in Chapter 13, and the guidelines in this chapter on selecting the appropriate spokesperson and tours and demonstrations to ensure successful fairs.

## Training

As mentioned in Chapter 3, "Laws That Mandate Risk Communication," the Occupational Safety and Health Act requires that employees be trained in the use of hazardous materials associated with their jobs. Training can also be used to teach concepts related to other forms of risk and to build a crisis response unit.

Developing effective training materials is a science unto itself. The primary considerations are the audience, the purpose of the training, and the resources available, including time. For example, the type of presentation and amount of material you can cover will differ greatly between the training of a group of clerical staff on ergonomic issues in the office at a 1-hour lunch meeting and the training of a group of firefighters on hazardous materials in the community at a week-long retreat. In general, consider these guidelines:

- Visual is always better than oral and hands-on is always better than visual—there is an old teaching adage, "I hear and I forget, I see and I remember, I do and I understand." Given audience, purpose, and resource constraints, try to provide opportunities for those being trained to experience the risk in question. For example, one instructor of basic radiation safety at a nuclear facility brings in a variety of items such as a smoke detector, gas lantern mantle, and pottery as well as a radiation detector to allow his students the chance to determine for themselves what is radioactive in their world.

- Focus your training—articulate clearly what you want the students to gain from attending the training and how you will provide that information. Too often, training related to preventing, managing, analyzing, or monitoring a risk fails because the content of the course is too broad. Better to ensure your students learn a few key concepts than to try to cram the equivalent of an advanced degree into a week-long course.

- Don't attempt training for a hostile audience—if your intended audience is highly hostile toward the organization in charge of communicating the risk or the risk in general, training is not your best option to communicate risk. Start by understanding and dealing with the source of the hostility.

Chapter 18 has additional information on computer-based training.

> Developing effective training materials is a science unto itself. The primary considerations are the audience, the purpose of the training, and the resources available, including time.

## CHECKLIST FOR FACE-TO-FACE COMMUNICATION

The spokesperson communicating the risk or leading the interaction:

- ❏ is acceptable to both the audience and organization
- ❏ has written material that the audience can take away to supplement the oral presentation
- ❏ has visuals that are easy for the audience to read and understand
- ❏ speaks in the language of the audience
- ❏ won't promise information or changes in policy unless these can be delivered
- ❏ has been coached if inexperienced
- ❏ has practiced
    - ❏ the presentation
    - ❏ answering questions
    - ❏ dealing with the media
    - ❏ dealing with hostility in the audience
- ❏ will be presenting in a neutral setting
- ❏ is dressed appropriately for the setting
- ❏ can be heard to the back of the audience
- ❏ knows how to work the microphone
- ❏ can reach the dimmer switch if needed
- ❏ knows how to work the visual aid equipment and has spare parts in case they are needed
- ❏ knows who to contact to run the heating, ventilation, and air conditioning system.

The organization's speakers bureau:

- ❏ uses speakers who are credible with the audience
- ❏ has trained speakers in risk communication
- ❏ is armed with consistent messages.

Tours and demonstrations:

- ❏ are scheduled at convenient times for the audience
- ❏ are accessible to the audience
- ❏ have appropriate spokespersons
- ❏ have clear goals
- ❏ consider audience and organization needs
- ❏ have been practiced.

Video presentations:

- ❏ follow general guidelines for information materials as well as selecting spokespersons
- ❏ have known distribution networks to reach the audience
- ❏ have supplemental materials to support the setting in which they will be shown
- ❏ are comprehensive enough to stand on their own should a spokesperson be absent at showing
- ❏ have quality appropriate to meet audience expectations.

Audience interviews:

- ❏ cover a wide range of audience perspectives
- ❏ are held in settings comfortable for the audience
- ❏ begin with an explanation of process
- ❏ start with a consideration of how to deal with misperceptions or inaccuracies.

Information fairs:

- ❏ follow the general guidelines for information materials and choice of spokesperson
- ❏ follow the general guidelines for tours and demonstrations.

Training:

- ❏ emphasizes hands-on or visual communication methods
- ❏ is focused
- ❏ will be given to a receptive audience.

## REFERENCES

McCallum, D. B., S. L. Hammond, and V. T. Covello. 1991. "Communicating about Environmental Risks: How the Public Uses and Perceives Information Sources." *Health Education Quarterly*, 18(3):349-361.

## ADDITIONAL RESOURCES

Peters, R. G., V. T. Covello, and D. B. McCallum. 1997. "The Determinants of Trust and Credibility in Environmental Risk Communication: An Empirical Study." *Risk Analysis*, 17(1):43-54.

# Working with
# the Media

*T*he mass media—including television, newspapers, radio, magazines, and the Internet—
are arguably the largest source of information
in today's society. Many people form their opinions
about health, environmental, and safety risks by what
they read in the newspaper and watch on the evening
news. In communicating risk-related information,
administrators, technical and health professionals, and
communication specialists often deal with the mass
media as a key provider, interpreter, gatekeeper, or channel of risk-related information. We have devoted a chapter to working with media representatives—reporters,
journalists, editors, and producers—because of the
distinct and significant role they play in communicating
risk information to the public. Use of the Internet for risk
communication is described in Chapter 18, "Technology-
Assisted Communication."

*"Every news story about
. . . risk is a collaboration
between the journalists
working on the story and
the sources they talk to."*
—Peter Sandman,
*Explaining Environmental
Risk* (1986, page 13).

## THE ROLES OF MASS MEDIA IN RISK COMMUNICATION

Media organizations—such as television producers
and newspapers—can choose among several roles, or

levels of participation, to address a given risk-related issue. Participation can span a wide range from least to most involvement: (1) reporting existing information, (2) influencing the way an issue is portrayed, (3) independently bringing an issue to the public's attention or restricting its coverage, and (4) proposing solutions to a risk-related decision, including taking a stand on an issue.

This section describes the levels of participation a media organization can take and corresponding strategies that those who communicate risk may wish to consider. At all levels, but especially the higher levels, it is important to develop and maintain productive relationships with media representatives.

Many factors affect which role, or combinations of roles, media organizations take. One factor is the type of communication situation: care, consensus, or crisis. When a crisis presents imminent danger, reporters are likely to start with reporting existing information, when the public must be alerted quickly to protect themselves. Later, media organizations may turn to a more investigative role to attempt to uncover the factors that led to the crisis. This may involve working with official investigating organizations, citizens' groups, policy-makers, and others to portray a more complete picture of the risk, its causes, and its potential solutions.

At the lowest-participation end of the scale, those responsible for communicating risks may be interviewed by reporters or otherwise asked to provide information for a story. In addition, those who are communicating risk may need to seek out media representatives to provide information on breaking news or current events. This can be done through press kits, media events, press releases, and other avenues. For providing information to reporters, see the tips later in this chapter under the heading, "Guidelines for Specific Situations."

In care communications, media organizations may choose to take an active role in illuminating and reducing a given risk such as gang-related crime, a low child-immunization rate, or a lack of adequate nutrition for seniors. In this role, media organizations will often describe the negative consequences of the risk on the community and suggest ways that individuals, groups, and entire communities can act to reduce risks. This approach casts media organizations in a stakeholder role, where they participate with others in characterizing the problem and its potential solutions. At this level of involvement, policy and technical professionals may work directly with media and other community representatives to characterize risks and their alternatives. Use the appropriate guidelines later in this chapter for working with media representatives.

In the highest-involvement end of the scale, individual editors or producers occasionally feel that a particular issue is significant enough that their organizations must get more involved, sometimes to the point of going on record with a stated position. This often involves an issue that affects the community, affects many stakeholders with different opinions about the risk, and requires a consensus decision informed by many views. Examples of such consensus-required issues are whether a new federal prison should be sited in the community, whether field burning should be made more or less restrictive, whether a new dam should be built or an existing one taken out, or whether two hospitals should merge services to cut costs.

Media organizations may choose to participate more strongly in such issues by taking an advocacy role. For example, editors or producers may participate in discussions with opinion leaders about the nature of the risk, its benefits and consequences, alternatives, various points of view, and potential solutions. They may even establish an editorial position and publish or air stories supporting that position. This is generally done through editorials or similar commentary rather than news coverage. At this level of participation, media representatives such as editorial boards may work actively and regularly with other stakeholders to fully describe the nature and consequences of a particular risk and propose solutions.

At all levels of media participation, it is important to establish productive relationships with media representatives, as described later in this chapter. Good working relationships between media representatives and those who are communicating risk increase the chances for accurate, balanced coverage. In addition, when media organizations publish or air something you disagree with regarding a particular risk, they are more likely to listen to your concerns if you have established yourself as a credible, reasonable source.

## MEDIA CONTRASTED WITH OTHER STAKEHOLDERS

Two broad characteristics distinguish media representatives from other stakeholders and limit involvement. The first is mission. A media organization's primary purpose is to provide the public with current information, often a combination of news and entertainment. This mission takes priority over involvement in a given risk-related issue. Other participants such as a citizens' group may be held responsible for crafting workable solutions, hammering out a myriad of details in agreements, and even implementing the agreements and evaluating their outcomes. Media organizations are there primarily to report on and illuminate issues. Though media involvement can be a very powerful voice in the ultimate outcome of risk issues, media organizations' responsibility in a decision-making process usually does not extend past proposing solutions.

The second characteristic that distinguishes media representatives from other stakeholders is one of position and representation. Non-media stakeholders participating in a risk-related group decision process often represent the views of a specific "constituency" such as health professionals, homeowners, or recreational enthusiasts. In group discussions, these members reflect the values and judgments of those whose views they represent.

Reporters and journalists, in contrast, generally aim for objectivity and balance in their stories. Thus media representatives may be hesitant to become directly involved in an issue, viewing such involvement as a professional conflict that could subject them to allegations of bias. In fact, the U.S. Supreme Court ruled in 1997 that a Washington State newspaper could rightly take a reporter off news assignments because her outside-of-work activities—

including activism on various social causes—could be perceived as biasing the new stories she wrote, thus risking the newspaper's reputation of objectivity (Nelson v. McClatchy Newspapers, Inc., et al. 1997).

## PRODUCTIVE INTERACTION, NOT POLARIZATION

Regardless of the media's level of involvement, agreeing on how risks should be portrayed can be challenging. Science and policy experts sometimes view mass media coverage of health and environmental risks as oversimplified, inaccurate, and sensationalized. Journalists and reporters, for their part, are occasionally frustrated by technical and policy professionals who appear unhelpful, arrogant, or controlling.

Nevertheless, experts who deal with issues involving health and environmental risks cannot afford to ignore media representatives or criticize them from afar. Entire industries have discovered the power of the mass media to influence their financial bottom lines. The Washington apple industry lost about $130 million in sales in the season following a CBS *60 Minutes* television program in 1989 about the dangers of the agricultural chemical Alar (O'Rourke 1990). Makers of silicon implants for breast augmentation faced bankruptcy after numerous consumer lawsuits followed extensive media coverage in the early 1990s.

It is equally true—and the position we advocate—that working productively with reporters and journalists can lead to a more informed, empowered, solution-oriented public. A good example of the benefits of this approach is broad public awareness of AIDS and *E. coli* bacteria risks through media coverage.

The first step in working effectively with media representatives is to understand their goals and constraints. Only then can risk communicators apply the guiding principles for care, consensus, or crisis communication. The rest of the chapter deals with mass media sources most familiar to the general public: television, newspapers, and radio. Use of the Internet is discussed separately in Chapter 18, "Technology-Assisted Communication."

—— ◇ ——

Working productively with reporters and journalists can lead to a more informed, empowered, solution-oriented public.

## UNDERSTAND "CULTURAL" DIFFERENCES

A researcher at a national laboratory was interviewed for the first time by a reporter about a technology destined for eventual use by the public. The researcher, flattered by the reporter's interest and questions, carefully explained the detailed technical workings of his invention and its uses. When asked, he freely discussed some of the technology's potentially controversial characteristics, downplaying the potential for public rejection. When the resulting news article was published, the researcher felt betrayed by its tone, viewing it as a misrepresentation of the technology that emphasized its controversial aspects rather than its benefits. "I thought the reporter was my friend," the researcher lamented.

The problem lay in the fact that the researcher had approached the interview as he would an informal discussion with one of his peers. Lacking an understanding of the reporter's mission and without his own goals for the conversation, the researcher inadvertently contributed to an article that disparaged his own technology.

This incident illustrates some of the differences between the ways subject matter experts and mass media representatives traditionally approach risk communication. We call them cultural differences because the two groups have their own—sometimes competing—values, traditions, and practices. Understanding the following differences can help risk communicators more effectively work with reporters and journalists.

### The Media are Event-Focused

Reporters, especially when covering the news, are largely reactive, reporting on the facts surrounding an event or an ongoing risk. The Environmental Risk Reporting Project, for example, found that scientific risk had little to do with the environmental coverage presented on the nightly news. Instead, the coverage appeared driven by the traditional journalistic news values of timeliness, geographic proximity, prominence, consequence, and human interest, along with the television criterion of visual impact (Greenberg et al. 1989).

Because of limited staff expertise in technical issues and constraints on space and time, the media may give

—◇—

News coverage is driven by timeliness, geographic proximity, prominence, consequence, human interest, and visual impact.

little emphasis to explaining the likelihood of the hazard occurring under various conditions, broader societal or policy issues surrounding the risk, or other contextual information. Technical and policy experts, in contrast, are highly concerned about fostering rational decision-making by the public—meaning providing information about immediate and long-term consequences, costs and benefits of a hazard and its alternatives, and the moral and economic issues that are inherent in hazardous processes and events. Thus risk communicators, especially in dealing with complex decisions, should not rely on the mass media alone to fully provide the contextual and background information necessary for well-informed decision-making.

## Certain Kinds of Risks Get More Coverage

Research has shown that the U.S. mass media disproportionately focus on hazards that are catastrophic and violent in nature, new, and associated with the United States (e.g., Adams 1986; Combs and Slovic 1979; Singer and Endreny 1993). Drama, symbolism, and identifiable victims, particularly children or celebrities, make risks more memorable. Controversy ensures greater coverage.

Risks are not covered in the mass media commensurate with their probability of occurrence. For example, airline crashes with fatalities are covered far more extensively than heart disease, though diseases take 16 times as many lives as accidents. The result, adding to the risk communicator's challenge, is that people consistently misjudge the frequency of certain lethal events, according to studies (e.g., Combs and Slovic 1979). Thus those communicating risks in a crisis situation may find it very easy to get media attention while those in care or consensus communication situations may have more difficulty reaching their audiences through media forums.

> Risks are not covered in the mass media commensurate with their probability of occurrence.

## Journalistic Independence and Deadlines Affect Content

Many technical professionals view the media as a conduit or pipeline, responsible for transporting technical information to the public (Nelkin 1996). Regarding the media as a technique to further their own goals, they expect to control the flow of information to the public just as they do within their own domains, and feel betrayed when their views are challenged.

In industry, government, and academia, extensive peer review systems ensure that information is approved by the appropriate authorities before release. This process is designed to eliminate technical errors and ensure that all parties have a chance to agree on how the material is presented. In contrast, journalists are charged with being independent watchdogs on society. Allowing a source to review an article is seen as opening the door to media censorship. Reporters pride themselves in giving their audiences an independent view of a situation, untainted by corporate or academic "propaganda." Though most reporters want to get the facts right, they do not appreciate being told how to say something.

Deadlines are another reason for lack of source review. Most newspaper, television, and radio reporters simply do not have time to call back each source. Many find that when they do take the time, their sources want to add material, change their quotes, nit-pick about wording, argue about the interpretation or theme of the article, and ignore word limitations. Both of these factors—independence and deadlines—mean that the risk communicator often has little control over the published or broadcast story.

## The Need for Balance Invites Opposing Views

The American view of fair and impartial reporting is to present divergent points of view on a given issue. Ironically, this attempt at balance sometimes results in an unwitting imbalance—the view of a vocal, self-proclaimed expert or media-savvy special interest group can be made to seem just as valid as that of a peer-reviewed group of scholars or even a worldwide scientific consensus. Many reporters are reluctant to characterize the non-scientific or special interest viewpoint as such for fear of appearing biased.

Adding to the reporter's challenge is the fact that members of the scientific community sometimes disagree among themselves on the same topic. Unfortunately, the resulting "dueling experts" stories may leave audiences both confused and concerned that the risk is unknowable if not even the experts can agree on it.

## Information is Condensed, Simplified, and Personalized

In today's information-glutted world, media stories must grab and keep the audience's attention. Stories for television, radio, newspapers, and magazines do not generally lend themselves to long discourses. In addition, many reporters are generalists with little or no background in science and technology.

When describing risks, journalists see their responsibility as informing people of potential dangers and identifying ways people can respond. To do this, they want to give people specific warning signs to alert them to danger, and tell them whom to go to for help and how to alleviate the risk. Concepts important to technical professionals, such as probabilities, uncertainties, risk ranges, acute versus chronic risks, and risk tradeoffs, do not translate well in many mass media formats.

To humanize and personalize the risk story, news organizations often use the plight of an individual affected by a hazard, regardless of how representative the person's situation is.

These approaches of condensing, simplifying, and personalizing information may make information more accessible to the public, but may result in incomplete and sometimes unbalanced information for making personal risk decisions.

## GUIDELINES FOR SPECIFIC SITUATIONS

Understanding the differences between risk experts and media professionals is the first step in effective interaction. We don't mean to suggest that the two groups are mutually exclusive. It is possible to find places where the interests of the two "cultures" converge, fostering a jointly beneficial working relationship.

For successful media interactions, we suggest the following broad guidelines. They apply equally to care, consensus, and crisis communications unless specified.

——— ◇ ———

*"Many accusations of inaccuracy follow less from actual errors than from efforts to present complex material about risk in a readable and appealing style."*

—Dorothy Nelkin, Professor at New York University's Department of Sociology and the School of Law (1996).

——— ◇ ———

When describing risks, journalists see their responsibility as informing people of potential dangers and identifying ways people can respond.

## Develop Relationships with Local and Regional Media Representatives

Journalists need information and ideas for stories that have importance for the local community. Risk communicators should think of themselves as resources who can make it easier for journalists to do a good job. Lawrence Wallack, professor at the University of California-Berkeley's School of Public Health and Director of the Berkeley Media Studies Group, recommends providing journalists with timely, accurate information; examples of local activities; summaries of key issues; and names of potential sources (Wallack et al. 1993).

An ongoing working relationship with media representatives makes it much more likely that you will get a fair hearing when a reporter is doing a story about a particular event. Demonstrating you want to serve as a source of information, rather than merely satisfying your self-interests, is the best way to build a long-term relationship. The goal is to build a reputation as a trustworthy, articulate source on one or more topics, so that you will be sought out in the future.

Go beyond individual reporters. Joann Rodgers, Director of Media Relations at Johns Hopkins Medical Institute in Baltimore, recommends expanding to include other media gatekeepers such as newspaper editors and television producers who influence what becomes news and how news is reported (Lebow and Arkin 1993).

## Know When to Approach Media Representatives or When They May Approach You

When there is a potential for immediate public health or environmental risk, it is necessary to contact media representatives without delay so people can be informed about how to avoid or reduce the risk. We recommend that organizations who may face such crisis communication situations pre-establish media protocols, including the use of trained spokespeople. The organization's top leaders—including presidents, operations managers, and agency heads—should be ready to speak clearly and candidly to the public through mass media channels.

> Demonstrating you want to serve as a source of information, rather than merely satisfying your self-interests, is the best way to build a long-term relationship.

The intent of such preparations is not to downplay the risk situation or deflect blame, but to respond as quickly and effectively as possible to alert people to danger. (See Chapter 2, "Approaches to Communicating Risk," for more information about crisis communications and Chapter 15, "Face-to-Face Communication," for more information on choosing and coaching a spokesperson. See Part V, "Bioterrorism and Other Emergencies," for advice on working with the media in crisis situations.)

Be aware of work you are involved with that may prompt media attention. This work may be a topic that has been featured recently in the media (such as the dangers of front-seat airbags for small passengers), has local applicability (a study about drinking water contamination from flooding would get more coverage in communities subject to overflowing rivers), or is of broad public interest (anything that could raise or lower cancer risks, for example). Inventors at one company developed an airport scanner that detects concealed plastic or metal weapons on pre-boarded passengers. Whenever there is a publicized airline incident thought to involve weapons, the inventors prepare themselves for a flurry of media inquiries regarding airport security technologies.

Timing and accuracy are important in releasing information to the public through the media. Make sure the information you are releasing is mature enough to be credible and defensible. One scientist independently released his highly preliminary findings about potential electromagnetic hazards of cellular phones right before the Christmas season. The research had not been reviewed by others, and it was presented without explanation of its preliminary nature. The resulting media coverage prompted enough controversy that his company faced potential lawsuits from cell phone manufacturers angry about losing business.

## Prepare Messages and Materials Carefully

Planning is critical for successful media interaction. When preparing to talk with a reporter, understand what might be asked and consider in advance how to

> The intent of establishing media protocols for potential crises is not to downplay the risk situation or deflect blame, but to respond as quickly and effectively as possible to alert people to danger.

respond. Table 16-1 gives examples of questions that help you prepare interview responses.

For a newspaper, television, or radio interview, have two or three short, crucial messages that you want to leave with the audience. In developing these, consider what the audience most needs to know, most wants to know, and is most concerned about. (See Chapter 9, "Develop Your Message," for more details on message development.) Find ways to "bridge" the conversation to these points even if you aren't asked questions that directly reflect them. This way, you answer the reporter's questions but also focus on the most critical information.

Take advantage of advice and training provided by public affairs specialists in your organization or through consultants. Many organizations use professional train- ers with media backgrounds when a finding of high pub- lic interest is about to be released. These trainers put technical and managerial staff who will be spokes- persons through extensive rehearsals, giving them realistic practice in explaining the significance of findings and responding to challenging questions. For more information on selecting an appropriate spokesperson

**TABLE 16-1**
Questions to Ask Before an Interview

| | |
|---|---|
| **Background Questions** | What is the reporter's name, organization, and phone number? |
| | What stories has the reporter previously covered? |
| | Who generally reads, sees, and/or hears the publication or program? |
| **Logistics Questions** | Where and when will the story appear? |
| | What is the deadline for the story? |
| | Where will the interview take place? |
| | How long will the interview take? |
| | How long will the story be? |
| | Does the reporter verify the accuracy of specific quotes attributed to the person being interviewed? |
| **Topical Questions** | What is the story's theme? |
| | What topics does the reporter want to cover in the interview? |
| | What types of questions will be asked? |
| | Has the reporter done any background research? |
| | Does the reporter want to receive background material before the interview? |
| | Who else has been interviewed? What did they say? |
| | Who else will be interviewed? |

(Adapted from work by Vince Covello, CDC et al. 2003.)

for various situations, see "Choosing a Spokesperson" in Chapter 15, "Face-to-Face Communication."

Offer to provide photos or video footage appropriate to the medium. Remember that for television, pictures, rather than words, usually determine what the audience remembers.

## Know Where to Draw the Line

Reporters often will ask questions outside the scope of your expertise. When you are asked a question for which you do not know the answer, it is perfectly acceptable to say, "I don't know"—or give the reporter another source who will know the answer. Avoid speculating about a hypothetical situation. Avoid guessing, especially in matters that involve quantities. For example, when asked how many people in your community may be affected by a certain risk, one response is to give a range based on various conditions.

Be aware of the limits of your position in representing your organization on a particular issue. One technical expert declined to be interviewed on radio with the head of a nationally known civil liberties organization. The reporter was asking them to discuss public acceptance aspects of a new technology that the expert was developing. Sensing a potentially contentious debate that held little value for his project, the technical expert declined that particular format. "I'm an engineer, not a constitutional lawyer," he explained to the reporter. He did, however, agree to do other, selected media interviews that focused on the need for the technology and its applications.

When being interviewed, don't feel obligated to answer every question. Never say anything you don't want to see in the paper or on the air. There's no such thing as "off the record"—despite what we see in the movies. Don't say "no comment," especially in a crisis communication situation; many audiences will interpret that as an assumption of guilt on the part of the organization. A better response would be to explain when you will be able to give a statement.

When being interviewed, don't feel obligated to answer every question.

## Put Your Message in Terms the Reporter's Audience Can Understand

When providing printed or visual information to media representatives, or when being interviewed, remember that you are not speaking to your peers, but to a general audience. Many of them know far less than you do about the risk in question. Guide journalists in interpreting the results of studies. Replace all technical jargon with terms and concepts to which the public can relate. It may be helpful to pretend you're talking with your neighbors or to a relative who doesn't know what you do.

People need a "yardstick" to evaluate a new or unfamiliar risk. For example, in reported studies of electromagnetic fields from electrical power lines, the levels of exposure often are compared with levels received from home appliances. (But be cautious about comparisons. See "Principles for Comparing Risks" in Chapter 6, "Principles of Risk Communication.") And get to the point—what is the bottom-line message about the risk that people should know? Audiences typically want to know two things: How does this affect me and my family, and what can I do about it?

Prepare press kits to give media representatives. The kits should contain factual, explanatory background information on a particular topic or event. Reporters may use the information as reference material to help them put the story in context or as self education about technical details. A typical situation where press kits are used is an event that media representatives have been invited to attend, such as a major release of information about a local or regional risk. Press kits can be offered to media representatives who are doing a story on a topic that involves your organization, especially if the topic is complex.

A kit might include some of the following materials: a fact sheet, a published article from a magazine or trade publication, a question-and-answer sheet, a press release, a photo depicting a visual aspect of the topic, a list of contacts, and a business card. The materials should use nontechnical, straightforward language; the closer the language to what the reporter will write or produce, the better. Keep the press kits lean; overstuffed packets are a big turnoff to reporters. Busy reporters will ignore press kits crammed with technical journal articles,

> ◇
>
> Audiences typically want to know two things: How does this affect me and my family, and what can I do about it?

official reports, or promotional materials that have been doctored with the organization's "spin."

## Put the Risk in Perspective

In providing printed, visual, or oral information, tell how new findings build on or contradict previous studies. This kind of "big picture" approach helps audiences evaluate the risk. A way to help audiences evaluate the magnitude of the risk is to differentiate between relative and actual risk. Cristine Russell, Special Health Correspondent to the *Washington Post*, uses the following example: A finding that a drug poses nine times greater risk of cancer (its relative risk) is misleading without explaining that the cancer has an *actual risk* of one in a million of occurring in the first place (Russell 1993). Similarly, Russell encourages communicators to distinguish between individual and societal risk. Is the risk a public health problem, or is it significant only for a localized or specialized population with certain characteristics?

Recommend that the reporter interview other people who see the risk from a different angle—those who cause, manage, benefit from, study, or prevent it. Including such a variety of people is especially useful in a press conference. This holistic approach gives audiences a clearer picture of the risk by illuminating more dimensions and points of view.

## Respect the Reporter's Deadlines

Return calls as soon as possible. Provide additional oral or printed information, video clips, photos, and reviews of materials when you say you will. Most reporters will identify their deadlines, but ask if you are unsure. You may only get one chance to provide information. If you don't respond in time, the story will appear or air without your input.

## Maintain Ethical Standards of Disclosure

When talking with media representatives, disclose any proprietary interest or other potential conflict of interest. This applies especially to scientific findings or risk-reduction technologies with direct personal benefit to you or your organization. The Jacobs Institute of Women's Health describes the increasing use of self-serving information release that actually is advertising—such as highlighting premenstrual syndrome and menopause programs—as two examples that have been used to generate revenue for health institutions (Lebow and Arkin 1993).

An example of ethical disclosure is identifying a research sponsor that could be seen as biasing the results, such as studies on lung cancer sponsored by the tobacco industry. If you fail to disclose an aspect of the work that is later shown as covertly benefiting you, your organization, or your sponsor, you and your work risk losing credibility.

### Take Action When Inaccurate or Misleading Material is Published or Aired

Reporters almost never ask a source to review a story before it is aired or published, though you can encourage reporters to fact-check a story with you before it runs. You do have the right to ask the reporter what the gist of the story will be. You can also ask to have your quotes read back to you during an interview.

It is also possible to alert reporters about factually inaccurate, incomplete, or misleading reporting after it has appeared. Use this option judiciously. Avoid complaining about the journalist's writing style, omission of superfluous details, or elements that do not change the main message of the story. Keep your end goal in mind: to get a more correct story next time, not to badger the reporter for an apology.

Most journalists appreciate being alerted to inaccuracies; they want to be viewed as credible. However, do not expect an automatic correction; it is the decision of the media representative, the editor or producer, and sometimes the media organization's policy.

### USING TECHNOLOGY

As the speed of information delivery increases, organizations are increasingly using the Internet and other technology tools to make their interactions with reporters faster and more efficient. Many organizations have entire multimedia sections on their web sites for media professionals and the public to access. The World Bank Group, for example, provides video and radio news releases, B-roll (extra footage that helps tell a story), a photo library, and downloadable public service announcements. It also contains a password-protected online media briefing center, which contains embargoed news (advance news that is requested not to be reported until a certain time) for accredited journalists.

The following sections describe some of the more common technology tools used when working with the media. For more on using technology in risk communication, see Chapter 18, "Technology-Assisted Communication."

## Distribution Services

Many organizations distribute their news releases using subscription-based web services that make news available to journalists. For risk-related news, many of these services are in the science and technology realms. The leading such service is EurekAlert!, operated by the American Association for the Advancement of Science. EurekAlert! is an online press service where research institutions, universities, government agencies, corporations, and others can distribute science-related news to reporters and news media. EurekAlert! also archives its press releases for the public. As with many online press services, you must register on the site as a public information officer to submit a news release. Only those who have registered as a reporter or freelancer can access embargoed news for use in a news story.

Another web service, Newswise, specializes in research results and news from research institutions worldwide. Some reporters also use a service called Profnet, part of PR Newswire, which matches reporters and sources. A reporter sends a topical query to the service at no charge, and Profnet compiles the queries and dispatches them as an e-mail once, sometimes several times daily, to institutional subscribers, who then contact

—— ◇ ——

Many organizations have entire multimedia sections on their web sites for media professionals and the public to access.

the reporter directly with their information that fits the query.

Many organizations use created and self-subscribe e-mail lists to distribute their news releases on a regular basis. Make sure each release contains an e-mail link to a contact person and the organization's web site address. To capture the attention of busy reporters, use a descriptive subject line in the e-mail (not "Press Release from ABC Company" but "New Discovery Reduces Health Risk from Asbestos"). Link to online background information and photos when available. Include an "unsubscribe" option.

Many organizations use e-mail lists to distribute their news releases on a regular basis. Make sure each release contains an e-mail link to a contact person and the organization's web site address.

## Video and Audio News Releases

Video and audio news releases provide broadcast-ready information. The Broadcast Media & Technology Center of the U.S. Department of Agriculture (USDA), for example, produces more than 90 video news releases annually, on stories including biotechnology, water quality, food safety, and other issues. The news releases usually air on nationally syndicated programs for rural audiences, as well as on commercial television stations. The Center also makes its news releases available to the public as streaming media files on its web site. USDA's radio news stories and news conferences, more than 2,000 annually, are available to radio stations via telephone dial-up service and MP3 audio files on the USDA's web site. This way, broadcasters can use the web to directly access nightly radio feeds that have CD sound quality.

One note of caution is that some reporters shun video news releases as manufactured propaganda. In keeping with journalistic objectivity, they'd rather explore all the angles and issues, not just what the producing organization wants to convey. On the other hand, media outlets with more restricted budgets, such as in smaller markets, may welcome video news releases as high-quality products without the hefty production price tag. As with any communication method, it's important to determine whether video news releases will be used and whether the costs are worth the return.

## Public Service Announcements

Public service announcements (PSAs) are advertising that serves the public interest. PSAs educate and raise awareness about significant social issues in a way that will change attitudes and behaviors and create positive social change. PSAs are not intended to promote a commercial product, brand, or service, and are usually put out by government and non-profit organizations. PSAs are common in care communication, such as anti-obesity campaigns, and crisis communication, such as the Federal Emergency Management Association telling people how to get help after a flood. TV and radio are the most common media outlets, but newspapers, magazines, and web sites may also accept PSAs.

Most PSAs run as a community service at no charge by the media, but some run in purchased time and space. Some non-profit organizations and government agencies, such as the Office of National Drug Control Policy and the Centers for Disease Control and Prevention, purchase media time and space for some of their PSAs. This gives them more control over placement and scheduling.

PSAs were more common in the past, when the Federal Communication Commission imposed stricter requirements for broadcasters to demonstrate that they were operating in the public interest. Today, with deregulation, most stations are setting their own standards on what constitutes fulfillment of their public service programming responsibilities to their local communities. Some stations run their own community-affairs program instead of PSAs. Others air public service-type messages from paying advertisers and use on-air promotions featuring their own network TV stars. Stations may run PSAs in the early morning hours when audiences are almost nonexistent, thus meeting the letter of the law if not the spirit. To counter this trend of diminishing PSAs, some organizations are delivering more content through video news releases and B-roll to the same markets that used to run PSAs.

Nevertheless, PSAs may be one strategy in an overall risk communication program. Sometimes a local ad agency may develop a PSA for your organization at no

⬦

Most PSAs run as a community service at no charge by the media, but some run in purchased time and space.

charge; local media may also lend their development support. The Advertising Council supplies dozens of free, high-quality PSAs; risk-related topics range from fire safety to childhood asthma to homeland security. In creating PSAs, it's important to tailor the message to audiences you are trying to reach and restrict the content to one take-away message. Understand the various media's policies, lead times, and required formats. If the PSA relates to a specific event, make sure it gets to the stations at least two weeks in advance, to allow them time to schedule it. Evaluate the results based on the broadcast statistics from the media outlet and the contact phone number and/or web site you've provided in the PSA. The PSA Research Center is a good source of additional information, including articles and case studies by PSA topic.

## Telebriefings

Telebriefings use a conference call format that replaces or augments the traditional press conference. Similar to a conference call, they can be conducted anywhere, not requiring participants to travel to a news conference location. Sometimes the telebriefing is broadcast via streaming audio on the web. The Centers for Disease Control and Prevention (CDC) has conducted more than 40 telebriefings each year since 2001, on public health topics including anthrax, smallpox, West Nile virus, severe acute respiratory syndrome, and many others. The CDC sends an e-mail message to its listserv of media, public health, and Congressional contacts, giving them a toll-free number to call and a time for the briefing. CDC leads the briefing with a group of experts, and reporters ask questions. CDC posts transcripts and audio of its telebriefings on its web site.

When considering a telebriefing, plan accordingly for capacity. The CDC, for example, pays for 100 phone lines to handle the deluge of callers during and after each telebriefing.

## SPECIAL CASE: THE USE OF MASS MEDIA IN PUBLIC HEALTH CAMPAIGNS

Public health campaigns represent a care communication situation where the mass media often play a central role. Risk-related issues frequently take center stage. Campaigns are designed to prompt long-term changes in knowledge, attitudes, behaviors, and sometimes public policy. For example, campaigns may encourage people to stop smoking, reduce pesticide use, drive sober, increase regular exercise, reduce yard-waste burning on high-smog days, wear seatbelts and motorcycle helmets, know what to do in case of fire, reduce AIDS risks, and handle raw food safely.

A large body of research and case studies exists on the design, implementation, and measurement of public health campaigns. A sample of these published studies is listed in "Additional Resources" at the end of this chapter. The wise campaign planner will draw on the lessons of others to make the best use of the significant time and funding necessary for an effective campaign. Because others have written extensively about public health campaigns, we provide only a brief overview here.

### Paid Placements or Independent Coverage

Media messages associated with public health issues can be either paid or independent. Paid placements—such as television and radio spots or newspaper ads—enable you to control the content of the message, the audience it reaches, and its timing. The success of the effort is more easily measured because the audience is receiving a consistent, predetermined message. One disadvantage is that the message can be seen as biased or self-serving, for example beer distribution companies warning about the dangers of underage drinking. Another disadvantage of mass media advertising is that it can require a large chunk of the campaign budget and may not necessarily target the population most at risk, especially if they do not use the traditional mass media channels.

◇

*"The press is a grand piano waiting for a player. Working in concert, unbiased reporters and smart advocates can make music together."*

—Susan Wilson, New Jersey Network for Family Life (Wallack et al. 1993, page 86).

Health campaign managers also can provide information to the media through press releases and public service announcements. Media representatives then decide whether and how they pass along the information to the public. This is a low- or no-cost option, but with reduced control by the health campaign managers. Campaign planners should know their media gatekeepers' interests and potential conflicts of interest, whether reporters may feel compelled to obtain an opposing point of view, and whether this works to the advantage or disadvantage of the campaign.

Media outlets also can independently cover a health campaign or the issue the campaign is featuring. Such coverage can create a tremendous support for the issue at hand. The *Alabama Journal*, a regional newspaper, took an advocacy position in a series of stories published in 1987 on state infant mortality. The series focused on real peoples' lives, how Alabama officials had failed to address the issue, the economic and social costs to the state, and what other states had done to reduce the problem. The newspaper sent reprints to 5,000 Alabaman opinion leaders, who used them as lobbying tools. Citizens and reporters kept the pressure on the governor and legislators, urging them to take action to reduce the problem. In the two years after the series was published, the state legislature instituted several policy changes to combat the problem, and infant mortality rates dropped. Researcher Kim Walsh-Childers concluded that the newspaper series, which won a Pulitzer Prize, was the critical factor in accelerating public support for policy changes and creating pressure on legislators to make those changes (Walsh-Childers 1994).

A potential downside of independent coverage is possible inconsistency with the message of a paid campaign. One example is mass media coverage in the 1980s about the connection between aspirin and Reye's syndrome, a potentially fatal illness occurring in children with flu or other viruses (Soumerai et al. 1992). A commonly occurring theme in media coverage was the battle between the consumer groups and the aspirin industry, which was fighting the Food and Drug Administration's proposal for warning labels on aspirin.

## Guidelines

Research into public health campaigns involving the mass media points to several success factors, upon which the following guidelines are based.

### Use Research to Design Campaigns

Campaign planners have long practiced two kinds of research for message design: (1) research to determine audience predispositions, and (2) research to pretest messages and materials for comprehensibility and response. A mass media campaign in South Carolina was designed to promote public action to reduce abuse of children in families plagued by alcohol or other drugs (Andrews et al. 1995). A public survey was conducted one year before the campaign to gauge opinions about child abuse and the respondents' likelihood of helping families where abuse was occurring. The results of this survey were used to design specific themes, messages, and materials for the campaign. One of the media forums was a televised talk show, which attracted higher viewership than the regular program, *Entertainment Tonight*—almost unheard of for a public affairs show. Most encouraging was a 62% increase in the number of people who called a phone service each month for information about how to help abused children.

One example of the benefits of pretesting messages comes from the Stanford heart disease prevention project, a multi-community campaign designed to improve cardiovascular health. One of the project's planned messages recommending all-season jogging was modified when it was realized that California winters can be too rainy and jogging paths too muddy for the less than highly motivated runner (Rogers and Storey 1987).

The U.S. Environmental Protection Agency presumably did not pretest its advertisement to alert Americans to radon gas in the home, where children were shown turning into skeletons after they were exposed to radon (Moore 1997). The ad created such protest that it was cancelled.

————— ◇ —————

Pretesting messages and materials in advance will help reveal problems or inadvertent misconceptions that may arise among the target audiences.

For ideas about how to research your audiences and their perceptions of the issues, see Chapter 8, "Analyze Your Audience."

### Use Multiple Media Channels to Reach People

More exposure means more opportunities to reach people. Base your selection of media channels on your audience analysis. Understand your community's media access points—where and how certain topics are covered in various media channels (Wallack et al. 1993). Consider going beyond traditional news programming. Television, for example, has magazine news shows, public affairs programming, and free speech or editorial announcements. Health topics may fit well with lifestyle, financial, and business sections of newspapers as well as editorial content. Radio has talk shows, editorials, and public service announcements.

In a campaign to lower cardiovascular disease in two California communities, public health experts found that certain channels and formats are accessible only to certain segments of the community (Fortmann et al. 1995). For example, a regular newspaper column on health was read by some members of the community and not others. In contrast, the child abuse prevention campaign in South Carolina, mentioned earlier, used an effective combination of media delivery channels and other formats. People heard about the problem of child abuse through television, billboards, posters, and print publications. After public service announcements were broadcast, people were invited to call a toll-free number for help or information.

A multimedia project directed at reducing teen pregnancy in the Ohio area used paid air time on radio, supplemented by public service announcements in other media. People could call a hotline number for information and appointments. The campaign reached 80% of teens in Columbus over seven weeks, resulting in 1,000 calls per month at its peak (Taplin 1981).

The M.D. Cancer Center in Houston ran a campaign to reduce sun exposure behavior in several large cities in Texas from 1990 through 1992. In addition to radio and TV interviews, public service announcements in English and Spanish, and press conferences, the campaign also used one-minute segments on six children's TV shows, live radio interviews with listener call-ins, and "Day at the Dome" baseball game publicity that included ticket giveaways on the radio before the game. The campaign reached more than 1 million people in three cities and a significant increase in people saying they had taken actions to reduce the risk of skin cancer (Gelb et al. 1994).

### Use Approaches that Go Beyond Media

Research on public health campaigns shows that the mass media are important sources, but not the only ones people pay attention to, and not necessarily the most credible for changing attitudes and behaviors (Rogers and Storey 1987). For the greatest chance of success, the message must be reinforced through other communication channels such as opinion leaders and community groups. An anti-alcohol abuse campaign targeting Michigan State University used media interviews and public service announcements, flyers, e-mails to college students, letters to alcohol vendors, theatre troops, and alcohol-free events (Witte et al. 2001).

Interpersonal communication has been shown to play a crucial role in changing strongly held attitudes and motivating behavior change. The Stanford heart health campaign used community leaders and support groups to disseminate information and to persuade by example (Kim 1985). In "neighborhood watch" programs to reduce crime, neighbors keep an eye on each others' houses, watching for any suspicious activities (O'Keefe 1985).

Some practitioners use an approach they call media advocacy, wherein community organizations and ad hoc groups work with the media to promote health policies aimed at fundamental social change (Wallack et al. 1993, 1999).

### Consider a Variety of Ways to Evaluate Success

Evaluating media-based public health campaigns by one or two broad measures—individual attitude or behavior change—is difficult because many factors other

———— ◇ ————

For the greatest chance of success, the message must be reinforced through other communication channels such as opinion leaders and community groups.

than media coverage contribute to change at the personal level.

Lawrence Wallack, professor at the University of California-Berkeley and Director of the Berkeley Media Studies Group, advocates broad avenues of inquiry to assess campaign effects. These include surveying and observing individuals in the target population; examining institutional records of individual behavior; interviewing those who interact with the individuals; and investigating institutional changes in the legal, business, industrial, or education systems. Official statistics—such as drunk driving arrests, sales data, and hospital emergency room data—also can be used as indicators of success (Wallack 1981). Some of the advice in Chapter 19, "Evaluating Risk Communication Efforts," may be helpful in evaluating public health campaigns.

## CHECKLIST FOR MEDIA APPROACHES

When planning to work with media representatives,

❑ the role and mission of mass media are understood and have been factored into risk communication goals as appropriate

❑ productive relationships have been developed with key members of the media who are most likely to cover specific risk issues

❑ a plan has been prepared for when to approach the media and/or what to do if events prompt them to approach you

When working with media representatives,

❑ risk messages and materials have been carefully prepared and tailored for specific media

❑ reporters are given the information they need and you want to convey, in language aimed at your target audiences

❑ questions outside the scope of your expertise or role in the organization are referred to others

- ❏ reporters' deadlines are known and respected
- ❏ ethical standards of disclosure are understood and maintained
- ❏ appropriate action is taken when inaccurate or misleading material is printed or aired.

For public health campaigns,
- ❏ the audience is researched in advance
- ❏ the audience analysis is used to identify the desired public health outcomes, themes, messages, and channels
- ❏ the campaign is evaluated for mid-course corrections, to determine success, and for lessons learned.

## REFERENCES

Adams, W. C. 1986. "Whose Lives Count?: TV Coverage of Natural Disasters." *Journal of Communication*, 36:113-122.

Andrews, A. B., D. G. McLeese, and S. Curran. 1995. "The Impact of a Media Campaign on Public Action to Help Maltreated Children in Addictive Families." *Child Abuse and Neglect*, 19:921-932.

CDC (U.S. Centers for Disease Control and Prevention), Agency for Toxic Substances and Disease Registry, Oak Ridge Institute for Science and Education, and the Prospect Center of the American Institutes of Research. 2003. *Emergency Risk Communication CDCynergy* (CD, February 2003). Online at http://www.orau.gov/cdcynergy/erc/.

Combs, B. C., and P. Slovic. 1979. "Newspaper Coverage of Causes of Death." *Journalism Quarterly*, 56:837-849.

Fortmann, S. P., J. A. Flora, M. A. Winkleby, C. Schooler, C. B. Taylor, and J. W. Farquhar. 1995. "Community Intervention Trials: Reflections on the Stanford Five-City Project Experience." *American Journal of Epidemiology*, 142:576-586.

Gelb, B. D., W. B. Boutwell, and S. Cummings. 1994. "Using Mass Media Communication for Health Promotion: Results from a Cancer Center Effort." *Hospital and Health Services Administration*, 39(3):283-293.

Greenberg, M. R., D. B. Sachsman, P. M. Sandman, and K. L. Salomone. 1989. "Network Evening News Coverage of Environmental Risk." *Risk Analysis*, 9(1):119-126.

Kim, Y. 1985. *Opinion Leadership in a Preventive Health Campaign.* Unpublished doctoral dissertation, Stanford University, Stanford, California.

Lebow, M., and E. B. Arkin. 1993. "Women's Health and the Mass Media: The Reporting of Risk." *Women's Health Issues*, 3(4):181-190.

McCall, R. B. 1988. "Science and the Press: Like Oil and Water?" *American Psychologist*, 43(2):87-94.

Moore, C. C. 1997. *Haunted Housing: How Toxic Scare Stories are Spooking the Public out of House and Home.* Cato Institute, Washington, D.C.

Nelkin, D. 1996. "Reporting Risk: The Case of Silicone Breast Implants." In *Technical Risk in the Mass Media*. Franklin Pierce Law Center. Online at http://www.fplc.edu/risk/vol5/summer/nelkin.htm.

Nelson v. McClatchy Newspapers, Inc., et al., No. 97-187-CSX, U.S. Supreme Court (1997).

O'Keefe, G. 1985. "Taking a Bite Out of Crime: The Impact of a Public Information Campaign." *Communication Research*, 12:147-178.

O'Rourke, A. D. 1990. "Anatomy of a Disaster." *Agribusiness*, 6(5):417-424.

Rogers, E. M., and J. D. Storey. 1987. "Communication Campaigns." *Handbook of Communication Science*, pages 419-445. Editors C. Berger and S. H. Chaffee, Sage Publications, Newbury Park, California.

Russell, C. 1993. "Hype, Hysteria, and Women's Health Risks: The Role of the Media." *Women's Health Issues*, 3(4):191-197.

Sandman, P. M. 1986. *Explaining Environmental Risk.* U.S. Environmental Protection Agency, Office of Toxic Substances, Washington, D.C.

Singer, E., and P. M. Endreny. 1993. *Reporting on Risk: How the Mass Media Portray Accidents, Diseases, Disasters, and Other Hazards.* Russell Sage Foundation, New York.

Soumerai, S. B., D. Ross-Degnan, and J. S. Kahn. 1992. "Effects of Professional and Media Warnings About the Association Between Aspirin Use, Children, and Reye's Syndrome." *The Milbank Quarterly*, 70:155-183.

Taplin, S. 1981. "Family Planning Communication Campaigns." *Public Communication Campaigns*. Editors R. E. Rice and W. J. Paisley. Sage Publications, Beverly Hills, California.

Wallack, L. M. 1981. "Mass Media Campaigns: The Odds Against Finding Behavior Change." *Health Education Quarterly*, 8:209-260.

Wallack, L., L. Dorfman, D. Jernigan, and M. Themba. 1993. *Media Advocacy and Public Health: Power for Prevention*. Sage Publications, Newbury Park, California.

Wallack, L., K. Woodruff, L. Dorfman, and I. Diaz. 1999. *News for a Change: An Advocate's Guide to Working with the Media*. Sage Publications, Newbury Park, California.

Walsh-Childers, K. 1994. "A Death in the Family - A Case Study of Newspaper Influence on Health Policy Development." *Journalism Quarterly*, 71:8220-8829.

Witte, K., G. Meyer, and D. Martell. 2001. *Effective Health Risk Messages: A Step-By-Step Guide*. Sage Publications, Inc., Thousand Oaks, California.

## ADDITIONAL RESOURCES

Advertising Council. Online at http://www.adcouncil.org/psa.

Atkin, C., and L. Wallack (Eds.). 1990. *Mass Communication and Public Health: Complexities and Conflicts*. Sage Publications, Newbury Park, California.

Clement International Corporation. 1991. *Risk Communication Manual for Electric Utilities, Volume 1: Practitioner's Guide*, EPRI EN-7314. Electric Power Research Institute, Palo Alto, California.

EurekAlert! Online at http://www.eurekalert.org.

Flynn, J., P. Slovic, and H. Kunreuther (Eds.). 2001. *Risk, Media, and Stigma: Understanding Public Challenges to Modern Science and Technology*. Earthscan Publications, Ltd., London.

Newswise. Online at http://www.newswise.com.

PR Newswire. Online at http://www.prnewswire.com.

Profnet. Online at http://www.profnet.com.

PSA Research Center. Online at http://www.psaresearch. com/index.html.

Rice, R. E., and C. Atkin (Eds.). 1989. *Public Communication Campaigns* (2nd ed.). Sage Publications, Newbury Park, California.

Rice, R. E., and C. Atkin. 1994. "Principles of Successful Public Communication Campaigns." *Media Effects: Advances in Theory and Research*. Editors J. Bryant and D. Zillman, Lawrence Erlbaum Associates, Hillsdale, New Jersey.

Sandman, P. M. 1986. *Explaining Environmental Risk*. U.S. Environmental Protection Agency, Office of Toxic Substances, Washington, D.C.

Sandman, P. M., D. B. Sachsman, and M. L. Greenberg. 1988. *The Environmental News Source: Providing Environmental Risk Information to the Media*. Risk Communication Project, Hazardous Substance Management Research Center, New Jersey Institute of Technology, Newark, New Jersey.

U.S. Department of Health and Human Services, Public Health Service and National Institutes of Health. 1992. *Making Health Communication Programs Work: A Planner's Guide*. NIH Publication No. 92-1493, Office of Cancer Communications, National Cancer Institute. Online at http://www.cancer.gov/pinkbook.

Walters, L. M., L. Wilkins, and T. Walters. 1989. *Bad Tidings: Communication and Catastrophe*. Lawrence Erlbaum Associates, Hillsdale, New Jersey.

West, B., P. M. Sandman, and M. R. Greenberg. 1995. *The Reporter's Environmental Handbook*. Rutgers University Press, Piscataway, New Jersey.

# Stakeholder Participation

*H*aving the audience or stakeholders interact directly with those who are communicating, assessing, and/or managing the risk can be an extremely effective way to communicate risk. Stakeholder participation can take many forms, such as self-help groups, focus groups, and advisory committees. Stakeholders can be involved in working through a particular risk issue, such as in a workshop. Stakeholders can also participate in how the risk is assessed or managed, for example, members of the public taking surveys or operating monitoring stations. The least effective but most often used form of stakeholder participation is the formal hearing or public meeting, for which the organization sets a time and place for the audience to present formal testimony, which is transcribed and used later in the risk management process.

Some stakeholder participation programs fail because of a lack of early and continuing involvement (Kasperson 1986). Stakeholder participation is most effective when key choices concerning the risk have yet to be made. Once an organization is locked on a course of action, participation opportunities dwindle to those that will educate the audience. Using stakeholder participation

Stakeholder participation is most effective when key choices concerning the risk have yet to be made. Once an organization is locked on a course of action, participation opportunities dwindle to those that will educate the audience.

solely to educate is more costly and time-consuming than other forms of risk communication that can be used to educate. Further, many stakeholders willing to participate expect a more substantial involvement and will become hostile when they realize their activities are limited, further constraining the risk communication effort.

Stakeholder participation is rapidly becoming the premiere way to communicate risks in consensus communication and planning for crises. Two blue-ribbon panels (the Presidential/Congressional Commission on Risk Assessment and Risk Management and the National Research Council's Committee on Risk Characterization) advocated stakeholder participation throughout the risk assessment, risk management, and risk communication process (Commission 1997; NRC 1996). Some research indicates that the public may be more supportive of decisions that were reached through a stakeholder participation process, even if they were not personally part of that process (Arvai 2003).

Advantages and disadvantages of stakeholder participation are discussed in Chapter 10, "Determine the Appropriate Methods." This chapter discusses requirements for successful stakeholder participation, provides guidelines for specific types of stakeholder participation activities, and gives advice on how to choose a form of stakeholder participation.

## REQUIREMENTS FOR STAKEHOLDER PARTICIPATION

To choose a form of stakeholder participation, you need to consider both organizational and stakeholder needs. Your organization must be comfortable with the way it interacts with stakeholders and vice versa. You can then evaluate the various forms of stakeholder participation for application to your situation.

### Organizational Requirements for Successful Stakeholder Participation

For any form of stakeholder participation to succeed, your organization must be fully committed to it. Everyone involved with the risk assessment and risk management process—the scientists and engineers, the public health professionals, the technicians, the communicators, the public affairs specialists, the risk managers, and the organization's line managers—must believe that stakeholders have a right to be and can be involved. If anyone has reservations, those reservations will be apparent to the stakeholders and spoil any chances for meaningful interaction. Because many organizations are less than committed to stakeholder participation, effective participation in risk communication has been limited. However, in those cases where participation has been successful, both the stakeholders and the organization have deemed the participation well worth the effort (see, for example, Aleknavage and Lyon (1997); Beierle (2002)).

To make the effort acceptable to all involved in the risk assessment and management process, you need a clear plan. You need to know your purpose and objectives, your audience (stakeholders), your schedule, and the resources at your disposal. If these factors show that stakeholder participation would be an effective way to communicate risk, you then need a compelling reason that will convince the organization. Perhaps stakeholders have perspectives that would be particularly valuable to the risk assessment or management process. Perhaps no other method will bring about the desired results. Perhaps a regulation or policy mandates stakeholder participation. Presenting your plan and this compelling reason to the others involved with communicating, assessing, and managing the risk, and having a list of cases where effective stakeholder participation made for a more effective risk management decision, can help convince management of the need to involve stakeholders in a meaningful way. (See Aleknavage and Lyon (1997); Arvai (2003); Beierle (2002); Imholz et al. (1990) in this chapter's reference list, and additional examples of case studies in Chapter 21, "Resources.")

What most organizations fear about stakeholder participation is that the organization might lose control over the risk decision. However, stakeholder participation can strengthen that decision by:

- identifying stakeholder perceptions early in the process, so that the organization doesn't find out

For any form of stakeholder participation to succeed, your organization must be fully committed to it.

after the decision is made that stakeholders are unwilling or unable to support or implement it

- developing a consensus among all parties affected by the risk, giving the decision a weight it can achieve in no other way

- helping to prevent conflicts such as lawsuits that can delay making or implementing the decision.

In addition, inviting stakeholders to participate in the communication, assessment, or management of the risk can raise their awareness, inform them, and motivate them to action more strongly than any other form of risk communication.

## Stakeholder Requirements for Successful Participation

Certain stakeholder characteristics can influence the success of interactions with the organization. These characteristics include the size and number of segments, their level of interest, and most important, their level of hostility.

If stakeholders are widely distributed and encompass a number of diverse constituencies, each with its own perception of the risk and your organization (for example, the entire American populace), it can be extremely difficult to develop a single kind of stakeholder participation that will meet everyone's needs. Even including just one representative from each segment may require a committee with hundreds of people. Many types of stakeholder participation are limited to no more than 10 people to be effective (for example, focus groups). With more people, it becomes extremely difficult to come to any level of agreement (in the case of **consensus** communication) or even to have any kind of meaningful discussion (in the case of **care** communication or **crisis** communication planning). With a stakeholder group whose representatives number in the hundreds, the forms of stakeholder participation that have a chance of being successful are formal hearings, multiple meetings held around the country or region of interest, and consensus-building committees run by an

Certain stakeholder characteristics can influence the success of interactions with the organization. These characteristics include the size and number of segments, their level of interest, and most important, their level of hostility.

expert in conflict resolution. Technology is also making large-scale involvement more feasible. See Chapter 18 for details.

Stakeholder participation can also be difficult if stakeholders are apathetic. If stakeholders truly care nothing about the risk, but your organization feels the risk is real, you may need to raise awareness before you can effectively involve stakeholders in decision-making or risk prevention.

Some people feel that silence or previous lack of involvement are signs of apathy. However, lack of attendance at meetings or lack of comments on documents may mean hostility, not apathy. Hostility is the primary obstacle to meaningful stakeholder participation. If stakeholders don't believe your organization and are angry about the way your organization is handling the risk assessment, risk management, or risk communication process, it may be difficult to bring in members to work with your organization. On the other hand, effective stakeholder participation can be one of the best ways to reduce hostility, by showing that the organization does listen to and address concerns. In a situation with hostile stakeholders, interactions with small groups to build consensus and make decisions is the best choice. The worst choice in a hostile situation is a formal hearing because (1) the layout of the meeting exacerbates the "us versus them" mentality, (2) the formal hearing process is not conducive to having organizations inform stakeholders how their concerns will be addressed or considered in the risk decision, and (3) communication tends to be one-way.

The International Association for Public Participation, a professional organization dedicated to promoting and improving the practice of public participation, provides another way to consider what stakeholders may expect from meaningful participation. The organization developed a list of core values to guide stakeholder participation efforts, such as those for risk communication:

- The public should have a say in decisions about actions that affect their lives.

- Public participation includes the promise that the public's contribution will influence the decision.

- The public participation process communicates the interests and meets the process needs of all participants.

- The public participation process seeks out and facilitates the involvement of those potentially affected.

- The public participation process involves participants in defining how they participate.

- The public participation process communicates to participants how their input affected the decision.

- The public participation process provides participants with the information they need to participate in a meaningful way (IAP2 2000).

## GUIDELINES FOR SPECIFIC TYPES OF STAKEHOLDER PARTICIPATION ACTIVITIES

Once you know what your organization will approve and what stakeholders need, you can determine which type of stakeholder participation activity will be most effective in your situation. For each of the types of participation mentioned above, there are certain things you can do to help ensure success.

### The Formal Hearing

Formal hearings are those in which the risk information is presented by a member of the organization, followed by formal testimony from members of the audience; an example is a scoping hearing for an environmental impact statement. These interactions tend to be primarily one-way communication and hence are often not very effective in involving stakeholders in risk assessment, risk management, or risk communication. In fact, some research indicates that formal hearings may increase participants' perception of risk and decrease their perception of the sponsoring organization's credibility (McComas 2001).

Formal hearings are those in which the risk information is presented by a member of the organization, followed by formal testimony from members of the audience; an example is a scoping hearing for an environmental impact statement. These interactions tend to be primarily one-way communication and hence are often not very effective in involving stakeholders in risk assessment, risk management, or risk communication.

However, as mentioned above, there are times when the formal hearing is a useful means of stakeholder participation (for example, when stakeholders are dispersed and encompass many segments). There are also times when the law appears to require that you hold such a hearing (for example, after a draft environmental impact statement has been released for public comment). (Note, however, that your organization can usually comply with the spirit of the law by holding workshops, open houses, or other less formal and more effective types of stakeholder participation.)

If you must conduct a formal hearing, following certain guidelines can help ensure success.

- Pick a time and place with which stakeholders have no associated negative feelings or even have associated positive feelings. Choose a room large enough to hold everyone. Pick a time that will allow them to attend without missing work or key social functions. (For example, few people attended a hearing held on St. Patrick's Day in a town with a large Irish Catholic population and those who did were hostile.)

- Make sure key decision-makers attend. Stakeholders often tend not to believe that an organization will do anything about their concerns and comments unless they see someone in authority at the meeting. This was illustrated by comments at several meetings concerning the potential dangers of hazardous waste storage tanks. While a number of concerns were expressed, the overriding comment was, "Why isn't the head of the organization here? We want to hear his views, and we want him to hear ours."

- Get a good moderator, one who (1) keeps the meeting on track without making anyone feel slighted, (2) can focus questions and concerns so that everyone understands them, and (3) is credible to the audience (which usually means one who is independent of the organization). We once listened to a moderator from a federal agency at a formal hearing address every member of the audience by name and provide seemingly sincere comments on their

———— ◇ ————

Sometimes stakeholder characteristics or legal requirements make formal hearings necessary, but often the spirit of the law can be met by less formal and more effective types of stakeholder participation.

testimony. We were greatly impressed, until a woman seated in front of us leaned over to her companion and whispered, "She's so hypocritical! As if she really cares!" The moderator seemed to be doing everything right, and still did not meet the needs of the stakeholders because, as a member of the organization, she had no credibility with stakeholders.

- Arrange for comments to be recorded. In many cases, the legal purpose of a formal hearing is to record audience concerns. This recording can be done by using a tape recorder, a court stenographer, or a video recorder. Just taking notes or writing words on a flip chart is insufficient, although both are excellent supplementary methods—they show your audience that you are listening to them and noting their concerns. However, neither is sufficient to recall exact phrasing or underlying concerns at a later date.

- Allow time for questions and answers. Too many meetings are structured to allow the organization and audience to speak at each other, but not to interact. Typically, the organization spokesperson makes a presentation concerning the risk, then members of the audience take turns coming to the podium or microphone and expressing their concerns. Allow time between the two presentations for the audience to ask questions about the risk. Answers to these questions may allay some concerns, which you will not have to deal with later.

- Respond to audience concerns. As soon as possible after the meeting, make sure those who attended and their constituencies know how their comments and concerns were used in making a decision about the risk. Often organizations publish the transcribed comments, with coding or annotation by the organization to indicate how comments were addressed. Unfortunately, few people ever see such documents, leaving most of the audience to wonder why they bothered, eroding your organization's credibility. It is better to contact each commenter personally, either by phone or by letter, to explain how their concerns were addressed. This can be a daunting job, given the hundreds to thousands of commenters at some formal hearings. Nonetheless, if your organization's credibility and the audience's level of hostility are important, you need the time and funds to do it.

## Group Interactions

Group interactions generally require some sort of meeting. Much has been written about how to make meetings more effective. For risk communication purposes, there are several circumstances under which group interactions in meetings will not work:

- data are confidential
- the subject is trivial related to the overall risk
- there is anger or hostility
- the decision has already been made (Doyle and Straus 1976).

For the various types of group interactions (self-help groups, focus groups, workshops, or advisory committees), there are certain factors that help ensure success.

- Pick a time when all members of the group can attend and a place with which they have no associated negative feelings and, at best, with which they have associated positive feelings. Both focus groups and advisory committees should meet away from the organization if the group is independent or at the organization if it is more important to reinforce the feeling that the organization is really listening to them. For self-help groups, choose a meeting place that is conducive to sharing feelings (private, with comfortable furnishings).
- Identify the purposes, objectives, and desired results at the beginning. Make sure both the group and the organization know why the group is meeting, what they hope to accomplish, any limitations

to their scope or ability to make decisions, and the expected results. For example, with a group that is determining possible future land uses after the cleanup of a Superfund site, the purpose could be to explore possibilities and make recommendations to the organization; the objectives could be to meet regularly, divide the work among representatives, consult legal authorities and stakeholders, and develop recommendations based on information gathered; and the results could be to present a report on their findings and recommendations to the organization by the end of a year.

- Set clear lines of command and communication. Who is in charge of the meetings, the organization's representative or the other members, perhaps on a rotating basis? How are decisions made, by written ballot or show of hands? Do all members discuss the information and allow an elected leader to actually make the decision? Who mediates in the case of conflicts? Is consensus necessary or is it more important to capture the range of concerns and comments? Who presents the information from the group and to whom? Who presents the information from the organization and to whom? Develop a plan for how the group will function and make sure everyone involved with the group and those involved from the organization agree to it.

- Make sure that the organization shows support for the group. This can be done by having someone from the organization whom the group respects attend the meetings; providing resources such as funding, meeting space, and support staff (for example, to type reports or provide guidance); or sending letters of support to the group or outside organizations such as the press. This last suggestion will be meaningless if no one attends meetings and no resources are provided. (In situations in which stakeholders are particularly hostile, it can also undermine the credibility of the group, so consider the situation before following this advice.) If the organization doesn't show support, the group interaction will soon wither. If the organization does show support, the group interaction can be an extremely effective way to communicate risk information.

- Provide technical support. Some members of stakeholder groups will lack the expertise to effectively participate in group discussions regarding risk.

Researchers have also studied various group interactions to determine what makes these interactions effective or not so effective. For example, researchers reviewed the work of a team of government agencies, contractors, Native American tribes, and stakeholders to evaluate potential risks to a major watershed from past releases from a nuclear facility. They found that perceptions of fairness and competence were key to process success. By fairness, they meant that everyone had the same opportunity to (1) determine the rules and the agenda, (2) speak and ask questions, and (3) access information and analysis. By competence, they meant the ability to understand language concepts and to agree on reality. Key problems that hindered the effort included lack of attention to process rules, refusal of management to support decisions made by organization representatives, no formal dispute resolution mechanisms, and lack of mutually understood meanings of terms and concepts (Kinney and Leschine 2002).

Below are additional guidelines for specific types of group interactions.

### Self-Help Groups

The general purpose of self-help groups is to motivate stakeholders already aware of personal risky behavior (such as alcoholism or drug addiction) to prevent the risk in their own lives. Self-help groups can also assist stakeholders who are dealing with the aftermath of a crisis. In general, self-help groups should be led by a trained facilitator, often a psychologist or other health care provider. Those who are communicating risk can listen to concerns raised by the group and provide or develop information materials to answer specific questions (more information on developing information materials can be found in

◇

The general purpose of self-help groups is to motivate stakeholders already aware of personal risky behavior (such as alcoholism or drug addiction) to prevent the risk in their own lives. Self-help groups can also assist stakeholders who are dealing with the aftermath of a crisis.

Chapter 13). Risk communicators can also assist the facilitator in finding ways to support the group members in managing the relevant risks.

### Focus Groups

Focus groups involve stakeholder representatives who meet for a specific purpose, usually for a specified period of time (a few hours to several months), for example, to evaluate the future land uses of a government Superfund site after it is cleaned up. Focus groups have been used in risk communication to explore risk perceptions, help develop content of risk messages, pretest risk communication messages and materials, select risk communication methods, develop alternative ways to manage a particular risk, and evaluate risk communication efforts (Desvousges and Smith 1988). As we use the term in this book, focus groups serve to inform those who are communicating risk to the wide variety of opinions, as well as the prevailing opinions, within a stakeholder group on a particular subject. Used in this way, their participatory nature is somewhat limited because information is still flowing in one direction. However, because the organization thought to ask stakeholder opinions, stakeholders sometimes perceive a greater degree of involvement than some other forms of one-way risk communication.

Focus group interactions require the use of a skilled moderator to probe attitudes and opinions on the specified topic. However, it is important that the moderator be independent—that is, the moderator cannot be perceived as an expert in the risk or the effort, or the meeting may turn into a question-and-answer session. Tasks or exercises are often used to focus discussion or identify perceptions (Desvousges and Smith 1988).

The key word is "focus." This applies to these groups in several areas:

- Focus membership—focus groups do not function well beyond about 10 members. More than that limits the amount of time each member can speak and may intimidate some members of the group, keeping them from speaking. If the stakeholder group is large and multifaceted, try holding several focus

---

Focus groups involve stakeholder representatives who meet for a specific purpose, usually for a specified period of time (a few hours to several months), for example, to evaluate the future land uses of a government Superfund site after it is cleaned up. Focus groups have been used in risk communication to explore risk perceptions, help develop content of risk messages, pretest risk communication messages and materials, select risk communication methods, develop alternative ways to manage a particular risk, and evaluate risk communication efforts (Desvousges and Smith 1988).

groups with specific characteristics. For example, you might meet separately with environmental group representatives, civic group representatives, labor representatives, etc.

- Focus time—keep the meetings short and on schedule, preferably no more than two hours (Desvouges and Smith 1988). Nearly everyone who might belong to your focus group will have limited time to contribute. Make their time count and they will be more likely to find the process useful.

- Focus effort—as mentioned previously, make sure all members know the purpose of the meetings and how their comments will be used.

- Focus results—make sure you act on what you hear. Don't avoid problems that surface. And once you have acted or at least have a plan to act, let the wider group know how you are responding to their concerns.

Again, having a trained facilitator at a focus group meeting can help ensure meaningful results for both the group members and those who are communicating risk.

### Workshops

Workshops are similar to focus groups in that the purpose of the meeting is specific (for example, to reach a decision on which alternative to propose to clean up a Superfund site). However, the nature of the workshop is more educational than participatory in that the stakeholders will be provided with presentations and information before conducting their evaluation. These presentations serve to ensure that all members of the workshop have a common language for the topic being discussed and have a similar understanding of the risk on which to build discussions. Another area that is frequently overlooked, however, is the development of a common understanding of the purpose of the workshop, the process the workshop deliberations is supporting, and how the results of the workshop will be used.

To develop the presentations for the workshop, follow the guidelines in Chapter 15 on speaking engagements.

Workshops are similar to focus groups in that the purpose of the meeting is specific (for example, to reach a decision on which alternative to propose to clean up a Superfund site). However, the nature of the workshop is more educational than participatory in that the stakeholders will be provided with presentations and information before conducting their evaluation.

To develop information materials to supplement the presentations, follow the guidelines in Chapter 13. To set up the workshop, follow the general guidelines for group interactions earlier in this chapter.

### Advisory Groups

An advisory committee is made up of stakeholder representatives who advise the organization about concerns, usually over a variety of subjects over an extended time. Advisory groups are becoming an increasingly popular way to involve stakeholders in how a risk is being managed and communicated, across care, consensus, and crisis communication. One of the reasons for this increased use is that the Comprehensive Environmental Response, Compensation, and Liability Act (CERCLA or Superfund) strongly suggests the use of citizen advisory groups and makes provisions for technical assistance grants to support these groups. Technical assistance grants provide citizen advisory groups with the resources to hire their own risk consultants to help them understand and respond to the information in a risk assessment. In addition, the Emergency Planning and Community Right-to-Know Act establishes emergency planning activities, many of which include citizen advisory groups. Federal guidance on bioterrorism preparedness planning in 2003 also encouraged the development of advisory groups. Industry uses employee groups to advise on health and safety issues. Many industries have also developed their own citizen advisory groups to assist them in maintaining a positive relationship with local communities.

The U.S. Department of Defense has established Restoration Advisory Boards (RABs), advisory groups for environmental restoration processes at specific military installations. An RAB includes representatives of the military installation, the U.S. Environmental Protection Agency, state and local governments, tribal governments, and the affected local community. RAB members share community views with the installation decisionmakers and report information back to the community on the military's environmental restoration activities.

An advisory committee is made up of stakeholder representatives who advise the organization about concerns, usually over a variety of subjects over an extended time. Advisory groups are becoming an increasingly popular way to involve stakeholders in how a risk is being managed and communicated, across care, consensus, and crisis communication.

RABs are not decision-making bodies; they advise the military installation's commanding officer.

Since 1994, the Department of Defense has established more than 300 RABs in the United States and its territories. The web site of the Defense Environmental Restoration Program contains many resources about RABs, including policies, guidance, operations manuals, and a directory of RABs operating nationwide (see Resources in this chapter). The Department of Energy has established similar boards (Site-Specific Advisory Boards) at various sites where they are cleaning up the legacy from the Cold War.

Advisory groups usually meet for a longer time than other types of group interactions (except for some self-help groups that go on for years), requiring a large commitment of time from stakeholder participants. This time commitment often limits who can serve as members of these groups. There are two common ways around this limitation.

The first way is to find a method to compensate members for their time. For employees meeting on safety issues, the solution may be to make group membership an equal part of their job and ensure they are paid for their time to attend meetings and provide information back to their fellow employees. For stakeholders outside the organization, the solution may be to make arrangements with their employers for time off as well as to pay them for their time. A drawback to this solution is that some members may look upon this pay as an entitlement and fight to stay in the group even when they are no longer in a position to contribute.

The second way to counter this limitation is to allow for a continuing rotation of membership, so that no member has to spend excessive time in meetings. Members representing specific groups could serve for a quarter, a year, or a few years, depending on the frequency of group meetings. The drawback to this solution is that with continued membership turnover comes the need for continued education on the same issues, slowing the progress of the entire group.

Because of the popularity of these types of groups, much as been written as to characteristics of the group that ensure success:

- Include members from across stakeholder groups. In care communication efforts, this would include a member of each group at risk. For example, in developing an employee safety committee, you would need members to represent common classes of employees such as clerical, managerial, physical labor, and scientific/engineering/white collar workers. In crisis communication planning efforts, members could include representatives from all groups who will assist in emergency response efforts, both inside and outside an organization, for example, county and city governments, local firefighters, and the news media. In consensus communication efforts, this would include representatives from each group with which consensus is sought. For example, advisory groups for environmental cleanup efforts often contain representatives of environmental groups, elected officials, business interests, regulatory agencies, Native American governments, and that nebulous group called "the public" (Serie and Dressen 1992). This latter group is the most difficult to recruit. Tactics include putting ads in the newspaper and contacting already organized groups with noncompeting agendas (for example, the local parent-teacher association might be able to identify a representative of the general public for an environmental cleanup effort but might be already deeply involved in an effort to reform the science curriculum in the education system).

- Provide for independent technical advisors. Regardless of whether the advisory group is chartered under Superfund (and thus can apply for a technical assistance grant), advisory groups can benefit from having their own expert advisor. This advisor can serve to help clarify risk information and provide additional review and perspective to the risk assessment and management process. When the advisor and the organization in charge of managing the risk agree on the interpretation of risk data, the organization's credibility is enhanced. When they disagree, the disagreement points to areas that require additional information and communication. Edward Scher of the Massachusetts Institute of Technology's Department of Urban Studies and Planning and Sarah McKearnan of the Public Disputes Program of the Harvard Law School suggest that to be successful, these technical advisors must be credible with all segments of the stakeholder group, understand the process as well as the technical issues, guide but refrain from driving the interactions, and have the ability to work closely with participation facilitators (Scher and McKearnan 1997).

## Interactions Involving Risk Assessment

More and more, stakeholders are demanding to participate in how a risk is determined, for example, in how regulations are set for particular chemicals, preparations are made for for public health emergencies, and risks are characterized in environmental cleanup decisions. A few years ago, many scientists, engineers, and other decision-makers would have balked at the thought of a layperson conducting complex risk analyses. However, the advent of widely available risk assessment models in the form of software that can be used on a personal computer has helped make such participation a reality.

Stakeholders can get access to much of the raw data used by scientists and engineers to calculate risks. Government agencies have to make such information available, even if they do so unwillingly as is often the case when a stakeholder group issues a Freedom of Information Act request. Industries that use hazardous chemicals must provide information on the types of chemicals and amounts to local communities when complying with the Emergency Planning and Community Right-to-Know Act. Some generic cancer registry information may also be available. With such raw data and a computer model, many stakeholder groups can calculate their own risk numbers, which, not surprisingly, may

◇

More and more, stakeholders are demanding to participate in how a risk is determined, whether in how regulations are set for particular chemicals or in how risks are characterized in environmental cleanup decisions.

differ from those being issued by the organization in charge of assessing the risk because different assumptions and scenarios were used. When the two estimates differ by more than a small amount, the organization's credibility can be eroded and subsequent risk communication efforts severely hampered.

It only makes sense, then, to assist stakeholders in their efforts to assess risk. Welcome the chance for an independent review (for that is what their assessment will be) of the risk assessment as an opportunity to improve the assessment. Meet with stakeholder groups from the beginning to identify assumptions, model limitations, and scenarios being developed. Whenever possible, incorporate their suggestions of assumptions and scenarios into your own risk assessment effort. When it isn't possible (perhaps because of time or funding constraints or model limitations), explain why. Offer to provide training in the use of their chosen model. Allow them to view the data being input to your model and provide an overview of how your model functions. These steps will likely increase the similarities in the two risk assessments. However, even if the two estimates still differ, stakeholders will have a better appreciation for what you were trying to accomplish and instead of open hostility, you are more likely to find a receptive audience to discuss the differences and continue the risk communication effort.

## Interactions Involving Decision-Making

As noted by James Creighton, consultant on stakeholder involvement, the American public has increasingly demanded a bigger role in how decisions about risk are made (Creighton 1992). It is not uncommon to find regulatory agencies, other government agencies, and industry moving toward consulting with stakeholders before making key decisions regarding environmental, safety, and health risks. Most of the activities described in this chapter can be adopted to allow stakeholders to participate in decision-making. Key considerations will be:

- The scope of the involvement—what does "stakeholder participation" mean for this decision? Will

As noted by James Creighton, consultant on stakeholder involvement, the American public has increasingly demanded a bigger role in how decisions about risk are made (Creighton 1992). It is not uncommon to find regulatory agencies, other government agencies, and industry moving toward consulting with stakeholders before making key decisions regarding environmental, safety, and health risk.

they provide criteria for ranking alternative ways to assess or manage the risk? Will they provide input on preferred ways to assess or manage the risk? Will they provide input on how various stakeholders might respond to different risk management strategies? Both the stakeholders and the organization in charge of managing the risk must agree on the exact parameters of involvement or the effort will not succeed.

- Results of the involvement—what will happen once input has been received? The ultimate decision maker in most risk situations is the organization in charge of managing the risk, and these organizations seldom relinquish that power. Indeed, in the case of government organizations, laws and regulations prohibit the relinquishing of that power. For organizational credibility, and the success of the risk communication effort, it is vital that stakeholders understand where their decision-making power ends and the organization's begins.

The following subsections discuss specific types of stakeholder participation related to decision-making involving risks. These types include facilitated deliberation and alternative dispute resolution.

### Facilitated Deliberation

Facilitated deliberation usually refers to groups of people discussing issues and recommending solutions, led by a facilitator. Methods can be as casual as "Internet café" discussion groups and as formal as AmericaSpeaks electronic "21st Century town hall meetings" involving thousands of citizens nationwide. For risk-related issues involving affected communities, two methods—Citizens Juries® and study circles—have been particularly useful.

**Citizens Juries.** The Jefferson Center, in Minneapolis, Minnesota, developed and trademarked the process known as the Citizens Jury. The Citizens Jury is designed to enable citizens to engage in informed discussions, generating findings for decision-makers and the broader community. Randomly selected and demographically representative panels of citizens meet for several

Facilitated deliberation usually refers to groups of people discussing issues and recommending solutions, led by a facilitator.

days using a prescribed, facilitated process to examine public policy issues and present their findings. The juries hear from "witnesses" in "hearings," deliberate on complex issues, and report their findings and recommendations.

Citizens Juries have been used for public policy issues of local, regional, or national importance. Risk-related issues have included comparing environmental risks, land use plans, agriculture and water policy, genetically modified food (Opinion Leader Research 2003), solid waste disposal (Jefferson Center 2001), and global climate change (Jefferson Center 2002). The Institute for Public Policy Research began its own series of Citizens Juries in the United Kingdom in the 1990s (Coote and Franklin 1999), with more than 100 projects conducted in Britain since 1996. Many other countries have adopted Citizens Juries as well. The Jefferson Center disbanded in 2002, but Citizens Juries continue in various forms.

Citizens Juries have many similarities to advisory groups. They are independent of the organization that formed them. Sessions are open to observers, and the final report is in the public domain. The commissioning organization is expected to either follow the jurors' recommendations or to explain publicly why not.

Unlike most advisory boards, Citizens Juries are useful for one-time decisions or input where intense discussion and deliberation occur over a condensed time period. The planning process usually takes three or four months, but the deliberation process itself typically runs only four or five days. Jurors disband afterward, so they can't address policy issues as they develop over time.

**Study Circles.** The study circle is another deliberation and problem-solving process. Groups of 8 to 12 people from diverse backgrounds and viewpoints meet several times to talk about an issue, often related to a community policy or need. They usually meet over a period of weeks or months and are guided by a trained facilitator. The emphasis is on examining an issue from many perspectives. The process does not require consensus, but it uncovers areas of agreement and common concern, ultimately generating strategies for action.

---

◇

Citizens Juries are useful for one-time decisions or input where intense discussion and deliberation occur over a condensed time period.

---

In a large-scale study circle program, people all over a neighborhood, city, county, school district, or region meet in diverse study circles over the same period of time. All the study circles work on the same issue and seek solutions for the whole community. At the end of the round of study circles, people from all the circles come together in a large community meeting to work together on the action ideas. According to the Study Circles Resource Center, in Pomfret, Connecticut, more than 100 communities have instituted community-wide study circles since 1992.

Risk-related topics in study circles have included community growth issues, land use, and neighborhood crime. Study circles involving nearly 400 people in Portsmouth, New Hampshire, prompted the city's Planning Board to endorse a 10-acre land purchase as public conservation habitat in 2003. Study circles of 350 people in Buffalo, New York, created programs such as "Walk and Park," where police officers park their cars for an hour a day to visit neighborhood businesses, and an anti-crime program called "Putting the Neighbor Back in the 'Hood'."

Study circle proponents say the process helps citizens gain ownership of the issues, discover a connection between personal experiences and public policies, gain a deeper understanding of their own and others' perspectives and concerns, create a greater ability to work collaboratively, and spark new connections between citizens and community leaders. The Study Circles Resource Center web site contains resources to help communities institute study circles, including operations guidelines, facilitator training guidelines, evaluation forms, and best practices reports.

Study circle proponents say the process sparks new connections between citizens and community leaders.

### Alternative Dispute Resolution

Risk-related decision-making often sparks conflicting points of view, sometimes leading to disputes. Alternative dispute resolution, in all its forms, represents ways to settle disputes without litigation or administrative adjudication, thus avoiding a solution that is imposed on the parties by an outsider. Research has shown that disputants often prefer alternative dispute resolution to the court process, because of rapid processing, low costs, and the perception of the process being satisfying, fair, understandable, and ultimately resolving the conflict (Cook et al. 1980).

Federal and state statutes have enacted resolutions for alternative dispute resolution, and many agencies have implemented their own programs (Herring 2001). An emerging area is resolving disputes using the Internet, called online or electronic dispute resolution (Katsh and Rifkin 2001).

Three of the most commonly used methods of alternative dispute resolution are facilitation, negotiation, and mediation. All three use a neutral third party to facilitate an agreement. They typically share certain goals: allow voluntary participation by the disputants in a fair process, craft a creative and mutually satisfactory resolution, and enhance the parties' relationships while enabling them to save face (Renken 2002). All three methods have been used extensively in public participation processes involving risk. The following sections briefly summarize each method. Note that these definitions are fluid and somewhat interchangeable; even practitioners and professional associations disagree among themselves on what each method entails.

**Facilitation.** Facilitation uses a neutral third party to help groups accomplish their work by providing process leadership and expertise. Facilitators improve the flow of information and enhance mutual understanding. The facilitator remains impartial about the substantive issues under discussion and focuses on the communication process, leading the parties and providing procedural direction. A facilitator uses skills and techniques that enable the group to clarify issues, generate ideas, prioritize goals or solutions, and solve problems. If conflicts arise, the facilitator uses process skills to help people get past their individual agendas and get on with the group task.

Unlike other alternative dispute resolution techniques, facilitation does not usually involve caucuses (private meetings with the facilitator), except for initial meetings to launch the proceedings.

The International Association of Facilitators recommends the use of an independent facilitator (not a member of the group working on the task) under the following circumstances:

- When distrust, bias, or rivalry are present

- When participants have disparate educational, social, or economic status; are at different hierarchical levels; or are in relationships with significant power disparities

- When the task or problem is poorly defined or defined differently by various participants

- When group members all want to participate in the decision process rather than focusing only on the group process and logistics.

The International Association of Facilitators offers a Certified Professional Facilitator© credential and maintains a directory of certified facilitators by country and state. Certification is based on demonstrated competencies. These include the ability to create collaborative client relationships, plan appropriate group processes, create and sustain a participatory environment, guide the group to appropriate and useful outcomes, build and maintain professional knowledge, and model a positive professional attitude.

In risk communication, facilitation has been used extensively to address issues such as environmental cleanup, resource management, siting of facilities and electric transmission lines, and habitat restoration. Risk communicators typically serve in one of two roles. They may serve as the trained facilitator. They may also serve as the liaison who selects and/or recommends a facilitator and provides that person with background information and resources for the facilitation exercise.

**Negotiation.** In negotiation, a third party helps the parties come to an agreement and may recommend a particular settlement. A long-established approach to negotiation considered it a "zero-sum" game, assuming that one party's gain is the other party's loss. But in the 1980s, Harvard Law School professors Roger Fisher and William Ury developed a highly regarded method called

In negotiation, a third party helps the involved groups come to an agreement and may recommend a particular settlement.

principled negotiation. It's based on the premise that it is possible to meet one's own needs and those of others, and that conflict provides such opportunities (Fisher et al. 1991). Four principles define the method:

- People problems (negative emotions, differences in perceptions, and communication difficulties) are separated from substantial issues.

- Positions are transformed into underlying interests.

- Many options for gain are generated before deciding.

- Mutually agreed-upon objective criteria are developed that are legitimate, practical, reciprocally applicable, and independent of each side's will.

Negotiators can be found and evaluated in the same manner as mediators; the following section suggests a process.

**Mediation.** Mediation helps people resolve or better manage disputes by reaching agreements about what the parties will do differently in the future. Originally adapted from labor-management negotiations, mediation is often used with families, businesses, schools, and workplaces, as well as with stakeholders in public policy issues. With the involvement of a neutral mediator, the parties identify the roles of the participants and ground rules, identify and discuss the problem, identify common goals and issues, generate options, bargain, and reach agreement. Private caucuses between the parties and the mediator may be used to build support or trust, explore settlement options, or break down barriers to negotiation in a confidential setting. The agreement is put in writing and signed by representatives of the parties, and it carries the same legal weight as any contract.

The Alaska Judicial Council (1999) recommends the following process for selecting a mediator:

- **Identify your mediation goals.** What do you expect the mediator to do, based on the nature of the dispute and context for resolving it? Consider your budget and time frame. Mediator organizations can help you understand which services would be best for your situation.

◇

Mediation helps people reach agreements about what they will do differently in the future.

- **Compile a list of names.** Mediator organizations often maintain listings by state, such as the Association for Conflict Resolution Mediator Directory.

- **Contact several mediators and request information.** This could include their promotional materials, resume, references, and a sample of their written agreements. Evaluate the materials in terms of training, experience, certification, and fee structure. Do they offer an orientation session after which the parties decide whether they want to continue?

- **Interview the mediators.** Your goal is to learn more about their training, knowledge, experience, style, confidentiality policies, logistics, and cost.

- **Compare among the mediators and decide.** You may wish to suggest two or three mediators so that all parties can agree on at least one.

Several programs and associations certify mediators. Some states and agencies also have their own certification requirements.

Environmental mediation, or environmental dispute resolution, as it's sometimes called, is a subset of mediation. Environmental disputes typically involve issues such as land use, agricultural and water rights, hazardous waste, tribal-state natural resource agreements, facility siting, and growth management. In South Carolina, for example, certified mediators throughout the state help citizens resolve disputes over environmental health and natural resources. Government officials are increasingly turning to negotiators for assistance when attempting to build public consensus on permitting decisions, public project specifications, and natural resource allocations (Blacklocke 2001). In California, an environmental mediation process brought agreement on technical issues that had stalled an ecological risk assessment for Vandenberg Air Force Base for two years (Poncelet and Widman 2001).

Public participation and dispute resolution expert Jim Creighton cautions that environmental mediation can succeed only if the following conditions are met (Creighton et al. 1998):

- The parties have reached the point that they no longer believe they can impose their will on each other.

- The relative power of the interests is close enough that no one worries unduly about being exploited.

- The parties are convinced that they will achieve more through an agreement than by continuing to fight.

- The parties are well defined.

- The parties agree on the need for all of them to be at the table.

- The parties have the ability to commit their respective constituencies to the agreement.

- The agreement is binding.

An even more specific kind of environmental mediation is negotiated rulemaking, or regulatory negotiation. It uses techniques of multiparty mediation to deal with large disputes over public policy. Representatives of stakeholder groups from industry, consumer and environmental organizations, and government agencies work with a mediator to negotiate government regulations. If they reach consensus, the agency can use the outcome as the basis for a proposed rule. The rule is still subject to public review and all other steps in the formal rulemaking process.

The U.S. Institute for Environmental Conflict Resolution maintains a directory of specialists in environmental mediation.

### Interactions Involving Risk Management

Risk management interactions involve stakeholders in managing the risk. In care communication involving personal risks to health and safety, those at risk are often the only ones who can manage the risk. Involving stakeholders in risk management is becoming more common in consensus and crisis communication too, for example, by having stakeholders collect and analyze environmental samples near a facility to determine whether contaminants are affecting the local area. Successful stakeholder participation in how a risk is managed is becoming more common, mostly because such interactions can be an extremely effective means of informing and raising awareness about a risk. To effectively involve stakeholders in managing the risk, certain guidelines should be followed.

- Determine the purposes and objectives. What do you want to gain by this interaction and how will you accomplish it? If your purpose is to inform your audience, a reasonable objective is to provide them with hands-on experience with the scientific assessment of risk. For example, they might join the scientists in running risk calculation models and explore how changes in various parameters equating to changes in lifestyles affect results. If your purpose is to raise awareness, your objective might be to show them how the risk is managed. For example, they might tour a new facility being built to identify safety features. If your purpose is to build consensus on the management of a risk, your objective might be to begin a dialogue on the issues at stake. For example, they might hold a workshop on strategies to communicate the dangers of drug addiction to teenagers. Each case will require slightly different arrangements.

- Determine the scope of the interaction. Exactly what will you have them do? If they will work in the field or laboratory, what will they be doing and who will be accountable for them? If they are working alongside management, who will determine what they can do within the organization and what information they are allowed to access? How long will they work? What will be the final product, a report to their constituencies, a press release, a journal article? Establishing this scope in the beginning will help you plan a meaningful interaction.

- Make sure those chosen to help manage the risk represent stakeholder groups. Risk management interactions take a lot of time to set up. If the people you choose to help manage the risk do not represent stakeholders, the effort will be for nothing. No stakeholder will be interested in what they have to say unless they are otherwise credible.

- Make sure those chosen to help manage the risk are properly trained. For safety reasons as well as for technical credibility, those who will be working with the risk must have the proper training. Allow them to attend the organization's training courses, or hold special sessions targeted to their needs.

- Make sure those chosen to help manage the risk are capable of disseminating information and mechanisms and resources are available for them to do so. For example, you might provide clerical assistance in typing an article by those involved in the risk management activity for a stakeholder newsletter. The main reason for conducting this type of stakeholder participation is to share risk management information. The information will be far more credible if it comes from stakeholder members who have been involved with the risk. If you disseminate the information on their behalf, it may have no greater credibility than if your organization gathered it. Make sure the workers chosen are articulate and can write or speak well enough to present the risk to their peers in language that stakeholders will understand.

- Show organizational support. With this type of interaction, the organization must be heavily involved in planning, training, overseeing, and evaluating the workers. However, releasing press information, mentioning the workers by name in organization literature (if the workers agree to this), and even treating them to dinner with the organization's top management are good ways to show you appreciate their efforts. (But first make sure stakeholders or the workers won't see this last token of appreciation as the organization's paying off the workers.)

- Watch out for union conflicts. Some of the jobs assigned to these workers may fall under union rules. Discuss the importance of these workers with union representatives beforehand. If the union workers understand that the organization's future reputation and business depend heavily on the audience understanding of a particular risk, they are more likely to accept such encroachment on their areas of expertise.

## Evaluating Stakeholder Participation Based on Your Situation

Table 17-1 lists advantages and disadvantages of the various types of stakeholder participation. The type of interaction you choose also depends on whether you are conducting care, consensus, or crisis communication. Table 17-2 shows which types of interaction are most effective for the three types of risk communication.

### TABLE 17-1
Advantages and Disadvantages of Stakeholder Participation in Risk Communication

| Type of Interaction | Advantages | Disadvantages |
|---|---|---|
| Formal hearings | Are easy to implement; meet minimum legal requirements for some laws; allow geographically dispersed groups to participate | Can increase hostility; give time to only vocal concerns; leave some members of the audience dissatisfied; provide insubstantial involvement |
| Self-help groups | Motivate audience to act; empower audience | Will be effective only if audience can affect risk; require long-term commitment from both organization and stakeholders |
| Focus groups | Are small scale and have well-defined purpose and time frame so may be less intimidating to some organizations | Have limited scale and time; may not represent full audience; may not be substantial enough involvement for some stakeholders |
| Workshops | Educate as well as involve; gather disperse viewpoints | Require technical knowledge; require teaming between organization and stakeholders that may not be possible in hostile situations |
| Advisory groups | Have longer time frame so stakeholders can learn about risk; can help develop decisions | May be less effective over time; commit organization to respond; requires considerable resources (time, money, staff) |

*continued*

**TABLE 17-1** *(continued)*
Advantages and Disadvantages of Stakeholder Participation in Risk Communication

| Type of Interaction | Advantages | Disadvantages |
|---|---|---|
| Risk assessment interactions | Provide credible review of process; increase chances of acceptable assessment | Require technical knowledge; feel too much like "challenge" to some technical experts |
| Decision-making interactions | Can lead to more acceptable decision; are highest form of involvement | Require organization to relinquish some control; may not be legal in some situations |
| Risk management interactions | Teach stakeholders about risk; empower them | Require technical knowledge; will be effective only if audience can affect risk |

**TABLE 17-2**
Effective Stakeholder Participation for Care, Consensus, and Crisis Risk Communication

| Level of Effectiveness | Care Communication | Consensus Communication | Crisis Communication* |
|---|---|---|---|
| Most effective | Self-help groups; risk management interactions | Decision-making interactions; advisory groups; workshops; risk assessment interactions | Focus groups |
| Moderately effective | Focus groups | Focus groups; risk management interactions | Self-help groups |
| Least effective | Formal hearings | Formal hearings | Formal hearings |

*Stakeholder participation cannot be conducted during a crisis unless the interaction has been planned months in advance. If planned, focus groups can meet quickly to help those who are communicating the risk to understand the needs of the audience and disseminate information. Self-help groups can be used after the crisis to help the audience come to terms with what has happened.

## CHECKLIST FOR STAKEHOLDER PARTICIPATION

❏ The involvement starts early and runs throughout the risk assessment and management process.

❏ The organization is committed to providing stakeholder participation.

The type of stakeholder participation was chosen based both on:

❏ organizational needs

❏ stakeholder needs.

❏ There is a written plan for the interaction.

For formal hearings:

❏ the time and place are comfortable to the audience

❏ key decision-makers have been invited to attend

❏ the services of a good moderator have been arranged

❏ comments will be recorded

❏ time has been allowed for questions and answers

❏ how audience concerns were used in the risk decision will be communicated to them after the meeting.

For group interactions:

❏ the time and place are comfortable to participants

❏ the purpose and objectives of the group have been agreed upon

❏ the lines of communication have been defined

❏ the group has decided how it will operate

❏ someone credible from the organization will attend

❏ the organization will provide resources

❏ technical support has been provided.

For self-help groups:

❏ the group is led by a trained facilitator

❏ additional information has been made available to meet audience needs.

For focus groups:

❏ the moderator is seen as independent

❏ there are no more than 10 members who represent stakeholders

❏ each meeting lasts no longer than two hours

❏ the group has an agreed-upon purpose

❏ the group knows how its comments will be used.

For workshops:

☐ guidelines for speaking engagements have been followed for presentations

☐ guidelines for information materials have been followed for those materials

☐ guidelines for group interactions have been followed.

For advisory groups:

☐ the organization has developed a mechanism to manage time commitments

☐ the group includes members from across stakeholder constituencies

☐ the group has a credible technical advisor.

For risk assessment interactions:

☐ assumptions, limitations, and scenarios for the assessment have been related to stakeholders

☐ stakeholder assumptions and scenarios have been included when possible and an explanation provided when it was not possible

☐ the stakeholders have been offered training in model use

☐ the stakeholders have viewed the data being input to the model

☐ the model functioning has been explained to the stakeholders.

For decision-making interactions:

☐ the scope of involvement has been delineated

☐ stakeholders know how their input will be used in the decision.

For risk management interactions:

☐ the purposes and objectives are clear to all involved

☐ scope has been determined and agreed upon

- ❏ those who are working represent the audience
- ❏ workers have received the appropriate training
- ❏ workers are capable of disseminating risk information
- ❏ the organization will show support for the workers
- ❏ the union has been consulted about possible conflicts.

## REFERENCES

Alaska Judicial Council. 1999. *A Consumer Guide to Selecting a Mediator*. Anchorage, Alaska. Online at http://www.ajc.state.ak.us/Reports/mediatorframe.htm.

Aleknavage, J., and B. Lyon. 1997. "Citizens and Manufacturers Work Together." *ChemEcology*, June-July:7-9.

Arvai, J. L. 2003. "Using Risk Communication to Disclose the Outcome of a Participatory Decision-Making Process: Effects on the Perceived Acceptability of Risk-Policy Decisions." *Risk Analysis*, 23(2):281-290.

Beierle, T. C. 2002. "The Quality of Stakeholder-Based Decisions." *Risk Analysis*, 22(4):739-750.

Blacklocke, S. 2001. *Alternative Environmental Dispute Resolution in South Carolina: Emerging Opportunities to Build More Sustainable Communities*. Online at http://www.mediate.com/articles/blacklocke.cfm#9.

Commission (Presidential/Congressional Commission on Risk Assessment and Risk Management). 1997. *Risk Assessment and Risk Management in Regulatory Decision-Making*. Commission, Washington, D.C.

Cook, R., J. Roehl, and D. Sheppard. 1980. *Neighborhood Justice Centers Field Test: Final Evaluation Report*. U.S. Government Printing Office, Washington, D.C.

Coote, A. and J. Franklin. 1999. "Negotiating Risks to Public Health—Models for Participation." In *Risk Communication and Public Health*, P. Bennett and K. Calman, editors. Oxford University Press, Oxford, Great Britain, pages 183-194.

Creighton, J. 1992. "What Does it Take for a Decision to 'Count'?" Presentation to the U.S. Department of Energy, Richland Operations Office, Richland, Washington. Creighton and Creighton, Palo Alto, California.

Creighton, J. L., C. M. Dunning, J. Delli Priscoli, D. B. Ayres (Eds.) 1998. *Public Involvement and Dispute Resolution: A Reader on the Second Decade of Experience at the Institute for Water Resources*. Institute for Water Resources, U.S. Army Corps of Engineers, Alexandria, Virginia.

Desvousges, W. H., and V. K. Smith. 1988. "Focus Groups and Risk Communication: The 'Science' of Listening to Data." *Risk Analysis*, 8(4):479-484.

Doyle, M., and D. Straus. 1976. *How to Make Meetings Work*. Wyden Books, Chicago.

Fisher, R., B. Patton, W. Ury. 1991. *Getting to Yes. Negotiating an Agreement Without Giving In* (2nd ed.). Penguin Books, New York, New York.

Herring, M. 2001. *Summary of State Alternative Environmental Dispute Resolution Institutions*. Online at http://www.mediate.com/articles/scsg1.cfm.

IAP2 (International Association for Public Participation). 2000. "Core Values for the Practice of Public Participation." Online at http://www.iap2.org/corevalues/index.html.

Imholz, R. M., T. B. Hindman, and D. M. Brubaker. 1990. "Lessons Learned from Applying External Input to DOE Policy Decision Making." *Proceedings of the International Topical Meeting on Nuclear and Hazardous Waste Management, Spectrum '90*, pages 12-15. American Nuclear Society, La Grange Park, Illinois.

Jefferson Center. 2001. *Citizens Jury®, Metro Solid Waste*. June 18-22, 2001, St. Paul, Minnesota. Jefferson Center, Minneapolis, Minnesota.

Jefferson Center. 2002. *Citizens Jury®, Global Climate Change*. March 18-22, 2002, Baltimore, Maryland. Jefferson Center, Minneapolis, Minnesota.

Kasperson, R. E. 1986. "Six Propositions on Public Participation and Their Relevance for Risk Communication." *Risk Analysis*, 6(3):275-281.

Katsh, E. and J. Rifkin. 2001. *Online Dispute Resolution: Resolving Conflicts in Cyberspace*. Jossey-Bass, San Francisco, California.

Kinney, A. G., and T. M. Leschine. 2002. "A Procedural Evaluation of an Analytical-Deliberative Process: The Columbia River Comprehensive Impact Assessment." *Risk Analysis*, 22(1):83-100.

McComas, K. A. 2001. "Public Meetings and Risk Amplification: A Longitudinal Study." Presented at the Society for Risk Analysis Annual Meeting, December 2-5, 2001, Seattle, Washington.

NRC (National Research Council). 1996. *Understanding Risk: Informing Decisions in a Democratic Society*. National Academy Press, Washington, D.C.

Opinion Leader Research. 2003. *FSA Citizens' Jury: Should GM Food Be Available to Buy in the UK?* Final Report. Prepared for the Food Standards Agency, London, England.

Poncelet, E. C. and G. Widman. 2001. *Better Together: Mediating an End to an Ecological Risk Assessment Dispute at Vandenberg Air Force Base.* Online at http://www.mediate.com/articles/poncelet.cfm.

Renken, D. 2002. *The ABC's of ADR. A Comprehensive Guide to Alternative Dispute Resolution.* Online at http://www.mediate.com/articles/renkenD.cfm#_edn2.

Scher, E., and S. McKearnan. 1997. "Do's and Don't's from a Philadelphia Story: How to Find Helpful Expert Advice." *Consensus*, April 1997, No. 34, pages 1, 8, and 12. MIT-Harvard Public Disputes Program, Cambridge, Massachusetts.

Serie, P. J., and A. L. Dressen. 1992. "Creating a Context for Public Confidence in Environmental Remediation Programs." *ER '91, Proceedings of the Conference for the U.S. Department of Energy,* pages 31-35. U.S. Department of Energy, Washington, D.C.

## ADDITIONAL RESOURCES

American Bar Association Section on Dispute Resolution. Online at http://www.abanet.org/dispute.

Association for Conflict Resolution. Online at http://www.acrnet.org.

Carpenter, S. L. and W. J. D. Kennedy. 2001. *Managing Public Disputes: A Practical Guide for Government, Business and Citizens' Groups.* John Wiley & Sons, Inc., New York, New York.

Center for Information Technology and Dispute Resolution. Online at http://www.ombuds.org/center/about.html.

CR Info: The Conflict Resolution Information Source. Online at http://www.crinfo.org.

Defense Environmental Restoration Program. Online at http://www.dtic.mil/envirodod.

Imholz, R. M., G. E. Rubery, and D. M. Brubaker. 1992. "Case Studies on Designing Meetings for Effective Institutional Interactions." *ER '91: Proceedings of the Environmental Restoration Conference for the U.S. Department of Energy*, pages 27-30. U.S. Department of Energy, Washington, D.C.

International Association of Facilitators. Online at http://www.iaf-world.org.

Jefferson Center. Online at http://www.jefferson-center.org.

Lynn, F. M., and G. J. Busenberg. 1995. "Citizen Advisory Committees and Environmental Policy: What We Know, What's Left to Discover." *Risk Analysis*, 15(2):147-162.

National Association for Community Mediation. Online at http://www.nafcm.org.

National Coalition for Dialogue and Deliberation. Online at http://thataway.org.

National Institute for Dispute Resolution. Online at http://www.sustainable.doe.gov/database/314.html.

Moore, C.W. 2003. *The Mediation Process: Practical Strategies for Resolving Conflict* (3rd ed.). Jossey-Bass, San Francisco, California.

Study Circles Resource Center. Online at http://www.studycircles.org.

U.S. Institute for Environmental Conflict Resolution. Online at http://www.ecr.gov.

# Technology-Assisted Communication

Computers and other forms of technology are becoming increasingly popular tools for communicating information about risks. Web sites raise risk awareness and provide options to mitigate risks. Telebriefings and streaming audio and video convey risk information quickly to media outlets and consumers. Listservs, CDs, and wireless devices deliver multimedia content for training, health information, and alerts. Electronic forms invite stakeholders to provide comments on risk decisions, computer models help them calculate their own risks, and group software aids decision-making processes.

Yet technology applications are not always superior to other forms of communication; in fact, they are sometimes less useful and more expensive. Advantages and disadvantages of technology-based applications are discussed in Chapter 10, "Determine the Appropriate Methods." This chapter discusses how to choose technology applications based on objectives and provides advice on how to use these applications when communicating risk in the workplace and in care, consensus, and crisis communication efforts. All web addresses given here were correct at the time of publication.

## CHOOSING TECHNOLOGY-BASED APPLICATIONS

As with any form of risk communication, purpose and objectives should be key factors in choosing technology-based applications to communicate risks. Table 18-1 gives some examples.

Audience needs are another important consideration. For effective technology-based applications, participants must have access to the equipment and software and know how to use it efficiently. Pretesting the application with target audiences is critical. This is especially true in situations where people will be using the applications on their own, without a person there to answer questions or facilitate the process.

A third consideration is the medium itself. Technology-based applications should be designed to use the characteristics specific to that medium. For example, web sites and CDs should use navigation patterns that enable people to go immediately to particular sections of interest, and drill down for more detail if desired. In computer-based training, immediate feedback about right and wrong answers should be provided to students

> ——— ◇ ———
>
> Technology tools should be designed specifically to use the characteristics of the medium, rather than merely substituting for another medium.

**TABLE 18-1**

Communication Objectives and Corresponding Technology-Based Applications

| Risk Communication Objectives | Potential Technology Tools |
|---|---|
| Provide safety and health training | Computer-based training or course work |
| Keep employees informed about risks, including during and after emergencies | E-mail, shared databases, shared file space |
| Provide current risk information | Web sites, e-mail, listservs, telebriefings, kiosks, streaming audio and video, CDs |
| Share information and receive feedback from interested individuals about a particular risk (participatory process) | Web, e-mail, local area networks, shared file space, computers in central areas. Tools must have a feedback feature or at least a point of contact to receive comments and discuss issues |
| Compile and analyze public comments | Tailored software |
| Support group decision processes | Tailored software or software/hardware combination with facilitator |

when possible. E-mail messages to employees during an emergency should be updated frequently, keeping workers continually up to date. On the other hand, computer-based applications should not be relied upon as the primary source to communicate crisis information in situations such as natural disasters, because electrical power may be lost.

Alexa Kierzkowski and colleagues of McKinsey, a prominent business consulting firm, identified several factors to determine whether an organization should use computer-based applications to convey information to others. Factors included whether the intended audiences were regular users of such applications, whether the organization was willing to build its capabilities to effectively create and maintain such applications, and whether the information was suited to such applications (Kierzkowski et al. 1996).

The following sections suggest ways to use technology to communicate about risks. For advice about how to design or adapt tools for specific situations, work with a technology specialist. "Additional Resources" at the end of this chapter lists helpful materials that provide more detail on each application described here.

## COMPUTERS IN THE WORKPLACE

Organizations such as government agencies, commercial companies, and universities often use computer applications to share risk-related information with their employees. Risk-related communication in these situations often fits into two categories: (1) ensuring that workers receive required training, and (2) keeping employees informed about current health, safety, and environmental issues, including emergency situations.

### Computer-Based Training

Computer-based training is a broad term encompassing everything from self-paced CDs to interactive, real-time multimedia training that links people and instructors in dispersed geographic locations. Computer-

Computer-based training can be a cost-effective, consistent, fast, and relatively easy way to impart information about risks and test employee knowledge of what to do on the job.

based training can be a cost-effective, consistent, fast, and relatively easy way to impart information about risks and test employee knowledge of what to do on the job. Common risk-based training topics are equipment operation, handling hazardous chemicals, fire safety, and general office safety.

General Physics, for example, developed a computer-based training program based on information and guidelines contained in regulatory documents (Lobbin 1997). The software includes more than 60 scenarios that constitute an "exam bank" that can be used by nuclear plant personnel to test and evaluate their understanding of requirements for reporting nuclear "events."

More organizations are using live online training, where a group of people in various locations receive simultaneous training via their desktop computers, linked to an instructor. To access the training, participants use their web browsers to log onto a server, where they are automatically connected. The trainees can watch and listen, via teleconference or Internet-based phone conference, in real time as the instructor shows and demonstrates information onscreen. Trainees can practice the exercises online. The instructor can share additional documents that all trainees download to their computers with a click of a mouse. Trainees can talk with the instructor and each other via teleconference or send e-mail messages to the instructor during training. A web camera can be used to show students what the instructor is doing. Don Clark, an information technology specialist at Pacific Northwest National Laboratory, recommends the following guidelines for live online training:

- People typically can't stay engaged in online training for more than an hour at a time, so keep training short or split it into several sessions.

- Trainees should be in quiet locations, ideally rooms where the doors can be shut. The background must be quiet enough so that all participants can hear each other on speaker phone; any ambient noise is transmitted to everyone on the conference call.

- Trainees must prepare in advance not to be interrupted in their offices during training. Unlike the seclusion of a traditional classroom, employees are sitting at their desks, and colleagues may unknowingly drop in while training is in process. People who answer multiple phone lines at their desks should arrange to forward the calls or use a different workstation, so they won't constantly have to break away to answer calls.

Distance education is another application for the Internet. Distance education enables learners to obtain instruction on their own time, at their own sites. Such learning often includes correspondence courses via the Internet. Depending on the setup, instructor and students can do projects, discuss issues, and share assignments and tests via the web, e-mail, various forms of shared file space, or shared multimedia spaces. One example is the Oak Ridge Institute for Science and Education, which provides a variety of courses and certifications on safety and health risk management. They use a variety of technologies including satellite uplink and downlink transmissions, video conferencing, and use of company web sites and intranets.

Another example is the Walter Reed Army Medical Center in Washington, D.C., which developed a web-based interactive distance learning tool to increase the clinical risk communication skills of Department of Defense health care providers. The Health-e Voice tool uses interactive simulated experiences to teach physicians how to better communicate with recently deployed veterans about medically unexplained physical symptoms, rather than disregarding them as merely psychological or stress-related. The Defense Department hopes that improved clinical risk communication may alleviate unnecessary patient distress and physical health concerns, reduce frustration and tension in the doctor-patient relationship, and reintroduce patient trust in care providers and the health system.

As in any kind of training, it is important to build a strong foundation. This includes researching the applicable regulations and laws that apply, determining the organization's responsibilities in specific training areas, understanding what employees know and need to know, identifying training objectives and effective ways

◇

Distance education enables learners to obtain instruction on their own time, at their own sites.

to impart information via technology, pretesting the training materials, and evaluating success.

Remember that some kinds of training—where an instructor needs to watch someone do something or students need to practice a hands-on skill—are still best conducted in a traditional classroom environment. Some training works well as a hybrid. For training equipment operators, for example, students could use an online course to understand the basics, and then meet as a group to practice operating actual equipment under the guidance of an instructor.

When adding a new computer-based training program or replacing a traditional program with a computer-based one, trainers often must justify the increased technology cost to management by showing a return on investment. Typical benefits measured are reduced travel and labor costs, delivery to more people in a shorter time, and automation of testing and scores. Of course, computer-based training, as with all training, should also measure learning outcomes such as changes in knowledge, skills, job performance, and/or business impact.

In developing risk-related computer-based training, additional factors must be considered:

- **Be aware of the possibility of generating or increasing hostility.** Some off-the-shelf computer-based training as well as some in-house developed applications has obviously been created with little knowledge of risk communication principles. Watch for inappropriate risk comparisons, technical jargon, downplaying of non-technical or opposing viewpoints, and other factors that may inadvertently generate or increase audience resentment, thereby reducing the chance that the risk communication effort will be successful.

- **Tailor off-the-shelf courses.** While many large organizations create their own computer-based training courses, smaller organizations often rely on courses developed by others. Supplement these off-the-shelf courses with information materials, presentations, and other forms of risk communication to ensure that the training fully meets the needs of the participants and reflects organization-specific information.

---

◇

Some kinds of training are best conducted in a traditional classroom environment.

---

Organizations such as the American Society for Training and Development, the Society for Applied Learning Technology, the United States Distance Learning Association, and the Distance Education and Training Council can provide additional guidance and resources.

## Informing Employees about Risks

In organizations where most employees have access to a networked computer, certain risk-related information can be effectively and quickly disseminated. One common way is to warn employees of potential upcoming risks so that they can prepare themselves. For example, through an all-staff e-mail message, workers can be alerted to approaching storm fronts and told to leave work early to avoid hazardous weather.

All-staff e-mail bulletins or electronic newsletters also can be used to remind workers to follow certain safety procedures, or that a safety audit or fire drill is coming up and what they should expect.

When sending all-staff messages, consider the following:

- **Keep the message short.** As one information specialist put it, "If they have to scroll, they won't." Try to keep the information to a size that is no larger than a standard computer screen. If you must go longer, insert topical headings in the message so staff can get an overview quickly.

- **Tell them why they should care.** As close to the front of the message as possible, state why this message is important. In some organizations, employees receive several hundred electronic mail messages each day. Even one from the president of the company is less likely to stand out in such a crowd. Give them a reason to continue reading.

- **Give them direction.** Let employees know what is expected of them. Do you want them to take some action? Do you want them to be more aware of an issue? For what purpose? Explaining what you expect of them will help them see the value of the message as well as encourage a response.

---◇---

Keep the message short. As one information specialist put it, "If they have to scroll, they won't."

- **Always provide a point of contact for additional information.** Because you're keeping it short, it is all the more important to provide sources of additional information for staff who want to know more.

Another way companies use e-mail is to keep employees informed after an accident or other unforeseen event has occurred—in other words, in-house crisis communication. After a chemical release, for example, a company may tell its employees what happened, define any known health or environmental consequences, and explain what is being done to rectify the situation. This kind of message usually comes from the president or other high-placed official. Often, a contact name and phone number are given so that employees may get more information.

Another way to use internal electronic communication is to use shared databases or intranets (in-house web sites) to keep users up to date on particular issues. AT&T's Environmental, Health, and Safety Engineering Center developed an integrated set of electronic tools for sharing current environmental information with its various divisions (Davis 1995). The Center must help its divisions worldwide stay on top of environmental issues, including constantly changing environmental regulations worldwide.

The Center used an internal customer survey and a needs analysis to develop the features of its electronic information system and the databases that support it. Users require a password to access the system. Users can download information and generate a variety of reports directly from the databases. In some cases, users can instruct the systems to fax the desired information to the user's local fax machine.

Based on the results of the survey and needs assessment, the Center instituted the following computerized databases for its internal organizations:

- an online database that gives access to general environmental and safety information such as AT&T policy and practices and training opportunities
- a single corporate chemical inventory, including a current list of approved chemicals, and a database

on all chemical substances manufactured, imported, exported, processed, or used within AT&T. This database is the primary tool for showing compliance with the Toxic Substance Control Act and Hazard Communication compliance. Any chemical substance not listed on the inventory must be checked for regulatory compliance before it can be approved for use by AT&T.

- a system for recording on-the-job injuries and illnesses. The system produces Occupational Safety and Health Administration reports and other customized reports for accident statistics and analysis.

- online Material Safety Data Sheets for chemicals and hazardous materials and products used by AT&T employees in the work area.

Center representative Thomas Davis cautions that it is easy to give customers enormous amounts of information without prioritizing it or making sense of it (Davis 1995). So much information already exists that people do not have time to digest it all. It is important to prioritize information provided via computer and evaluate its usefulness to users on a regular basis.

The advantage of using computers to keep staff informed is that everyone linked to a computer gets the message immediately and consistently, a central point of contact is given, and updates can easily be provided. One possible disadvantage is the potential spreading of sensitive information. Company officials should assume that anything they send to employees via computer can be distributed outside the company, including to the media.

For environmental, health, and safety issues that have a longer life, some organizations also use computers for two-way discussions. This approach often involves shared file space, such as computer bulletin boards or electronic question and answer forums. Employees can have informal discussions on particular topics, or, more formally, pose questions that are then answered by designated people in the company that everyone can see.

AT&T's Environmental, Health, and Safety Engineering Center uses an electronic folder on a shared e-mail

◇

It is all too easy to give people enormous amounts of information via computer without making sense of it (Davis 1995). Prioritize information and evaluate its usefulness to users on a regular basis.

◇

Company officials should assume that anything they send to employees via computer can be distributed outside the company, including to the media.

system for two-way dialogue between the Center and its internal customers. The folder contains a variety of environmental and safety information, including technical developments, new regulations and laws, recommendations, updates on progress toward environmental and safety goals, and comments and tips from employees. Unlike traditional mailing lists, which are notoriously difficult to keep up to date, the electronic folder enables users to self-select material of interest to them. The Center is cautious not to place highly sensitive or restricted information on this shared folder.

## TECHNOLOGY IN CARE COMMUNICATION

When risk managers, technical and public health professionals, members of the public, and other individuals need to find current information about a given risk, the Internet has become a starting point. Though the Internet is unregulated and thus subject to abuse and commercial exploitation, many credible organizations are represented online. Table 18-2 shows some examples of risk-related information on the Internet. This is not intended to be a comprehensive list, but to show the types of organizations that provide health, environmental, safety, and risk communication information online.

Many publications give guidelines and standards for properly preparing information to be viewed on the web; see the resource list at the end of this chapter. When designing web sites to communicate, a few points should be emphasized:

Establish your credibility in the "About" section of your web site by describing your organization, its role, and your accountability.

- **Establish your organization's credibility.** Anyone can put risk-related advice on the web, and it's difficult for users to know whom they should trust, especially when they receive conflicting information. Establish your credibility in the "About" section by describing your organization, its role, and your accountability. It helps to have testimonials from others. The Department of Engineering and Public Policy at Carnegie-Mellon University, for example, has a "What Others Say" page that includes quotes from notable third parties endorsing the Department's programs. Include contact

**TABLE 18-2**

Some Organizations that Provide Online Risk-Related Information

## GOVERNMENT ORGANIZATIONS—EXAMPLES

| Source | Content Highlights |
|---|---|
| *American Cancer Society*<br>http://www.cancer.org | Information about various cancers, treatments, statistics, research. Includes Treatment Decision Tools, interactive exercises that help patients understand and choose customized treatments |
| *Agency for Toxic Substances and Disease Registry*<br>http://www.atsdr.cdc.gov | Information on hazardous substances and sites in the United States |
| *Centers for Disease Control and Prevention*<br>http://www.cdc.gov<br>*Communication at CDC*<br>http://www.cdc.gov/communication/index.htm | Searchable by health topic. Contains strategies and materials for entire intervention campaigns for a variety of health issues, e.g., antibiotic use, diabetes, Hepatitis C, skin cancer, immunization. Research-tested intervention programs are searchable by age, race, and setting (e.g., urban, school, workplace). Many have their own web sites and/or are downloadable. |
| *National Cancer Institute*<br>http://www.cancer.gov | Downloadable, research-tested intervention programs and a risk communication bibliography |
| *National Institutes of Health*<br>http://www.nih.gov | Medical and behavioral research under the U.S. Department of Health and Human Services. Represents more than two dozen institutes and centers, including the National Cancer Institute |
| *Occupational Safety and Health Administration, U.S. Department of Labor*<br>http://www.osha.gov | Workplace safety and health |
| *U.S. Department of Homeland Security*<br>http://www.dhs.gov | Threat advisories, emergency planning, contacts, and resources. Includes the Federal Emergency Management Agency for emergency planning and disaster assistance |
| *U.S. Environmental Protection Agency*<br>http://www.epa.gov | Searchable list of environmental protection topics, laws and regulations, resources and contacts by state |
| *U.S. Food and Drug Administration*<br>http://www.fda.gov | Information on U.S. Food and Drug Administration activities and regulated products. Searchable by demographic category (e.g., consumers, patients, health professionals, industry, press) |

## UNIVERSITY RESEARCH CENTERS—EXAMPLES

| | |
|---|---|
| *Department of Engineering and Public Policy, Carnegie-Mellon University*<br>http://www.epp.cmu.edu | The Risk Analysis and Risk Communication Section of this Department conducts research, including behavioral decision-making and policy. Researchers pioneered approaches including mental models and internationally recognized risk rankings |

*continued*

**TABLE 18-2** *(continued)*
Some Organizations that Provide Online Risk-Related Information

| Source | Content Highlights |
|---|---|
| **UNIVERSITY RESEARCH CENTERS—EXAMPLES** *(continued)* | |
| ***Environmental Risk Analysis Program, Cornell University in the Department of Communication and Center for the Environment*** <br> http://environmentalrisk.cornell.edu | Resources for citizens and policy-makers about environmental risks |
| **Harvard Center for Risk Analysis** <br> http://www.hcra.harvard.edu | Decision science applied to risk analysis, including public response to risk |
| ***Institute for Risk Analysis and Risk Communication, University of Washington*** <br> http://depts.washington.edu/irarc | Research and training |
| ***Johns Hopkins Bloomberg School of Public Health*** <br> http://www.jhsph.edu/risksciences | The Risk Sciences and Public Policy Institute focuses on environmental policy to improve public health. The School's Center for Communication Programs focuses on public health interventions |
| **PROFESSIONAL ASSOCIATIONS AND SOCIETIES—EXAMPLES** | |
| ***American Industrial Hygiene Association*** <br> http://www.aiha.org | Occupational and environmental health and safety issues |
| ***Association of State and Territorial Health Officials*** <br> http://www.astho.org | Includes public health contacts by state |
| ***International Association for Public Participation*** <br> http://www.iap2.org | Advancing public participation in decision-making and policy-making |
| ***National Safety Council*** <br> http://www.nsc.org | Resources for protecting life and health |
| ***Society of Environmental Toxicology and Chemistry*** <br> http://www.setac.org | Science-based environmental quality |
| ***Society for Risk Analysis*** <br> http://www.sra.org | Multidisciplinary, international focus on risk analysis, including risk assessment, characterization, communication, management, and policy. A subgroup, the Risk Communication Specialty Group (http://www.sra.org/rcsg), focuses on risk perception, public participation, mass media coverage of risk, trust and credibility, social influence, and evaluation. It includes a listserv for information sharing |
| ***Society for Technical Communication*** <br> http://www.stc.org | Resources for technical communicators |

*continued*

**TABLE 18-2** *(continued)*
Some Organizations that Provide Online Risk-Related Information

| Source | Content Highlights |
|---|---|
| **DATABASES—EXAMPLES** | |
| ***ATSDR's Hazardous Substance Release and Health Effects Database***<br>http://www.atsdr.cdc.gov/hazdat.html | U.S. hazardous sites, searchable by state and contaminant |
| ***Combined Health Information Database Online***<br>http://chid.nih.gov/subfile/subfile.html | Searchable by health topic. Maintained by a coalition of government agencies |
| ***EnviroFacts Data Warehouse***<br>http://www.epa.gov/enviro | U.S. Environmental Protection Agency database searchable by environmental information and geographic area |
| ***HealthComm Key Database***<br>http://www.cdc.gov/od/oc/hcomm/hcomm_about.html | U.S. Centers for Disease Control and Prevention database of health communication literature, focusing on communication research and practice in public health |
| ***National Library of Medicine***<br>http://www.nlm.nih.gov | Health-related databases of publications and resources, including MEDLINE and PubMed |
| ***National Priorities List***<br>http://www.epa.gov/superfund/sites/npl/npl.htm | U.S. Environmental Protection Agency database of Superfund sites, searchable by state |
| ***Risk Analysis Center***<br>http://www.risk-analysis-center.com/newhome.asp | Database of abstracts about risk-related information, including media articles (leading newspapers are scanned daily), journals, books, papers, and technical reports |
| **COMMERCIAL ORGANIZATIONS—EXAMPLE** | |
| ***Risk World***<br>http://www.riskworld.com | Information on the analysis and management of health, environmental, financial, and technological risks. Includes press releases, news, book reviews, links to other resources |

information (e-mail, phone, and postal mail) for people to get in touch or ask questions.

- **Put your risk information in context and qualify it.** When including risk information, tell how it was prepared and how accuracy is ensured. Include any qualifying statements about the limitations of risk estimates. Medical professionals, for example, caution that online cancer risk calculators often neglect to state whether the risk is from getting a disease or dying from it, how the risk compares with those of other people or other cancer risks, and the level of uncertainty inherent in the estimate (Woloshin et al. 2003). Say when the risk information was last updated. Make sure all downloadable papers, presentations, and other information include publication dates and are traceable back to their sources.

- **Be ethical.** Specify the purpose of the site, including any commercial purposes and advertising. Identify any potential conflicts of interest or biases. Explain how the privacy and confidentiality of any personal information collected are protected.

- **Collaborate with credible others.** View the Internet as a way to collaborate, especially for skeptical or hostile audiences. Provide links to related regulatory agencies, environmental or civic groups, universities, and other such sites. Common Internet courtesy is to request such linking beforehand and to provide reciprocal linking if possible (you link to them, and they link to you). Check with your organization first before linking. Some government agencies and industrial organizations have policies about linking to certain other sites to avoid the appearance of endorsing them.

- **Conduct usability testing.** Content is king, so make sure users can find the information they want and need, in language to which they can relate. Make sure content, including graphics and downloaded files, comes up within seconds on a variety of computer platforms and bandwidth speeds. Make sure the site structure, navigation, and "search" function are clearly and logically organized to let users find

Make sure all downloadable papers, presentations, and other information include publication dates and are traceable back to their sources.

what they need, know where they are, and get back to where they were.

- **Consider the guidelines** for the visual representation of risk (Chapter 14) as well as the development of information materials (Chapter 13).

## STAND-ALONE AND WEB-DELIVERED MULTIMEDIA PROGRAMS

Consumers are increasingly expecting risk information in multimedia formats. The use of computer-assisted audio, video, animation, and other tools makes risk information and discussions more salient, immediate, and interactive than ever.

### CDs and Web Tools

CDs are becoming common for communicating about risk-related topics, especially those related to health issues. The multimedia format makes them ideal for combining video, graphics, text, animation, virtual tours, interactive tools, and other options. Users control the flow of information and can move around to various topics of interest. For example, the Centers for Disease Control and Prevention offers a highly regarded CD series called CDCynergy, with programs on health communication planning and education, including cardiovascular health, immunization, and communicating in emergencies (CDC et al. 2003).

Many organizations provide audio and video programs online. For example, the Occupational Safety and Health Administration web site offers streaming video and PowerPoint® presentations, on a wide range of worker safety topics from asbestos safety to workplace violence.

Many online tools are interactive and customizable. One example is the American Cancer Society's Treatment Decision Tools, interactive exercises that help patients understand and chose customized treatment decisions. The user answers questions about his or her cancer diagnosis and test results, then gets customized information about treatment options and rates of survival and recurrence. A number of online smoking

> ◇
>
> CDs are becoming common for communicating about risk-related topics, especially those related to health issues. The multimedia format makes them ideal for combining video, graphics, text, animation, virtual tours, interactive tools, and other options.

cessation programs use customizable online tools for self-monitoring of behaviors, social support, and reinforcement timed to match enrollees' efforts to quit.

Often these tools contain an educational component. The web site of the Agency for Toxic Substances and Disease Registry, for example, includes an extensive interactive learning program about the process used to evaluate whether people will be harmed by hazardous materials from waste sites. It includes a description of how community members can get involved in the assessment process, along with interactive self-quizzes and other exercises to test the user's knowledge while going through the learning program.

In creating CDs or web media tools, make sure they can be used as intended by the target audience. Take advantage of the interactive, multimedia nature of the medium, including audio, video, movement, sound, and interactive exercises as appropriate. Make sure the tool works properly on all standard computer platforms. Specify the program duration. For CDs, specify the computer system requirements and how to start the program. It helps to include a web site that contains more information about the subject of the program and a way to contact the organization for more information and troubleshooting.

## Web and Satellite Broadcasts

Telebriefings, web seminars (also called webinars), webcasts, live streaming video and audio, and satellite broadcasts are increasingly used for communication to select or large populations. Like traditional mass media, they quickly reach many people at the same time, but often with the added benefit of being interactive, enabling discussion among participants.

Telebriefings are similar to press conferences or updates, but using a conference call format. The advantage of telebriefings is that they can be conducted anywhere, not requiring participants to travel to a news conference location. The organizers plan the briefing in advance, often to address urgent or time-sensitive issues, and invite people to call in. Sometimes telebriefings are

> Take advantage of the interactive, multimedia nature of the medium, including audio, video, movement, sound, and interactive exercises as appropriate.

broadcast in streaming audio on web sites and people have the option of calling in to ask questions. For toll-free lines, participation is usually controlled in advance by using a listserv, e-mail list, or password-protected area on the web. Organizers can send electronic presentations or other materials in advance to participants, or put them on a web site.

The Centers for Disease Control and Prevention has conducted more than 40 telebriefings each year since 2001, on public health topics including anthrax, small-pox, West Nile virus, severe acute respiratory syndrome, and many others. The organization posts transcripts and audio of its telebriefings on its web site.

Webcasts and streaming video are audio and video programs that are converted into files for hearing and/or seeing on a web site. They can be live, or taped and archived on the web for on-demand viewing later. Live broadcasts are advertised in advance, then people log on by clicking on a web site link that becomes active when the webcast occurs. Viewing requires access to a standard media player program and sufficient bandwidth connection to hear and see the program clearly. Participants can be given access to audio files, transcripts, and related reference materials.

Good examples of web-delivered audio and video abound. A nine-part Centers for Disease Control and Prevention webcast that first occurred in December 2001, "CDC Responds: Risk Communication and Bioterrorism," was widely viewed on the web for years afterward. It also came with PowerPoint® slides and text excerpts, and was also available as a videotape. The American Cancer Society's Cancer Survivors Network® makes good use of the multimedia nature of the web by including downloadable talk shows, interviews with transcripts, and webcasts, along with its chat and discussion board areas and other web-based resources. The U.S. Food and Drug Administration (FDA) web site includes archived 15-minute news programs for health professionals called "FDA Patient Safety News." The programs cover products recently approved by the FDA, product recalls and safety alerts, and tips on protecting patients and preventing medical errors. Viewers can see video

—— ◇ ——

Webcasts and streaming video can be live, or taped and archived on the web for on-demand viewing later.

segments, find more information on each story, and report problems with products through an online link.

Satellite broadcasts are good for reaching sites around the country simultaneously. Viewers congregate at downlink host sites that have the proper coordinates to link to the broadcast. Many satellite broadcasts are interactive. The Centers for Disease Control and Prevention, for example, broadcasts programs simultaneously in the United States and Canada via satellite, dish network, webcast, and web conference. Panels of experts answer questions posed by viewers throughout the broadcast via fax, e-mail, and telephone.

For computer-delivered multimedia programs, consider the following guidelines:

- Clearly state user access instructions in introductory materials or on the web.
- Specify the program duration. For live programs, note the time zone.
- List the requirements to view or hear the program. It's easiest for the user to click on a link to see whether his or her system is configured properly to handle the program. Consider having various bandwidth speeds to accommodate various users.
- Have a mechanism, such as a technical support person standing by or a person to e-mail, in case participants have problems.
- Tell people where to get more information about the topic, online and elsewhere.
- For telebriefings, clearly introduce the speakers at the beginning. Make sure all participants (including questioners) state their names and affiliations.
- Use a password for online access if you want to limit the information to specific audiences.
- Consider making a very short questionnaire available at the end of web-based programs for user evaluation, for program planning.

### Interactive Multimedia Programs in Public Places

User-navigated computer programs contained in kiosks are another option for risk communication. Many of these programs are similar to interactive CDs, where the user selects information at will and can skip around to various topics. Many use touch screens for easier user interface than a mouse. Nevertheless, the degree of sophistication varies widely. Kiosks may range from a self-contained computer program to those that connect to the Internet or other networks. Computer kiosks can let users browse the web, send e-mail photos, send video, conduct business transactions, view virtual reality exhibits, and print information.

A kiosk in a public place, such as a community center, university, library, or health center, can be one component of a broader communication plan. Being unstaffed, kiosks can add efficiency and reduce labor costs by freeing up employees to do other things. Through questions, computer programs can tailor information to the user's demographics, experience, literacy level, and other characteristics. Kiosks are especially useful for populations without widespread computer access.

Staff from a federally funded climate change research program created an educational, interactive touch-screen program that runs on a kiosk in a community center in Alaska (Figure 18-1). The kiosk uses a custom-built multimedia program running on a standard desktop computer. The program consists of interviews of Alaskan community members, primarily Iñupiat tribal elders, with additional animations and material from program

◇

Kiosks are especially useful for populations without widespread computer access.

**FIGURE 18-1.** Touch-screen program in a kiosk in Barrow, Alaska. The program, which uses video clips and animation, describes climate change and research being conducted in the surrounding North Slope of Alaska.

(Source: Mike Ebinger, ARM Climate Research Facility Education and Outreach.)

scientists. The program is designed to answer questions about the research program and describe how the climate has changed over time.

In the video clips, a local whaling captain speaks about how he's seen the sea ice become thinner over time, and how this makes the spring whale hunt more difficult and more dangerous for the hunters. One elder speaks about how it freezes later each year, which affects when people can put their nets through the ice. Scientists speak about what they're measuring and what causes climate change. Residents and visitors have been very excited about the program; an elaborate tribal celebration with dancing and singing was held when the kiosk was first unveiled.

Kiosks have been shown effective in health interventions, when risks are communicated but the underlying goal is to encourage behavior change. Researcher Armando Valdez designed a successful kiosk-based information program designed to promote breast cancer screening among low-income, low-literacy Latinas in California (Valdez 2002). Extensive formative research had revealed misconceptions and information gaps among the target audience that were directly addressed in the ten-module program. Video clips showed Latina women speaking about their experiences, getting mammograms, and giving advice about early screening. The program also directly addressed common misconceptions such as, "Breast cancer is an automatic death sentence," "Breast cancer risk decreases with age," and "Putting off treatment gives the cancer a chance to get better."

The kiosk used a standard desktop computer, a head-phone jack for privacy or for the hard-of-hearing, and a thermal printer. Using the touch screen, women were asked a few introductory questions about their spoken language, age, and personal screening history, then given access to various customized modules, which they could choose at will. Every module emphasized the importance of taking action to get early screening. Women were also given the option of printing out information about where to get a mammogram, including clinics offering low-cost or free services.

◇

Kiosks have been shown effective in health interventions.

Results showed increased knowledge and, most importantly, a very high rate of behavior change. Fifty-one percent of women got mammograms after viewing the program, as opposed to other interventions, which typically range from 20% to 40%. The kiosk format was effective when other intervention methods—videos, public service announcements, and print media—weren't working well for the target population.

In 1997, the University of Michigan's Health Media Research Laboratory developed its "Health-O-Vision" software and placed 100 interactive, touch-screen health kiosks in shopping malls, supermarkets, medical centers, libraries, community centers, and other high-traffic settings. The kiosks are designed to convey a range of topics, including smoking cessation and prevention, cancer screening, bicycle helmet safety, immunizations, cardiovascular disease prevention, alcohol problem detection, and sexually transmitted disease prevention. The kiosk is designed to look like a television, allowing users to select and interact with risk factor "channels." Each kiosk is linked via the Internet to a central data collection system at the University of Michigan's Health Media Research Laboratory, allowing data collection on usage and satisfaction. Public health and medical specialists, computer programmers, graphic artists, and Hollywood Screen Writers Guild writers joined forces on the project, which was funded by proceeds from the state tobacco tax. More than 400,000 people use the kiosks each year (Strecher et al. 1999).

When designing kiosk programs, keep these things in mind:

- Understand how a kiosk fits into your overall communication strategy.

- When estimating the cost, include not just hardware and software, but also network connections, implementation, maintenance, and upgrades.

- Understand what your audiences want and need to know, and design information accordingly.

- Test the information with the intended audience for usability. The Alaska kiosk program, for example, was developed and tested for more than a year before it was installed in 2003.

- Make sure there's a way for users or administrators to report any problems, fix technology glitches, and update information as necessary.
- Build in ways to evaluate effectiveness.

## ONLINE DISCUSSION FORUMS

For online risk-related discussions, several electronic forums are available. The most common are e-mail lists, listservs, and newsgroups.

E-mail lists and listservs enable subscribers to receive and sometimes send messages. Traditional mailing lists are often one-way, with organizations sending information to subscribers, though a contact name is often provided for inquiries. For example, the Centers for Disease Control and Prevention has more than two dozen mailing lists on topics ranging from ambulatory care to preventing chronic disease. The Food Safety Network has several e-mail lists that provide current public risk perception information about food-related issues, generated from journalistic and scientific sources worldwide and distributed daily to subscribers from academia, industry, government, the farm community, journalism, and the public. The Leukemia and Lymphoma Society uses an online live chat feature on its web site to convey expert information. Users click on a link and are instantly connected to someone who can answer their questions in real time.

Some listservs are set up as a discussion forum, where any subscriber can send a message that goes to all other members, to which anyone can respond. The Society for Risk Analysis, for example, runs separate listservs on risk analysis and risk communication. The listserv for the European Risk Communication Network fosters discussion between researchers and practitioners in Europe about best practices for risk communication. Some listservs archive past postings. Risk World, an online commercial site, contains several online discussion groups on risk-related topics including risk analysis, risk management, and technology.

Usenet is a very general source of discussion forums accessible via the Internet, consisting of newsgroups with names that are classified hierarchically by subject. People post articles or messages to these newsgroups. In some newsgroups, the articles are first sent to a moderator for approval before appearing in the newsgroup. Many Usenet sites are commercial entities, but universities, research labs, or other academic institutions also operate Usenet sites.

Because of their "viral" propagation with little or no controls, be aware that e-mail, listservs, and newsgroups have significant potential to affect risk perceptions. One study looked at the power of Usenet to affect risk perceptions about NASA's plutonium-powered space probe, Cassini. A study of Usenet messages about the probe from 1995 through 1999 showed that six people originated messages that ultimately evolved into more than 8,000 messages by more than 900 authors (Rodrigue 2001).

Additional guidance on using e-mail, listservs, and newsgroups to communicate about risk includes the following:

- **Focus the topic.** E-mail lists are proliferating and readers are being asked to choose which they will join based on content and information. At the same time, more users are blocking spam or filtering out information from lists on a particular topic. So, for example, instead of hosting a list for employees related to all safety risks at your company, you might want separate lists on laboratory safety, equipment operations safety, and office safety to better meet audience needs.

- **Establish ground rules.** Clearly state the kind of e-mail behavior you expect. Many lists have rules against posting personal information, advertisements for products or services, inflammatory or obscene language (sometimes called flaming), and attachments—which can overload some mail programs and carry viruses.

◇

Because of their "viral" propagation with little or no controls, be aware that e-mail, listservs, and newsgroups have significant potential to affect risk perceptions.

- **Clearly state whether the list is moderated.** Many lists have a host who ensures that messages arrive and are sent to all list subscribers appropriately. Sometimes these hosts act as moderators, screening postings to ensure nothing proprietary, inflammatory, redundant, or off the subject is sent to the subscribers. Especially for lists communicating risk information, let all subscribers know in advance whether a moderator will be used, what rules the moderator will use to screen information, and how to appeal if a decision inadvertently censors important information. When the moderator does reject a message, make sure the subscriber is aware of the reason and has the opportunity to rephrase the message in more appropriate terms. If subscribers post information that does not appear, with no explanation, resentment will increase and participation will fall off.

## TECHNOLOGY IN CONSENSUS COMMUNICATION

Computers can be used effectively in risk communication that involves groups or individuals in a decision-making process. This section summarizes some of the most common tools and guidelines for each.

### Web Sites

In consensus communication, web sites can describe a risk and its options for mitigation and invite public input that can be used to craft a decision. The U.S. Department of Energy and other federal agencies, as part of public involvement on environmental analyses, often put draft publications online for review and comment. Stakeholders can use a feedback form on the web site to submit comments. Web sites can also keep stakeholders updated on events in the decision-making process. For example, a web site can show a timeline of the decision process with public involvement steps clearly marked. A calendar of public involvement activities also can be displayed.

## Local Area Networks, Extranets, and Bulletin Boards

Community-level decision-making may benefit from the use of a local area network (LAN). A LAN enables electronic communication among users within an organization or area, such as a neighborhood. All those who are hooked up to the LAN can communicate with each other. Users of a LAN aren't necessarily on the Internet. A site may use a LAN to place documents for comment, meeting notifications, announcements, and multimedia. The U.S. Department of Agriculture's Broadcast Media & Technology Center, for example, uses a LAN to carry messages, press conferences, and taped events throughout the Washington, D.C., metro area. To span a larger geographic area, two or more LANs can be linked to form a wide area network.

Extranets are external intranets. By setting up an extranet, a company can allow selected people outside an organization to connect via the web to information that is normally internal to the company. The extranet can be set up to maintain security for sensitive or proprietary company information. Companies typically use extranets for business communication and commerce among employees, suppliers, customers, and other business partners. However, extranets also can be used for consensus-type communication such as community-wide workgroups. An extranet can be used to give participants access to internal information such as documents and databases. A feedback mechanism can be included for making comments or requesting additional information.

An electronic bulletin board can be internal to an organization, on a LAN, or on the Internet. Newsgroups, or collections of people with a common interest, talk to each other via bulletin boards that focus on specific topics. Everyone who logs onto the bulletin board can see all the other messages in the discussion and can jump into the discussion as well. For those who have access, bulletin boards are a good way to get the current "pulse" on an issue, share information, address rumors, and correct misinformation.

Electronic bulletin boards are a good way to get the current "pulse" on an issue.

Some of the same guidelines apply to LANs, bulletin boards, and extranets as to e-mail lists. Make sure your audience knows the ground rules, let them know whether a moderator will be used and define that person's role, and focus the topic of the discussion to ensure appropriate information is being communicated in a way that meets audience needs.

## Computers in Centralized Public Locations

Environmental regulations such as the Comprehensive Environmental Response, Compensation, and Liability Act and the National Environmental Policy Act often require that information supporting an organization's decision be provided in a central location for public access. These locations are called information repositories or reading rooms. They can be located within existing libraries or elsewhere.

Most centralized information centers have computers available for users. Several established government reading room sites use computers and electronic databases where users can search for specific documents or topics at that site. Other stand-alone computer tools are increasingly being used as well. For example, the U.S. Department of Energy made its Waste Management Preliminary Environmental Impact Statement available on CD in a searchable, menu-driven format. One-third of the agency's 120 reading rooms nationwide requested the CD version of the statement. (Another third wanted it in microfiche; the rest, in hard copy.)

If you decide to provide information for such an electronic repository, consider these guidelines:

- **Know the software and hardware that will be supporting the information.** You will need to provide information in a format that meets the existing infrastructure unless you are starting a new information center. While many industries have the latest computer software and hardware, some public libraries exist on donations of outdated equipment. Make sure what you provide can be accessed on the machines available.

---

◇

Provide indexes, summaries, and other navigational cues in computer-based information, even more than you would in a hardcopy document.

---

- **Organize and locate pertinent information in a way that makes it easy to find and use.** Provide indexes, summaries, and other navigational cues through the information, even more than you would in a hardcopy document. In a hardcopy document, readers can thumb through the pages to locate the information they want. With thousands of pages online, this is even harder without some kind of searching capability.

- **Provide hardcopy backups for important information.** Some members of the public are not comfortable accessing information on the computer. Be sure to provide point-of-contact information and other key pieces of information in hardcopy for those who want it in that form.

## Tracking and Analyzing Comments and Responses

Software programs are increasingly being used to track stakeholder comments and issues and an organization's or agency's responses. The idea is to track who commented, when, what they said, and what the response was. One government organization tailored a standard database software application to record information associated with its public briefings during the public consultation process (McMakin et al. 1995). Database fields included date, commenter's name and affiliation, commenter's location, comment summary, comment category (topic), recorder (note-taker at meeting), and follow-up actions and dates. The fields could be searched and summary reports generated. Database input and maintenance time depend on the number of briefings, comments, and responses.

The U.S. Forest Service adapted commercially available software for objective and systematic analysis of public input (U.S. Department of Agriculture 1994). This process groups comments by subjects and categories and reports the information back in a concise display for consideration in the decision-making process. This approach involves coding comments into categories, such as which type of organization is commenting, how the comment was received (e.g., letter, phone call), subject, and responses. The software can report and sort by numerous fields. Direct quotes from comments and responses are easily selected for use in response letters to commenters. The Forest Service also uses the software to generate a summary report containing comments and responses that can be placed directly into final summary documents, such as environmental impact statements.

This level of detail is especially useful for formal public involvement processes, such as those required by certain environmental regulations. Because the process is so thorough, it is also labor intensive and requires skilled clerical support to run it. The Forest Service content analysis team needs two weeks to several months to set up the coding structure, code responses, input them to the database, run the software, and report the summary results.

The Regional Municipality of Ottawa-Carleton in Ottawa, Ontario, has adapted for public consultation commercial software originally designed for managing sales and telemarketing contacts (McMakin et al. 1995). The Municipality is a regional government responsible to 750,000 citizens for transportation, environmental services, health, social services, and planning. The Municipality adapted the software to make a several-thousand-person mailing list available to Municipality staff with criteria for when and how to contact citizens regarding policy and program consultation. The software also keeps track of who was contacted and can track public comments. The database outputs addresses to mailing labels and reports. The Municipality is putting the database on a community-based net system so that all constituency groups in a particular area can access the database. The net system also enables people to send e-mail to the Municipality.

### Facilitating Group Decision Making

The increase in community and technical advisory panels, as well as public and technical workshops, means that many viewpoints must be fairly considered and balanced, especially to reach consensus. This process is made more difficult when viewpoints are polarized and issues are complex.

An increasing number of software and hardware combinations are available to help facilitate group decision processes. These technologies help with brainstorming ideas, presenting and weighing group members' viewpoints, visualizing "what-if" scenarios of processes or systems, ranking or rating items, voting, and reaching consensus. One way to use these systems is to have all group members in a meeting room, or in diverse geographic areas but in a shared web area, where they type comments via computer terminals and comments are redisplayed on an electronic whiteboard or on each others' screens. If the comments are anonymous, participants experience more freedom to verbalize and criticize others' ideas without fear of reprisal (Jessup et al. 1990; Valacich et al. 1992). Though this process may thus cause greater conflict within the group, the conflict tends to be substantive rather than interpersonal, and decision-making may be enhanced (Watson et al. 1988).

One caution from research studies is that situations in which the group must reach consensus appear to work best when combined with face-to-face interaction. More social interaction than just working individually on computers is needed to reach agreement, especially when the group is given restricted time periods (Hiltz et al. 1986; Siegel et al. 1986). One such study showed the highest decision quality was achieved with a two-phase arrangement. Anonymous computer-mediated communication was used for brainstorming ideas, and face-to-face interaction was used for evaluation and reaching consensus (Olaniran 1994).

CH2M Hill, an environmental engineering firm, created a software application that they use to help groups reach consensus (McMakin et al. 1995). They use the software in conjunction with a nominal group technique, a structured method for discussing and evaluating issues. The process involves developing criteria that capture the salient points of the issues, assigning weights to the criteria (each participant does this), conducting a statistical analysis of the weights, and discussing the results as group. This process can be repeated several times, in

> Studies show that situations in which a group must reach consensus work best when computer-mediated communication is combined with face-to-face interaction.

which group members often move closer together in their views as they carve out common ground. This process requires not only mastery of the software that documents the statistical analysis, but excellent facilitation skills to capture and clarify viewpoints while keeping the process moving.

A national program to clean up the U.S. Department of Energy's former sites used computer-mediated communication in its public participation process to rank criteria, vote, and conduct other group activities. The software they used displayed visual results, such as bar charts. Group members used remote touchpads for recording input and voting. Agency representatives report that the software has saved hours of discussion time that would ordinarily be required by traditional methods (McMakin et al. 1995).

Professional facilitator and dispute resolution expert Jim Creighton offers some recommendations for using technology in group decision-making (Creighton and Adams 2002):

> "Focus the process on the user and the purpose, not the technology."
> —Jim Creighton (Creighton and Adams 2002, page 180).

- **Put the collaboration first, rather than the technology.** Technology does not magically transform diverse people, especially adversaries, into collaborative partners. A group decision process must be expertly designed to involve all participants, resolve disputes, and achieve the goals of the collaboration.

- **Match the technology to the process.** Information briefings from a trusted source may require only e-mail or intranet communication, while conflict resolution may require more elaborate technologies that demonstrate that all points of view have been heard and recorded.

- **Count the costs and benefits.** Costs can include software and equipment, technicians to set up and troubleshoot it, transaction charges for telecommunications, and leader and/or facilitator labor. But remember to balance that with likely cost reductions—less travel by participants, less time spent in meetings, and a more efficient decision process.

## TECHNOLOGY IN CRISIS COMMUNICATION

Web sites that are updated frequently can be good resources in helping the public know what to do in case of an emergency and how to respond when one occurs. The web sites of the Department of Homeland Security, Federal Emergency Management Agency, and American Red Cross, among others, tell citizens what to do in case of various threats. Web sites for localized threats can be more specific. For example, a chemical weapons depot in Oregon has a web site containing a wide variety of emergency response information. Among the items is a map showing school locations in each surrounding county with designated emergency plans for each (shelter in place, evacuate, etc.). The site also includes instructions for citizens in how to prepare for an emergency, including sound clips of warning sirens, and what to do during an emergency.

Wired and wireless telecommunications are increasingly being used to convey critical information and updates in crisis situations. Several communities and states have so-called reverse 911 telecommunication systems that phone citizens in targeted geographic areas with a recorded message to notify them about specific threats. Reverse 911 also includes a number citizens can call to hear pre-recorded information, such as emergency evacuation procedures. Emergency communication systems send information instantly to subscribers' mobile devices (cell phones, pagers, handheld computers) as well as to e-mail systems. Government organizations are increasingly using these emergency communication systems to keep their first responders, employees, and citizens informed. Part V of this book includes more information about technology-assisted communication in emergencies.

Ironically, as much as we rely on technology in emergencies, it can be the first thing to fail. In recent years, various crises in the United States have crashed the Internet, overloaded phone lines, rendered cell phone towers inoperable, and triggered multi-state electrical blackouts extending into Canada. Organizations responsible for communicating risks should have backup

Reverse 911 telecommunication systems phone citizens in targeted geographic areas with a recorded message to notify them about specific threats.

communication plans that account for failure of standard public communication methods. The Oregon chemical weapons depot, for example, distributes battery-powered tone alert radios to citizens in surrounding communities. Some organizations put their emergency risk communication plans, including a list of people to contact in emergencies, on CDs that run on battery-powered laptop computers.

## CHECKLIST FOR TECHNOLOGY-BASED APPLICATIONS

❏ The particular type of technology is determined to be appropriate and useful to meet the communication objectives.

❏ Tools are designed to use the special characteristics of the medium, not just as a substitute for other forms of communication.

❏ Computer-based information is prioritized and organized so users can easily find what they need.

❏ When possible, technology applications are pretested with the intended audiences before implementation.

❏ The participants have access to the equipment and software needed to use the tools.

❏ The participants are willing to use the tools and know how to use them effectively, or training and/or facilitation are provided.

❏ Proprietary or sensitive information is not used on networked computer systems.

❏ Information provided on the Internet is updated as appropriate to maintain its usefulness.

❏ In public participation situations, technology tools include feedback systems to support a two-way communication process.

❏ In crisis communication, a backup plan for communication is in place in case of electricity loss or other disaster.

# REFERENCES

CDC (U.S. Centers for Disease Control and Prevention), Agency for Toxic Substances and Disease Registry, and Oak Ridge Institute for Science and Education, and the Prospect Center of the American Institutes of Research. 2003. *Emergency Risk Communication CDCynergy* (CD, February 2003). Online at http://www.orau.gov/cdcynergy/erc.

Creighton, J. L. and J. W. R. Adams. 2002. *Cyber Meeting: How to Link People and Technology in Your Organization.* Xlibris Corporation, Philadelphia, Pennsylvania.

Davis, T. S. 1995. "Communicating Environmental, Health, and Safety Information to Internal and External Audiences." *Journal of the Society for Technical Communication,* 42(3):460-466.

Hiltz, S. R., K. Johnson, and M. Turoff. 1986. "Experiments in Group Decision Making: Communication Process and Outcome in Face-to-Face Versus Computerized Conferences." *Human Communication Research,* 13:225-252.

Jessup, L. M., T. Connolly, and J. Galegher. 1990. "The Effects of Anonymity on Group Decision Support System Group Process with an Idea-Generating Task." *MIS Quarterly,* 14:312-321.

Kierzkowski, A., S. McQuade, R. Waitman, and M. Zeiser. 1996. "Marketing to the Digital Consumer." *The McKinsey Quarterly,* 3:5-21.

Lobbin, F. 1997. "10 CFR 50 Event Reporting Computer-Based Training Program." *Nuclear Plant Journal,* 15(5):45.

McMakin, A. H., D. L. Henrich, C. A. Kuhlman, and G. W. White. 1995. *Innovative Techniques and Tools for Public Participation in U.S. Department of Energy Programs.* PNL-10664, Prepared for the U.S. Department of Energy, Pacific Northwest National Laboratory, Richland, Washington.

Olaniran, B. A. 1994. "Group Performance in Computer-Mediated and Face-to-Face Communication Media." *Management Communication Quarterly,* 7:256-282.

Rodrigue, C. M. 2001. "The Internet in the Social Amplification and Attenuation of Risk." Presented to the 26th Annual Natural Hazards Research and Applications Workshop, Boulder, Colorado, July 15-18, 2001.

Siegel, J., V. Dubrovsky, S. Kiesler, and T. W. McGuire. 1986. "Group Processes in Computer-Mediated Communication." *Organizational Behavior and Human Decision Processes,* 37:157-187.

Strecher, V. J., T. Greenwood, C. Wang, and D. Dumont. 1999. "Interactive Multimedia and Risk Communication." *Journal of the National Cancer Institute Monographs,* 25:134-139.

U.S. Department of Agriculture, Forest Service, Northern Region. 1994. *Content Analysis Training.* U.S. Department of Agriculture, Missoula, Montana.

Valacich, J. S., A. R. Dennis, and J. F. Nunamaker. 1992. "Group Size and Anonymity Effects on Computer-Mediated Idea Generation." *Small Group Research,* 23:49-73.

Valdez, A. 2002. "Innovative Multimedia Cancer Education Interventions for Latinas." Presented at the 130th Meeting of the American Public Health Association, November 9-13, 2002, Philadelphia, Pennsylvania.

Watson, R. T., G. DeSanctis, and M. S. Poole. 1988. "Using Group Decision Support Systems to Facilitate Group Consensus: Some Intended and Unintended Consequences." *MIS Quarterly,* 12:463-478.

Woloshin, S., L. M. Schwartz, and A. Ellner. 2003. "Making Sense of Risk Information on the Web." *BMJ,* 327:695-696.

## ADDITIONAL RESOURCES

American Society for Training and Development. Online at http://www.astd.org.

Distance Education and Training Council. Online at http://www.detc.org.

Eng, T. R. 2000. *Wired for Health & Well-being: The Emergence of Interactive Health Communication.* U.S. Government Printing Office, Washington, D.C.

McGovern, G. and R. Norton. 2002. *Content Critical: Gaining Competitive Advantage Through High-Quality Web Content.* Financial Times Prentice Hall, Pearson Education Limited, Edinburgh Gate, Great Britain.

Rice, R. E., and J. E. Katz (Eds.). 2000. *The Internet and Health Communication: Experiences and Expectations.* Sage Publications, Thousand Oaks, California.

Society for Applied Learning Technology. Online at http://www.salt.org.

Spyridakis, J. H. 2001. "Guidelines for Authoring Comprehensible Web Pages and Evaluating Their Success." *Technical Communication,* 47(3):301-310.

Tsagarousianou, R., D. Tambini, and C. Bryan (Eds.). 1998. *Cyberdemocracy: Technology, Cities and Civic Networks.* Routledge, New York.

U.S. Distance Learning Association. Online at http://www.usdla.org.

U.S. Food and Drug Administration web site, video programs called "FDA Patient Safety News." Online at http://www.fda.gov/psn.

Usability.gov. National Cancer Institute's web site of resources for "usable, useful and accessible websites and user interfaces." Online at http://usability.gov/guides/index.html

Van Duyne, D. K., J. A. Landay, and J. I. Hong. 2002. *The Design of Sites: Patterns, Principles, and Processes for Crafting a Customer-Centered Web Experience.* Addison-Wesley Publishing Company, Boston, Massachusetts.

# Part IV

# EVALUATING RISK COMMUNICATION EFFORTS

Every risk communication effort can benefit from being evaluated. Evaluation can help a current effort achieve its purpose and objectives and make future efforts more successful.

# Evaluating Risk
# Communication Efforts

 $\mathcal{E}$ very risk communication effort should undergo some sort of evaluation. Whenever possible, evaluations should be conducted during as well as at the end of a project; the former tells you changes to be made to reach your objectives, the latter tells you what you should change in future efforts. However, the thoroughness and timing of the evaluation will depend on your objectives and purpose (for example, evaluation of crisis communication may have to wait until the worst is over), funding and resources, and organizational constraints.

## WHY EVALUATE RISK COMMUNICATION EFFORTS?

Evaluating risk communication efforts takes time and resources. Given the fact that both are limited for many risk communication efforts, why should you bother with evaluation?

Information from the evaluation can be used to refine risk communication policies, procedures, and practices. Most organizations involved in risk communication efforts communicate risk more than once. Information gained from one effort can be applied to strengthen future efforts.

Evaluation can serve to prove that laws are being followed. As noted in Chapter 3, "Laws That Mandate Risk Communication," many risk communication efforts are in some way responses to a law or regulation. Showing a regulatory agency that you have evaluated your efforts can help to prove that you are complying with both the letter and the spirit of the law.

Evaluation can serve to prove to your organization's management that risk communication efforts are valuable. If results show that efforts have met organizational goals, management will be more likely to continue funding. If, on the other hand, results show that efforts have failed to communicate risk, the information gained in the evaluation should show where improvements are needed.

Carnegie-Mellon researchers Granger Morgan and his colleagues offer several arguments for using the mental models approach to risk communication (see Chapter 2, "Approaches to Communicating Risk," for more information), but these arguments could easily apply to any risk communication evaluation effort:

1. "You'd never design a new product on the basis of an engineer's best guess. You'd insist on careful empirical design and testing. The same standard should apply to risk communication."

2. "Why balk at spending an amount of money on getting the message right that is a tiny fraction of the stakes riding on correct public understanding?"

3. "We wouldn't release a new drug without adequate testing. Considering the potential health (and economic) consequences of misunderstanding risks, we should be equally loath to release a new risk communication without knowing its impact." (Morgan et al. 2002, p. 180).

## THE MEANING OF SUCCESS

How can you tell whether risk communication efforts have been successful? Success for risk communication efforts relates back to your risk communication plan: did you meet your objectives? If you met your objectives, you succeeded.

There are additional factors to evaluate, however, that will give you useful information for refining future risk communication efforts, particularly when using the methods of information materials, face-to-face communication, pictorial representation of risk, mass media, and computer-based applications. David Dozier and colleagues at the University of Maryland, who studied excellence in communications and public relations programs, suggest that at a minimum, evaluation should measure awareness, knowledge, opinions, and behaviors of the target audience before and after the risk communication program was implemented (Dozier et al. 1995). They also encourage the evaluation of outcomes, not process.

Risk communication experts Neil Weinstein and Peter Sandman (1993) recommend the following be considered to measure the success of risk communication efforts:

- Does the audience understand the content of the communication?

- Does the audience agree with the recommendation or interpretation contained in the message?

- Do people facing a higher level of the risk perceive the risk as greater or show a greater readiness to take action than people exposed to a lower level of the risk?

- Do audience members facing the same level of risk tend to have the same responses to this risk?

- Does the audience find the message helpful, accurate, and clear?

For stakeholder participation methods, another set of factors must be considered. Early work at Tufts University (Rosenbaum 1978) suggested the following factors:

- Accessibility—did the risk communication effort increase the audience's opportunities to obtain relevant information, air views before decision-makers, and hold officials accountable?

How can you tell whether risk communication efforts have been successful? Success for risk communication efforts relates back to your risk communication plan: did you meet your objectives? If you met your objectives, you succeeded.

- Fairness—were all views given equal consideration in the decision-making process?

- Responsiveness—did the risk communication effort foster recognition of public views on decisions?

More recent work suggests that evaluating stakeholder involvement efforts may be far more difficult. What appears to be success from one side may be abject failure from the other. For example, if litigation was avoided, some organizations may mark the effort as a success while stakeholders leave the tables feeling disenfranchised and still in the dark as to the risks they face. For example, risk communication luminaries Susan Santos of FOCUS GROUP and Caron Chess of Rutgers University used two different approaches to evaluate citizen boards advising the Department of Defense on environmental cleanup issues. The more theoretical approach, which considered some of the issues addressed above (such as fairness), would have ranked the efforts rather low, while using stakeholder perceptions, the efforts were deemed successful from both a process and outcome point of view (Santos and Chess 2003).

Other factors to consider depend on your particular situation. Consider your communication effort. Did you accomplish the most you could with the funding and resources available? Would a significant change have been made by additional funding or more staff? Consider your organization's requirements. Did the fact that all materials had be to approved by seven layers of management delay production or lessen the organization's credibility with the audience? Consider your audience's needs. Did a recent election affect the way they view a particular risk, and should you have predicted that and planned for it? Table 19-1 lists possible additional factors for care, consensus, and crisis communication.

## TYPES OF EVALUATION

Once you have decided to evaluate the risk communication effort, you must determine what type of evaluation you need. Kasperson and Palmlund (1989) developed a set of factors to consider when determining

Kasperson and Palmlund (1989) developed a set of factors to consider when determining how to evaluate risk communication efforts, including the objectives of the evaluation, the choice of evaluators, timing, training and monitoring of evaluators, how the audience is to be involved, boundaries of the evaluation, and how success is measured.

**TABLE 19-1**

Evaluation Factors to Consider for Care, Consensus, and Crisis Communication

| Care Communication | Consensus Communication | Crisis Communication |
|---|---|---|
| Did the audience change to less risky behavior? | Were all segments of the audience represented in building the consensus? | Have all members of the audience been alerted to the risk? |
| How long did the behavior change last? | Does the audience understand enough about the risk to make decisions? | Does the audience understand enough about the risk to make decisions? |
| Have all members of the audience been alerted to the risk? | Was a consensus reached about the decision? | Did the audience change to less risky behavior? |
| Does the audience understand the risk well enough to make decisions? | Can the decision be implemented? | Was consistent information given regarding the risk? |

how to evaluate risk communication efforts, including the objectives of the evaluation, the choice of evaluators, timing, training and monitoring of evaluators, how the audience is to be involved, boundaries of the evaluation, and how success is measured.

First determine the objectives of the evaluation effort. Why are you conducting the evaluation? Possible reasons include determining how the current effort is going so that you can revise it, determining what to improve in future efforts, demonstrating to management the results of your program, and proving compliance with regulations. These reasons apply to care, consensus, and crisis communication.

Another factor is who conducts the evaluation. Who will evaluate your efforts? Possible evaluators include those involved in the risk communication efforts, upper management, an outside organization that specializes in such evaluations, and your audience. Which you choose will depend on organizational requirements and the situation. Table 19-2 lists the advantages and disadvantages of these evaluators.

Another factor to consider is timing. When should the evaluation be conducted to best get the information you want? Choices include before the effort begins (i.e.,

Who will evaluate your efforts? Possible evaluators include those involved in the risk communication efforts, upper management, an outside organization that specializes in such evaluations, and your audience.

**TABLE 19-2**

Advantages and Disadvantages of Using Various Evaluators

| Evaluator | Advantages | Disadvantages |
|---|---|---|
| Risk communication staff | Staff intimate with program and risk communication practices; approvals generally not needed; staff trusted by organization | May lack credibility with regulating agencies or audience; may have difficulty being objective |
| Upper management | Positive interactions can increase support; less costly than outside evaluations; staff intimate with organization's constraints | Negative interactions can decrease support; may lack credibility with regulatory agencies or audience |
| Outside organization | Staff intimate with risk communication practices; may have more credibility with regulators and audience; may be more objective | May be more costly than in-house evaluations; may not understand organization's constraints |
| Audience | Interactions can increase support; audience understands own needs best; highly credible to audience | May be difficult to get approvals; doesn't understand organization's constraints or risk communication practices |

evaluating the plan), during the effort, and after the effort. Evaluations conducted during the effort should be timed so that there has been enough activity conducted to provide the information needed and so that no activity will be compromised by rescheduling staff time and resources for the evaluation. Evaluations conducted after the effort should generally be conducted soon enough that facts are still clear in people's minds. Evaluations may be conducted later if retention is a factor to be evaluated.

Training of evaluators should also be considered. Do the evaluators know what to look for and are they capable of getting the kind of information you need? If you are using inexperienced evaluators, have someone experienced in risk communication programs train them in what to look for and how to go about it. Even if you are using experienced evaluators, you will need to acquaint them with your situation. One project manager with whom we worked always had his risk communication messages evaluated by a team of technical experts to make sure the technical information was correct. With them, he also sent descriptions of the laws he was trying to comply with, his expected audience, and other background information along with the message so that the evaluators could judge the effort in context. He found that this helped to eliminate suggestions and comments that were unreasonable given his situation.

You will also want to monitor the work of the evaluators to ensure that they are collecting their information without hindering your efforts and that you receive their input in time to use it.

Another consideration is how the audience is to be involved. How and when should the audience be involved in the evaluation effort? The audience can be involved in several ways. They can serve as the evaluators themselves, particularly if you have an interactive advisory committee or focus group. They can also serve as the research subjects of a questionnaire or survey.

Also consider the boundaries of the evaluation. Boundaries to consider are access to proprietary data (especially if an outside group will be conducting the evaluation) and access to the audience. Organizational requirements should be considered. Setting a time limit for the evaluation may also be necessary.

The final factor to consider is how the success of the risk communication effort should be judged. How will the evaluators determine whether your efforts have been successful? As noted above, they should evaluate your efforts based on your plan. Did you meet your objectives? If they are evaluating the plan itself, they should evaluate it relative to your reasoning for its content.

Based on these factors and your ultimate purpose and objectives, you can design an evaluation effort that will bring you the information you need.

## CONDUCTING THE EVALUATION

Little literature has been devoted to evaluation in risk communication as opposed to other aspects of the field (examples include Kasperson and Palmlund 1989; Regan and Desvousges 1990; Weinstein and Sandman 1993; and Santos and Chess 2003). Obviously, your evaluators will need to determine whether your efforts have achieved your purposes and objectives. Because your purposes and objectives will most likely involve how your audience will react to your efforts (changing behavior, gaining awareness), your evaluators must consider your audience's reactions to determine whether your efforts have been successful.

The best ways to determine audience reactions are surveys and interviews. Surveys may be conducted by mail, phone, electronic mail, or in person, depending on the situation. Consider your resources and the availability and disposition of your audience. For example, David Chrislip and Carl Larson, in their research that led to their 1994 book, *Collaborative Leadership: How Citizens and Civic Leaders Can Make a Difference*, developed a measurement device that could be used for consensus communication activities. The survey, which covers five dimensions (context of the effort, design of the effort, stakeholder skills and attitudes, consensus process, and results) asks respondents to mark statements as true, more true than false, more false than true, or false. The instrument has been shown to accurately correlate with success of the effort, as judged by comparisons with results of other instruments (Chrislip and Larson 1994).

Interviews can be conducted separately with representative members of your audience or in focus groups. See Chapter 15 for advice on conducting interviews with individuals and Chapter 17 for advice on conducting focus group meetings.

Occasionally, time or organizational constraints sometimes make it impossible to use surveys or interviews. For example, some government organizations must receive permission from the federal Office of Management and Budget before conducting any survey of more than 10 people. Alternative methods to evaluate audience reactions to risk communication efforts include:

- Reviewing risk communication plans—evaluators can look at your plan and evaluate it against the audience's, organizational, and regulatory requirements. For example, regulators often evaluate an organization's community relations plan for Superfund sites to ensure that the community will be kept informed of and involved in activities.

- Reviewing specific messages for content—if the evaluators are sufficiently schooled in the theories, principles, and practices of risk communication, they may be able to point to problems by reviewing the information you are disseminating. For example, J. Harrison Carpenter of Michigan Technological University found that the way technical terms are defined in text can result in potential manipulation of the content (either to paint too rosy a picture or to create fear). He goes on to present a possible tool for classifying terms and their definitions that might be used to test risk communication messages to ensure appropriate presentation of information (Carpenter 1997).

- Reviewing entire efforts for such factors as continuity of content, timing, and follow-through—how the risk is communicated is often as important as the content of the risk messages themselves. Evaluators may be able to determine patterns that should be changed or maintained. For example, evaluators might review the timing, scope, and content of health care campaign messages to ensure appropriate coverage across time and audiences.

Regardless of which technique is employed, evaluations are generally conducted in a similar manner. Michael Regan and William Desvousges, in their risk communication evaluation handbook for the U.S. Environmental Protection Agency (1990), suggest five steps to this evaluation process:

- Clarify the risk communication goals and objectives—you must know what you are trying to accomplish before you can evaluate how well you did it. See Chapter 7 of this book for additional information on setting purpose and objectives.

- Determine information needs for evaluation—what kinds of information will you need to prove that you are meeting your objectives? For example, if your objective is to raise awareness of an issue, you might want to conduct a survey at the beginning of your risk communication effort to understand the current level of awareness among your intended audience. After conducting the risk communication effort, you would do another survey to see how awareness had changed.

- Collect the information—as part of your risk communication effort, you would gather the information you had identified as needed for evaluation purposes.

- Analyze the data—you would then look at the information you had gathered to identify any trends or difficulties.

- Draw conclusions—you would determine what might be changed to enhance any positive trends or resolve any difficulties.

They further suggest that this activity be included in the original risk communication plan to ensure timing, resources, and information gathered are appropriate.

## CHECKLIST FOR EVALUATING RISK COMMUNICATION EFFORTS

❑ What constitutes success in my risk communication efforts has been determined.

The following were determined before the evaluation:
❑ evaluation objectives
❑ evaluators
❑ timing
❑ training of evaluators
❑ monitoring of evaluators
❑ audience involvement
❑ possible boundaries
❑ judgment of success.

My purpose in evaluation is
❑ refining practices

❏ justifying continuation of the efforts

❏ proving compliance with the law.

To evaluate the risk communication efforts, evaluators will

❏ conduct audience interviews

❏ survey the audience

❏ review risk communication plans

❏ review specific messages for content

❏ review the effort for continuity of content, timing, and follow-through

Evaluators will follow this process for the evaluation:

❏ Clarify the risk communication goals and objectives

❏ Determine information needs for evaluation

❏ Collect the information

❏ Analyze the data

❏ Draw conclusions

❏ Share results with risk communication team.

## REFERENCES

Carpenter, J. H. 1997. "Define and Conquer: Technical Definitions and the Rhetoric of Risk Communication." *Proceedings of the Fourth Biennial Conference on Communication and Environment*, State University of New York-Syracuse, New York.

Chrislip, D. D., and C. E. Larson. 1994. *Collaborative Leadership: How Citizens and Civic Leaders Can Make a Difference*. Jossey-Bass, Inc., San Francisco.

Dozier, D. M., L. A. Grunig, and J. E. Grunig. 1995. *Manager's Guide to Excellence in Public Relations and Communication Management*. Lawrence Erlbaum Associates, Publishers, Mahwah, New Jersey.

Kasperson, R. E., and I. Palmlund. 1989. "Evaluating Risk Communications." *Effective Risk Communication: The Role and Responsibility of Government and Nongovernment Organizations*, editors V. T. Covello, D. B. McCallum, and M. T. Pavlova, pages 143-158. Plenum Press, New York.

Morgan, M. G., B. Fischhoff, A. Bostrom, and C. J. Atman. 2002. *Risk Communication: A Mental Models Approach.* Cambridge University Press, New York.

Regan, M. J., and W. H. Desvousges. 1990. *Communicating Environmental Risks: A Guide to Practical Evaluations.* EPA 230-01-91-001, U.S. Environmental Protection Agency, Washington, D.C.

Rosenbaum, N. 1978. "Evaluating Citizen Involvement Programs." *Citizen Participation Perspectives*, pages 82-86. Lincoln Filene Center for Citizenship and Public Affairs, Tufts University, Medford, Massachusetts.

Santos, S. L., and C. Chess. 2003. "Evaluating Citizen Advisory Boards: The Importance of Theory and Participant-Based Criteria and Practical Implications." *Risk Analysis*, 23(2):269-280.

Weinstein, N. D., and P. M. Sandman. 1993. "Some Criteria for Evaluating Risk Messages." *Risk Analysis*, 13(1):103-114.

## ADDITIONAL RESOURCES

Desvousges, W. H. 1991. "Integrating Evaluation: A Seven-Step Process." *Evaluation and Effective Risk Communications Workshop Proceedings*, editors A. Fisher, M. Pavlova, and V. Covello, pages 119-123. EPA/600/9-90/054, U.S. Environmental Protection Agency, Washington, D.C.

Desvousges, W. H., and V. K. Smith. 1988. "Focus Groups and Risk Communication: The 'Science" of Listening to Data." *Risk Analysis*, 8(4):479-484.

Kline, M., C. Chess, and P. Sandman. 1989. *Evaluating Risk Communication Programs: A Catalog of "Quick and Easy" Feedback Methods.* Rutgers University, Cook College, Environmental Communication Research Program, New Brunswick, New Jersey.

Santos, S. L. 1990. "Developing a Risk Communication Strategy." *Management and Operations*, November:45-49.

Smith, V. K., W. H. Desvousges, A. Fisher, and F. R. Johnson. 1987. *Communicating Radon Risk Effectively: A Mid-Course Evaluation.* U.S. Environmental Protection Agency, Office of Policy Analysis, Washington, D.C.

*Part*

# V

# BIOTERRORISM AND OTHER EMERGENCIES

he terrorist attacks of September 11, 2001, and subsequent perceived public health emergencies like anthrax and mad cow disease have shown that emergency risk communication requires different strategies and tactics to be effective.

◇

*"In emergency risk communication, it's your job to provide the public with information that allows them to make the best possible decisions within nearly impossible time constraints."*

— Linda Sokler, Managing Regional Director of American Institutes for Research, Prospect Center, 2002.

# Risk Communication Before, During, and After Emergencies

*T*he first two editions of this book were written under a paradigm that divided risk communication into care, consensus, and crisis communication based on a number of factors such as agreement on the magnitude of the risk between scientific experts and those at risk, the level and type of involvement by audiences or participants, and the urgency of the risk. Like many things in the United States, this paradigm was challenged by the terrorist attacks of September 11, 2001. Since then, other challenges to public health, for example, the threat of severe acute respiratory syndrome (SARS) in 2002 and 2003, have caused risk communicators to reconsider how risks should be communicated in the face of terrorism or public health emergencies.

Thus, we make a distinction in this chapter between a crisis and an emergency. A traditional definition of a crisis is a turning point that will decisively determine an outcome. Medical practitioners once spoke of a crisis as a critical point in a disease. Thus, a crisis follows a process, even if it is an undesirable one, and is not altogether unexpected. An emergency, on the other hand, has traditionally been defined as a sudden or unforeseen situation that requires immediate action. Emergencies are random, they often don't follow predictable processes, and they are unexpected. By these definitions, the sudden rupture of an underground oil tank that has been leaking for some time would be a crisis, while a bioterrorist attack would be an emergency. Other recent examples of emergencies include disease outbreaks (SARS, West Nile virus) and terrorism-related events (9/11, anthrax).

Risk communicators have long dealt with crises such as natural disasters (floods, earthquakes, hurricanes), industrial accidents (hazardous releases internal to a facility, environmental releases), and routine disease outbreaks (flu, measles). Indeed, crisis communication, as our paradigm implies, is a distinct branch of risk communication, with its own strategies and tactics. What's different about risk communication in an emergency? At times, communication principles, strategies, and tactics in emergencies fit within the boundaries of crisis, care, and even consensus communication. Nevertheless, those communicating risk must understand the unique characteristics of emergency risk communication, so they can plan for the unexpected and communicate during and after an emergency.

## UNDERSTANDING EMERGENCY RISK COMMUNICATION

Emergencies have their own unique characteristics that affect how risk communication is put into practice. Table 20-1 shows some of these characteristics. The following text explains these characteristics in more detail.

### Emotions and Public Actions

People's reactions during an emergency, especially one involving potential bioterrorism, can be intense and complex. Fear may prompt a debilitating response, with people acting in extreme and sometimes irrational ways to avoid a perceived or real threat. People may feel apathy or hopelessness, that nothing they do will help. They may experience denial, leading to avoiding

> A crisis follows a process. An emergency is a sudden or unforeseen situation that requires immediate action. The sudden rupture of an underground oil tank that has been leaking would be a crisis, while a bioterrorist attack would be an emergency.

**TABLE 20-1**
Characteristics of Emergency Risk Communication

| What's Different | The Result | Practices |
|---|---|---|
| Purpose | Communicators must explain, put in context, correct misperceptions, give options for action, empower people to make decisions, move people to recovery, and help them attain a new level of readiness. | Use principles of care and crisis communication as appropriate. |
| Sense of urgency, rapid rate of change | Decisions must be made within a narrow timeframe, with an uncertain outcome, to reduce risks that are still unknown and to rapidly recover from an event that is still unfolding. | Recognize that communication may be confusing, contradictory, and subject to change as the event evolves. Pre-planning can reduce confusion. |
| Disrupted logistics | Normal or pre-planned communication channels and actions may not be available, such as electrical power, cell phones, Internet connections, and transportation to scenes. | Use pre-planning and be flexible during the event to identify alternatives. |
| Potential for large numbers of ill or injured people across wide jurisdictions | Lines of authority cross for responders, family and friends demand immediate information, and the health care infrastructure can be severely stressed. | Team with a wide variety of agencies and organizations and look for creative communication alternatives. |
| Intense media attention | Reporters are seeking and reporting information nonstop. | Designate and train spokespeople, but prepare others to speak as well. |
| Emotional response | People may experience a range of strong emotions including fear, anger, panic, denial, laying blame, solidarity with others, desire to help victims, and need for personal control. All these may affect how people respond to a risk. | Develop and implement communications that account for these responses, including giving people reasonable and appropriate actions to take. |
| Incomplete or unknown information | Misunderstanding facts about the risk may affect people's response. Uncertainty may increase fear and panic. | Address factual misperceptions in planning and during an emergency. Explain what is known at the time and what is unknown, saying that it is preliminary. Say what you're doing to find out more. Concede errors and modify previous statements as more information comes to light. |

*continued*

**TABLE 20-1** *(continued)*
Characteristics of Emergency Risk Communication

| What's Different | The Result | Practices |
| --- | --- | --- |
| Involvement of multiple organizations, sometimes with competing agendas, including possible criminal/regulatory investigation | Sources may issue conflicting information, leading to confusion and reduced credibility. | Get buy-in of organizations during emergency planning. Understand agency roles, jurisdictions, and preservation of evidence/documentation for law enforcement followup. Draw clear lines of authority and responsibility, and make sure everyone understands the roles. |
| Security and privacy issues | Some information, such as victims' names, can't be released. | Explain the kind of information that can't be released and why. Say whether it will be released later and under what circumstances. |
| Backlash | After the emergency is over, people may seek those to blame. | Evaluate deficiencies. Take responsibility for things that were your organization's fault. Explain what's being done differently now. |

warnings, not believing the threat is real, or not believing it applies to them. These attitudes can result in not taking action until the last minute or until it's too late.

Despite these negative responses, a national survey after the September 11 attacks showed that Americans want honest and accurate information about terror-related situations. They want this information even if it makes them worried, angry, or fearful. They want the facts, want to know whom to blame, and want to feel solidarity with fellow citizens (Fischhoff 2002).

They don't want leaders to hide their own response to tragedies. Risk communication consultant Peter Sandman likes to use the example of former New York City Mayor Rudy Giuliani. When asked about the number of casualties just hours after the World Trade Center attacks, Giuliani simply answered, "More than we can bear." Giuliani's impact in the days that followed resulted not just from his calmness, competence, and compassion,

◇

Americans don't want leaders to hide their own response to tragedies. Risk communication consultant Peter Sandman likes to use the example of former New York City Mayor Rudy Giuliani. When asked about the number of casualties just hours after the World Trade Center attacks, Giuliani simply answered, "More than we can bear."

Sandman says, but from the fact that these traits were accompanied by Giuliani's readily detectable pain, which enabled people to identify with him. Sandman also argues that communication should not try to "over reassure," or convince people that there's nothing to be afraid of. People may rightly be afraid. Instead, acknowledge and accept that the fear is legitimate, then tell people what's being done and what they can do.

This concept of giving people reasonable actions to take is very important in an emergency, especially one involving public health. You want people to be concerned and vigilant, and to take reasonable precautions. Through actions, people share control of the situation, and in some cases, they can keep it from getting worse. Having a constructive role engages people in a common mission and provides a sense of control. People can do things to help themselves, victims, and emergency responders. They can also be prepared to do things to minimize the risk of more bad things happening.

Sandman suggests giving people a choice of three actions matched to their level of concern: a minimum precaution, a maximum response, and a recommended middle response. For example, for drinking water safety, a public health official might give three options: use chlorine drops (minimum), buy bottled water (maximum), or boil water for two minutes (the recommended middle response). Another way of looking at this is: you must do X, you should do Y, and you can do Z.

◇

Having a constructive role engages people in a common mission and provides a sense of control.

## Credibility and Trust

The need to establish credibility and trust is a common theme in risk communication. Ideally, trust is built over time and is the result of ongoing actions, listening, and communication skill. In an emergency, it helps if the responding organizations have already built trust in the affected communities. If they haven't, or if people haven't come in contact with them enough to build trust, there are still things the organization can say and do to build trust in a crisis.

Research has shown that several factors affect trust: caring and empathy, dedication and commitment, competence and expertise, and honesty and openness (Slovic 1999). Trust and credibility are eroded when there is disagreement among experts; lack of coordination among risk management organizations; lack of listening, dialogue, and public participation; an unwillingness to acknowledge risks; not disclosing information in a timely manner; and not fulfilling risk management responsibilities (Chess et al. 1995; Covello et al. 1989).

Three examples in recent years underscore the importance of establishing trust in emergency risk communication: SARS, mad cow disease, and anthrax. Beijing was widely criticized for its initial cover-up of SARS cases, which surfaced in southern China in 2002 and killed more than 800 people worldwide before subsiding in 2003. In Hong Kong, which suffered 299 deaths, the health department first learned about the emergency through media reports. To its credit, China has since instituted a 24-hour online monitoring and consultation system to gather information and answer medical questions to prepare for future outbreaks. Similarly, the British government was criticized about covering up facts in the early stages of the mad cow disease epidemic that began in the 1980s in the United Kingdom. Perhaps learning from that experience, when the disease surfaced in the United States in 2003, government agencies and industry groups immediately began communicating with the public about actions to recall meat, trace the affected cow's history, and ensure the safety of the food supply. In the early days of the 2001 anthrax attacks, the Centers for Disease Control and Prevention (CDC) mistakenly said anthrax spores couldn't escape a sealed envelope to threaten postal workers. Later, they corrected that information and admitted their error, adding to the agency's trust for handling future incidents. The SARS, mad cow, and anthrax examples demonstrate that it's important to tell people what you know, what isn't known, and to correct misinformation as soon as it is discovered.

Trust is also affected by who delivers the message. Surveys indicate that certain organizations and individuals, including citizen advisory groups, health and safety professionals, scientists, and educators, are perceived to have medium to high levels of trust on health, safety,

*"The British government's big mistake, at the time of that [mad cow disease] epidemic, was to cover up facts and hide statistics. Official secrecy led to increased anxiety. The British lesson is clear: If more facts are revealed, consumers will feel safer, and the industry is less likely to suffer permanent damage."*
—The Washington Post, December 28, 2003.

and environmental issues (EPA 1990). A city or state government agency, for example, may wish to involve these groups and seek third-party endorsements from them, if appropriate, during an emergency.

Individual trust still overrides organizational trust. Research has shown that direct personal contact has the most significant effect on a person's willingness to trust and act on health-related information (Covello et al. 2001). Throughout the duration of the Washington, D.C., anthrax case, a CDC Epidemiologic Investigation Service officer met repeatedly with the Brentwood postal workers to discuss antibiotics. In a public situation, when the officer gave the recommendation of 30 days of antibiotic therapy in addition to the anthrax vaccine, an activist in the crowd started shouting inflammatory comments. But because the officer had established himself as a credible and trusted source of information, instead of rallying around the activist, the crowd told him to be quiet so they could hear what the officer had to say.

Trust is also affected by how an organization responds to a diverse community. During the 1999 West Nile virus outbreak, New York City officials commendably issued brochures and fact sheets in at least ten languages. However, trust was diminished when communications were neglected for sensitive populations, such as alerting asthmatics about spraying locations and schedules (Covello et al. 2001).

—— ◇ ——

Individual trust overrides organizational trust.

## PLANNING FOR THE UNEXPECTED

Planning involves understanding the needs and desires of the community and organizational jurisdictions in an emergency situation, creating and getting approval for a written plan, training staff, educating the public, getting the resources required in the plan, and making sure the infrastructure is in place to carry it out. Planning should be done with the help of stakeholders and partners, including citizens, who could be affected by or will respond to an emergency, as well as those who will implement the plan. The following text provides guidance on making sure your organization is ready, teaming with other organizations, working with communities in advance, determining appropriate communication methods, and developing an emergency communication plan.

## Preparing Your Organization

Many organizations are expected to play a role in responding to emergencies. In the public sector, state and local emergency response units stand ready to save lives and bolster damaged infrastructure. In the private sector, organizations provide needed volunteers and donations of critical goods and services. While effective response requires the teamwork of many organizations, each one understands its niche in the process. It's the same in risk communication.

To prepare your organization to effectively communicate risk during an emergency takes time and effort. Some of the most critical preparations, however, have to do with attitude and process rather than simply gathering communication tools. What often hinders communication in emergencies is not the lack of infrastructure or skills but the lack of consensus on roles and responsibilities. Also important is making sure that the organization's own employees receive and share information during an emergency.

### Check Your Attitudes at the Door

Organizations charged with communicating risk during an emergency must first take inventory of their attitudes and processes. Chapter 4, "Constraints to Effective Risk Communication," discusses ways to combat such nonproductive attitudes as malicious compliance with regulations, a pessimistic attitude toward the public, an unwillingness to share power, and management apathy or hostility. That chapter also describes how to overcome ineffective organizational processes such as inappropriate resources, inappropriate review and approval procedures, conflicting organizational requirements, and access to staff and information. While such difficulties can limit any type of risk communication endeavor, they become magnified when trying to deal with an emergency. It's best to deal with them when calm heads are more likely to prevail.

Organizations also must deal with ethical issues well before an emergency occurs. Chapter 5, "Ethical Issues," deals with such issues as determining those who are potentially at risk, the acceptable magnitude of a risk, representation of those at risk, and the use of persuasion. Each organization will likely respond differently to such issues, but working with teaming agencies to come to consensus in how these issues will be addressed in an emergency is also critical to communicating with the news media and the public during an emergency.

### You Want Me to Do What? Determining Staff Roles

Because of the extensive teaming necessary to respond to an emergency, organizations also need to be clear internally as well as externally about their roles. Are you first responders, on the scene immediately and gathering information about the depth and breadth of the situation for other team members to communicate while at the same time working to minimize panic and maximize appropriate responses by the public? Does your organization gather information from all sources, distill it, and provide a cohesive message so that team members speak with one voice? Are you the spokesperson, interfacing with the news media and public? Do you provide support with staff or equipment and thus communicate needs and capabilities to those making decisions? All staff likely to be involved in emergency response need to understand the organization's role in the risk communication process, and all organizations expected to work together on a response need to understand and agree on each other's roles.

Staff within an organization also need to understand their roles within the wider organizational mandate. Who is the contact person for the organization? Who serves as spokesperson? Who analyzes risks and responses? Who ensures communication within the organization? Table 20-2 shows how typical organizational roles fit within the emergency risk communication process. Note that the roles are patterned after the Incident Command Structure used by many emergency

*All organizations expected to work together on a response need to understand and agree on each other's roles.*

**TABLE 20-2**

Typical Staff Roles in the Emergency Risk Communication Process

| Role in Emergency Response | Role In Emergency Risk Communication | Example Activities |
|---|---|---|
| *Incident Commander*—manages the response | Ultimate authority on response, manager of the public information officer | • Holds hourly to daily briefings with response leaders, including public information officer<br>• Shares information with public information officer<br>• Reviews and approves information to be released |
| *Safety Officer*—ensures responders have adequate protection | Subject matter expert, providing information on safety (precautions, limitations, etc.) | • Initially briefs public information officer followed by additional briefings as the situation evolves |
| *Public Information Officer*—ensures public and news media have appropriate information | Spokesperson or coach of spokesperson, conduit of information | • Attends briefings with various command staff<br>• Monitors public and media information needs<br>• Suggests data that should be gathered to planning and intelligence functions<br>• Crafts messages to public and media<br>• Serves as or coaches spokesperson<br>• Responds to public and media information requests |
| *Agency Liaison*—ensures cooperation with appropriate organizations | Subject matter expert, providing information on their agency's support to the effort (number of staff, roles, etc.) | • Initially briefs public information officer followed by additional briefings as the situation evolves |
| *Agency Representative*—manages agency's portion of response | Subject matter expert, providing information on agency's role, and sharing response information with own agency; may also serve as agency spokesperson | • Responds to questions from public information officer as requested<br>• May serve as agency spokesperson |
| *Planning and Intelligence*—collects and analyzes information and recommends actions | Data gathering and sharing with response team, including public information officer | • Gathers communication information as well as other emergency information<br>• Briefs public information officer on regular basis |
| *Logistics*—provides support, necessary infrastructure, and supplies | Providing necessary equipment for communication internally and externally | • Understands communication needs<br>• Supplies equipment, infrastructure, and other items necessary for communication |
| *Finance/Administration*—manages costs, payment, and procurement | Collecting and paying costs of communication | • Accrues costs<br>• Pays bills |

management organizations across the United States. While titles in some areas may vary, functions should be analogous.

### Ensuring Worker Communication

In a wide-scale emergency such as a terrorist attack or outbreak of a major disease, organization staff are as likely to be affected as the public. Even for staff not directly affected or involved in the response effort, loss of infrastructure such as phone lines may prevent information from reaching them in traditional ways. In addition, emergency communication plans often direct communications externally—to the news media and public—and not internally to staff and management. Thus, organizations need to consider how to get information to staff during an emergency.

Workers generally have several broad information needs in an emergency. They need to know what is expected of them from a work perspective. If the emergency occurs on off hours, do they come in as usual? Come in on different shifts? Report to a different location? Shelter in place? If the emergency happens while they are at work, do they evacuate the building? Move to an emergency shelter? Return home?

Some government organizations use the security levels from the Department of Homeland Security to inform staff of their actions under particular scenarios. For example, the Nevada Division of Health translated these security levels into specific actions staff should take. When levels changed, the staff of the public information office sent a mass e-mail to all of their employees and posted printed copies on all entry and exit doors at the facility.

During an actual emergency, staff members need to know the same things the general public wants to know, including the depth and breadth of the emergency, what is being done to respond, and what they can do to help. Before an emergency, however, staff members need to know how emergency information is going to reach them and where to go for additional information. Some organizations make emergency communication with staff the responsibility of the communications staff, but

Before an emergency, staff members need to know how information is going to reach them and where to go for additional information.

this can prove problematic if communications staff are also serving as the public information officers in an emergency. The information officer must look outward, to other organizations, to the news media, and to the public. This outward focus and the time commitment associated with it make reaching staff difficult. It's better to make organizational communication the responsibility of another function, such as human resources.

To ensure that staff know their roles in an emergency, they must be trained and their training reinforced. Emergencies happen too rarely for people to remember how to respond without frequent reminders. Some organizations that use security badges have included information on emergency response directly on the badge or on another card worn with the badge. Others issue refrigerator magnets, business-card-size information pieces to be carried in wallets, or small booklets to be kept at home. Another method is a telephone hotline for staff only, often using the weather alert hotline.

## Teaming with Other Organizations

Once your organization knows its role in an emergency, it's time to find its role with other responding organizations. It takes a number of functions to adequately respond to an emergency, particularly one of regional or national significance. Health care providers, emergency medical technicians, fire, police, and civic organizations respond at a local level. Most have state- and national-level counterparts. Some emergencies involve private organizations as volunteers or critical equipment donors. Local organizations sometimes worry that they will have to shoulder the burden alone, but experience with the September 11 attacks and the anthrax events in recent years has shown that a serious event brings help from expected and not-so-expected places. As the Health Officer of Palm Beach County eloquently put it after anthrax surfaced there, "If you have an incident, they will come." The question is: what are you going to do with this help?

The Federal Emergency Management Agency suggests organizing responses around emergency support

*"If you have an incident, they will come."*
—Health Officer, Palm Beach County, Florida, commenting on people who responded when anthrax was found there.

functions (ESFs). Those most closely related to risk communication are ESF 8, which relates to public health, and ESF 5, which relates to public information. Teaming organizations need to determine who takes the lead and who supports each function. They also need to determine what that support entails, how teaming organizations will be notified, and where they will meet to respond. Such details are typically outlined in an emergency response plan, which all organizations should review and approve.

With organizational roles agreed upon, team members need to train internally and with each other. Such training helps find potential pitfalls in the plan before an emergency occurs and helps staff remember their roles.

Note, however, that training is more necessity than luxury. In the aftermath of the World Trade Center bombing in 1993 and the Oklahoma City bombing in 1995, a 1998 Congressional mandate called for practice operations for a terrorist attack. Such exercises are designed to assess the nation's crisis management capabilities under extreme conditions and to identify areas needing additional training and preparations.

One of these, a multi-state biowarfare attack exercise in 2000 called Operation Topoff, showed participants in Colorado that they had not thought through the consequences of imposing quarantine. In the exercise, the governor had issued a travel restriction order for all of metropolitan Denver, and the CDC had quarantined the entire state of Colorado. The orders created many unforeseen problems, including how to enforce the restrictions, maintain essential community services, and distribute food and medicine (Hoffman 2003).

Topoff 2, a mock nuclear and biological terror attack, was staged in 2003 in Chicago and Seattle by the Department of Homeland Security. Over a week, hundreds of "casualties" filtered through emergency rooms in both cities. The $16-million drill involved more than 85,000 people from more than 100 federal, state, and local agencies, plus several hundred more participants in British Columbia. Participants gained first-hand knowledge about large-scale triaging and isolation to prevent contamination to caregivers and other patients in the facility.

## Working with Communities in Advance

Besides identifying organizational and team roles, you need to consider teaming with the public. Emergency services personnel, when focused on carrying out their duties, tend to think of the public as passive bystanders. At the scene of a traffic accident or crime scene, for example, the public is separated from the response operation by the familiar barrier of yellow tape. But a disaster is an event that generates casualties beyond available resources, shattering the yellow tape phenomenon, argue researchers Glass and Schoch-Spana (2002).

In the September 11 terrorist attacks in New York, volunteers and groups converged at ground zero to offer aid and support, despite hazardous conditions and uncertainty about the risks of further attack or collapse of the towers. Volunteers responded rapidly and in large numbers to support search and rescue efforts while professional operations were still being put in place. After the attacks, affected communities organized through local government, relief groups, and civic organizations, such as churches, neighborhood associations, and labor organizations. Since then, more preparedness programs across the country have been discussing ways to capitalize on the work of nonprofessionals, especially in identifying, surveying, and containing a disease outbreak and caring for large numbers of casualties.

Beyond harnessing public volunteers, participatory decision-making processes should be used in developing emergency risk plans. During the West Nile virus outbreak in 1999, risk communication researcher and consultant Vince Covello argues that city officials didn't do enough to understand stakeholder concern about certain actions the city took. For example, wildlife experts and environmental groups became outraged about the City's decision to use the pesticide Malathion for disease control, using aerial spraying by highly visible helicopters (Covello et al. 2001). He advocates using citizen advisory panels or other community leaders for

> "A legitimate sense of control can be given to those under threat, especially in advance of an attack, by public education, by public participation in the preparation process, and by providing the public a voice in the decisions that will affect them."
> —Vince Covello et al., "Risk Communication, the West Nile Virus Epidemic, and Bioterrorism: Responding to the Communication Challenges Posed by the Intentional or Unintentional Release of a Pathogen in an Urban Setting" (2001).

responses that require a community's ethical judgment. These might include setting priorities for use of scarce medical resources, such as antibiotics and vaccines, or instituting epidemic control measures that compromise civil liberties.

A response to bioterrorism or other emergencies should capitalize on peoples' desire to help others, especially through the use of existing social groups. Population responses to a wide range of emergencies, including the terrorist acts in New York and Washington, D.C., in 2001 and mass electrical blackout in the Eastern United States in 2003, show that there is a tendency toward adaptability, cooperation, and resourcefulness in times of disaster (Glass and Schoch-Spana 2002). After the 9/11 terrorist attacks, in the absence of an organized response, people flocked to health centers to give blood. During the Persian Gulf War in 1991, Israel effectively used a network of community information centers to dispense medical information, medication instructions, and reports indicating which hospitals, clinics, and pharmacies were open (Sachs et al. 1991).

In responding to a bioterrorism incident, health and biodefense researchers suggest that church groups could distribute antibiotics, convene vaccination meetings, or arrange visits to the home of people who are ill (Glass and Schoch-Spana 2002). Social groups such as the Kiwanis or Rotary Clubs might activate phone trees to gather case reports, trace contacts, or disseminate instructions on appropriate use of medications. In its SARS communication plan, the CDC recommended that the American Lung Association and other groups could be helpful in disseminating educational messages to community groups about SARS (CDC 2003).

## Determining Appropriate Communication Methods

When disaster strikes, people want as many information sources as possible, and technology is increasingly being used to inform people about emergencies. Media such as television, radio, and newspapers are the most commonly used communication methods in emergencies, and are described in more detail in Part III of this

---◇---

A response to bioterrorism or other emergencies should capitalize on people's desire to help others, especially through the use of existing social groups.

book and in a later section in this chapter called "Working with the Media in an Emergency." This section describes other forms of communication to consider in emergencies.

### Web Sites

Web sites that are updated frequently can be good resources in helping the public know what to do in case of emergency and how to respond when one occurs. For example, the chemical weapons depot in Oregon has a web site containing a wide variety of emergency response information. Among the items is a map showing school locations in each surrounding county with designated emergency plans for each (shelter in place, evacuate, etc.). The site also includes instructions for citizens to prepare for an emergency, including sound clips of warning sirens, and what to do during an emergency. Also included is an archive of press releases, updated as new ones are issued, as well as contact information for public information officers. Chapter 18, "Technology-Assisted Communication," describes web-delivered communication in more detail.

### Telecommunications

While telecommunications systems can be severed during an emergency, many communities rely on them for emergency communication. Several communities and states have so-called reverse 911 telecommunication systems that phone citizens in targeted geographic areas with a recorded message to notify them about specific threats. Reverse 911 also includes a phone number citizens can call to hear pre-recorded information, such as emergency evacuation procedures. In Florida, the Orange County Sheriff's Department used its reverse 911 system in 2002 to warn trailer park residents to evacuate when a hurricane bore down on Orlando. Colorado's system warns homeowners of approaching wildfires.

Electronic communication systems that send information and track responses in real time are becoming more common. Information is communicated instantly to subscribers' mobile devices (cell phones, pagers, hand-held computers) as well as to e-mail systems. Government organizations are increasingly using these wired or wireless emergency communication systems to keep their first responders, employees, and citizens informed. Arlington County, Virginia, used its system to deliver information in English and Spanish about Hurricane Isabel in 2003. Subscribers received weather warnings, messages about the safety of Arlington's drinking water, and locations of ice distribution centers. The County also uses the system to activate teams of emergency responders.

The New Brunswick provincial government in Canada is developing a phone network that alerts residents in emergencies, activating a blinking red light similar to a phone's voice message light. In 2003, RCA introduced a TV with a built-in early warning system. Using a dedicated emergency alert tuner and antenna, the TV constantly monitors emergencies and issues warnings and advisories, even when the TV is turned off. It gathers data from government agencies such as the Federal Emergency Management Agency and the National Oceanic and Atmospheric Administration, finds events that threaten local residents, and displays alerts on the screen. The TV translates government-issued radio codes into text messages, audio alarms, and colored warning lights.

### Creative Alternatives

Lower-tech communication options may be necessary when electricity is out, cell phone towers are inoperable, or computers are slowed by traffic and viruses. In 2003, a soy-based baby formula lacking vitamin B1 was found to have caused several infant deaths in Israel. The milk substitute had been widely used in orthodox Jewish communities because of its kosher certification. When the problem was discovered, the Jewish Sabbath, which forbids electricity use, had already begun. Lacking access to electricity-powered mass media to reach the target audience, Israeli health authorities sent trucks equipped with loudspeakers into Orthodox Jewish neighborhoods, warning parents not to use the formula.

◇

Lower-tech communication options may be necessary when electricity is out, cell phone towers are inoperable, or computers are slowed by traffic and viruses.

Community groups in several states have organized their ham radio operators for systematic emergency communication, especially when electricity fails.

The public warning system for a chemical emergency at a munitions depot in Oregon includes outdoor sirens and electronic highway message reader boards. To augment the standard TV and radio emergency advisory systems, depot staff have distributed battery-powered tone alert radios to thousands of homes and businesses in surrounding communities. In an emergency, the radios would be activated to provide warnings and emergency instructions.

### Developing an Emergency Risk Communication Plan

Chapter 12, "Develop a Communication Plan," includes most of what is needed for emergency risk communication. However, because of the differences alluded to earlier, emergency risk communication plans include additional elements or cover some elements in greater detail.

Many of the following suggestions are adapted from guidance by the CDC, which has done extensive public health emergency planning and training. See the "Additional Resources" section of this chapter for other organizations with emergency communication plans. You can also request the emergency communication plan for your state and other public jurisdictions. By law, these plans must be created and maintained.

In addition to the elements in a typical risk communication plan, an emergency risk communication plan needs to pay particular attention to the following areas:

- **Identification of organizations and individuals who are responsible for various activities**. These groups include the public information team, public health officials, emergency responders, law enforcement agencies, elected officials, and community organizations. A key role is spokesperson for various issues. According to Catherine DesRoches of the Harvard School of Public Health, the most credible sources on an emergency such as a disease outbreak or bioterrorism are a person's doctor, the director of the local fire department, director of the local hospital, director of state or local police, and director of the state or local health department (DesRoches 2003).

- **Identification of organizations and stakeholders who need to receive and, in some cases, convey information during the emergency**. Emergency risk communication plans should describe stakeholders' likely concerns and how those will be addressed. Table 20-3 shows some examples of concerns associated with various groups.

- **The process for information verification and approval.** Especially when many organizations are required to team to respond to an emergency, the process for determining which information is accurate and who can approve its issuance is vital to successful communication. The simpler the process, the better, for time is always a scarce commodity in an emergency.

- **Procedures to get needed resources.** In an emergency, public information offices will need space, equipment, staff, and supplies, around the clock. The Texas Division of Emergency Management, for example, suggests in its emergency management plan that the public information office be given separate space adjoining the emergency command center, with a dedicated phone line, computer, and direct links to key personnel (Texas DEM 2003).

- **Identification of communication methods.** Include how information will be disseminated and gathered (such as about disease spread) and how questions will be answered (media, hotlines, web sites, e-mail lists or listservs, phone banks, town hall meetings, broadcast fax, conference calls, telebriefings, door-to-door canvassing, stakeholders, partners, etc.). Include alternative methods for times when regular channels of communication are disrupted.

- **How special populations will be informed.** These populations could include, for example, the elderly, unvaccinated, non-English-speakers, and people with chronic respiratory illness.

**TABLE 20-3**
Examples of Stakeholders and Their Concerns in an Emergency

| Stakeholder | Likely Concerns |
|---|---|
| Public in the disaster, for whom action messages are intended | Personal, family, and pet safety; stigmatization; property protection |
| Public immediately outside the disaster, for whom action messages are not intended | Personal, family, and pet safety; interruption of normal life activities |
| First responders | Resources to accomplish response and recovery; personal, family, and pet safety |
| Public health and medical professional responders | Personal safety, resources adequate to respond |
| Family members of victims and first responders | Personal safety, safety of victims and response workers |
| Health care professionals outside response | Vicarious rehearsal of treatment recommendations, ability to respond to patients with appropriate information, access to treatment supplies |
| Civic leaders: local, state, and national | Leadership, response and recovery resources, quality of response and recovery planning and implementation, expressions of concern, liability; international relations |
| Congress | Informing constituents, review of statutes and laws for adequacy and adjustment needs, expressions of concern |
| Trade and industry | Business issues (protection of employees, loss of revenue, liability, business interruption) |
| National community | Vicarious rehearsal, readiness efforts |
| International neighbors | Vicarious rehearsal, readiness efforts |
| International community | Vicarious rehearsal, exploration of readiness |
| Stakeholders and partners | Included in decision-making and access to information specific to the emergency |
| Media | Personal safety, access to information and spokespersons, deadlines |

(Adapted from "Immediate Response Communication Plan," from CDC et al. 2003.)

——— ◇ ———

Vicarious rehearsal occurs when those not susceptible to the risk believe themselves to be at risk and act accordingly. Those "worried well" may flood hospital emergency rooms or otherwise overload public health resources. They may also divert resources away from more urgent use elsewhere.

• **Methods for analyzing media content and public information calls.** Emergency risk communication, like other forms of risk communication, needs to be two-way. Determine how you will gather information from stakeholders in real time during an emergency. Use stakeholder input to make sure accurate information is conveyed and to understand what still needs to be addressed.

The emergency risk communication should also include a contact list for local and regional media, with information on after-hours news desks. Also useful is a list of subject matter experts outside your organization who can speak to other aspects of the emergency and can augment your recommendations during an emergency.

Besides completing the emergency risk communication plan, organizations need to make sure the following equipment will be readily available during an emergency:

- Fax machines with a preprogrammed number for broadcast fax releases to media and partners
- Computers on a local area network with e-mail list-servs designated for partners and media
- Web site capability around the clock, so new information can be posted as quickly as possible
- Printers, copiers, paper, audio-visual equipment, and office supplies
- Cell phones, pagers, and handheld computers
- Visible calendars, flow charts, bulletin boards, message boards, and easels
- Portable microphones, podium, and TV with cable hookup
- Small refrigerator and microwave for staff working around the clock.

In addition, the CDC recommends portable "go kits" for public information specialists who may have to abandon their normal place of operation. These kits should include a computer capable of linking to the Internet and receiving e-mail, a CD or disks containing the elements of the emergency risk communication plan as well as contact information, a cell or satellite phone and/or pager, a credit card or other funding mechanism to purchase operational resources, and background information to provide to the public and media.

> "Go kits" include a computer, the risk communication plan, a cell or satellite phone, and other pieces of equipment and information communicators need if they must abandon their normal place of operation.

## COMMUNICATING DURING AN EMERGENCY

When disaster strikes, implement your plan, adapting it as necessary. The first 48 hours of an emergency are likely to be the most challenging. Table 20-4 shows communication actions the CDC recommends in this critical time period.

**TABLE 20-4**

Communication Actions in the First 48 Hours of an Emergency

| Action | Details |
| --- | --- |
| Verify the situation | Determine the type, scope, and severity of the event. To get as accurate information as possible, verify each piece of information with more than one source if possible. |
| Conduct notifications | Notify the appropriate organizations and individuals using the call list in your communication plan. This should include your organization, stakeholders (including elected officials), and partners. Tell them about the emergency and what actions are being taken. Determine how often the decision-making team will get back together during the day to update each other. |
| Assess the level of crisis | Identify the severity and character of the crisis to help make decisions about hours of operation for communication team, jurisdictions, and other factors. |
| Organize and delegate assignments | Activate the teams identified in the communication plan, including spokespeople. Communication team members may be conducting activities like media interaction, staffing the hotline, updating web sites, developing information materials, and clearing information for release. Science or medical team members may be defining medical issues and treatments and communicating with health professionals. Various team members may be interacting with emergency responders and law enforcement. |
| Prepare information and obtain approvals | Include information that addresses questions and concerns of stakeholders and information they need to know including protective actions, while expressing empathy and caring. |
| Release information | Try to get each new wave of information out to all audiences, all venues, at the same time in a coordinated way. Methods and audiences can include media, web sites, hotlines, employees, partners, legislators and special interest groups, and community members. |

Remember that during an event, it is your responsibility to communicate. If the public or news media misunderstands, you bear the responsibility to adapt methods or messages to get critical points across. Lessons learned from emergencies in recent years also suggest the following:

- **One of the biggest issues is control.** Nobody wants to feel like a victim, even vicariously. To help people regain some sense of control, give them something to do. This "something" needs to be positive ("do this," rather than "don't do that"), actionable (they know what to do and when they have accomplished it), and real (no placebos). One of the frustrating things for Americans following the September 11 attacks was the call from the nation's leaders to "be vigilant." While positive, it was difficult to implement and thus not satisfying as a personal response.

- **Transparency and process still matter.** In stakeholder involvement, the process of communicating risk has often been just as important to the success of the effort as the actual risk communication product. This fact is proving even more so for emergency situations. Jennifer Leaning of the Harvard School of Public Health looked at ethical issues for public-health-related terrorist events and found that the integrity of the search for answers was just as important as the answers themselves (Leaning 2003).

- **Remember the individual as well as the group.** Leaning also found that while public health practitioners are taught to seek the greatest good for the greatest number, the needs of individuals in emergencies cannot be ignored. Leaning also stresses attention to psychological distress (Leaning 2003).

The following text provides additional advice on communicating during an emergency, including communicating from an emergency operations center, working with the media, answering public questions, and supporting a family assistance center.

## Emergency Operation Centers

An emergency operation center, which may include or be called a joint information center, is activated in an emergency to distribute consistent and accurate information. More and more, these centers are run according to the Incident Command Structure mentioned earlier. In a public health emergency such as SARS, such centers have the following communication responsibilities (CDC et al. 2003):

- Issue local public health announcements and updated information on the outbreak and the response

- Disseminate information about the crisis, its management, and the possible need for travel restrictions, isolation, and quarantine

- Establish a news desk operation to coordinate and manage media relations activities

- Provide a location for state, local, and federal communication and emergency response personnel to meet and work side by side in developing key messages, handling media inquiries, and writing media advisories and briefing documents

- Respond to frequently occurring questions by developing fact sheets, talking points (key messages), and question-and-answer documents

- Coordinate requests for spokespersons and subject matter experts

- Issue media credentials

- Address other local/regional information requests related to the outbreak that require distribution to the media and the public

- Develop, coordinate, and manage local web sites, as required.

Such centers may also house the public information hotline and operators (see below).

A chemical weapons depot in Oregon has created a "Smart Book" that guides operations in its joint information center in case of an emergency. Topics range from tips for answering calls to information about agricultural and livestock exposure to steps for sheltering in place.

Those who are charged with communicating risk must understand their role in the structure of an emergency operations center (public information officer, subject matter expert, gathering and analyzing information, etc.), and provide for around-the-clock staff trained in that role.

### Working with the Media in an Emergency

TV and radio are still the top information sources for most people in an emergency (Hasson and Holmes 2003). Newspapers remain important, especially for describing the final result of an event and putting it in context. What can you do to make media interactions as productive as possible? Start by finding a method to coordinate public information personnel from a range of federal, state, and local agencies, working together to respond to media inquiries, writing releases, and providing information on their agencies. If a joint information center is not activated for this, the participants should establish a daily briefing among themselves to coordinate and communicate on media briefings and materials.

The Emergency Management Laboratory (2001) has several suggestions to accommodate reporters on the scene of an accident or disaster. First, try to make sure they have access to the resources necessary to do their jobs:

- Ample electrical power
- Sufficient light for auditorium and meeting space
- Sufficient phone lines for filing stories electronically
- Use of a multiplex remote sound box
- Access to high-quality graphics
- Access to parking near the scene
- Arrangements with local police/city agencies to block off congested streets or areas.

Next, recognize that the media will seek certain information and behave in a certain way during an emergency. They tend to

- Search for background information
- Dispatch reporters/resources to the scene (may include local and national coverage)
- Get access to the site or spokesperson
- Dramatize the situation (which includes looking for the most dramatic video or photo possible)
- Expect an instant briefing, complete with written information
- Find immediate victims and other affected people
- Find filler for stories if credible information is not available, using sources such as nearby residents and volunteer rescue workers.

What can you do to make media interactions as productive as possible? Start by finding a method to coordinate public information personnel from a range of federal, state, and local agencies, working together to respond to media inquiries, writing releases, and providing information on their agencies.

TV, radio, and web-based media usually have faster deadlines than print media. These media outlets might need just the basics within 30 minutes, and more later.

TV, radio, and web-based media usually have faster deadlines than print media. They can go with very brief information at the beginning and don't need to wait to have a more thorough story before distributing it. These media outlets might need just the basics within 30 minutes, and more later. Thus in an emergency, organizations need to be thinking about "what's good enough for now" instead of waiting 2 hours to respond with a full description of the incident.

Be prepared to answer the following questions:

- What happened and where?
- Who was affected and how?
- What's the extent of damage?
- What caused the problem?
- Who is to blame?
- Has anyone broken the law?
- Has this ever happened before?
- Is there danger now?
- What else can go wrong?
- What are you doing about it?
- How can we find out more?

The CDC makes the following recommendations about working with media during an emergency:

- Have staff assigned to answer calls before you release information.
- Put media info out via blast fax, newswire, phone, briefing, and web site.
- Set up a media command post where media can consolidate information to deliver to their viewers and listeners.
- Have areas for TV media to do their "stand ups." If it's at your site, it will usually be where the building displays your organization's logo.
- Let the media know when updates will be given. Give them as promised, even if there's nothing new to say.
- Distribute a copy of any official statements and a fact sheet on the situation and the organization.

When doing a news conference, personnel involved in handling the emergency, spokespersons, and technical advisors should agree on the following before the news conference:

- What information is most important?
- Who will speak for what specific issues?
- What are the key messages?
- What questions are likely to arise?
- What visuals could be used?
- Who will take notes about any information or resources that need to be followed up?

During the news conference, each person who speaks should give his or her name, role, and organization represented. With many organizations involved, it helps to have the news conference manager moderate the question-and-answer session by referring the questions to the appropriate person. Tell reporters when the next news conference will occur, if known. Tell them how they can get questions answered in the mean time. After the news conference, debrief with the team to see if any misinformation needs to be corrected later or other changes made for the next interaction.

After the first 48 hours, the public and media will begin to focus harder on why this event happened, what lessons were learned, and what's being done to keep it from happening again. Media competition may intensify to keep the story going with new angles. Monitor the event for new information, monitor media coverage, and continue implementing the plan, making adjustments as necessary. Determine whether the emergency is changing in any way, and address any rumors or points of conflict. Add any new resources needed; relieve staff or return them to normal duties.

◇

After the first 48 hours, the public and media will begin to focus harder on why this event happened, what lessons were learned, and what's being done to keep it from happening again.

## Answering Questions

One of the most frequently used methods in emergency risk communication is the hotline. This single, publicized phone number should be available toll-free to anyone looking for more information. Operators must be available 24 hours a day, although some organizations have found that calls can be serviced by starting with a short, pre-recorded message (1 minute or less) that outlines answers to most frequently asked questions.

When planning for an emergency hotline, plan big. During the 1999 West Nile virus outbreak in New York City, hotline staff, 27 to 75 per shift, answered calls around the clock, fielding a total of more than 150,000 inquires during 7 weeks (Glass and Schoch-Spana 2002). The anthrax incident in Palm Beach County, Florida, in 2002, saw such an influx of questions to the hotline, by callers who were remarkably well-informed, that operators were quickly overwhelmed.

Giving hotline employees the answers to frequently asked questions, prepared in advance, is one way to help them field calls more efficiently. People typically have the following basic questions:

- What happened?
- Who is/will be affected, and how?
- What is being done?
- What can I do?
- How long will it last?
- Will it happen again?
- Who was at fault?

The following categories suggested by the CDC may be helpful for organizing responses to questions, especially where public health is involved:

- Information about the event or threat
- Tip line, with actions people can take to protect themselves and others
- Reassurance/counseling
- Referral information for health care workers
- Referral information for epidemiologists or others to report cases
- Lab/treatment protocols.

In developing responses in advance, consider people's mental models. Understanding what people don't know and what misperceptions they have helps you provide accurate information and counter rumors. When the Allegheny County Department of Health in Pennsylvania was dealing with the flood of anthrax-related calls in 2001, they realized that people didn't know they had to be exposed to be at risk. Risk communication researcher Baruch Fischhoff helped them develop a model of the probability of anthrax exposure that could be used to design risk communications. The model included concepts such as exposure route, dose, anthrax strain, vaccination status, and health status of recipient (CDC et al. 2003).

## COMMUNICATING AFTER AN EMERGENCY

When the emergency situation stabilizes, the work of the risk communicator continues. Information is needed to help stakeholders (affected people, the broader public, media) move from the emergency situation to resolution and recovery, improve public response to future similar emergencies, and learn from experience. Information is also needed to convey relief and thanks to the response team, evaluate the response effort, and conduct public education.

In the case of mass casualties, one of the more difficult tasks of those communicating risk may be to support the family assistance centers or medical examiner's/coroner's offices (Office for Victims of Crime 2001). In its November 2002 *OVC Bulletin*, the Office for Victims of Crime in the U.S. Department of Justice issued an outstanding template for communities and agencies considering crisis response plans (Blakeney 2002; online at http://www.ojp.usdoj.gov/ovc/publications/bulletins/prf mf_11_2001/188912.pdf). The report was written by Ray L. Blakeney, Director of Operations for the Office of the Chief Medical Examiner of the State of Oklahoma; Blakeney was a key responder to the Oklahoma City bombing and the Oklahoma City tornado of 1999. The bulletin describes lessons learned from mass fatalities on how to provide relief to victims' families. Overarching recommendations include the need for all communities to have an effective crisis response plan and the need for all agency personnel who will interact with families to be

◇

After an emergency, communicators should help move stakeholders to resolution and recovery, improve future public response, and learn from experience.

trained in communicating effectively, compassionately, and sensitively.

Of particular interest to risk communicators is the list of questions most often asked by families and how to respond. For example:

1. **How will families be notified if their loved ones are recovered and identified?** Responders must identify who will pass on this information and how. While a central point of contact is critical, some organizations such as the police, fire department, and military have their own systems. Families must know who will provide them with accurate information.

2. **What is the condition of the body?** Describing the horrific condition of bodies after an airplane crash or bombing requires compassion, honesty, and tact. While risk communication advice generally suggests specific language, Blakeney instead suggests more general words like "severe," "significant," and "trauma." Responders should listen to the family and give only the information wanted. Anything more may overwhelm.

3. **How do families know that the information they receive is accurate?** Responders must identify authorized sources of information and make arrangements such as conference calls to relay information to families who would otherwise have to travel to the site. Responders should also provide written information to augment verbal communications, as people under stress have a hard time recalling information.

Those who remain also need risk information. Research has shown that a community is most responsive to risk avoidance and mitigation education directly after a disaster has occurred, because they have been sensitized. People want to hear about lessons learned and steps taken to prevent the situation from recurring. People want to be reassured of their safety and attain closure. Particularly in emergencies involving violence such as terrorism or bioterrorism, people need help to deal with the issues. Example reactions include shock and

A community is most responsive to risk avoidance and mitigation education directly after a disaster has occurred, because it has been sensitized.

numbness, intense emotion, fear, guilt, anger and resentment, depression and loneliness, isolation, and panic. Those who live through such attacks may also exhibit physical symptoms like headaches, fatigue, nausea, sleeplessness, loss of sexual feelings, and weight gain or loss. Many find it difficult to resume normal activity. Some ways that risk communicators can help include the following:

- Make counselors, clergy members, and other survivors available to talk to those having difficulty coping.

- Be ready to answer questions about types of assistance, payment for travel and other expenses, and how to query insurance companies.

- Remember children, who are often overlooked in times of crisis.

- Give victims and families of victims opportunities to help others.

## REFERENCES

Blakeney, R. L. 2002. "Providing Relief to Families After a Mass Fatality: Roles of the Medical Examiner's Office and the Family Assistance Center." *OVC Bulletin*, November 2002.

CDC (Centers for Disease Control and Prevention). 2003. *Public Health Guidance for Community-Level Preparedness and Response to Severe Acute Respiratory Syndrome (SARS), Draft*. October 2003. Online at http://www.cdc.gov/ncidod/sars/.

CDC (Centers for Disease Control), Agency for Toxic Substances and Disease Registry, Oak Ridge Institute for Science and Education, and the Prospect Center of the American Institutes of Research. 2003. *Emergency Risk Communication CDCynergy* (CD-ROM, February 2003). Online at http://www.orau.gov/cdcynergy/erc/.

Chess, C., K. L. Salomone, B. J. Hance, and A. Saville. 1995. "Results of a National Symposium on Risk Communication: Next Steps for Government Agencies." *Risk Analysis*, 15(2):115-125.

Covello, V. T., D. B. McCallum, and M. T. Pavlova. 1989. "Principles and Guidelines for Improving Risk Communication." *Effective Risk Communication: The Role and Responsibility* of Government and Nongovernment Organizations. pages 3-16. V. T. Covello, D. B. McCallum, and M. T. Pavlova, editors, Penum Press, New York,

Covello, V. T., R. G. Peters, J. G. Wojtecki, and R. C. Hyde. 2001. "Risk Communication, the West Nile Virus Epidemic, and Bioterrorism: Responding to the Communication Challenges Posed by the Intentional or Unintentional Release of a Pathogen in an Urban Setting." *Journal of Urban Health: Bulletin of the New York Academy of Medicine*, 78(2):382-391.

DesRoches, C. M. 2003. "Opinion Surveys and Risk Communication," quoting the *Harvard School of Public Health/Robert Wood Johnson Foundation Survey Project on Americans' Response to Biological Terrorism*, October 24 – 28, 2001. Harvard School of Public Health presentation to the Maine Institute for Public Health.

Emergency Management Laboratory. 2001. *Emergency Public Information Pocket Guide*. Oak Ridge Institute for Science and Education, Oak Ridge, Tennessee. Online at http://www.orau.gov/eml.

EPA (U.S. Environmental Protection Agency). 1990. *Public Knowledge and Perceptions of Chemical Risks in Six Communities: Analysis of a Baseline Survey*. EPA 230-01-90-074, U.S. Government Printing Office, Washington, D.C.

Fischhoff, B. 2002. Remarks delivered at the 27th Annual AAAS Colloquium on Science and Technology Policy on April 11-12, 2002, Washington, D.C.

Glass, T. A. and M. Schoch-Spana. 2002. "Bioterrorism and the People: How to Vaccinate a City Against Panic." *Chemical Infectious Diseases*, 34:217-23.

Hasson, J. and A. Holmes. 2003. "Who We Believe." *Federal Computer Week*, 17(30):18-25.

Hoffman, R. E. 2003. "Preparing for a Bioterrorist Attack: Legal and Administrative Strategies." *Emerging Infectious Diseases*, 9(2):1-11. Online at http://www.cdc.gov/ncidod/EID/vol9no2/02- 0538.htm.

Leaning, J. 2003. "Bioterrorism and Public Health: The Ethics of Public Health Practice in Crisis Settings." Harvard School of Public Health, Harvard Medical School, presentation to the Maine Institute for Public Health.

Office for Victims of Crime. 2001. *OVC Handbook for Coping After Terrorism, September 2001*. NCJ 190249, Office for Victims of Crime, Office of Justice Programs, U.S. Department of Justice, Washington, D.C.

Sachs, Z., Y. L. Danon, R. Dycian, et al. 1991. "Community Coordination and Information Centers During the Persian Gulf War." *Israel Journal of Medical Sciences,* 27:696-700.

Slovic, P. 1999. "Trust, Emotion, Sex, Politics, and Science: Surveying the Risk-Assessment Battlefield." *Risk Analysis,* 19(4):689-701.

Texas DEM (Division of Emergency Management). 2003. "Media and Public Information Office (PIO) Observations." Texas DEM Web Site for WMD/Terrorism Domestic Preparedness. Online at http://www.demwmd.net.

## ADDITIONAL RESOURCES

Agency for Toxic Substances and Disease Registry. Online at http://www.atsdr.cdc.gov.

Association for Professionals in Infection Control and Epidemiology. Online at http://www.apic.org.

Association of State and Territorial Health Officials. 2002. *Communication in Risk Situations: Responding to the Communication Challenges Posed by Bio-terrorism and Emerging Infectious Diseases.* Washington, D.C.

California Governor's Office of Emergency Services. 2001. *Risk Communication Guide for State and Local Agencies.* Office of Emergency Services, Sacramento, California.

Canadian Centre for Emergency Preparedness. Online at http://www.ccep.ca.

Federal Emergency Management Agency. Online at http://www.fema.gov.

U.S. Department of Health and Human Services. 2002. *Communicating in a Crisis: Risk Communication Guidelines for Public Officials.* Substance Abuse and Mental Health Services Administration, Rockville, Maryland. Online at http://www. riskcommunication.samhsa.gov/RiskComm.pdf.

U.S. Department of Homeland Security, *Ready.gov.* Online at http://www.ready.gov.

Part
VI

**RESOURCES**

**GLOSSARY**

**INDEX**

# Resources

*W*hile the field of risk communication is relatively new, a number of studies have been conducted, articles written, and seminars constructed that present information that can be useful to the risk communicator. Below are listed some of these resources. Resources are first grouped topically, by the type of communication (general, environmental, safety, and health) and then by purpose (care, consensus, and crisis communication). References used in the book and additional resources can be found at the end of each section and are only repeated here if they provide more general resource material.

## GENERAL RISK COMMUNICATION RESOURCES

Chess, C., B. J. Hance, and P. M. Sandman. 1989. *Planning Dialogue with Communities: A Risk Communication Workbook.* Rutgers University, Cook College, Environmental Communication Research Program, New Brunswick, New Jersey.

Covello, V. T., and F. W. Allen. 1988. *Seven Cardinal Rules for Risk Communication.* OPA-87-020, U.S. Environmental Protection Agency, Washington, D.C.

Covello, V. T., D. B. McCallum, and M. T. Pavlova, editors. 1989. *Effective Risk Communication: The Role and Responsibility of Government and Nongovernment Organizations.* Plenum Press, New York.

Covello, V. T., P. M. Sandman, and P. Slovic. 1988. *Risk Communication, Risk Statistics, and Risk Comparisons: A Manual for Plant Managers.* Chemical Manufacturers Association, Washington, D.C.

Davies, J. C., V. T. Covello, and F. W. Allen, editors. 1987. *Risk Communication: Proceedings of the National Conference on Risk Communication,* held in Washington, D.C., January 1986. Conservation Foundation, Washington, D.C.

Hance, B. J., C. Chess, and P. M. Sandman. 1988. *Improving Dialogue with Communities: A Risk Communication Manual for Government.* New Jersey Department of Environmental Protection, Division of Science and Research, Trenton, New Jersey.

Hance, B. J., C. Chess, and P. M. Sandman. 1990. *Industry Risk Communication Manual.* CRC Press/Lewis Publishers, Boca Raton, Florida.

International Research Group on Risk Communication, R. E. Kasperson, Chair, CENTED, Clark University, Worcester, Maine 01610, (508) 751-4622.

Kasperson, R. E. 1986. "Six Propositions on Public Participation and Their Relevance for Risk Communication." *Risk Analysis,* 6:275-281.

Lundgren, R. E., consultant and trainer in risk communication, public involvement, and science communication. Offers free quarterly newsletter, *The Risk Comminque,* on risk communication policies, philosophies, and practices. See web site at http://www.rlriskcom.com for more information.

Morgan, M. G., B. Fischhoff, A. Bostrom, and C. J. Atman. 2002. *Risk Communication: A Mental Models Approach.* Cambridge University Press, Cambridge, UK.

National Research Council. 1989. *Improving Risk Communication*. National Academy Press, Washington, D.C.

National Research Council. 1996. *Understanding Risk: Informing Decisions in a Democratic Society.* National Academy Press, Washington, D.C.

Navy Environmental Health Center. No Date. *Risk Communication Primer: A Guide for Conveying Controversial or Sensitive Environmental, Health, and Safety Information to a Concerned Audience.* Environmental Programs Directorate, Norfolk, Virginia.

Professional Interest Committee for Environmental, Safety, and Health Communication, Society for Technical Communication, 901 N. Stuart St. Suite 304, Arlington, Virginia 22203, (703) 522-4114.

Santos, S. L. 1990. "Developing a Risk Communication Strategy." *Management and Operations*, November:45-49.

Society for Risk Analysis, 8000 Westpark Drive, Suite 400, McLean, Virginia 22102; http://www.sra.org.

U.S. Environmental Protection Agency. 1987. *Risk Assessment, Management, and Communication: A Guide to Selected Sources.* EPA 1MSD/87-002, U.S. Environmental Protection Agency, Office of Information Resources Management and Office of Toxic Substances, Washington, D.C.

U.S. Environmental Protection Agency. 2002. *Community Culture and the Environment: A Guide to Understanding a Sense of Place.* EPA 842-B-01-003, Office of Water, Washington, D.C.

## ENVIRONMENTAL RISK COMMUNICATION RESOURCES

Hance, B. J., C. Chess, and P. M. Sandman. 1988. *Improving Dialogue with Communities: A Risk Communication Manual for Government.* New Jersey Department of Environmental Protection, Division of Science and Research, Trenton, New Jersey.

Hance, B. J., C. Chess, and P. M. Sandman. 1990. *Industry Risk Communication Manual.* CRC Press/Lewis Publishers, Boca Raton, Florida.

Krimsky, S., and A. Plough. 1988. *Environmental Hazards: Communicating Risks as a Social Process.* Auburn House, Dover, Massachusetts.

National Consortium for Environmental Education and Training. University of Michigan, 2546 Dana Building, Ann Arbor, Michigan 48109-1115; http://eelink.umich. edu.

North American Association for Environmental Education. 1255 23rd St., NW Suite 400, Washington, D.C. 20037; http://eelink.umich.edu/eetap.html.

Sachsman, D. B. 1991. "Environmental Risk Communication and the Mass Media." Paper presented at the 41st Annual Conference of the International Communication Association, Chicago. School of Communications, California State University, Fullerton, California.

Sachsman, D. B., M. R. Greenberg, and P. M. Sandman, editors. 1988. *Environmental Reporter's Handbook.* Rutgers University, Cook College, Environmental Communication Research Program, New Jersey Agricultural Experiment Station, New Brunswick, New Jersey.

Sandman, P. M. 1986. *Explaining Environmental Risk.* U.S. Environmental Protection Agency, Office of Toxic Substances, Washington, D.C.

Sandman, P. M., D. B. Sachsman, and M. R. Greenberg. 1988. *The Environmental News Source: Providing Environmental Risk Information to the Media.* New Jersey Institute of Technology, Hazardous Substance Management Research Center, Risk Communication Project, Newark, New Jersey.

U.S. Environmental Protection Agency. 1992. *Community Relations in Superfund: A Handbook.* EPA/540/G-88/002, U.S. Environmental Protection Agency, Office of Emergency and Remedial Response, Washington, D.C.

U.S. Environmental Protection Agency. 2002. *Community Culture and the Environment: A Guide to Understanding a Sense of Place.* EPA 842-B-01-003, Office of Water, Washington, D.C.

## SAFETY RISK COMMUNICATION RESOURCES

American Industrial Hygiene Association. No date. *Hazard Communication: An AIHA Protocol Guide.* AIHA Publication Orders, P.O. Box 27632, Richmond, Virginia 23261-7632; http://www.aiha.org/pubs/content/hazcomm.html

National Institute for Occupational Safety and Health, Hubert H. Humphrey Bldg., 200 Independence Ave., SW, Room 715H, Washington, D.C. 20201; (202) 401-6997; http://www.cdc.gov/niosh/homepage.html.

National Safety Council, 1121 Spring Lake Drive, Itasca, Illinois 60143-3201, (630) 285-1121; http://www. nsc.org.

No author. 1995. *Chemical Hazard Communication.* OSHA 3084, Occupational Safety and Health Administration, Washington, D.C.

Occupational Safety and Health Administration, 200 Constitution Avenue, N.W., Washington, D.C. 20210; http://www.osha.gov.

Society for Risk Analysis, 8000 Westpark Drive, Suite 400, McLean, Virginia 22102; http://www.sra.org.

## HEALTH RISK COMMUNICATION RESOURCES

Agency for Toxic Substances and Disease Registry, 1600 Clifton Rd., Atlanta, Georgia 30333; http://atsdr1. atsdr.cdc.gov:8080/atsdrhome.html.

Agency for Toxic Substances and Disease Registry. No date. *A Primer on Health Risk Communication Principles and Practices.* http://atsdr1.atsdr.cdc.gov:8080/HEC/primer. html.

Baram, M. S., and P. Kenyon. 1986. "Risk Communication and the Law for Chronic Health and Environmental Hazards." *Environmental Professional,* 8(2): 165-179.

Centers for Disease Control, Agency for Toxic Substances and Disease Registry, Oak Ridge Institute for Science and Education, and the Prospect Center of the American Institutes of Research. 2003. *Emergency Risk Communication CDCynergy* (CD-ROM, February 2003). Online at http://www.orau.gov/cdcynergy/erc/.

Centers for Disease Control and Prevention, 1600 Clifton Rd., Atlanta, Georgia 30333; http://www.cdc.gov.

Cohen, A., M. J. Colligan, and P. Berger. 1985. "Psychology in Health Risk Messages for Workers." *Journal of Occupational Medicine,* 27(8):543-551.

Fischhoff, B. 1989. "Helping the Public Make Health Risk Decisions." In *Effective Risk Communication: The Role and Responsibility of Government and Nongovernment Organizations,* editors V. T. Covello, D. B. McCallum, and M. T. Pavlova, pages 111-116. Plenum Press, New York.

McCallum, D. B. 1995. "Risk Communication: A Tool for Behavior Change." *NIDA Research Monograph,* 155:65-89.

Witte, K., G. Meyer., and D. Martell. 2001. *Effective Health Risk Messages: A Step-By-Step Guide.* Sage Publications, Inc., Thousand Oaks, California.

U.S. Department of Health and Human Services, Public Health Service and National Institutes of Health. 1992. *Making Health Communication Programs Work: A Planner's Guide.* Office of Cancer Communications, National Cancer Institute, NIH Publication No. 92-1493, Washington, D.C.

## CARE COMMUNICATION RESOURCES

Agency for Toxic Substances and Disease Registry, 1600 Clifton Rd., Atlanta, Georgia 30333; http://atsdr1.atsdr.cdc.gov:8080/atsdrhome.html.

Centers for Disease Control and Prevention, 1600 Clifton Rd., Atlanta, Georgia 30333; http://www.cdc.gov.

Cohen, A., M. J. Colligan, and P. Berger. 1985. "Psychology in Health Risk Messages for Workers." *Journal of Occupational Medicine,* 27(8):543-551.

Levitson, L. C., C. E. Needleman, and M. A. Shapiro. 1997. *Confronting Public Health Risks: A Decision Maker's Guide.* Sage Publications, Thousand Oaks, California.

Sandman, P. M. 1993. *Responding to Community Outrage: Strategies for Effective Risk Communication.* American Industrial Hygiene Association, Richmond, Virginia.

## CONSENSUS COMMUNICATION RESOURCES

Chess, C., B. J. Hance, and P. M. Sandman. 1989. *Planning Dialogue with Communities: A Risk Communication Workbook.* Rutgers University, Cook College, Environmental Communication Research Program, New Brunswick, New Jersey.

"Consensus" the quarterly newsletter; Massachusetts Institute of Technology-Harvard Public Disputes Program, Harvard Law School Program on Negotiation, 516 Pound Hall, Cambridge, Massachusetts 02138.

Creighton, J. L. and J. W. R. Adams. 2002. *Cyber Meeting: How to Link People and Technology in Your Organization.* Xlibris Corporation, Philadelphia, Pennsylvania.

Flynn, J., P. Slovic, and H. Kunreuther. 2001. *Risk, Media and Stigma: Understanding Public Challenges to Modern Science and Technology.* Earthscan, London.

Hance, B. J., C. Chess, and P. M. Sandman. 1988. *Improving Dialogue with Communities: A Risk Communication Manual for Government.* New Jersey Department of Environmental Protection, Division of Science and Research, Trenton, New Jersey.

Kasperson, R. E. 1986. "Six Propositions on Public Participation and Their Relevance for Risk Communication." *Risk Analysis,* 6:275-281.

National Research Council. 1996. *Understanding Risk: Informing Decisions in a Democratic Society.* National Academy Press, Washington, D.C.

Ortwin, R. 1992. "Risk Communication: Toward a Rational Discourse with the Public." *Journal of Hazardous Materials,* 20:465-519.

Walker, G. B., and S. E. Daniels. 1997. "Collaborative Public Participation in Environmental Conflict Management: An Introduction to Five Approaches." *Proceedings of the Fourth Biennial Conference on Communication and Environment,* State University of New York-Syracuse, New York.

Wilson, T. 1989. "Interactions between Community/Local Government and Federal Programs." *Effective Risk Communication: The Role and Responsibility of Government and Nongovernment Organizations*, editors V. T. Covello, D. B. McCallum, and M. T. Pavlova, pages 77-81. Plenum Press, New York.

## CRISIS COMMUNICATION RESOURCES

Caernarven-Smith, P. 1993. "Managing a Disaster." *Technical Communication*, 40(1):170-172.

Carney, B. 1993. "Communicating Risk." *IABC Communication World*, May:13-15.

Centers for Disease Control, Agency for Toxic Substances and Disease Registry, Oak Ridge Institute for Science and Education, and the Prospect Center of the American Institutes of Research. 2003. *Emergency Risk Communication CDCynergy* (CD-ROM, February 2003). Online at http://www.orau.gov/cdcynergy/erc/.

Cipalla, R. 1992. "Dealing with Crisis the United Way." *IABC Communication World*, August:23-26.

Clawson, S. K. Date Unknown. "Crisis Communication Plan: A Blueprint for Crisis Communication." Northern Illinois University, DeKalb, Illinois 60115; http://www.niu.edu/newsplace/crisis.html.

Governor's Office of Emergency Services. 2001. *Risk Communication Guide for State and Local Agencies*. Office of Emergency Services, Sacramento, California. Online at http://www.oes.ca.gov/oeshomep.nsf/all/RiskGuide/$file/RiskGuide.pdf.

International Association of Business Communicators (IABC). 1993. *Crisis Communication Handbook*. International Association of Business Communicators, Washington, D.C.

Lave, T. R., and L. B. Lave. 1991. "Public Perception of the Risks of Floods: Implications for Communication." *Risk Analysis*, 11(2):255-267.

Lerbinger, O. 1996. *The Crisis Manager: Facing Risk and Responsibility*. Lawrence Erlbaum Associates, Mahwah, New Jersey.

No author. 1991. "Communicating in a Crisis: How Phillips Petroleum and Other Companies Avoid 'the Chernobyl Response.'" Editor's Workshop, Lawrence Ragan Communications, Inc., Chicago, Illinois.

*Nuclear Plant Journal*, EQES Inc., 799 Roosevelt Road, Building 6, Suite 208, Glen Ellyn, Illinois 60137-5925.

U.S. Council for Energy Awareness, Annual Crisis Communication Workshop, 1776 I Street N.W., Suite 400, Washington, D.C. 20006-3708, (202) 293-0770.

U.S. Department of Health and Human Services. 2002. *Communicating in a Crisis: Risk Communication Guidelines for Public Officials*. Substance Abuse and Mental Health Services Administration, Rockville, Maryland. Online at http://www.riskcommunication. samhsa. gov/RiskComm.pdf.

U.S. Department of Justice. 2001. *OVC Handbook for Coping After Terrorism*. Office of Justice Programs, Office of Victims of Crime, Washington, D.C.

U.S. Department of Justice. 2002. "Providing Relief to Families After a Mass Fatality: Roles of the Medical Examiner's Office and the Family Assistance Center." *OVC Bulletin*, November 2002.

# Glossary

*T*he way a number of terms in this book are used may differ from standard usage in the field of risk communication. These terms are defined below, as are other terms related to risk communication.

**alternative dispute resolution**—Methods of settling disputes without litigation or administrative adjudication, often involving a neutral third party to solve a disagreement. Methods include facilitation, negotiation, and mediation.

**audience**—those who may be affected by or perceive that they may be affected by a risk.

**bioterrorism**—the release of a disease-causing substance with the intent to inflict harm and increase fear for political or ideological reasons.

**care communication**—communicating about a risk for which the risk assessment is completed and the results are accepted by the majority of the audience. This can include communication about industrial hazards and health risks.

**community relations**—developing a working relationship with the public to determine the acceptable ways of cleaning up a Superfund site. This relationship is mandated by the Comprehensive Environmental Response, Compensation, and Liability Act.

**consensus communication**—communicating risk to bring a number of groups or individuals to a consensus on how the risk should be managed. Often the extent and nature of the risk is not agreed upon by the various groups when the communication effort begins.

**crisis**—crisis is a turning point that will decisively determine an outcome, for example, the rupture of a leaking underground storage tank.

**crisis communication**—communicating risk in the face of a crisis, such as an earthquake or a fire at a chemical plant.

**ecological risk**—the hazards posed to specific components of the ecological system. This area of risk is getting renewed interest from the U.S. Environmental Protection Agency in regard to the Natural Resource Damage Assessments.

**emergency**—sudden or unforeseen situation that requires immediate action, for example, a terrorist attack.

**emergency communication**—communicating risk and appropriate responses in the face of an emergency such as a major disease outbreak.

**facilitated deliberation**—A facilitator leads groups of people in discussing common issues and recommending solutions, often for consideration by decision makers. Ranges from online discussion groups to thousands of citizens nationwide.

**facilitation**—A process that uses a facilitator to help groups accomplish their work. The facilitator uses skills and techniques that enable the group to clarify issues, generate ideas, prioritize goals or solutions, and solve problems.

**hazard**—danger; peril; exposure to a situation that could cause loss or injury.

**health risks**—hazards to human health, usually from diseases or lifestyle factors.

**health risk communication**—communicating about how to prevent, mitigate, or manage hazards to human health (a kind of care communication).

**interactive multimedia**—Communication methods where the user has some control over the content, format, order of presentation, level of detail, language, delivery speed, sound, and/or other aspects. Sometimes involves conversations or questions and answers. Examples are multimedia CDs, computer-based kiosks, and live web-based seminars.

**mediation**—A process that uses a neutral mediator to help people resolve or better manage disputes by reaching agreements about what the parties will do differently in the future. Private caucuses between the parties and the mediator may be used to build support or trust, explore settlement options, or break down barriers to negotiation.

**misperception**—something a person believes to be related to a risk probability or hazard outcome but that experts agree is irrelevant to the actual probability or outcome.

**negotiation**—A third person helps parties negotiate an agreement, sometimes recommending a particular settlement. The concept of "principled negotiation" rejects a "win-lose" mentality and is instead based on the premise that it is possible to meet one's own needs and those of others, and that conflict provides such opportunities.

**public**—people who may or may not be interested in the risk but who are not charged with communicating, assessing, or managing the risk.

**public affairs**—that division of an organization which is charged with the task of developing a positive relationship with the public.

**public information**—information to communicate with the public as opposed to scientists or managers. Because the topic may not be risk, public information and risk communication materials are not necessarily synonymous. However, most risk communication materials will be sent to the public.

**public involvement**—involving the public and other interested groups and individuals such as activities groups, community leaders, regulators, and scientists in making some decision. Because the decision may not involve an environmental, safety, or health risk, public involvement is not synonymous with risk communication. The two can, however, overlap.

**public participation**—*see* public involvement.

**public relations**—the efforts involved in developing a positive relationship with the public, with the goal of getting the public to view your organization in a positive light.

**risk**—probability of adverse outcome. Risk is inherent in any action, even in inaction.

**risk assessment**—determining the risks posed by a certain hazard, usually to human health or the environment; can also include legal and financial risk.

**risk/benefit analysis**—determining and weighing the relative risks and benefits of taking a certain action. It includes determining who receives the risks and benefits.

**risk communication**—the interactive process of exchange of information and opinions among individuals, groups, and institutions concerning a risk or potential risk to human health or the environment. Any risk communication effort must have an interactive component, if only in soliciting information about the audience in the beginning or evaluating success in the end.

**risk decision**—a decision about how to mitigate or prevent a risk.

**risk management**—evaluating and deciding how to cope with a risk. Risk management may or may not include public participation.

**risk message**—message that communicates information about the hazard, its probability, the potential outcomes, and actions that can be taken to manage the risk.

**risk perceptions**—the set of beliefs that a person holds regarding a risk, including beliefs about the definition, probability, and outcome of the risk.

**stakeholder**—person who holds a "stake," an interest in how a risk is assessed or managed.

**stakeholder involvement**—*see* stakeholder participation.

**stakeholder participation**—involving those who hold an interest in the risk, or in how the risk is assessed or managed.

**technology-assisted communication**—technology (web pages, pagers, etc.) used as a conduit for risk communication information as opposed to simply a tool to create it.

**terrorism**—an act of violence intended to inflict harm and increase fear for political or ideological reasons.

# Index

Pages containing figures are denoted by *f*. Pages containing tables are denoted by *t*.

caucuses, 322, 324

CDC. *See* U.S. Centers for Disease Control and Prevention

CDCynergy, 43, 351

CDs. *See* compact discs

celebrity spokespersons, 84*t*, 254

census data, 136

Center for Environmental Communication (Rutgers University), 50

Center for Health Systems Research and Analysis, 144

Center for Mass Media Research (Marquette University), 14

CERCLA. *See* Comprehensive Environmental Response, Compensation, and Liability Act

certifications, 323, 325

Certified Professional Facilitator©, 323

CH2M Hill, 365–366

*Challenger* explosion, 91, 243

Chambers of Commerce and audience analysis, 136

chartjunk, 241, 243

checklists
audience analysis, 140–141
communication methods, 169
communication planning, 191–192
evaluating risk communication efforts, 384–385
face-to-face communication, 268–270
information materials, 209–211
mass media, 296–297
message development, 154
purpose and objectives, 121–122
schedules, 175, 179
stakeholder participation, 330–333
technology-assisted communication, 368
visuals, 245

chemicals, hazardous, 34, 39–40, 41–42, 54–55

Chess, Caron, 50, 378

child abuse, 293, 294

children, 35, 293, 294, 419

church groups, 403
*See also* volunteer support during an emergency

citizen advisory groups. *See* advisory groups

Citizens Juries®, 319–320

Clark Atlanta University, 79

Clark, Don, 340

classified information, 88

Clean Air Act Amendments of 1990, 41–42

climate change, 148, 355–356

clothing for face-to-face communication, 258, 265

cocaine epidemic, 240–241*f*

collaboration, 350, 366, 397, 400–403, 413

Combined Health Information Database, 349*t*

comments and responses, 363–364

communication methods
approaches, 134, 157–170, 337–371
in communication plan, 184–190

communication methods *(cont.)*
emergencies, 403–405, 407
incorporating audience analysis, 139*t*
message development, 153
principles of, 95–111
public health campaigns, 294–295

communication plans
community relations, 31, 32*f*–33*f*, 135, 381
developing, 181–190
evaluating risk efforts, 381, 382

communication process approach, 14–15

communications skills challenge, 19, 20

communicators
audience representative, 77
constraints, 47–59, 67–69, 89–91
evaluating risk communication efforts, 380*t*
listening to audience, 61
mass media, 273–274
roles, 90–91, 323
values, 57
*See also* organizations communicating risk

Communism, 74–75

*Community Culture and the Environment: A Guide to Understanding a Sense of Place,* 128

*Community Relations in Superfund: A Handbook,* 34, 186, 187

community relations plans, 31, 32*f*–33*f*, 135, 381

compact discs, 351, 352, 362

compact discs (CDs), 351, 352

comparisons and risks, 105–109, 197, 229–230, 284

competence and group interactions, 311

comprehensive audience analysis, 127, 132*t*

Comprehensive Environmental Response, Compensation, and Liability Act (CERCLA), 30–34, 44*t*, 135, 186–187, 314
*See also* Natural Resource Damage Assessment

computers in the workplace, 339–346
*See also* technology-assisted communication

concept loading, 140

conference calls. *See* telebriefings

consensus communication
advisory groups and panels, 316
alternatives in information materials, 197
approaches to, 17, 19–20, 23, 145
audience analysis, 126, 127, 137, 138*t*
audience interviews, 264
audience needs, 120
audience profile sections, 182–183
audience's decision-making steps, 175, 177*t*
celebrity spokespersons, 254
communication methods, 302
definition of, 4*f*, 5–6
evaluating risk communication efforts, 379*t*
laws, 44*t*
media attention, 277
message development, 143

frequently asked questions, 414, 416, 418
frustration. *See* hostile audience
funding. *See* resources

**G**

Gallup (company), 136
General Physics (company), 340
genetic counseling and odds ratios, 231
Giuliani, Rudy, 392–393
glossary in information materials, 199
go kits, 409
Gore, Albert, 35
government, 65–66, 74–75, 88, 134
government inducements, 42–43
grants, technical assistance, 314
graphics. *See* visual representations of risk
Gregory, Robin, 67, 82
Griffin, Robert, 220
groundwater contamination, 62, 221–224
group interactions, 309–317
    *See also* stakeholder participation
Grunig, James, 50, 88, 189
Grunig, Larissa, 50, 88, 189

**H**

Hager, Peter J., 221
ham radios, 406
hardware, computer. *See* technology-assisted
    communication
Harris (company), 136
Harvard University, 323, 348*t*, 406, 411
hazard communication program and
    Occupational Health and Safety Act, 40
Hazard Communication Standard, 39, 345
hazardous materials
    accessibility, 317
    computer-based tools, 54–55, 344–345, 352
    regulations, 30–34, 37–38, 39–40, 41–42
hazard plus outrage approach, 21–22
    *See also* outrage
Hazcom, 39, 345
HealthComm Key Database, 349*t*
Health-e Voice, 341
Health Insurance Portability and Accountability
    Act, 42
health intervention and technology, 356–357
health messages, 150–152
    *See also* public health campaigns
Health-O-Vision, 357
health records, 42
    *See also* Privacy Rule
hearings. *See* Citizens Juries®
heart disease, 233*f*, 234, 241–243, 294, 295
helpful hints sections, 199
HIV and AIDS, 147*f*, 148
home pages. *See* web sites
honest imbeciles, 236

hormone replacement therapy, 233*f*, 234
hostile audience
    analysis avoidance, 134
    causes of, 59–62, 79–80, 96–97, 256, 342
    constraints caused by, 60–62
    decision process, 200
    formal hearings, 309
    information release, 53–54
    internal management as, 50, 51
    listening/responding to, 102–103
    ranges to communicate to, 106–107
    stakeholder participation, 305
    training, 267, 342
hotlines. *See* telecommunications
human figures and probability graphics, 231–234
human subjects research, 126, 382

**I**

idiom, risk, 76–79
illiteracy, 66–67
images. *See* visual representations of risk
inaccurate or misleading material, 265–266, 286
inclusion and audience interviews, 265
independent coverage, mass media, 291, 292
indexes, 200, 363
Indians, use of the word, 202
individual risk, 285
individuals and groups in emergencies, 411
industrial community definition, 190
infant mortality, 292
information fairs, 266
    *See also* face-to-face communication
information flow, 32*f*–33*f*
    *See also* information release
information materials
    audience concerns covered in, 102
    creating, 195–211
    definition of, 157–158
    Executive Order 12898, 35
    with face-to-face communication, 254
    scientific information, 58–59
    speakers bureaus, 260
    visual considerations, 217*t*
    *See also* writing
information needs, 144, 216, 392–393, 407, 408*t*
information processing, 22, 144–145
information release, 86–89, 98–99, 261–262, 281
Information Repository, 31
information volume, 219–220, 343, 345
Institute for Public Policy Research, 320
intellectual property and trade secrets, 54, 261
internal communications in communication
    plans, 184
International Association for Public
    Participation, 166, 305, 348*t*
International Association of Facilitators, 323
Internet. *See* technology-assisted communication

Society of Environmental Toxicology and
        Chemistry, 348*t*
sociologists, 135
sociopolitical environment, 74–76, 77*t*
software
    databases, 344–345, 349*t*, 363–364
    decision-making applications, 364–366
    risk analyses, 79
    training, 342
    *See also* technology-assisted communication
Sokler, Linda, 387
solid waste and RCRA, 41
space shuttles, 91, 243
speakers bureaus, 259–260
speaking engagements, 256–260
spokespersons
    credibility, 152, 261, 394–395
    emergencies, 406–407, 415
    legitimacy, 83–85
    mass media, 164
    selection of, 84*t*, 250–254
    skills required, 162
    training, 84*t*, 256–259
    video presentations, 263–264
staff. *See* employees; resources
stakeholder participation
    advantages and disadvantages, 77*t*, 329*t*–330*t*
    advertisements for, 34
    CERCLA, 31, 32–33*f*, 34
    communication method, 165–166, 167*f*
    conducting, 301–336
    consensus communication, 5–6
    emergency planning and response, 402–403, 408
    evaluating risk communication, 377–378
    historical view of, 74–76
    timing, 77–79
    *vs.* face-to-face communication, 161, 250
stakeholders
    CERCLA, 31, 186–187
    communication approaches to, 13–28, 187–190
    comparisons in communication products,
        105–109
    confusion, 80–81, 279
    constraints, 59–69, 158
    decision-making steps, 175, 176*t*, 177*t*, 178*t*
    emotions, 14, 21–22, 59–64, 305
    evaluating risk communication efforts,
        376–378, 380*t*, 381
    expectations from, 96–97, 256, 305–306, 407, 408*t*
    factors influencing involvement, 305
    internal management as, 49–51, 85–86,
        184–185
    mass media as, 273, 274–275
    patronizing approach to, 56–57, 102, 261–262
    perceptions as reality, 99–100
    in risk and technical communication, 2–3
    science-phobic attitude assumed by, 58–59

stakeholders *(cont.)*
    spokespersons to, 251–252
    technology, 338
    use of the word, 202
    values, 57–58, 65
    *See also* hostile audience
standards, comparisons to, 107, 221
Stanford University, 293
state emergency response commissions, 34
State Environmental Policy Act, 30
state laws. *See* laws
stigma, 24, 67–68, 81–82
storyboarding, 185–186
strategic planning, 190–191
streaming video, 353
structure
    group interactions, 308, 312
    information materials, 200, 208–209
    stakeholder participation, 326–327
    technology-assisted communication, 338–339
    visuals, 224, 235–236
study circles, 320–321
Study Circles Resource Center, 321
suicides, 220
Superfund. *See* Comprehensive Environmental
        Response, Compensation, and Liability Act
Superfund Amendment and Reauthorization Act
        (SARA), 30–31, 34
    *See also* CERCLA
surrogate audiences, 133
surveys, 264–265, 293, 382
    *See also* audience analysis
survivors and post-emergency communication,
        417–419

# T

Tal, Alon, 64
technical advisors, 316–317
technical assistance, 310, 314, 318, 328
technical communication, 2–3
technical reports, 208–209
    *See also* information materials
technical writers, 159
technology-assisted communication
    advantages and disadvantages, 166, 168–169,
        367–368
    audience analysis, 135
    choosing and using applications, 337–371,
        403–405
    databases, 344–345, 349*t*, 363–364
    decision tools, 244, 317–318, 364–366
    dispute resolution, 322
    media delivery, 286–290
    risk analysis, 79
    training, 339–343, 352
    *See also* writing
technophiles, 168

# W

Waddell, Craig, 21
Wallack, Lawrence, 213, 280, 296
Walter Reed Army Medical Center, 341
warfarin, 241–243
web broadcasts, 352–354
webcasts, 353
web sites
    consensus communication, 360
    crisis communication, 367
    emergency communication, 404
    indirect audience analysis, 135
    intranets, 344–345
    media resources, 287–288
    sources of risk information, 347*t*–349*t*
    *See also* technology-assisted communication
Weinstein, Neil, 377
Western Washington University, 203
West Nile virus, 99, 395, 416
wheelchair access, 260–261
whistleblower, 91
wide area networks, 361
Wilson, Susan, 291

Wilson, Thomas, 193
wind energy project, 81, 255
Witte, Kim, 150
workers. *See* employees
workshops, 309–311, 313–314
    *See also* face-to-face communication;
        information materials
worst-case scenario, 41
writing
    acronyms and abbreviations, 199, 204–205
    comprehension, 62, 81, 159
    concept loading, 140
    e-mail, 343
    health communication, 151–152
    incorporating audience analysis, 140
    Internet, 346, 350
    mass media, 279
    scientific notation and formulas, 106, 201
    style, 101–102, 134, 201, 202–203
    video presentations, 263
    *See also* language; message; structure